The Instal

Ad Rotator Component

Properties
Border
Clickable
TargetFrame

Methods
GetAdvertisement

Content Linking Component

Methods
GetListCount
GetListIndex
GetNextDescription
GetNextURL
GetNthDescription
GetNthURL
GetPreviousDescription
GetPreviousURL

Content Rotator Component

Methods
ChooseContent
GetAllContent
Unlock

Counters Component

Methods
Get
Increment
Remove
Set

Logging Utility Component

Properties
BytesReceived
BytesSent

ClientIP
Cookie
CustomFields
DateTime
Method
ProtocolStatus
ProtocolVersion
Referer
ServerIP
ServerName
ServerPort
ServiceName
TimeTaken
URIQuery
URIStem
UserAgent
UserName
Win32Status

Methods
AtEndOfLog
CloseLogFiles
OpenLogFiles
ReadFilter
SendLogRecord
WriteLogRecord

MyInfo Component

Properties
PageType
PersonalName
PersonalAddress
PersonalPhone
PersonalMail
PersonalWords
CompanyName
CompanyAddress
CompanyPhone
CompanyDepartment
CompanyWords
HomeOccupation
HomePeople
HomeWords

SchoolName
SchoolAddress
SchoolPhone
SchoolDepartment
SchoolWords
OrganizationName
OrganizationAddress
OrganizationPhone
OrganizationWords
CommunityName
CommunityLocation
CommunityPopulation
CommunityWords
URL(n)
URLWords(n)
Style
Background
Title
Guestbook
Messages

Page Counter Component

Methods
Hits
PageHit
Rest

Permission Checker Component

Method
HasAccess

Tools Component

Methods
FileExists
Owner (Macintosh only)
PluginExists (Macintosh only)
ProcessForm
Random
Test

ASP 3

Instant Reference

Evangelos Petroutsos

SYBEX®

San Francisco • Paris • Düsseldorf • Soest • London

Associate Publisher: Richard Mills
Contracts and Licensing Manager: Kristine O'Callaghan
Acquisitions & Developmental Editor: Denise Santoro-Lincoln
Editors: Susan Berge, Pete Gaughan, Patrick J. Peterson
Production Editors: Leslie E. H. Light, Teresa Trego
Technical Editor: Greg Guntle
Book Designer: Franz Baumhackl
Graphic Illustrator: Tony Jonick
Electronic Publishing Specialist: Franz Baumhackl
Proofreaders: Dennis Fitzgerald, Dave Nash, Camera Obscura, Laurie O'Connell, Nancy Riddiough
Indexer: Nancy Guenther
Cover Designer: Design Site
Cover Illustrator: Sergie Loobkoff

Library of Congress Card Number: 00-103810

ISBN: 0-7821-2781-9

Manufactured in the United States of America

10 9 8 7 6 5 4 3 2 1

ACKNOWLEDGMENTS

My gratitude to the talented staff at Sybex, especially the developmental editor Denise Santoro-Lincoln for turning a manuscript into an actual book; the technical editor Greg Guntle for ensuring the correctness and accuracy of this book's information; the editors Susan Berge, Pete Gaughan, and Patrick J. Peterson and the production editor Leslie E. H. Light for their keen remarks and constant editing of my revisions; the proofreaders Dennis Fitzgerald, Dave Nash, Camera Obscura, Laurie O'Connell, and Nancy Riddiough for eliminating mistakes from the manuscript; and the electronic publishing specialist Franz Baumhackl for laying out the book.

CONTENTS AT A GLANCE

CONTENTS

INTRODUCTION

An increasing number of VB programmers apply their programming skills to the Web by writing ASP (Active Server Pages) applications. An ASP application is a collection of scripts written in VBScript and HTML pages. VBScript is a subset of Visual Basic and a VB programmer is, by definition, a VBScript programmer too. The difficulty is learning how to build applications that use HTML to interact with the user. HTML is a simple language, and the elements at your disposal for building interfaces are simple controls, the HTML controls.

ASP applications run on the server, where all the processing takes place. The scripts communicate with the client by reading the viewer-entered data on the page and supplying the results of the processing in the form of HTML documents. Although the client is limited to HTML and simple scripts (mostly written in JavaScript), the scripts running on the Web server are as functional as any VB application. This functionality is achieved through the ASP objects, which represent the items you need to develop a server-side script that interacts with the client. The ASP objects expose methods and properties that simplify the development of server-side scripts. Before ASP, the most basic operation of a server-side script, the retrieval of the client-submitted data values, was a major task. Actually, for years VB developers were unable to write an application that could interact with the client. ASP makes this task very simple—this functionality is practically built into the VBScript.

To develop ASP applications, VB programmers needn't learn anything new, short of the six ASP objects, also known as built-in objects. To send the client some text (plain text or HTML code), for example, you can call the Write method of an ASP object, appropriately named the Response object. Likewise, to read the values on a Form's controls on a page, you can call the Form collection of the Request object. If you want to use cookies in your application, and most ASP applications do, you use the Response object to send cookies to the client and the Request object to read the cookies' values. Finally, the Server object exposes the CreateObject method, allowing you to contact any COM Server application on the server. A COM Server is an application like Excel, but it can be a custom component designed specifically for your Web application. Appendix A describes how to build custom components in VBScript.

In addition to the built-in objects, several installable components work in the context of an ASP application—but they're not limited to ASP applications. You can use the installable components just like the built-in components. The only difference is that you must instantiate them in your script with a call to the Server.CreateObject method. The ActiveX Data Objects, for instance, allow your scripts to access databases on the Web server, and the Ad Rotator component simplifies banner management on your site's pages.

Who Should Read This Book

This book is addressed to VB programmers who wish to start writing ASP applications, as well as to VBScript developers who need a reference to the members exposed by the ASP objects. Once you've understood the role of each ASP object in the development of server-side scripts, you'll be able to find the member that does the job. The ASP objects expose a relatively small number of members, the syntax is quite simple, and most VB or VBScript developers don't need extensive tutorials to learn how to use them in their scripts. A reference book that demonstrates how to use these objects through examples should be adequate for people familiar with Visual Basic.

This book is for people who would prefer to read a short book that demonstrates the syntax of the properties and methods with simple examples rather than lengthy tutorials explaining relatively simple topics. There's nothing really complicated about ASP and this is especially true for VB developers.

The Structure of the Book

This reference book is structured after the ASP object model. The only way this book deviates from a typical reference book is that the various objects are not listed alphabetically—although the members of each object in each chapter are listed in alphabetical order. I first introduce the more basic objects, so that I can use them in the examples of the following chapters.

The book is organized into three parts. The first part introduces Web applications and the ASP objects. It explains the structure of a Web application and the role of VBScript and the ASP objects.

The second part, which is the book's core, discusses the built-in ASP objects in detail. This part also discusses the ADO component, not because it's a built-in ASP object, but because you'll be using this object most often in your scripts. The ADO chapter is the book's longest and is not meant for readers unfamiliar with database programming. However, I've included some detailed examples to demonstrate a few important operations from a Web developer's point of view. These operations are the generation of paged Recordsets (pages that display a small number of rows and allow viewers to move to any other group by clicking a hyperlink at the bottom of the page), how to code multiple actions in transactional mode, and so on.

The last part of the book discusses the installable components, which are distributed with the Web server and can be used like the built-in object. The difference is that the installable components must be instantiated in the script that uses them. Practically, this only amounts to a single additional statement. The installable components address some of the problems faced by a large number of Web developers, like the Ad Rotator component, which simplifies the process of displaying banners on your site's pages; the File Access component, which allows you to access the server computer's file system; and so on. Most of the installable components are quite simple and will probably be replaced by more complicated components in the next version of ASP.

Finally, this book contains two appendices. One summarizes the VBScript and ASP error codes. The other appendix is a tutorial on building Windows Script components. If none of the built-in or installable components offers the functionality you need, you can write your own component and use it from within your scripts as if it were another installable component. You can even distribute the component so that other developers can use it in their scripts. Although you can develop custom components in languages like Visual Basic or Visual C++, the beauty of Windows Script components is that they can be coded in VBScript. This means that any Web developer can now develop his or her own custom components.

How to Reach the Author

Despite our best efforts, the first edition of a book is bound to contain errors. If you have any problems with the text and/or the applications in this book, you can contact the author directly at:

76470.724@compuserve.com

Although I can't promise a response to every question, I will address any problem in the text and/or examples and provide updated versions. I would also like to hear any comments you may have about the book regarding topics you liked or disliked and how useful you found the examples.

chapter 1

Web Applications
and ASP

I n the early days of the Web, just being able to navigate through the pages of a site, or jump from one site to another with a mouse click, was a major breakthrough. This interaction model that was based on the single click of the mouse, not even the double click, was responsible for the tremendous success of the Web. Yet, in a few short years, this model of interaction was proven inadequate, because it didn't allow viewers to interact with the Web server in the way they interacted with a typical Windows application.

The Web was based on the premise that clients request documents from Web servers. This was a reasonable assumption for the early days of the Web, but the unexpected adoption of this technology lead very quickly to the need for a more elaborate scheme of information flow between clients and servers. We are no longer interested in simply requesting documents from a server. People need up-to-date, live information. They need to search databases, look up stock prices, place orders, and in general send, as well as retrieve, information from the server.

To allow for a better two-way communication between clients and servers, the HTML standard was enhanced with Forms and controls. A Form is a section of a page where users can enter information (enter text in Text controls, select an option from a drop-down list, or check a radio button). The controls are the items that present or accept information on the Form. The values of the controls are sent to the server by the browser, where they're processed by an application, or a script, that runs on the server. HTML Forms and controls are quite rudimentary when compared to VB Forms and controls, but they are the only means of interaction between clients and servers (excluding the click of the mouse on a hyperlink).

Therefore, if you want to build a Web application, you must limit yourself to these controls. Your page may not look quite like a Windows application, but this is something you must live with and it doesn't seem like it's going to change any time soon. Yet, these controls coupled with hyperlinks are adequate for building applications that run over the Internet.

There was another limitation that had to be overcome. Browsers are designed to communicate with Web servers in a very simple manner. They request documents by submitting a string known as a URL (Uniform Resource Locator). URLs are the addresses of HTML documents on the Web. The URL of the desired document is embedded in the document itself. The browser knows how to extract the destination of the selected hyperlink and request the document. Alternatively, you can specify the URL of the desired document by entering its name in the browser's Address box. To interact with servers, clients should be able to request not only static HTML pages, but also programs (executable files or scripts) on the server. A script can create a new HTML page on the fly; moreover, this page can be different for different clients. If a client requests the details of an item, you could look up the item in a database the moment it's requested and retrieve the most up-to-date information. For instance, the units in stock is a piece of information that can't be stored in a static page; it must be looked up in a database the moment it's requested.

Requesting Server-Side Scripts

It is possible for the browser to request the name of a script on the server just as it would request an HTML page. The browser doesn't really have to know anything about the requested document. It simply sends a request for the document specified in each hyperlink and the server submits another HTML page. If the requested document is a script, the script is executed on the server and it generates an HTML page on the fly, which is returned to the client in response to the initial request.

For a richer interaction model, browsers should be able to pass more than a single URL to the server. Sometimes, they have to pass a lot of information back to the server, such as query criteria, registration information, and so on. To enable this two-way communication, the client attaches all the information to be passed to the server in the destination's URL. The URL of a page that contains a Form is the name of the script that will process the Form, followed by the parameter values entered by the viewer on the Form. Figure 1.1 shows what happens when you use the AltaVista search engine to locate articles on database programming. The search argument is "+ASP +programming" (this argument will return all the titles on ASP programming) and the browser passes the following URL to the server. The following line won't be broken in your browser's Address box and you may not see the entire string.

```
http://www.altavista.com/cgi-bin/query?pg=q&sc=on&hl=on&
    q=%2BASP+%2Bprogramming&
    kl=XX&stype=stext
```

This is not a common URL. The first part is the URL of an application that runs on the server. It's the query application in the *cgi-bin* folder under the Web server's root folder. The question mark separates the name of the application from its arguments, while the ampersand symbol separates multiple arguments. The query application accepts six arguments: the *pg*, *sc*, *hl*, *q*, *kl*, and *stype* arguments. Most of the arguments are of no interest to us. The *q* argument is the search string. Notice that spaces are replaced by the plus (+) sign. The plus sign itself (which is a special symbol in URLs) was replaced by the string %2B (the hexadecimal representation of the plus character). The query application will read the information passed by the client, query the database with the specified keywords, and return another HTML document with the results of the query (you will probably see different documents at the top of the page if you perform the same query).

FIGURE 1.1: Invoking a server application and passing arguments to it from within the browser

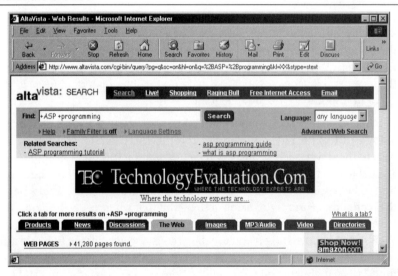

In effect, we fool the browser into thinking that the destination document has a really long URL. The Web server will figure out what the URL means; it will invoke the query application and pass the specified parameters to it.

The application that runs on the server is not an EXE file. Different Web servers allow different types of applications to be invoked. IIS works with ASP (Active Server Pages) scripts. An ASP script is a program written in VBScript (or JavaScript) that uses several objects to communicate with the client. These objects are the ASP objects and they're explained in this guide. In the future, more objects may be added (you can actually write your own components for use with ASP pages). VBScript need not be changed in major ways. Additional functionality will be supported through new objects.

VBScript is a simple scripting language, based on Visual Basic. Likewise, JavaScript is another scripting language based on Java. Both languages support the basic flow-control statements, the same functions as Visual Basic (or Java), and can manipulate variables. They're core languages and don't provide any mechanisms for interacting with the client. If you're familiar with Visual Basic, you're ready to write ASP scripts in VBScript. The real power of VBScript is that it can access the ASP built-in objects, as well as any COM+ component installed on the server. For example, you can use the ADO objects to access databases, or the File Access component to access the server's file system. If you have developed middle-tier components for use with an application that runs on a local area network, you can use the same components to interface a Web application to a database.

Most ASP developers use VBScript. VBScript comes with Windows and it's fine for developing scripts. The scripts run on the server and they produce HTML code that can be viewed on any browser. In addition to server-side scripts, there are client-side scripts. These scripts are executed on the client and they can be written either in VBScript or in JavaScript. Internet Explorer supports both VBScript and JavaScript, but Netscape's Communicator supports only JavaScript. In a few cases where I'll have to include a client-side script in the examples of this book, I'm going to use JavaScript, so that the script can be executed on all browsers. This book, however, is about server-side scripts and I'm going to use VBScript for all scripts that run on the server.

Server-Side Scripts

A server-side script is a script that's executed on the server. It is possible to write scripts that are downloaded to the client, along with the HTML page (client-side scripts), and are executed on the client, but this is beyond the scope of this book. A server-side script is a mix of HTML statements and VBScript statements. The following script generates a simple page that displays the date and time on the server computer:

```
<HTML>
<H1>Active Server Pages</H1>
The date on the server is <% =Date() %>
and the time is <% =Time() %>
</HTML>
```

The tags <% and %> delimit the VBScript statements in the HTML document. When this script is executed, all HTML elements are sent to the client without any processing. The VBScript statements are executed and the output they produce is transmitted to the client in the place of the actual statements. The expression =Date() will be replaced by the output of the function Date(), which is the current date. Likewise, the expression =Time() will be replaced by the output of the function Time().

If you store the previous lines in a text file with the extension ASP in your Web server's root folder, and then open the file from within the browser, the following HTML code will be transmitted to the client:

```
<HTML>
<H1>Active Server Pages</H1>
The date on the server is 4/5/00
and the time is 8:02:53 AM
</HTML>
```

This is straight HTML. All VBScript statements embedded in a pair of <% and %> tags were replaced by the output they produced.

NOTE Unlike HTML pages, ASP pages can't be opened by double-clicking their names. You must start your browser and connect to the server where the file is stored. If you're using a single machine to test the samples in this book, you must start the Web server (the Personal Web Server or Internet Information Server) and connect to the URL of the desired file. To test the file Test.asp, use the URL 127.0.0.1/Test.asp. 127.0.0.1 is the address of the local Web server and the file Test.asp is assumed to be in the server's root folder. If the Web server is running on another computer on the LAN, replace the address 127.0.0.1 with the name, or IP address, of the server. If the file is stored in a virtual folder under the root folder, replace the filename Test.asp with the appropriate relative path (Samples/Test.asp, for example).

You can also explicitly create output to be transmitted to the client by using the Response object (one of the ASP objects discussed in detail later in the book):

```
<%
Response.Write "<HTML>"
Response.Write "<H1> Active Server Pages</H1>"
Response.Write "The date on the server is" & Date()
Response.Write "and the time is " & Time()
Response.Write "</HTML>"
%>
```

The tags <% and %> delimit an entire section of the script, consisting of multiple lines.

Finally, you mix and match HTML and VBScript code by embedding VBScript statements in a pair of <% and %> tags. Here's a slightly modified version of the same script. The difference is that all VBScript statements are on separate lines and they're a bit more complicated than before. This script formats the date and time values with the FormatDateTime function.

```
<HTML>
<H1>Active Server Pages</H1>
The date on the server is
<%
Response.Write FormatDateTime(Date, 1)
%>
and the time is
<%
Response.Write FormatDateTime(Time(), 3)
%>
</HTML>
```

You can also use VBScript to generate Forms that would normally be coded in straight HTML. For example, you can create a List control and populate it from within a script. See the section "The Select Control" later in this chapter for an example.

The Structure of Web Applications

The Web started as a global network that simplified the sharing of information. Some people post information in the form of Web pages, or HTML pages, or HTML documents, and many more people view this information. With the introduction of HTML Forms and specialized software that runs on the server, the Web has become an environment for running applications. The Web is no longer a simple click-and-view environment. It has become a client/server environment for running elaborate applications. The browser is the client, which can display HTML documents and interact with the viewer through HTML controls and scripts that run on the server. The Web server processes the information and sends the results to the client in the form of HTML pages. Nowadays, we talk about Web applications. People using Microsoft's tools to build applications that run on the Web over the HTTP protocol call them ASP-based applications, because ASP plays such an important role in developing scripts on the server.

A Web application is a site with multiple HTML pages and server-side scripts. HTML pages call server-side scripts and pass parameters to the scripts. These scripts are executed on the server, just like applications would be. They process the values submitted by the client, format the results as HTML documents on the fly, and send the new documents to the client. One side of the script sees the client and interacts with the viewer by accepting information posted by the client and sending HTML pages to the client. The other side of the script sees the components on the server. Such components include databases, the server's file system, e-mail applications, and so on.

Web applications have a special requirement. Where typical desktop applications use Forms to interact with the user, Web applications are based on HTML pages. In a VB application, for example, there are many options for its Forms to communicate with one another. They can use public variables, they can read directly the values of the controls on any Form, and they can set each other's properties. The situation is different on the Web. Each page is a separate entity and it can't interact directly with another page of the same site. Not to mention that any user could bookmark any page and jump to this page directly.

A Web application is a site that works much like a Windows application, and specifically like a client/server application. Viewers enter information on a Form. This information is then transmitted to the server, and the result of the processing returns to the client as another HTML document. In most cases, the processing that takes place on the server is a database search. The results of the search are then furnished back to the client in the form of another HTML page.

Here's another major difference between a desktop application (like an application written in VB) and a Web application: the windows of a desktop application can remain open on the desktop and users can switch from one to the other with a mouse-click. This is not true with a Web application. A Web application can only display one Form (page) at a time. In order to switch to another page we must either select a link on the current page, or click the Back button to view a page we've already visited.

Creating a Web Site

A Web site is a collection of HTML documents that reside on the server. To access your site, a client must connect to a URL, which is the site's domain name. You could store all the documents making up the site in the folder C:\Web\MySite. Viewers need not know the actual name of the folder where the documents are stored. The C:\Web\MySite folder is the site's root folder and users can connect to it by specifying an address like www.ComputersRus.com. You can also specify the document that will be displayed by default when a viewer connects to your site. This document is usually a static HTML page named default.htm or index.htm.

Your documents can be organized in folders under the root virtual folder. As long as you use relative path names to call one document from within another, you can move a site to a different location on the hard disk and you won't have to change the references.

To create a new site with IIS under Windows 2000 Server, just start the Internet Information Services by selecting Start ➢ Programs ➢ Administrative Tools. If you're using Windows 2000 Professional, you will find the IIS in the Control Panel. When you see the IIS Console window, right-click the name of the server and select Properties to see the properties of the default site. Its root folder is in C:\InetPub\WWWRoot, but you can map the site's root folder to any folder on your system. You can also create virtual folders under the root folder and store the samples there. To test the samples, you must specify not only the Web server's domain name, but the name of the virtual folder as well. If you have a virtual subfolder named "Samples," use the following URL to open the Test.asp file in this folder: http://www.domain.com/Samples/Test.asp.

If you're using a server that doesn't have its own domain name, use the IP address of the local host, which is always `127.0.0.1`: `http://127.0.0.1/Samples/Test.asp`.

The root folder is where all the pages making up the site must be placed. Of course, you can place them in subfolders of the root folder. For example, you can create an Images folder and place all images there, or a Scripts folder and place all scripts there. As long as these pages are referenced relative to the root folder, you'll be able to move your site to another root folder, or computer, as is.

Since you're reading this book, I'm assuming some of your pages are ASP scripts. You can use the extension ASP for all the documents of the site, even if they don't contain any VBScript statements. ASP 3.0 is very efficient in processing ASP pages that don't contain any scripts (just HTML code).

In addition to the ASP scripts (and static HTML pages, if you have any), a typical site contain a few more special files. These are the GLOBAL.ASA files, which contain declarations, and one or more INCLUDE files, which contain declarations and useful functions that can be included in any other script of the same site. These files are discussed in the last section of this chapter.

For readers who are familiar with VBScript, or even Visual Basic, I will discuss briefly the HTML statements for creating Forms with HTML controls. These pages are the application's user interface and your task as a Web developer is to design the application's user interface and the scripts that will accept and process the data entered on the various Forms. The Web designers will dress up your pages. A Web designer is responsible for the look and feel of the page. Your task is to fill the page with different data, which are usually the result of the execution of a script. The designer will create a good-looking page with dummy data (a table with fake data, for instance). The developer will populate the table with data retrieved from a database. To do so, you must write a script that reads the parameter values submitted by the client, builds the appropriate SQL statement, executes it against the database, and formats the rows returned by the database as an HTML table.

HTML Forms and Controls

To interact with the viewer, besides the ubiquitous hyperlinks, HTML recognizes a few special tags that insert controls on a Form. An HTML control is a stripped-down version of the ActiveX controls you use to build Forms with Visual Basic. You can use controls to collect information from the user for registration purposes, take orders over the Internet, or let the user specify selection criteria for record retrieval from databases. HTML provides the following controls:

Text control   A box that accepts a single line of text, similar to Visual Basic's default TextBox control.

TextArea control   A box that accepts multiple lines of text, similar to a TextBox control with its MultiLine property set to True.

RadioButton control   A circular button that can be checked or cleared to indicate one of multiple options. This control is similar to Visual Basic's Option control.

CheckBox control   A box that can be checked or cleared to indicate that an option is selected.

Password control   A text control that doesn't display the characters as they are typed.

Select control   A list of options from which the user can select one or more. This control is equivalent to Visual Basic's ListBox control.

Command Button control   A usual button that can trigger various actions, similar to Visual Basic's Button control.

NOTE   The HTML keywords are not case sensitive, but I use uppercase to make it easy to distinguish them in the text. VBScript statements are also case insensitive, but we capitalize the first letter in each keyword (statement, keyword, and so on).

Before you place any controls on a page, you must create a Form, with the FORM tag. All controls must appear within a pair of FORM tags:

```
<FORM NAME = "myForm">
{your Controls go here}
</FORM>
```

The NAME attribute is optional, but it's a good practice to name Forms. Beyond the NAME attribute, the FORM tag accepts two more attributes, METHOD and ACTION, which determine how the data will be submitted to the server and how they'll be processed there. The METHOD attribute can have one of two values: POST and GET. These two attributes are discussed in detail in Chapter 6, *The Request Object*. The ACTION attribute specifies the script that will process the data on the server. To specify that the contents of a Form must be submitted to the script ReadValues.asp, use the following <FORM> tag:

```
<FORM NAME = "myForm" ACTION = "ReadValues.asp" METHOD="POST">
```

The values entered by the viewer on the Form's controls are sent to the server with the Submit button. Every Form has a Submit button (even if it's named something different), which extracts the ACTION attribute from the <FORM> tag and the values of the controls, creates a new URL, and sends it to the server. Because the name of the requested document is ReadValues .asp, the Web server executes the ReadValues.asp script, which in turn uses the Request object to read the values of the controls.

WARNING For security purposes, the Web server will not execute any executable file specified as a URL. By default, IIS will execute the ASP scripts in the site's root folder and its subfolders. It's also common to turn off the Write privileges of the root folder, so that no one can place scripts there except the administrator.

The values of the various controls can be retrieved through the Request.Form collection. There are other methods to retrieve the control values, which are discussed in Chapter 6. The simplest one is through the Form collection and I'll use this technique for the examples of this chapter. The Form collection has one member for each control on the Form and you can access the individual control's value by name. If the Form contains a control named "UserValue" you can access this control's value with the expression Request.Form("UserValue").

The CheckBox Control

The CheckBox control is a little square with an optional check mark. The check mark is a toggle, which turns on and off every time the user clicks the control. It is used to present a list of options, from which the user can select one or more. When the check mark is turned on, the check box is said to be checked, and when it's turned off, the control is said to be cleared.

The CheckBox control can be inserted in a document with the following tag: <INPUT TYPE = CHECKBOX NAME = "Check1"> where *Check1* is the control's name. You'll use it later to find out whether the control is marked or not, for instance. By default, a check box is cleared. To make a check box checked initially, you use the CHECKED option in its INPUT tag:

```
<INPUT TYPE = CHECKBOX NAME = "Check1" CHECKED>
```

To read the value of the Check1 control from within your script, use the following expression:

```
If Request.Form("Check1") = "on" Then
    ' these statements are executed if Check1 was checked
Else
    ' these statements are executed if Check1 wasn't checked
End If
```

The RadioButton Control

The RadioButton control is similar to the CheckBox control, only it's round, and instead of a check mark, a solid round mark appears in the center of a checked RadioButton. RadioButton controls are used to present a list of options, similar to a group of CheckBox controls, but only one option can be selected in a group of RadioButtons. Not only that, the responsibility of clearing the previously checked button lies on the control itself; there's nothing you must do in your code to clear the checked button every time the user makes a new selection.

To insert a RadioButton in a document, use a line similar to the one for the CheckBox, only this time replace the control type with RADIO: <INPUT TYPE = RADIO NAME = "Radio1">. Whereas each CheckBox on a Form has its own name, you can have several RadioButtons with the same name. All RadioButtons with the same name form a group and only one member of the group can be checked at a time. Every time the user clicks a RadioButton to check it, the previously checked one is cleared automatically. To initially check a RadioButton, use the CHECKED attribute, which works similarly to the attribute with the same name of the CheckBox control. Notice that the options are mutually exclusive and only one of them can be checked.

Since a number of RadioButton controls may belong to the same group, and only one of them can be checked, they must also share the same name. The following statements will place a group of RadioButton controls on a Form:

```
<B>Income Range:</B>
<P>
<INPUT TYPE=RADIO NAME="IncomeBracket" VALUE=1>Less than 10K<BR>
<INPUT TYPE=RADIO NAME="IncomeBracket" VALUE=2>More than 10K but
less than 30K<BR>
<INPUT TYPE=RADIO NAME="IncomeBracket" VALUE=3>More than 30K but
less than 100K<BR>
<INPUT TYPE=RADIO NAME="IncomeBracket" VALUE=4>More than 100K<BR>
```

To read the value of the IncomeRange control from within your script, use an expression like the following one:

```
Range = Request.Form("IncomeBracket")
```

The Text Control

The Text control is a box that can accept user input and is used for entering items such as names, addresses, and any form of free text.

To insert a Text control on a page, use the INPUT tag and set the TYPE attribute to TEXT. The line:

```
<INPUT TYPE = TEXT NAME = "Publisher" VALUE = "Sybex">
```

will display a Text control on the page, with the string "Sybex" in it. The viewer can enter any string, overwriting the existing one or appending more text at its end. The usual text editing and navigational keys (Home key, arrows, the DEL and INS keys) will work with the Text control. However, you can't format the text in a Text control, by using different fonts or even font attributes like bold and italic.

Finally, you can specify the size of the control on the page with the SIZE attribute, and the maximum amount of text it can accept with the MAXLENGTH attribute. For example, the TextBox control defined as:

```
<INPUT TYPE = TEXT NAME = "Publisher" SIZE = 40
    MAXLENGTH = 100 VALUE = "Sybex">
```

can accept user input up to 100 characters, while its length on the page corresponds to the average length of 40 characters in the current font.

To read the value of the Publisher Text control from within your script, use an expression like the following one:

```
PubName = Request.Form("Publisher")
```

The Password Control

The Password control is a variation on the Text control. Its behavior is identical to that of the Text control, but the characters entered are not displayed. In their places, the user sees asterisks instead. It's meant for input that should be kept private. To create a Password control you use an INPUT tag similar to that for a Text control, but specify the PASSWORD type:

```
<INPUT TYPE = PASSWORD NAME = "Secret Box"
SIZE = 20 MAXLENGTH = 20>
```

Other than a different TYPE attribute, Password controls are identical to Text controls.

The TextArea Control

You can also provide your users with a control that accepts multiple lines of text. It is the TextArea control, whose operation is quite similar to that of the TextBox control, but it handles the carriage return character, which causes it to change lines. All navigational and editing keys will work with the TextArea control as well. To place a TextArea control on a Form, use the TEXTAREA tag:

```
<TEXTAREA NAME = COMMENTS ROWS = 10 COLS = 50></TEXTAREA>
```

This tag creates a box on the page, whose dimensions are 10 rows of text, with 50 characters per line. The ROWS and COLS tags specify the dimensions of the control on the page (in units of the current font).

Besides its attributes, another difference between the TextArea control and the other controls you've seen so far is that the TextArea control must end with the </TEXTAREA> tag. The reason for this is that the TextArea control may contain lengthy, multiple-line default text, which must be enclosed between the two tags and can't be assigned to an attribute:

```
<TEXTAREA NAME = COMMENTS ROWS = 10 COLS = 50>
This is the greatest Web site I've seen in years!
Congratulations!!!
</TEXTAREA>
```

The text between the two TEXTAREA tags is displayed initially in the box. In the unlikely event that the user is less than excited about your pages, he can overwrite your initial comments. Notice that all line breaks in the text will be preserved. There's no need to use paragraph or line break tags to format the initial text of a TextArea control (and if you do include HTML tags in the text, they will be displayed in the Text box as you typed them). If the text can't fit in the space provided, the appropriate scroll bars will be added to the control automatically. Notice the lack of any HTML formatting tags in the text. The line breaks are preserved, but the control isn't going to process any HTML tags. Remember that the TextArea control doesn't insert line breaks on its own, so you must try not to exceed the maximum line length (as defined with the ROW attribute) if you want the contents of the control to be entirely visible along each line.

The Select Control

The Multiple Selection List control, as it's called, is a control that presents a list of options to the viewer, and lets him or her select none, one, or more of them. The tag for the List control is <SELECT> and it must be followed by a matching </SELECT> tag. The attributes that may appear in a <SELECT> tag are NAME (the control's name), SIZE (which specifies how many options will be visible), and MULTIPLE (which specifies whether the user may choose multiple items or not). To place a List control on your Form, use the following tag:

```
<SELECT NAME = "UserOptions" SIZE = 4 MULTIPLE = MULTIPLE>
</SELECT>
```

Between the two SELECT tags you can place the options that make up the List, each one in a pair of OPTION tags:

```
<SELECT NAME = "UserOptions" SIZE = 3 MULTIPLE = MULTIPLE>
<OPTION>Computer</OPTION>
<OPTION>Monitor</OPTION>
<OPTION>Printer</OPTION>
<OPTION>Modem</OPTION>
<OPTION>Speakers</OPTION>
<OPTION>Microphone</OPTION>
<OPTION>Mouse</OPTION>
</SELECT>
```

The control displayed on the Form with the statements shown above contains seven options, but only three of them are visible. The SIZE attribute will help you save space on your pages when you have a long list of options to present to the user. The user can also select multiple options (with the Shift and Control keys) even if some of them are not visible. To disable multiple selections, omit the MULTIPLE attribute.

To minimize the List control's size on the Form, omit the MULTIPLE attribute (if possible) and don't specify how many items will be visible. The result will be a list with just one visible element. If the user clicks the arrow, the list will expand and all its elements will become visible until the user makes a selection. Then, the list collapses back to a single item.

The OPTION tag has a VALUE attribute too. This attribute specifies the string(s) that will be sent back to the server when the user submits the Form with that option selected. In other words, it is possible to display one string in the list, but send another value to the server. Here's a modified version of the previous list:

```
<SELECT NAME = "UserOptions" SIZE = 6 MULTIPLE = MULTIPLE>
<OPTION VALUE=1>Computer</OPTION>
<OPTION VALUE=2>Monitor</OPTION>
<OPTION VALUE=3>Printer</OPTION>
<OPTION VALUE=4>Modem</OPTION>
<OPTION VALUE=5>Speakers</OPTION>
<OPTION VALUE=6>Microphone</OPTION>
<OPTION VALUE=7>Mouse</OPTION>
</SELECT>
```

When the selection on this list is submitted to the server instead of the actual string, the server sees a number, which corresponds to the viewer's selection.

Quite often, we use VBScript to create and populate Select controls on a Form. If the control's options are read from a database, for example, you don't know the options that will appear on the control at design time. You must write a script that reads the appropriate values and then produces the HTML code that will display the control and its options on the page.

The following example shows you how to create a Select control with the month names. First, it places the <SELECT> tag to the output stream and then it goes through the names of the 12 months with a For ... Next loop. At each iteration it outputs the month's number (this is the control's VALUE attribute) and the month's name (this is what the viewer sees). The If statement outputs a slightly different <OPTION> tag when the month happens to be the current month. The SELECTED attribute preselects the current month on the control.

```
<%
Response.Write "<SELECT NAME = 'Months' SIZE = 1>"
For iMonth = 1 To 12
    MName = MonthName(iMonth)
    If iMonth = Month(Date()) Then
        Response.Write "<OPTION VALUE=" & _
                        iMonth & " SELECTED>" &
                        MName & "</OPTION>" & vbCrLf
    Else
        Response.Write "<OPTION VALUE=" & _
                        IMonth & ">" & MName &
                        "</OPTION>" & vbCrLf
    End If
Next
Response.Write "</SELECT>"
%>
```

If you open this script from within your browser and examine the page's source code, you'll see the following HTML code:

```
<SELECT NAME = 'Months' SIZE = 1>
    <OPTION VALUE=1>January</OPTION>
    <OPTION VALUE=2>February</OPTION>
    <OPTION VALUE=3>March</OPTION>
    <OPTION VALUE=4 SELECTED>April</OPTION>
    <OPTION VALUE=5>May</OPTION>
    <OPTION VALUE=6>June</OPTION>
    <OPTION VALUE=7>July</OPTION>
    <OPTION VALUE=8>August</OPTION>
    <OPTION VALUE=9>September</OPTION>
    <OPTION VALUE=10>October</OPTION>
    <OPTION VALUE=11>November</OPTION>
    <OPTION VALUE=12>December</OPTION>
</SELECT>
```

To read the selected value(s) on a Select control from within your script, use a statement like the following one:

```
Options = Request.Form("Month")
```

The value of the Select control is the same as the selected option's VALUE attribute. The *Options* variable, for example, will be assigned a numeric value, which is the selected month's number.

If the viewer has selected multiple options on the control, you can access them with the same name and an index value:

```
Option1 = Request.Form("Month")(1)
Option2 = Request.Form("Month")(2)
```

The Command Button

The Command Button is a control that can be clicked to trigger certain actions. Typically, Command Buttons are used to trigger two actions: Submit the data to the server, or reset all controls on the Form to their original values. Command Buttons can also be used to trigger any actions you can program in your pages with VBScript (or JavaScript) statements that are executed on the client, but we are not going to discuss client-side scripting in this book. If you want to include client-side scripts in your pages, use JavaScript to make sure your pages can be viewed on all browsers.

There are two types of Buttons you can place on a Form. The most important one is the SUBMIT Button; it transmits the contents of all controls on the Form to the server. The RESET Button clears the controls on the Form (or resets them to their initial values) and doesn't submit anything.

These two types of Buttons can be placed on a Form with the following INPUT tags:

```
<INPUT TYPE = SUBMIT VALUE = "Send Data">
```

and

```
<INPUT TYPE = RESET VALUE = "Reset Values">
```

where VALUE is the caption that appears on the Button. Each Form should contain at least a SUBMIT Button to transmit the information entered by the user to the server. (If the page contains a script, then you can submit the data to the server via the script and you don't have to include a SUBMIT Button.)

Figure 1.2 shows a Web page with a Form that contains all of the HTML controls we use in developing Web applications, with the exception of the TextArea and Password controls. The output of the AllControls.htm page is shown in Figure 1.2. We'll return to this page in Chapter 6, *The Response Object*, where you'll see how the values of the controls on this Form can be read from within a script.

FIGURE 1.2: The output of the AllControls.htm page

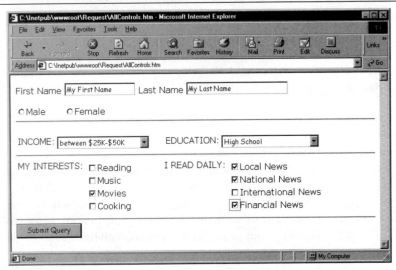

▶ *Listing 1.1: The AllControls.htm Page*

```
<HTML>
<FONT FACE="Verdana">
<FORM NAME=Personal ACTION=ReadParameters.asp METHOD=GET>
First Name
<INPUT TYPE=Text NAME=FirstName SIZE=20
       VALUE='My First Name'>
Last Name
<INPUT TYPE=Text NAME=LastName SIZE=30
       VALUE='My Last Name'>
<BR><BR>
<INPUT TYPE=Radio NAME="Sex" VALUE="Male">Male
    
```

```
<INPUT TYPE=Radio NAME="Sex" VALUE="Female">Female
<BR>
<HR>
<BR>
<TABLE>
<TR><TD VALIGN=TOP>INCOME:</TD>
<TD><SELECT NAME="IncomeRange">
<OPTION VALUE="invalid">Select your income range
<BR>
<OPTION VALUE="Low">less than $25K
<BR>
<OPTION VALUE="Med">between $25K-$50K
<BR>
<OPTION VALUE="High">more than $50K
</SELECT>
</TD>
<TD>    </TD>
<TD VALIGN=TOP>
EDUCATION:
</TD>
<TD>
<SELECT NAME="Education">
<OPTION VALUE="invalid">Select your highest degree
<BR>
<OPTION VALUE="HSchool">High School
<BR>
<OPTION VALUE="College">College
<BR>
<OPTION VALUE="University">University
</SELECT>
</TD>
</TR>
</TABLE>
<HR>
<TABLE><TR>
<TD VALIGN=TOP>MY INTERESTS:
</TD>
<TD VALIGN=TOP>
<TABLE>
<TR><TD>
```

```
<INPUT TYPE=CheckBox NAME="Books">Reading</TD></TR>
<TR><TD>
<INPUT TYPE=CheckBox NAME="Music">Music</TD></TR>
<TR><TD>
<INPUT TYPE=CheckBox NAME="Movies">Movies</TD></TR>
<TR><TD>
<INPUT TYPE=CheckBox NAME="Cooking">Cooking</TD></TR>
</TABLE>
</TD>
<TD>     
        </TD>
<TD VALIGN=TOP>I READ DAILY:</TD>
<TD VALIGN=TOP>
<TABLE>
<TR><TD>
<INPUT TYPE=CheckBox NAME=Local>Local News</TD></TR>
<TR><TD>
<INPUT TYPE=CheckBox NAME=National>National News</TD></TR>
<TR><TD>
<INPUT TYPE=CheckBox NAME=International>
International News</TD></TR>
<TR><TD><INPUT TYPE=CheckBox NAME=Financial>
Financial News</TD></TR>
</TABLE>
</TABLE>
<HR>
<INPUT TYPE=SUBMIT>
</HTML>
```

Directives and Server-Side Includes

Besides VBScript (or JavaScript) statements and HTML encoded text, ASP
files may contain two special items, *preprocessing directives* and *server-side
includes*. A preprocessing directive is a command to the ASP interpreter; it
tells the interpreter to execute some statements before it starts processing
the script. If you're familiar with C programming, you'll recognize that the
preprocessing directives are equivalent to compiler directives. A server-side
include is a statement that tells the interpreter to load a file and replace the

statements with the file's contents. If several of your scripts use the same code segment, you can place these statements in a text file and include it in any script by placing a server-side include at the beginning of the script.

The preprocessing directives have the following syntax:

```
<%@ directive=value%>
```

To specify multiple directives, separate them with a single space, as shown here:

```
<%@ directive1=value1 directive2=value2%>
```

Since the space delimits successive directives, there shouldn't be any spaces around the equals sign. Finally, the line with the directive must be the first one in the script. The only exception is the <% =var %> directive, which instructs the ASP interpreter to replace the entire directive with the value of the *var* variable.

ASP recognizes the following directives. Notice that most directives have an equivalent property in the Session object.

CODEPAGE   This property determines which code page will be used to prepare the output and it must match the code page used by the client. Different languages and locales use different code pages. The value 932 corresponds to the code page of Japanese Kanji.

ENABLESESSIONSTATE   This property determines whether ASP will maintain state across the pages of your application. The default value of this property is True and we rarely change it. ASP relies on client-side cookies to maintain state. If a client doesn't accept cookies, ASP won't be able to maintain state across pages, regardless of the setting of this directive. This directive doesn't have an equivalent property in the Session object.

LANGUAGE   This directive specifies the scripting language. It's equivalent to setting the LANGUAGE attribute of the <SCRIPT> tag. The language you set with the LANGUAGE directive becomes the default language. You can overwrite this setting in a script with the LANGUAGE attribute.

LCID   This directive sets the Locale ID for the current page. The Locale ID determines how numbers and dates will be formatted. The value 1036 corresponds to the French locale.

TRANSACTION The TRANSACTION directive tells the interpreter to treat the entire page as a transaction. For more information on transactional scripts, see Chapter 10.

A server-side include (SSI) is similar to a directive: it tells the interpreter to replace the SSI with the contents of a file or another value. ASP recognizes the following server-side includes:

#include Tells the interpreter to replace the SSI line with the contents of a file. The #include SSI is described in detail in the last section of this chapter.

#config Sets the format for error messages, dates, and file sizes.

#echo Inserts the value of an environment variable (a member of the Request.ServerVariables collection) at the current location in the script.

#exec Inserts the result of a command or application. The command or application is executed before the script is processed, so that the result can be inserted at the current location in the script.

#flastmod Inserts the date/time when the file was last modified.

#fsize Inserts the current file's size in the script (this is the script's file size).

The #include SSI

The most important server-side include is #include, which inserts an entire file into the script. The syntax of this SSI is:

```
<!-- #include fileType = filename -->
```

fileType specifies whether the file is referenced with a virtual or relative path and its value can be one of the literals "file" or "virtual." The following statement places the navigational buttons or hyperlinks at the top of the page:

```
<!-- #include virtual "/Common/NavBar.inc" -->
```

The NavBar.inc file contains the code for the navigational buttons and it resides in the Common folder under the Web server's root folder.

chapter 2

The ASP Objects

This chapter is an overview of the ASP objects. As you recall from the previous chapter, VBScript is a general scripting language and doesn't support the functionality you need to interface a script running on the server to the client. The ASP objects bridge this gap; they allow your scripts to access the information passed by the client in a request and to generate output to be returned to the client. In addition, they can help you maintain state among the pages of your application.

The first part of this chapter deals with the HTTP request and response headers. The client sends the request header to the server every time it requests a new document. The request header contains the requested document's name, information about the browser, and the cookies left on the client computer by the same application (in either the current session or a previous session). If the page contains a Form, the values of the controls on the Form are also submitted to the server as part of the request header. The response header contains information about the server that supplies the document, information about the document being sent (the document's type, for example), and cookie values (when the server needs to create a new cookie or change the value of an existing one). The main document follows the response header.

HTTP Headers

A basic understanding of how information moves back and forth between clients and servers will help you understand the role of the ASP objects in developing Web applications. You don't really need to understand how the HTTP protocol works, and you'll never have to build headers on your own; these are the responsibility of the Web server and ASP. The following brief discussion of the HTTP headers, however, will help you understand how the ASP objects fit into the picture of a Web application, and you'll be able to guess which object provides the functionality you need for each operation.

When a client makes a request to a server, it transmits the HTTP Request header. This header contains the version of HTTP in use and the URL of the requested document. The following is a typical HTTP header:

```
GET /MyDocument.htm HTTP/1.1
Connection: Keep-Alive
User-Agent: Mozilla/3.0 (Win95; I)
```

```
Host: 212.54.196.226
Accept: image/gif, image/x-bitmap,
        image/jpeg, image/pjpeg, *.*
```

This header uses the GET command to request the MyDocument.htm page. The Host field is the IP address of the client. You shouldn't use this value to identify viewers between sessions. Most viewers are assigned an address dynamically the moment they connect to their ISP, and different users can use the same address at different times. Actually, if a user is disconnected momentarily, the same user will have a different IP address upon reconnect.

The request header shown above requests an HTML page. The following request header comes from a page that contains a Form. The values of the controls on the Form are automatically transmitted to the client as part of the header. This header requests a script on the server and sends parameter values to the script:

```
POST /Scripts/ReadData.asp HTTP/1.1
Referer: http://212.54.196.226
Connection: Keep Alive
User-Agent: Mozilla/3.0 (Win95; I)
Host: 212.54.196.226
Accept: image/gif, image/x-bitmap,
        image/jpeg, image/pjpeg, *.*
Content-type: application/x-www-form-urlencoded
Content-length: 38

FirstName=Mary+Ann&LastName=Sylvester
```

The client uses the POST method to transmit the parameter values (the other method is GET). The Referer field is the address of the page from which the user jumped to the page with the Form. The Content-type field says that the parameters are encoded in a format suitable for transmission along with the URL of the requested document; then comes the number of bytes that follow, and finally the parameters and their values.

The Web server acknowledges the request by sending a Response header, followed by the requested HTML file. Here's a typical HTTP Response header:

```
HTTP/1.1 200 OK
Server: Microsoft-IIS/4.0
Date: Tue, 04 Apr 2000 00:26:34 GMT
```

```
Content-type: text/html
Set-Cookie: ASPSESSIONIDFFFYXKFR=ACMNFLJANKGBAMPBEGNGLEAB; path=/
Cache-control: private
Transfer-Encoding: chunked
<HTML>
{ the rest of the HTML file }
```

This response came from the Personal Web Server (PWS). The string "200 OK" is the status of the request. If the server couldn't handle the request, this string would be an error message like "404 Object Not Found." The SetCookie field sets the value of a cookie. This cookie identifies the current session; PWS (or IIS) will use this cookie to keep track of viewers while they remain connected to the site. *path* is a cookie attribute that tells the browser this cookie shouldn't be sent to pages that don't reside in the site's root folder.

The browser displays the document and waits for the viewer to follow a hyperlink to another page or another site. The document is interpreted as HTML code, because the Content-type field of the Response header is text/html. If the page contained an image, it would be transmitted to the client with another Response header, whose Content-type field would be image/jpeg.

The Set-Cookie string is inserted automatically by PWS or IIS and is used to identify the session. This value will be transmitted back to the client with all subsequent requests, so the Web server knows which requests belong to which session. For more information on cookies, see Chapter 5, *The Cookies Collection*.

If the page that requests a document contains a Form, then the values entered by the user on the Form are transmitted to the server as part of the request header. The requested document must be a script (an ASP file), which will process the parameter values passed by the client along with the request. Accessing the information in the request header is not a simple task; neither is the generation of response headers. To simplify the process of communicating with the client, Microsoft has included several objects in IIS, the ASP objects, which represent the entities of a Web server and can be used from within ASP files. The Request object represents a client request; all the information passed by the client in a request, including parameter values and cookies, can be accessed through the Request object. Likewise, the Response object represents the server's response to a request; everything you want to send to the client must be written to the output string with the Response.Write method. Other objects, such as the Session object, represent a viewer's session.

Using the ASP Objects

The first half of this guide discusses the ASP objects, which are necessary for building Web applications. VBScript was not designed specifically for developing Web applications, so ASP exposes a few objects that moderate between VBScript and the Web server. Figure 2.1 shows how a script interacts with the client and the Web server itself.

FIGURE 2.1: The built-in ASP objects

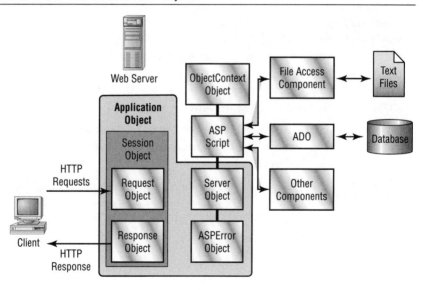

All the scripts of the application are executed in the context of the Application object. The script is not part of the Application object, but it's useless outside the context of an Application object. The Application object represents the Web application. All variables with Application scope, for example, are visible to all the scripts and all sessions.

Each client has its own Session object, which represents the viewer's session. A new Session object is created the first time a viewer connects to the application, and all subsequent requests made by the same client are executed in the context of the same Session object.

The Request and Response objects enable your script to interface with the client. The Request object returns information from the client (the parameter values passed by the client request, cookie values, and so on), while the Response object represents the stream from the Web server to the client.

While the script executes, it can request some of the server's functionality through the Server object. The ASPError object allows you to handle runtime errors. Another ASP object, the ObjectContext object, enables you to execute the statements in a script as a transaction.

In addition, the script can access the resources on the server computer through other components. These components come with Windows, but they're not part of ASP and they're called *installable* components, as opposed to the built-in ASP objects. The File Access component, for example, allows scripts to access the computer's file system and manipulate text files. The ADO component interfaces scripts with databases. You can also write custom COM+ components that can be used from within an ASP script.

The following sections are a brief overview of the built-ASP objects and the members they expose. The short descriptions of the various members will help you understand the type of functionality each object brings to the script and how this functionality is implemented in terms of properties and methods.

The Application Object

The Application object represents a Web application; we use this object to share information among all the users of the application. A Web (or ASP-based) application is a collection of ASP and HTML files in a virtual folder and its subfolders.

Collections

Contents   This is the most important member of the Application object; it contains all of the items that have been added to the application through the application's scripts. In addition to the usual properties of a Collection object, the Contents collection supports the Remove and RemoveAll methods for removing selected items or all the items in the collection, respectively.

StaticObjects   This collection contains all of the objects added to the application with the <OBJECT> tag.

Methods

Lock   The Lock method prevents other scripts from modifying an application variable while the current script is editing it.

Unlock   The Unlock method releases the hold placed on the Application object by the Lock method.

Events

Scripts for these two events are declared in the `global.asa` file.

Application_OnEnd   This event takes place when an application terminates (usually when the Web server is shut down). Use this event's handler to insert any clean-up code (to store the values of application variables to text files, for example).

Application_OnStart   This event takes place when an application starts (usually when the Web server is restarted). Use this event's handler to insert your initialization code (to create variables that must be visible by all the scripts of the application and read their values from a text file, for example).

The ObjectContext Object

We use the ObjectContext object to execute transactional scripts. A *transaction* is a set of actions that must either commit or abort as a whole: If one of the actions fails, then the subsequent actions will not take place. More important, the actions that have already taken place must be rolled back (that is, their effects must be reversed).

When an ASP contains the @TRANSACTION directive, the page runs in a transaction and does not finish processing until the transaction either succeeds completely or fails.

Methods

SetComplete   The SetComplete method declares that all the actions in the script have completed successfully and the transaction has been committed. If all components participating in the transaction also call SetComplete, the transaction will complete.

SetAbort   The SetAbort method declares that one of the actions in the script has failed and the transaction has been aborted. The effects of the actions that have already completed successfully (like changes in a database) must be rolled back. MTS will automatically roll back database operations, but it will not do the same with other actions, such as the modification of an application variable.

Events

OnTransactionCommit   This event takes place when a transaction completes successfully. Use the OnTransactionCommit event handler to confirm the successful commitment of a transaction.

OnTransactionAbort   This event takes place when a transaction aborts. Use the OnTransactionAbort event handler to undo operations that can't be rolled back automatically by MTS.

The Request Object

The Request object represents the HTTP request made by the client to the script. We use this object to retrieve information passed by the client during the request, such as parameter values and cookies.

Collections

ClientCertificate   The values of fields stored in the client certificate, sent in the HTTP request, are used to validate the client. You don't need a verified server to use the ClientCertificate collection, but the clients must be verified by a company like VeriSign.

Cookies   The Cookies collection contains the values of cookies sent in the HTTP request. The cookies are first created and stored on the client computer through the Cookies collection of the Response object. Then you can read their values with the Cookies collection of the Request object.

Form   The Form collection contains the values of all the controls on a Form. These values are transmitted to the server as part of the HTTP request body.

QueryString   This is the entire string with the parameter values in the HTTP request (the string following the question mark after the name of the script in the request). The QueryString collection contains the same information as the Form collection; it's just a different method to retrieve the values of control on the Form.

ServerVariables   These are the values of predetermined environment variables, which provide useful information such as the IP address of the client, the viewer's logon name (if viewers are required to log on to the server), and so on.

Property

TotalBytes   The total size of the request body sent by the client, in bytes. This property is used only when the client transmits binary information to the server.

Method

BinaryRead   This method retrieves data sent to the server from the client as part of a POST request; it isn't used commonly in Web applications.

The Response Object

The Response object represents the HTTP response sent to the client by a script. We use the Response object to send output (HTML code and cookie values) to the client. In addition, we use the Response object's properties to specify certain attributes of the output (such as the code page to be used in rendering the HTML page on the browser). Notice that the Response object supports the BinaryWrite method, which allows you to send binary information to the client (images, for example).

Collection

Cookies   This collection allows your script to create new cookies (or change the values of existing cookies) and store them on the client computer. If the cookie exists on the client, its value is changed. If not, a new cookie is created and set to the specified value.

Properties

Buffer   Indicates whether page output is buffered; by default, ASP 3.0 buffers the output. This means that you can clear the output at any time in the course of the execution of the script. When the script completes its execution, or when the Response.Flush method is called, the output is transmitted to the client. If you set the Buffer property to False, then the output is transmitted to the client as it's generated by the script.

CacheControl   Determines whether proxy servers are able to cache the output generated by ASP. Allows proxy servers to cache your site's pages if they don't change frequently.

Charset   Appends the name of the character set to the Content-type header field. Most developers specify the character set in the <META> tag at the beginning of each page.

ContentType   Specifies the HTTP content type for the response. The default value of this property is "text/html."

Expires   Specifies the length of time before a page cached on the browser expires.

ExpiresAbsolute   Specifies the date and time when a page cached on the browser expires.

IsClientConnected   Indicates whether the client has disconnected from the server. Use this property to interrupt the execution of lengthy scripts if the client has disconnected.

PICS   Adds the value of a PICS (Platform for Internet Content Selection) label to the Response header. This property allows you to rate the contents of your site.

Status   Gives the value of the status line returned by the server. The status code is interpreted by the browser, which acts accordingly.

Methods

AddHeader   Adds a custom field to the Response header. Custom headers are used in unusual situations.

AppendToLog   Appends a record to the Web server log file for the current request. The Web server logs all the operations on its own, but the AppendToLog method allows you to add custom records to the log file.

BinaryWrite   Writes binary information to the current HTTP output without any character-set conversion. You'll rarely have to transmit binary information to the client using this method. Insert the appropriate tags in your pages to transmit sounds, images, and other types of binary information to the client. Keep in mind that the client should be able to handle the information you send.

Clear   Erases any buffered HTML output; you can't call this method if the Buffer property isn't set to True. Call this method to clear any output generated by the script so far when you detect an unusual situation.

End   Stops processing the .asp file and sends any buffered output to the client.

Flush   Sends any buffered output to the client.

Redirect   Sends a redirect message to the browser, causing it to attempt to connect to a different URL.

Write   Writes a string (literal or variable) to the current HTTP output as a string. This is the method you'll be using more than any other, since it allows you to generate HTML documents on the fly from within your scripts.

The Server Object

The Server object exposes part of the server's functionality by providing access to methods and properties on the server. Most of these methods and properties serve as utility functions.

Property

ScriptTimeout   The amount of time that a script can run before it times out. A script must eventually time out, since the viewer can't interrupt its execution remotely.

Methods

CreateObject   Creates an instance of a server component. This is probably the most useful method of all ASP objects, because it extends the capabilities of VBScript by allowing it to contact any component running on the server. These components include the File Access component (which gives VBScript access to the server's file system), the Active Data Objects (ADO, which provides access to databases), and more.

Execute   This method calls another script on the same server. After the called script completes, the original script resumes its execution.

GetLastError   This method returns the most recent error in the script. Notice that the Err object represents the VBScript error and is reset after each statement's execution. The information about the error is stored in an ASPError object variable. See the upcoming section "The ASPError Object" for more details.

HTMLEncode   Applies HTML encoding to the specified string. Use this method to display HTML tags that would normally be interpreted by the browser.

MapPath   Maps the specified virtual path—either the absolute path on the current server or the path relative to the current page—into a physical path.

Transfer   Terminates the execution of the current script and transfers control to another script. The new script is executed in the context of the interrupted script (it has access to the session and transaction state of the calling script).

URLEncode   Applies URL encoding rules, including escape characters, to its argument. Use this method to prepare URLs with parameter values.

The Session Object

The Session object represents a viewer's session; we use this object to store information that applies to the entire session. Variables stored in the Session object are not discarded when the user jumps between pages in the application; instead, these variables persist for the entire session and are released when the session ends.

Session state is only maintained for browsers that support cookies. If a client doesn't support cookies (or the viewer has disabled the cookies), then each request made by the client corresponds to a new session. Notice also that when a user comes back to the application, or connects to the application through another instance of the browser, a new Session object is created.

Collections

Contents   Contains the variables that you have added to the session with script commands. In addition to the usual properties of a Collection object, the Contents collection supports the Remove and RemoveAll methods for removing selected items or all the items in the Collection, respectively.

StaticObjects   Contains the objects created with the <OBJECT> tag and given session scope.

Properties

CodePage   The code page that will be used for symbol mapping. This property is used by ASP to prepare the text before it's written to the output stream.

LCID   The locale identifier. This property is used by ASP to format currency, date, and time values for the current session.

SessionID   The session identification for this user. This is a long string generated by the server when the user connects to the site. The SessionID string is stored on the client as a cookie (it expires at the end of the session) and is read from the Request header as the viewer navigates through the pages of the site.

Timeout   The timeout period for the current session. The session will timeout automatically in 20 minutes, if the viewer doesn't visit another page or refresh the current one.

Method

Abandon   This method terminates a session by releasing its Session object.

Events

Scripts for these two events are declared in the global.asa file.

Session_OnEnd   This event takes place when a session terminates (usually when the client disconnects or when a script terminates the session with the Abandon method).

Session_OnStart   This event takes place when a new session is established (when a viewer connects to the application for the first time).

The ASPError Object

The ASPError object provides detailed information about the most recent ASP error and exposes the following properties. To retrieve the information stored in the ASPError object call the Server.GetLastError method.

Properties

ASPCode	The error number; this property is reported by IIS.
ASPDescription	A detailed description of the error.
Category	The source of the error (whether it's ASP itself, a VBScript error, or a component error).
Column	The character position (column number) where the error occurred in the script.
Description	A short description of the error.
File	The name of the script in which the error occurred.
Line	The line where the error occurred in the script.
Number	The COM error code.
Source	A string containing the statement that caused the error.

chapter 3

The Application Object

The Application object represents the Web application, and all the users of the application can access it. In other words, all viewers that request a page of your site will have access to the variables and objects created with the Application object. When a viewer requests an ASP page for the first time, an instance of the Application object is created. This instance is created by the ASP.DLL, which is responsible for retrieving user input, interpreting ASP scripts, and submitting their output to the client.

Most developers use the Application object as a depository for information (variables) that must be shared among all the users of the application. A Web application is a collection of pages, some straight HTML and some ASP-based script pages. These pages reside in a virtual folder (and its sub-folders) on the Web server. The Web server maintains the information you store in the Application object and distinguishes between multiple Web applications with the names of the virtual folders in which they reside. If you have two Web applications (two online stores) stored in the folders BOOKS and MUSIC, all ASP scripts that belong to the application in the BOOKS folder will share their common information through their Application object. They are not allowed to access the Application object of the ASP scripts in the MUSIC folder. For instance, both applications may maintain the count of their own visitors and use identical statements to increase their counter (they may even use the same name for the counter variable). The Web server will maintain two different variables, however, one for each application.

Application variables are in effect global variables—they can be accessed by any module in the application, as opposed to local variables, which can be accessed only from within the module in which they're declared. The equivalent of a module in a Web application is a script. Just as with any other application, you should try to not overuse global variables in your Web applications. Another good reason for avoiding the introduction of too many Application variables is that you must lock the Application object before setting them, and release it afterward. If not, another script might attempt to access the same variables and cause concurrency problems.

In addition to maintaining any number of variables, the Application object triggers two special events, *Application_OnStart* and *Application_OnEnd*, when the application starts and ends, respectively. Use these events to execute the startup and clean-up code (initialize variables when the application starts and store them to a file when the application ends).

Collections

Like several other ASP objects, the Application object exposes a property that is a collection. It is the Contents collection, which holds all the variables with application scope; this is the single most important property of the Application object.

The Contents Collection

The Contents collection of the Application object stores any number of variables, which can be created either in the Application_onLoad event or from within any script of the application. As a collection, it exposes the standard properties (Item, Key, and Count) of a collection object. All variables with application scope (or *application-wide variables*) can be accessed by all scripts and all users of the application. As you will see in Chapter 4, *The Session Object*, there's another set of variables for each viewer, maintained by the Session object; these variables are private to a session.

Item

This property lets you set or read the value of a specific member of the Contents collection. You can think of the elements of the collection as variables that have a name and a value. The members of the Contents collection can be accessed either through a numeric index (just like the elements of an array) or through a key value. Notice that the first member's index is 1 and not 0. If you attempt to use the element with the index of 0, ASP will *not* generate an error message; it will simply ignore the expression.

To add a new variable to the Contents collection, use an expression like the following one:

```
Application.Contents.Item(1) = "Guest"
```

If the Contents collection contains a variable already, its value will be overwritten with a new one. If it contains more than one variable, then the first one will be overwritten. If you don't want to overwrite the value of the first variable, use the Empty() function, which returns True if its argument is an empty variable (a variable that hasn't been initialized):

```
If IsEmpty(Application.Contents.Item(1)) Then
    Application.Contents.Item(1) = "Guest"
End If
```

To read the value of the first element of the Contents collection, use the expression:

```
UserName = Application.Contents.Item(1)
```

Key

The Item notation requires that you remember the order in which the variables are created. The members of a collection can be accessed by key too. Each member has its own unique key, which you can use in the place of the index. The following statement creates a new variable and names it *FirstName*:

```
Application.Contents.Item("FirstName") = "Evangelos"
```

This variable will be accessed by name, and you no longer need to worry about the order in which the variables were created. To retrieve the value of the variable *FirstName* use the statement:

```
Fname = Application.Contents.Item("FirstName")
```

The Item property is the collection's default property, so the previous expressions can be written as either:

```
Application.Contents(1) = "Evangelos"
FName = Application.Contents(1)
```

or

```
Application.Contents("FirstName") = "Evangelos"
FName = Application.Contents("FirstName")
```

The Contents collection is the default property of the Application object, which means that the previous expressions can be reduced to the following:

```
Application("FirstName") = "Evangelos"
FName = Application("FirstName")
```

In short, Key is the variable's name and Item is the variable's value. If you need to find out the name of a variable, use its ordinal position. You will see in the following section how you can iterate through the members of the Contents collection and retrieve variable names and values, or ordinal numbers and values.

Any script in the application can create or access variables with application scope. These are the scripts that reside in the same folder as the application's main page or a subfolder underneath it. Because scripts must be aware of these variables, we usually create them from within the Application_OnStart event handler (described later in this chapter). Each member of the Contents collection can be accessed by name, and this name is the collection's key.

Count

This is a read-only property that returns the total number of members in the collection. The following code segment uses the Count property to iterate through the members of the Contents collection:

```
For item = 1 To Application.Contents.Count
    Response.Write item & "     " &
                    Application.Contents.(item)
Next
```

There's an even better way to iterate through the elements of a collection, namely the For Each ... Next loop, which is shown next:

```
For Each item In Application.Contents
    Response.Write item & "   " & _
                    Application.Contents(item)
    Response.Write "<BR>"
Next
```

In this loop, *item* is the name of the element's name and *Application(item)* is the element's value.

Array Variables

In addition to simple variables you can create arrays with application scope. To do so, you must first create an array, populate its elements, and then assign the entire array to a member of the Contents collection. Conversely, to read the array elements, you must read the same member of the Contents collection into a new array and then access the array's elements.

The following statements will create an array with the names of several book categories:

```
<%
Dim Categories(9)
Categories(1) = "Mystery"
Categories(2) = "Horror"
Categories(3) = "Fantasy"
' INSERT STATEMENTS FOR MORE CATEGORIES HERE
Application.Contents("BookCategory") = Categories
%>
```

To read the elements of the *BookCategory* array variable in a script, assign the entire variable to a properly declared array, as shown next:

```
<%
Dim Categories(9)
Categories = Application("BookCategory")
'   NOW YOU CAN USE THE CATEGORIES ARRAY IN YOUR CODE
%>
```

If your site uses these categories frequently, you can store them in an array instead of a database table or individual variables. To add new categories or change the names of existing categories, you need only edit the statements that create the array. The most appropriate place for these statements is the code of the Application_OnStart event.

The StaticObjects Collection

The StaticObjects collection is similar to the Contents collection, but it contains only the objects added to the application with the <OBJECT> tag. Objects added to the application with the CreateObject method of the Server object are not listed in the StaticObjects collection.

You're probably familiar with the <OBJECT> tag that allows you to insert an object on a page. If the object exists on the client computer, it's displayed on the page. If not, the browser downloads a CAB file with the object's components (DLL files) and installs the object on the client computer. Then it displays the page with the object (or uses the object from within a client-side script). Of course, using the <OBJECT> tag on the client is not a good idea, because most viewers will not allow any site to install a component on their computer.

If the client is a Windows machine, for example, you can add an instance of the Common Dialog Control and call its methods from within your script to display the File Open, Select Color, and other common dialog boxes. The following <OBJECT> tag will create an instance of the Common Dialog Control on the client page:

```
<OBJECT NAME=CD
      CLASSID="CLSID:F9043C85-F6F2-101A-A3C9-08002B2F49FB">
</OBJECT>
```

Listing 3.1 is an HTML page that uses the Common Dialog Control to display the File Open dialog box and prompts the user to select a file. The client-side script doesn't do much; it simply displays the selected file's name in a message box:

▶ *Listing 3.1: The CommonDialog.htm Page*

```
<SCRIPT LANGUAGE=VBScript>
Sub OPEN
    CD.ShowOpen
    If CD.FileName = "" Then Exit Sub
    MsgBox "You selected the file " & CD.FileName
End Sub
</SCRIPT>

<OBJECT NAME=CD
    CLASSID="CLSID:F9043C85-F6F2-101A-A3C9-08002B2F49FB">
</OBJECT>
Click the button below to select a file
<FORM>
<INPUT TYPE=Button OnClick="Open" VALUE="Select a File">
</FORM>
```

If you open this page with Internet Explorer or Netscape Communicator on a Windows machine, you will see the File Open dialog box. However, it will not work on a non-Windows machine.

You can use the same notation to add an object to a Web application. The component must exist on the server computer and is used by the application's scripts; the client is not aware of the existence of this object. So it's safe to add any object to the Web application—as long as you think it's safe for your server. Most objects added to the application either with the <OBJECT> tag or with the Server.CreateObject method are developed by Web developers, so there is no security risk in adding objects to a Web application.

To add an object to your application with the <OBJECT> tag, insert the appropriate tag in the GLOBAL.ASA file. The following three tags will add three objects to the application: an ADO Connection object, an ADO Command Object, and an ADO Recordset object. These objects are required to access a database on the server and perform queries against it. All three objects, plus a few more ADO objects, are discussed in detail in Chapter 9, *ADO 2.5 For Web Developers*.

```
<OBJECT ID=CONN
    CLASSID="CLSID:00000514-0000-0010-8000-00AA006D2EA4">
</OBJECT>

<OBJECT ID=CMD
    CLASSID="CLSID:00000507-0000-0010-8000-00AA006D2EA4">
</OBJECT>

<OBJECT ID=RS
    CLASSID="CLSID:00000535-0000-0010-8000-00AA006D2EA4">
</OBJECT>
```

If you place these lines in the GLOBAL.ASA file, you will be able to access the properties and methods of the CONN, CMD, and RS object variables from within the application's scripts. You'll find many examples on using the ADO component later in this book, so I won't elaborate on using objects instantiated with the <OBJECT> tag. Adding objects to a Web application with the <OBJECT> tag is a rather antiquated method. Use the Server .CreateObject method instead, which is described in detail in Chapter 8, *The Server Object*. The difference between the two methods is that any objects added with the <OBJECT> tag are not created before they're being used—i.e., when a script calls a method of the object or sets one of its properties. The Server.CreateObject method creates the object the moment you call it, so just avoid calling this method before the script needs the object. Some developers believe the <OBJECT> tag is slightly more efficient than calling the CreateObject method, but its syntax is awkward, not to mention that if you revise the component you must also change its ClassID in your scripts.

As a collection, the StaticObjects property exposes the Item, Key, and Count members, which are described next.

Item

This property lets you set or read the value of a specific member of the Static-Objects collection. The members of the StaticObjects collection can be accessed either through a numeric index (just like the members of the Contents collection) or through a key value. Notice that the first member's index is 1 and not 0. If you attempt to use the element with the index of 0, ASP will simply ignore the expression; it will *not* generate an error message.

Key

The Item notation requires that you remember the order in which the object variables are created. The members of a collection can be accessed by key, too. In the case of the StaticObjects collection, the key is the ID attribute of the <OBJECT> tag. If you don't know the names of the objects at design time, you can iterate through the collection and find out the names of the objects.

Count

Count is the number of elements in the StaticObjects collection.

Methods

In addition to the Content collection, the Application object supports a number of methods. The Lock and Unlock methods eliminate concurrency problems while editing the values of Application variables. The Remove method allows you to remove selected variables from the Contents collection, while the RemoveAll method removes all the variables from the same collection.

Lock

While you're setting the value of a variable with application scope, there's always a chance that another script may attempt to access it at the same time. To make sure this doesn't happen, call the Lock method to prevent other scripts from accessing the same variable. Set the variable's value and then call the Unlock method to release the lock.

Syntax

The syntax of the Lock method is simply `Application.Lock`. The Lock method locks the Application object and not just a single variable. Other scripts will not be able to edit any variable, not even add a new one, while your application manipulates an Application variable. It is imperative, therefore, to lock the Application object as late as possible (just before changing a variable's value) and release the lock as early as possible (right after the variable's value was set). Notice that all locks are automatically released as soon as the script terminates or times out. To release the lock explicitly, call the Unlock method.

Example

If you want to execute multiple statements without any interference from other scripts, you *must* call the Lock and Unlock methods, as shown in the following example:

```
<%
Application.Lock
If (Application("Viewers") Mod 1000000) = 0 Then
    Mlns = Application("Viewers") / 1000000
    VLogo = "Over " & Mlns & "million clients served!"
End If
Application.Unlock
%>
```

Remove

The Remove method allows you to remove a variable from the Contents collection. You can remove items either with their index, or their key.

NOTE The Remove method of the Application object is new to ASP 3.0.

Syntax

The syntax of the Lock method is

```
Application.Contents.Remove index | key
```

where *index* is the index of the item to be removed and *key* is the same item's key value. To remove the first item of the collection, use this statement:

```
Application.Contents.Remove 1
```

It's simpler and safer to remove items by their keys, with a statement like the following:

```
Application.Contents.Remove "SessionDuration"
```

NOTE Even though Contents is the default property of the Application object, you can't omit the Contents qualifier when calling the Remove method. In other words, you must use the expression *Application.Contents .Remove*. The expression *Application.Remove* is not a valid shorthand notation, because Remove is a method of the Contents collection and not of the Application object.

RemoveAll

The RemoveAll method deletes all the variables with application scope, and it doesn't accept any arguments. Notice that all variables are automatically released when the application ends (which usually happens when the Web server is terminated), and they're re-created when the application starts again. You shouldn't have to release all application variables, but if you ever do, use the Lock method to lock the Application object while you remove the variables and create new ones.

NOTE The RemoveAll method of the Application object is new to ASP 3.0.

Unlock

The Unlock method releases the lock on the Application object placed with the Lock method. (See the description of the Lock method for more information on using both methods.)

As you have noticed, the Lock and Unlock method do not apply to individual variables. You must lock the entire Application object in order to set a single variable, and it's imperative that you place the lock as late as possible and release it as early as possible. If you forget to unlock the Application object, the lock will be automatically removed when the script ends or times out.

If another script attempts to read the value of a variable with application scope while the Application object is locked, the script will not abort. It will wait until the Application object is unlocked and then proceed with the read operation.

You need not call the Lock/Unlock methods if you're only going to set the value of a variable, because a single statement is executed in a single step; no other script will get a chance to access the variable while it's being written. However, it's customary to lock the Application and Session objects before setting a variable and unlock them immediately afterward.

Events

The Application object fires two events, OnStart and OnEnd. These events are fired when the application starts and ends, respectively. You can use the OnStart event to initialize variables with application scope, create object variables you plan to use in the application, and perform other initialization tasks. The OnEnd event is where you insert the clean-up code (save some of the variables to a text file and then release them).

OnEnd

The OnEnd event is fired every time the Web application is stopped. This happens when you stop the Web server, or you unload the application from the Web server. Here's where you insert the clean-up code to be executed when the Web application ends. The code of this event resides in the

GLOBAL.ASA file and is processed after any other code in that file is executed. The OnEnd event is optional and you may not code it. We usually release counters and other variables with application scope in this event's code.

The following script shows how to store the value of a variable to a text file when the application ends normally. The *TotalViewers* variable has an application scope; it's created when the application is started (from within the Application_OnStart event, which is described in the following section) and is incremented every time a new viewer connects to the application (from within the Session_OnStart event, which is described in the following chapter).

```
<SCRIPT LANGUAGE = VBScript RUNAT = Server>
Sub Application_OnEnd
    Set FS = CreateObject("Scripting.FileSystemObject")
    Set TS = FS.OpenTextFile("C:\MYSITE\COUNTER.TXT", True)
    Hits = Application.Contents("TotalViewers")
    TS.WriteLine Hits
    TS.Close
    Set TS = Nothing
    Set FS = Nothing
    End Sub
</SCRIPT>
```

This script uses the FileSystemObject object to access the text file. For more information on this object see Chapter 15, *The File Access Component*.

OnStart

The OnStart event is fired when the application starts. Technically, it's fired when first client connects to the application, but this is where you insert the code you want to execute when the application starts.

The code of this event resides in the GLOBAL.ASA file and is processed before any other code in the GLOBAL.ASA file is executed. Notice that the OnStart event is optional and you may not code it. We usually instantiate counters and other variables with application scope in this event's code. The following code creates a counter variable, which will be incremented by one every time a new viewer connects to the application. Obviously, the counter must be incremented from within the Session_OnStart event, which is fired once for each new viewer.

```
<SCRIPT LANGUAGE = VBScript>
Sub Application_OnStart
```

```
    Application.Contents("TotalViewers") = 0
End Sub
</SCRIPT>
```

This script sets the *TotalViewers* counter to 0. Since we don't want our visitor count to reset every time we start the application (that is, every time the server is restarted), we must store the value of the *TotalViewers* variable to a disk file. Here's how it's done:

```
<SCRIPT LANGUAGE=VBScript>
Sub Application_OnStart
    Set FS = CreateObject("Scripting.FileSystemObject")
    Set TS = FS.OpenTextFile("C:\WEB\MYSITE\COUNTER.TXT")
    Hits = TS.ReadLine
    TS.Close
    Set TS = Nothing
    Set FS = Nothing
    Application.Contents("TotalViewers") = Hits
End Sub
</SCRIPT>
```

This script reads the value of the total hits from a text file and assigns its value to the variable *TotalViewers*, which has application scope. It uses the FileSystemObject object, which is described in Chapter 15, *The File Access Component,* to access a text file on the server, where the total number of hits is stored. Each time the *TotalViewers* variable is incremented, it must also be stored in the same file. If the site is very busy, you may choose to update this file with every 100 hits or more. The code for storing the counter's value to a text file is shown in the description of the OnStart event of the Application object.

Alternatively, you can store the value of the *TotalViewers* variable to a text file when the application stops. This approach will work in all situations, except when the computer running the Web server crashes. See the example of the OnEnd event in the previous section.

WARNING Any objects that will be used in transactions with the ObjectContext object should not have session or application scope. The Microsoft Transaction Server destroys these objects at the end of the transaction, so you should create them when you need them and release them as soon as you're done. For more information see Chapter 10, *The ObjectContext Object.*

chapter 4

The Session Object

T he Session object represents a user session. It can be accessed by all the scripts of the application in the context of the same user. Each time a viewer connects to the site for the first time, a new Session object is created. This object is destroyed automatically at the end of the session. If the same viewer comes back to the site, a new Session object will be created.

Most developers use the Session object as a depository for variables with information about a specific viewer. The Session object is a rather peculiar object. The Web server maintains information about a session with the help of a special cookie, which is sent to the server along with every request. When the Web server sees this cookie, it immediately associates the request with a session. If the client doesn't support cookies, however, the Web server will not be able to associate the requests with the sessions. One script will set a variable with Session scope, for instance, and the other scripts won't see the value of the variable. To make the most of the Session object, you must understand the relationship between the Session object and cookies. For more information on this topic, see the section describing the SessionID property, later in this chapter.

Properties

The Session object exposes the properties discussed in the following sections. Most of the properties determine the overall appearance of the document— such as the code page that will be used to render the text on the browser, the formatting dates and so on.

CodePage

This property sets or returns the code page that will be used by the Web server to display text. A code page contains the English characters, digits, punctuation symbols and the characters that are specific to a locale (see the LCID for more information on the locale).

Syntax

```
Session.CodePage = intCodePage
myCodePage = Session.CodePage
```

intCodePage is an integer value that determines the code page. The code page you specify must match the character set installed on the server. Obviously, the same character set must be installed on the client, or else the viewer will see gibberish in the place of the local characters.

NOTE The default character set is specified with the CODEPAGE directive. The CodePage property temporarily overwrites this setting for the text sent to the client.

The code page you specify must be installed on the server. The following table lists the values of the most common code pages:

1252	Western language (U.S. English and most European languages). It's also referred to as the ANSI code page.
932	Japanese Kanji
935	Chinese simplified
950	Chinese traditional

LCID

The LCID property sets or returns the locale ID. This setting determines the formatting of certain information, such as date and time values, currency, and so on. Each locale is identified by an integer value and it's defined in the operating system. The locale ID for U.S. English is 2048 and the locale IDs for a few European languages are shown here:

German	1031
Greek	1032
Spanish	1034
French	1036

Syntax

```
Session.LCID = intLocaleID
mLocaleID = Session.LCID
```

intLocaleID is an integer value that determines the ID of the locale on the Web server.

NOTE Notice that you can't specify an invalid ID. If the locale ID isn't supported by the operating system, a run-time error will occur.

Example

The following script demonstrates the use of the LCID property. For each different locale ID, the system will format different currency and date values.

▶ *Listing 4.1: The Locale.asp Script*

```
<%
Dim LocaleIDs

LocaleID=Session.LCID
LocaleIDs=Array(2048, 1030, 1031, 1032, 1033, _
                1034, 1035, 1036, 1038, 1039, 1040)
origLCID = Session.LCID
For i = 0 To UBound(LocaleIDs)
    LocaleID=LocaleIDs(i)
    Session.LCID=LocaleID
    Response.Write "<B>LCID=" & LocaleID & "</B>"
    Response.Write "<BR>"
    Response.Write "The date in short format is " & _
                   Date & "<BR>"
    Response.Write "The date in long format is: " & _
                   FormatDateTime(Date, vbLongDate)
    Response.write "<BR>"
    Response.Write "Formatted currency value: " & _
                   FormatCurrency(104.35)
    Response.write "<BR><BR>"
Next
Session.LCID = origLCID
%>
```

FIGURE 4.1: The output of the LocaleID.asp script

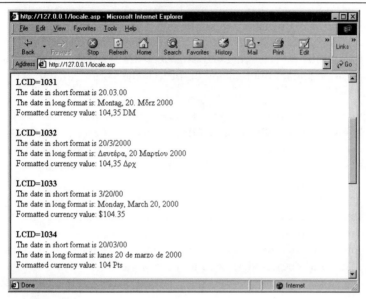

```
LCID=1031
The date in short format is 20.03.00
The date in long format is: Montag, 20. Mörz 2000
Formatted currency value: 104,35 DM

LCID=1032
The date in short format is 20/3/2000
The date in long format is: Δευτέρα, 20 Μαρτίου 2000
Formatted currency value: 104,35 Δρχ

LCID=1033
The date in short format is 3/20/00
The date in long format is: Monday, March 20, 2000
Formatted currency value: $104.35

LCID=1034
The date in short format is 20/03/00
The date in long format is: lunes 20 de marzo de 2000
Formatted currency value: 104 Pts
```

SessionID

This is a read-only property that identifies the current session. The SessionID property's value is a long integer and it's stored on the client computer as a cookie. The browser transmits this value to the server with every request to identify the viewer.

The SessionID value is generated automatically by the Web server the first time a new session object is created, and it's released when the session terminates or times out. If the same viewer disconnects and later establishes a new session, the Web server will use the same ID. The SessionID property can be used to identify a viewer during the same session, but not across multiple sessions.

The SessionID property is moved back and forth between the server and the client as a cookie. If the client has disabled cookies, then a new value is generated each time you call the SessionID property. The Web server does not receive the cookie with the session's ID from the client and ASP generates a new one every time a script calls the Session.SessionID property. As a result, using this property to identify sessions can be tricky. One idea would be to create a Session variable and set it to the SessionID property when a viewer connects to the main page of the site. It would be nice if you could use the Session_OnStart event to create the Session variable and set its value. But the SessionID value is generated when a viewer opens the first page of the application and it's not available at the time the Session_OnStart event is processed.

If the viewer has enabled the use of cookies, then you can identify the viewer's session either with the SessionID property or with the HTTP_COOKIE member of the ServerVariables collection. If the viewer has disabled the use of cookies, then you can't reply on the SessionID to monitor the viewer during the session. The solution is to create a unique value (string or numeric value) and pass it to every page on a hidden control. When the viewer clicks a hyperlink on the page, the value of the hidden control is also transmitted to the server and your scripts can extract this value through the Request.Form collection. For more information on this technique, see the section "Maintaining State without Cookies," later in this chapter.

Timeout

This property sets or returns the time interval for which the Web server will maintain a session alive without any viewer action. In other words, how long the session variables will maintain their value while the session is inactive (that is, for as long as the viewer hasn't followed a hyperlink to another page, or has not terminated the session.

Syntax

```
Session.Timeout = interval
```

Interval is the number of minutes for which the Web server will maintain information about the session. The default value of the Timeout property is 20 minutes (and 10 minutes for Windows NT).

There's no need to change this value unless you expect viewers to spend more time with a specific page. If a page contains animation or other material that may keep the user busy for more than 20 minutes, you can increase the timeout period. You may have to lower this value if the typical viewer doesn't spend more than a few minutes viewing your pages on the average. If your site gets too many hits, you'll make more efficient usage of the server's resource's by lowering this setting.

WARNING The Timeout property applies to all sessions, and it should belong to the Application object. If you change the value of the Timeout property in a single session, all sessions will inherit the same value.

Collections

The Session object exposes two collections, the Contents and StaticObjects collections, which are quite similar to the collections by the same name exposed by the Application object. The two collections of the Session object are described in the following sections.

Contents

All the variables created through scripts, that have an application scope, are contained in the Contents collection. As a collection, it exposes the standard properties of a collection object. They are described next. All variables with session scope can be accessed by all the scripts of the application in the context of the viewer that initiated the session. One session's variables can't be accessed by another session's scripts because session variables are private to a session.

Item

This property lets you set or read the value of a specific member of the Contents collection. The members of the Contents collection can be accessed either through a numeric index (just like the elements of an array), or through a key value. Notice that the first member's index is 1 and not 0. If you attempt to use the element with the index of 0, ASP will simply ignore the expression and it will *not* generate an error message.

To add a new variable to the Contents collection, use an expression like the following one:

```
Session.Contents.Item(1) = "Guest"
```

If the Contents collection contains a variable already, its value will be over-written with a new one. If it contains more than one variable, then the first one will be overwritten. If you don't want to overwrite the value of the first variable, use the Empty() function, which returns True if its argument is an empty variable (a variable that hasn't been initialized):

```
If IsEmpty(Session.Contents.Item(1)) Then
    Session.Contents.Item(1) = "Guest"
End If
```

To read the value of the first element of the Contents collection, use the expression Session.Contents.Item(1), as shown next:

```
UserName = Session.Contents.Item(1)
```

Key

The Item notation requires that you remember the order in which the variables are created. The members of a collection can be accessed by key too. Each member has its own unique key, which you can use in the place of the index. The following statement creates a new variable and names it *FirstName*:

```
Session.Contents.Item("FirstName") = "Evangelos"
```

This variable will be accessed by name and you no longer need to worry about the order in which the variables were created. To retrieve the value of the variable *FirstName* use the statement:

```
Fname = Session.Contents.Item("FirstName")
```

The Item property is the collection's default property, so the previous expressions can be written as either

```
Session.Contents(1) = "Evangelos"
FName = Session.Contents(1)
```

or

```
Session.Contents("FirstName") = "Evangelos"
FName = Session.Contents("FirstName")
```

The Contents collection is the default property of the Session object, which means that the previous expressions can be reduced to the following ones:

```
Session("FirstName") = "Evangelos"
FName = Session("FirstName")
```

In short, Key is the variable's name and Item is the variable's value. If you need to find out the name of a variable, use its ordinal position. You will see in the following section how you can iterate through the members of the Contents collection and retrieve variable names and values, or ordinal numbers and values.

Count

This is a read-only property that returns the total number of members in the collection. The following code segments uses the Count property to iterate through the members of the Contents collection:

```
For item = 1 To Session.Contents.Count
    Response.Write item & Session(item)
Next
```

There's an even better way to iterate through the elements of a collection, namely the For Each ... Next loop, which is shown next:

```
For Each item In Session.Contents.Count
    Response.Write item & Session.Contents(item)
Next
```

In this loop, *item* is the name of the variable and *Session(item)* is the variable's value.

Methods

The Session.Contents collection exposes two methods that allow you to remove individual items from the Contents collection (the Remove method), or all the items in the Contents collection (the RemoveAll method).

NOTE The Remove and RemoveAll methods of the Session object are new to ASP 3.0.

Remove

The Remove method allows you to remove a variable from the Contents collection. You can remove items either with their index, or their keys.

Syntax

The Syntax for the Remove method is:

```
Session.Contents.Remove index | key
```

Where *index* is the index of the item to be removed and *key* is the same item's key value. To remove the first item of the collection use this statement:

```
Session.Contents.Remove 1
```

It's simpler and safer to remove items by their keys, with a statement like the following one:

```
Session.Contents.Remove "SessionDuration"
```

> **NOTE** Even though Contents is the default property of the Session object, you can't omit the Contents qualifier when calling the Remove method. In other words, you must use the expression *Session.Contents .Remove*. The expression *Session.Remove* is not a valid shorthand notation, because Remove is a method of the Contents collection and not of the Session object.

RemoveAll

The RemoveAll method deletes all the variables with session scope, and it doesn't accept any arguments. Notice that all variables are automatically released when the session ends (which happens when the viewer disconnects or a script terminates the session with the Abandon method).

Array Variables

In addition to simple variables you can create arrays with session scope. To do so, you must first create an array, populate its elements, and then assign the entire array to a member of the Contents collection. Conversely, to read the array elements you must read the same member of the Contents collection into a new array and then access the array's elements.

The following statements will create an array with the names of several book categories the particular viewer is interested in:

```
<%
Dim Categories(9)
Categories(0) = "Mystery"
```

```
Categories(1) = "Horror"
Categories(2) = "Fantasy"
' INSERT STATEMENTS FOR MORE CATEGORIES HERE
Session("BookCategory") = Categories
%>
```

To read the elements of the *BookCategory* array variable in a script, assign the entire variable to a properly declared array as shown next (these statements will normally appear in a separate script):

```
<%
Categories = Session("BookCategory")
'  NOW YOU CAN USE THE CATEGORIES ARRAY IN YOUR CODE
%>
```

Notice that the Categories array is not declared. ASP will dimension the array according to the number of elements in the BookCategory array. If you declare the array, a Type Mismatch run-time error will occur.

The StaticObjects Collection

The StaticObjects collection is similar to the Contents collection, but it contains only the objects added to the session with the <OBJECT> tag. Objects added to the current session with the CreateObject method of the Server object are not listed in the StaticObjects collection.

You're probably familiar with the <OBJECT> tag that allows you to insert an object on a page. If the object exists on the client computer, it's displayed on the page. If not, the browser downloads a CAB file with the objects components (DLL files) and installs the object on the client computer. Then it displays the page with the object (or uses the object from within a client-side script). Of course, using the <OBJECT> tag on the client is not a good idea, because most viewers will not allow any site to install a component on their computer.

To add an object to your application with the <OBJECT> tag, insert the appropriate tag in the GLOBAL.ASA file. Use the same notation as explained in Chapter 3, *The Application Object,* but use the following attribute:

```
SCOPE = Session
```

This tag will add a Recordset object to every session:

```
<OBJECT ID=RS SCOPE=Session
```

```
CLASSID="CLSID:00000535-0000-0010-8000-00AA006D2EA4">
</OBJECT>
```

If you place these lines in the GLOBAL.ASA file, then a Recordset object variable will be created for each session. Each session's Recordset variable will be named RS, but each application will be able to see its own RS object variable. No session can access another session's RS object variable.

Maintaining object variables with Session scope is not a great idea, because you're wasting resources. Instead, you should create an instance of a Recordset object when you need it and release it when you're done with it.

NOTE Any objects that will be used in transactions with the Object-Context object should not have Session or Application scope. The Microsoft Transaction Server destroys these objects at the end of the transaction. For more information see Chapter 10, *The ObjectContext Object*.

As a collection, the StaticObjects property exposes the Item, Key, and Count members, which are described next.

Item

This property lets you set or read the value of a specific member of the Static-Objects collection. The members of the StaticObjects collection can be accessed either through a numeric index (just like the members of the Contents collection), or through a key value. Notice that the first member's index is 1 and not 0. If you attempt to use the element with the index of 0, ASP will simply ignore the expression; it will *not* generate an error message.

Key

The Item notation requires that you remember the order in which the object variables are created. The members of a collection can be accessed by key too. In the case of the StaticObjects collection, the key is the ID attribute of the <OBJECT> tag. If you don't know the names of the objects at design time, you can iterate through the collection and find out the names of the objects.

Count

This counts the number of elements in the StaticObjects collection.

Methods

The Session object exposes a single method that allows you to terminate a session from within your application.

Abandon

The Abandon method terminates a viewer's session and releases the memory allocated to maintain information about the viewer. If the user leaves the site, this information is maintained until the session times out. If the viewer returns before the session times out, the Web server doesn't create another a new Session object; instead, it uses the existing one.

Syntax

```
Session.Abandon
```

The Abandon method isn't used when a viewer disconnects, as much as it's used as a quick method to release all Session variables and create new ones. If you maintain viewer preferences or other viewer specific information in Session variables and you want to release them all, instead of iterating through all the variables of the Session.Contents collection, you can release them all with a single call to the Abandon method.

The Abandon method releases the Session variables after it has processed the page that called the method. It is possible to call the Abandon method and still see the values of the Session variables. You shouldn't assume that the Session.Contents collection has been cleared immediately after a call to the Abandon method. If you execute the following script, you will see that the variable UserName has its value even after the call to the Abandon method:

▶ *Listing 4.2: The Abandon.asp Script*

```
<%
Response.Write "USERNAME variable <B>" & _
               Session("UserName") & "</B>"
Response.Write "<BR>"
Session("UserName") = "Richard"
```

```
Response.Write "USERNAME variable <B>" & _
                Session("UserName") & "</B>"
Response.Write "<BR>"
Session.Abandon
Response.Write "USERNAME variable <B>" & _
                Session("UserName") & "</B>"
%>
```

The first time you open this page, the UserName variable has no value. However, after the call to the Abandon method, the UserName variable maintains its value. If you refresh the page by pressing F5, the UserName variable will be empty. If you comment out the line that calls the Abandon method, the variable UserName will maintain its value, because you haven't interrupted the session.

Maintaining State without Cookies

You can experiment a little further with this example. Comment out the line that calls the Abandon method and then disable the cookies in your browser (insert a single quote at the beginning of the line to comment it out). Open the Abandon.asp page again and refresh it a couple of times. The UserName variable doesn't maintain its value, even though it's a Session variable. The reason is that the Web server can't exchange cookies with the client. As a result, it can't maintain a session ID to identify the current session.

This experiment demonstrates the close relationship between sessions and cookies. Web server maintains session variables by passing a value to the client. This value is the HTTP_COOKIE server variable. If the client doesn't accept cookies (whether because the browser doesn't support them, or because the viewer has turned them off), then the Web server can't identify sessions and it can't maintain Session variables.

An interesting experiment, but it doesn't help you write scripts that maintain state even when the client doesn't accept cookies. If the client doesn't accept cookies, you must create a unique string for each session and pass it to the client on a hidden Text control. Alternatively, you can make this string part of every URL in your application. For example, if the unique string is stored in the Session variable USESSIONID, you can embed it in all the URL you build from within your scripts with a statement like the following one:

```
Response.Write "<A HREF='" & pageURL &
         "?ID=" & USESSIONID & ">" & sometext & "</A>"
```

If the destination of a hyperlink on a page is NewItemsPage.asp, you would normally embed the following hyperlink on the page:

```
Click <A HREF='NewItemsPage.asp'>here</A>
         to see the new items
```

This hyperlink will become:

```
Click <A HREF='NewItemsPage.asp?ID=XXX'>here</A>
         to see the new items
```

XXX is the unique string that uniquely identifies the current session.

If the script that processes the request expects additional parameter values, append them to the URL using the "&" character to separate multiple parameters. Assuming that a hyperlink's destination is the script ShowTitles-ByAuthor.asp, you should insert the following hyperlink in the HTML document:

```
<A HREF="ShowTitlesByAuthor.asp?UID=XXX&AuthorID=nnn>
AuthorName</A>
```

xxx is the value that uniquely identifies the viewer and *nnn* is the ID of the author. AuthorName is an author's name that you want to turn into a hyperlink. This hyperlink will invoke a script on the server, which will return a page with the books of the specified author. If you didn't care about maintaining state, you would pass only the author's ID to the script. As you can understand, this hyperlink's URL must be built on the fly.

After you have created the unique ID for the session, you can easily implement a basket by using Session variables with the same names and values as the cookies you'd leave on the client computer through the Response.Cookies collection. You must be aware that a shopping basket on the server will not maintain its contents between sessions. The basket will be released after the current session and you must warn users that their selections will be lost if they don't order them before the end of the session.

Many sites use this technique, regardless of whether the client supports cookies or not. You can tell how a site maintains state across pages by looking at the URL each pages passes back to the server (this URL appears in the Address Box of the browser). If all URLs contain an alphanumeric string that remains the same for all requests, then the application maintains state by passing a value to the client along with every request.

All sites created by Microsoft's Site Server, for example, pass a unique ID to the client with each page as part of the page. The same ID is returned to the server with every request and, as a result, the server knows where the request came from and it can maintain state. This technique allows you to design shopping baskets, but these baskets are limited in the current session and won't maintain their contents between sessions.

To maintain the basket across session, simply attempt to create the appropriate cookies on the client. If the viewer hasn't disabled the cookies, you'll be able to retrieve the basket's items the next time the same viewer connects to your site. You could also store the basket's contents to a local database on the server, but this entails that viewers will have to identify themselves every time they connect to your site, before they can see the contents of their baskets.

Events

The Session object recognizes two events: the OnStart event, which is triggered when a new session is created, and the OnEnd event, which is triggered when the current session terminates. Insert any code you want to execute when a new session is established, and when a session is terminated respectively.

OnStart

The OnStart event is fired when a new session is initiated (that is, every time a new viewer connects to your application). In this event you can read a user ID stored on the client computer as cookie, set up variables with session scope, and so on. All variables you create in the OnStart event handler must be released in the OnEnd event handler. If not, they will be automatically released.

The code of this event resides in the GLOBAL.ASA file and it's processed before any other code in the GLOBAL.ASA file is executed. Notice that the

OnStart event is optional and you may not code it. We usually instantiate counters and other variables with application scope in this event's code. The following code creates a counter variable, which will be incremented by one every time a new viewer connects to the application. Obviously, the counter must be incremented from within the Session_OnStart event, which is fired for each new viewer.

```
<SCRIPT LANGUAGE = VBScript>
Sub Session_OnStart
    Session.Contents("TotalViewers") =
        Session.Contents("TotalViewers") + 1
End Sub
</SCRIPT>
```

This script increases the *TotalViewers* counter by one every time a session is established. It's simpler to use the Counters component to maintain counters in your application, and not the OnStart event to maintain counters in your code, as we have done here. For more information on the Counters object, see Chapter 17.

When the OnStart event is triggered, many of the ASP objects have not been created yet. As you will see in Chapter 7, *The Request Object*, the expression: Request.ServerVariables("HTTP_IP") returns the IP address of the client. If you attempt to use this property in the Session_OnStart event, you'll find out that its value is an empty string.

OnEnd

The OnEnd event is fired every time a session terminates (in other words, when a viewer leaves your server). Here's where you insert the clean-up code to be executed at the end of a session, as well as maintain statistics about the viewers. For example, you can save the duration of the session to a text file or a database. However, you can't access any of the ASP object in the Session_OnEnd event, except for the Application object. This means that you can't store the values of the cookies on the user's computer to a local database from within this event's code. You do have access to other components that are instantiated with the Server.CreateObject method, For example, you can open a text file and append session variables to the file.

The code of this event resides in the GLOBAL.ASA file, and the Session_OnEnd subroutine is optional. We usually release counters and other variables with session scope in this event's code.

chapter **5**

The Cookies Collection

C ommercial sites on the Web usually maintain a list of items selected by the user in a so-called shopping basket. The items selected by each viewer are placed in the basket so the viewer can order them now, later, or empty the basket. The contents of the basket are maintained between sessions of the same user, and users can see the items they have selected a few days or a few months ago. Each customer has his or her own private basket which no other user can view the items in another user's basket.

Obviously, some product IDs (along with quantities and discount information) are stored somewhere and retrieved every time the same viewer connects to the site. There are two places where this information can be stored: either on the server computer or on the client computer. If each user had a fixed IP address, it would be possible (although not very practical) for the server to maintain a database with IP addresses and the preferences for each visitor. As you recall, the IP address of the client computer is given by the ServerVariables collection of the Session object. The ASP application could identify users by their IP address as soon as they connect to the site and retrieve their order from a local database. But most clients have different IP addresses each time they connect, so this approach is out of the question.

You could ask your visitors to log in with a user ID and password, but then you may lose business. Most people wouldn't offer much information (or many keystrokes, for that matter) so that they can browse your site.

If you think about it, you will see that the most efficient method for the server to maintain information about specific clients is to store this information on the client computer itself and recall it each time the client connects to the server. The information is stored, by the browser, in a special folder on the client computer, in the form of *cookies*. As you will see, each cookie has a name and a value, similar to a variable. Cookies are similar to the application and session variables you learned to create using the corresponding objects in earlier chapters, but they're stored on the client computer.

Why Use Cookies

HTTP is a stateless protocol, which means that you can't pass information directly from one page to the other. If you want to share information across the pages of your application, you can use session variables, and in some cases application variables, as you have seen in the last two chapters. Cookies are also used to pass information between pages on the same site. Let's say you want to provide custom pages. The site is made up of many pages and all pages should be aware of the viewer's preferences. To share a piece of information across multiple pages, you must store it in a session variable. Even so, you must be able to associate the session variables to the values specified by the viewer in an earlier session—obviously, users shouldn't have to specify their preferences every time they connect. The most efficient method of maintaining state across sessions of the same viewer is to store the information on the client computer. Each client maintains a set of cookies (variables) that the application can read them as soon as the client connects to the application.

Storing information on the client computer is not a problem-free method. Viewers may delete the cookies on their computers, and when this happens, your application will not recognize the viewer. It will prompt them for their preferences again, and any items in their basket will be lost for good. Because of the complexity of alternate approaches, this is a risk many sites take.

A safer approach is to store customer information to a local database on the server. Each customer will be assigned a unique ID. You can then store this ID on the client computer as a cookie. When the cookie is lost, you can prompt the viewer to enter his or her e-mail address and a password, and use this information to look up your database. Of course, if the user has disabled the cookies, the application must prompt the users every time for their login information.

Depending on the nature of your business and the type of customers, you will decide which method works best for you. No matter how you resolve the problem of maintaining state across sessions, you will eventually use client-side cookies.

How about the users who are skeptical about cookies and turn them off? Occasionally, some viewers will simply not accept cookies. If you can't leave cookies on the client computer, you will have to ask your viewers to identify themselves every time they connect to your site. In other words, you must maintain a database of viewers/customers and ask them to identify themselves with a user ID/password combination when they connect to your site. Once you have identified a viewer, you can retrieve his or her basket from the same database. This is a lot of work for the server, especially for a popular site. Fortunately, most people find this very inconvenient and allow Web sites to store cookies on their computers.

As far as security risks are concerned, the browser manages cookies. A Web page can't access the client computer's hard disk directly, and as a consequence, cookies are safe. Moreover, when a page requests the values of the cookies, the browser supplies only those cookies that were stored by the same page, or other pages of the same site. In other words, cookies left on your computer by Microsoft's Web site can't be read by pages of other sites. You can't even write an ASP script to read the cookies left on your computer by another site.

Cookie Files

If you're curious as to what each site you visit stores on your computer, you can view the cookies left by a site on your computer. Each site's cookies are left in a file in folder Documents and Settings\userid\Local Settings\Temporary Internet Files in Windows 2000. The cookie files are named

```
cookie:user_name@www.sitename.com
```

where *user_name* is your user name and *sitename* is the name of the site. Cookie files are not text files and you can't read the information stored in them. The developer decides what type of information must be stored on the client computer in the form of cookies, and this information may be coded too. If you have items in a shopping basket, however, you will probably recognize the IDs of these items in the basket. Some sites encrypt the information they store on your computer, so that you can't read it. Even so, a cookie can't harm your computer.

Cookies Expire

Cookies have expiration dates too. If a cookie is stored without an expiration date, it ceases to exist after the current session. A cookie with an expiration date remains on the client computer as long as specified by its expiration date. You should be careful as to which cookies will remain on the client's computer and when they'll expire. The same viewer may connect to your site a year later and the application may find in the basket product IDs that do not exist anymore. Do not leave too much information on the client computer, and make sure it won't stay there for very long. If a viewer hasn't come back to your site in a few weeks, chances are he has forgotten about the items in his shopping basket. If you decide to change the names of the cookies your application leaves to the client, you should check for old cookies and delete them every time a client connects to the new site.

To set the expiration date of a cookie, use the Expires property of the Cookies collection. This property's value must be a valid date, and it may include the time as well.

Saving and Reading Cookies

Cookies can be accessed through the Cookies collection. To set a cookie, use the Response.Cookies collection; to read the values of the cookies, use the Request.Cookies collection. When your application sets a cookie, its value is transmitted to the client along with the header of the response. It is therefore imperative to set any cookies before sending the page's main body to the client. If you attempt to set a cookie value after you have sent any HTML content to a client (even the <HTML> tag), an error message will be displayed.

To create a new cookie, use a statement such as the following:

```
<%
Response.Cookies("News")="Sports"
%>
```

This statement created a new cookie with the name *News* and set its value to the string "Sports". If a cookie by that name exists already on the client computer, its value is overwritten; if not, a new cookie is created. This cookie is released as soon as the current session ends.

You can specify the expiration date and time with the Expires property of the cookie, as follows (type this as a single line, but it won't fit in a single line on this printed page):

```
<% Response.Cookies("News").Expires =
        "December 31, 2005 12:00:00 GTM" %>
```

To read the *News* cookie from the client computer, use the Cookies property of the Request object and specify the desired cookie by name. To read the value of the *News* cookie, use a statement such as the following:

```
<%
interest = Request.Cookies("News")
%>
```

The *interest* variable holds the string "Sports" after the execution of this statement. The *News* cookie tells your application that the viewer is interested in sports news and, presumably, you will use this setting in your application to create a custom page for the viewer. You can also use this information to present ads about sporting items to the specific viewer.

To customize a page, however, you need more than a single cookie. A viewer might be interested in a dozen topics or be able to watch the prices of a number of stocks. Multiple related cookies are usually stored in a so-called dictionary of cookies. A dictionary is a structure similar to an array, but its elements can be accessed by name instead of a numeric index. Moreover, a dictionary may contain an entire array as an element.

Cookie Dictionaries

A cookie dictionary has a name like a regular cookie, and its members have names. To access individual members of the dictionary, use another name. If you want to create a dictionary of cookies and name it News and name the individual cookies Sports, Finance, and so on, use the following statements to create the dictionary:

```
<%
Response.Cookies("News")("Sports") = "Hockey"
Response.Cookies("News")("Finance") = "Funds"
Response.Cookies("News")("Technology") = "Computers"
%>
```

To read the same cookies, use the Cookies collection of the Request object and the same notation:

```
<%
SportsNews = Request.Cookies("News")("Sports")
```

```
FinanceNews = Request.Cookies("News")("Finance")
TechNews = Request.Cookies("News")("Technology")
%>
```

Iterating through the Cookies Collection

The number of cookies in the Cookies collection is given by the Request .Cookies.Count property. You can write a For ... Next loop that scans the collection, or you can write a For Each ... Next loop such as the following:

```
For Each cookie In Request.Cookies
    {process current cookie, which is Request.Cookies(cookie)}
Next cookie
```

and insert your own statements to read the cookie value and process it in the loop's body. If a cookie is a dictionary (in other words, it has keys), you must access them as elements of a collection. Let's assume you've sent a cookie with keys to the client with the following statements:

```
<%
Response.Cookies("Prefs")("Background") = "Planets.bmp"
Response.Cookies("Prefs")("Books") = "Mystery"
Response.Cookies("Prefs")("News") = "Sports"
%>
```

The first member in the *Prefs* dictionary determines the visitor's favorite background pattern. The next two members can be used to create a custom home page. The following loop reads all the cookies on the client computer, including cookie dictionaries. The If clause reads a cookie dictionary, while the Else clause reads the single cookies.

```
<%
For Each cookie In Request.Cookies
    If Request.Cookies(cookie).HasKeys Then

        For Each scookie In Request.Cookies(cookie)
' Process current cookie. Its name is:
' cookie and its value is:
' Request.Cookies(cookie)(scookie)
        Response.Write cookie & "=" & scookie
```

```
            Next
      Else
    ' Process current cookie. Its name is cookie
    ' and its value is Request.Cookies(cookie)
          Response.Write cookie & "=" &
                            Request.Cookies(cookie)
      End If
    Next
    %>
```

Normally, the script on the server knows the names of the cookies and can request them by their names:

```
Pattern = Request.Cookies("UserName")
```

or, if the cookie belongs to a dictionary of cookies, use a statement like the following one:

```
BookType = Request.Cookies("Prefs")("Books")
```

If you need to find out the names of the cookies, use the For Each ... Next structure. At each iteration, the value of the *cookie* variable is the name of the cookie, and *Request.Cookies(cookie)* is its value.

All members of a dictionary of cookies have the same expiration date. To set the expiration date of the dictionary, use the following expression:

```
Response.Cookies("Prefs").Expires = Now + 365
```

The elements of the *Prefs* dictionary will expire a year after their creation. You can't set the expiration date of individual cookies in the dictionary with a statement like the following one:

```
'    THE FOLLOWING STATEMENT IS INVALID
Response.Cookies("Preferences")("News") = Now + 30
```

Notice that the Expires property is write only, because the Request.Cookies collection doesn't support the Expires property.

Cookies Belong to the HTTP Header

Cookies are sent to the client as part of the HTTP header. Because this header is transmitted to the client before any other information, you can't call the Response.Cookies method after you have sent any output to the client. The following script sends some data to the client and then attempts to send a cookie:

```
<HTML>
<H1>Cookies are Great!</H1>
<%
Response.Cookies("UserName") = "Evangelos"
%>
</HTML>
```

If you attempt to execute this script by opening the page on the Web server, the following error message will be displayed when the Response.Cookies method is processed:

```
Header Error

/ExampleCookies.htm, line 4

The HTTP headers are already written to the client
browser.
Any HTTP header modifications must be made before
writing page content.
```

To fix the page, move the Response.Cookies line to the beginning of the script, before any other output is sent to the client. Remember, however, that once the <HTML> tag has been sent to the client, it's too late to set any of the properties that modify the response header.

Deleting Cookies

The Cookies collection doesn't expose a Remove method to delete individual cookies. To delete an existing cookie, you set its expiration date to a past date. As soon as the expiration date is set to a date before the current date, the cookie ceases to exist.

To delete the cookie "LastOrderDate", use the following statement:

```
Response.Cookies("LastOrderDate") = Date() - 1
```

This statement will set the cookie's expiration date 24 hours behind the current date and the cookie will be deleted. Of course, this will not happen if the client computer's date is incorrect. It wouldn't hurt to subtract 365 days from the current date, or set the expiration date to 1900.

It's already been mentioned that cookie dictionaries have a common expiration date for all of their members. As a consequence, you can't delete individual cookies from a cookie dictionary. You must delete the entire dictionary and then create a new one. The items of a shopping basket, for example, shouldn't belong to a dictionary, because some customers like to add and remove many items to and from their baskets before they actually place the order. It is simpler to use individual cookies to monitor the contents of a basket.

Implementing a Basket

This section's examples show you how to create a basket on the client computer with book ISBNs and quantities. I can't show you a real application that lets you select the items to purchase in every detail. The examples of this section are the core of the scripts that maintain a basket on the client computer with cookies.

We'll start with a script to place three cookies on the client computer. Each cookie's name will be an ISBN (which is equivalent to a product ID), and its value will be the quantity of items ordered. Normally, the cookies will be created from within an application that allows the viewer to browse and select book titles or other products. For this example, I will use a short script that leaves a few cookies to the client computer. These cookies are pairs of ISBNs and quantities and they expire three days later, so that you can test the application while you're still reading this book. Another script will read the cookies and display the ISBNs and corresponding quantities. Later in the book we'll revise this script to make it retrieve the corresponding titles and prices from the BIBLIO database.

Creating the Order

The following script stores three cookies to the client computer. Each cookie's name is the ISBN of the selected book and its value is the number of items ordered. Here's the OrderBooks.asp script that creates a basket on the client computer. Later you will see how you can remove some (or all) of the cookies from the client computer.

▶ *Listing 5.1: The OrderBooks.asp Script*

```
<%
OrderISBN="0-7821126-4-1"
Response.Cookies(OrderISBN) = "1"
Response.Cookies(OrderISBN).Expires = Date + 3

OrderISBN="1-8503219-6-5"
Response.Cookies(OrderISBN) = "1"
Response.Cookies(OrderISBN).Expires = Date + 3

OrderISBN="0-8958858-9-1"
Response.Cookies(OrderISBN) = "1"
Response.Cookies(OrderISBN).Expires = Date + 3

Response.Write "<HTML><FONT FACE='Comic Sans MS'>"
Response.Write "<H3>The following books were ordered</H3>"
Response.Write "<BR>0-7821126-4-1 (quantity 1)"
Response.Write "<BR>1-8503219-6-5 (quantity 1)"
Response.Write "<BR>0-8958858-9-1 (quantity 1)"
%>
```

Figure 5.1 shows the output of the OrderBooks.asp script. Notice that the same lines will be printed even if the client doesn't accept cookies. They're printed directly from within the script. This is not an indication that the cookies have been actually stored on the client computer. If the client doesn't accept cookies, then the next page that reads the cookies will simply not display their values.

Notice the lines that set the cookies' Expires property. All cookies will remain on the server for three days after their creation and will then expire. If you want to test the expiration of the cookies, you can change the computer's date and then attempt to read the cookies with the ReadOrder.asp script, which is discussed in the following section.

FIGURE 5.1: The output of the `OrderBooks.asp` script

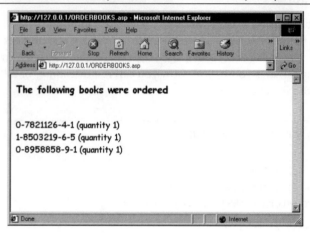

Reading the Order

Let's write another script to read the values of the cookies left on the client computer. We'll use a For Each ... Next loop to read all the cookies on the client computer. Here's the script that reads the books in the client's basket. In Chapter 9, *ADO 2.5 For Web Developers,* we'll revise the ReadOrder.asp script to actually receive the order, calculate the total, and record the order to a database.

▶ *Listing 5.2: The ReadOrder.asp Script*

```
<%
Response.Write "<HTML><FONT FACE='Comic Sans MS'>"
Response.Write "<CENTER>"
Response.Write "<H3>ReadOrder.asp Script Output<BR><BR>"
Response.Write "<TABLE BORDER=ALL>"
Response.Write "<TR><TD><B>Cookie Name</B>"
Response.Write "<TD><B>Cookie Value</B>"
For Each cookie in Request.Cookies
    Response.Write "<TR>"
    Response.Write "<TD ALIGN=CENTER>" & cookie
    Response.Write "   "
    Response.Write "<TD ALIGN=CENTER> "
    Response.Write Request.Cookies(cookie)
Next
```

```
Response.Write "</TABLE>"
Response.Write "</HTML>"
%>
```

To Test the Examples

To test the OrderBooks and ReadOrder scripts, follow these steps:

1. Copy the OrderBooks.asp and ReadOrder.asp files into the Web server's root folder (or a virtual folder under it).

2. Start your browser and enter the URL of the OrderBooks.asp file in the Address box. The address should be something like www.servername.com/vfolder/OrderBooks.asp. If the two files are not in a virtual folder, omit the vfolder segment of the path. If the Web server is running on your computer, the address will be 127.0.0.1/vfolder/OrderBooks.asp.

3. If the OrderBooks.asp script completes successfully, you will see a confirmation message. This means that the cookies have been saved on your computer and you can read them.

4. Enter the URL of the OrderBooks.asp file in the Address Box, as explained in step 2. You should see the ISBNs of the books already in the client computer's basket.

Notice that the same application may save other cookies on the client computer. If there are additional cookies on the client computer, the OrderBooks.asp script will display them as well. To select the cookies that correspond to books, prefix the names of the cookies by the string "ISBN." For example, change the following line in the OrderBooks.asp script:

```
OrderISBN="0-8958858-9-1"
```

to

```
OrderISBN="ISBN0-8958858-9-1"
```

You must also modify the ReadOrder.asp script, so that it processes only the cookies that correspond to ISBNs. To do so, change the loop to the following:

```
For Each cookie in Request.Cookies
    If Left(cookie, 4) = "ISBN" Then
        Response.Write "<TR>"
```

```
          Response.Write "<TD ALIGN=CENTER>" & Mid(cookie, 5)
          Response.Write "   "
          Response.Write "<TD ALIGN=CENTER> "
          Response.Write Request.Cookies(cookie)
      End If
   Next
```

Of course, for this trick to work there should be no cookies with the prefix "ISBN" other than the ones that relate to ordered items. If you create a cookie with a name like "ISBNCount", then this script will also be displayed on the output page.

Modifying the Basket

In this section we'll develop a script that displays the cookies on the client computer and allows the user to remove items from the basket. Going to Figure 5.2, it shows the SelectISBNs page, which displays the ISBNs of all the books in the basket, and a check box next to each ISBN. To remove an item from the basket, just check the box next to the quantity.

FIGURE 5.2: The SelectISBNs.asp script lets you remove items from your shopping basket.

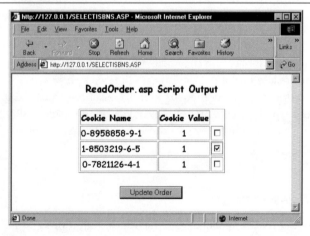

The SelectISBNs.asp file is shown next. It's very similar to the ReadOrder.asp script, only it displays the quantity and a check box next to each item, as shown in Figure 5.2.

You can revise the script so that it displays the quantity in a Text control and lets the user edit the quantity. Items with no quantity will be removed from the basket. The SelectISBNs.asp script calls the UpdateOrder.asp script on the server, which actually removes the cookies.

▶ *Listing 5.3: The SelectISBNs.asp Script*

```
<%
Response.Write "<HTML><FONT FACE='Comic Sans MS'>"
Response.Write "<CENTER>"
Response.Write "<H3>SelectISBNs.asp Script Output<BR><BR>"
Response.Write "<FORM ACTION='UpdateOrder.asp'
               METHOD=POST>"
Response.Write "<TABLE BORDER=ALL>"
Response.Write "<TR><TD><B>Cookie Name</B>"
Response.Write "<TD><B>Cookie Value</B>"
For Each cookie in Request.Cookies
    Response.Write "<TR>"
    Response.Write "<TD ALIGN=CENTER> " & cookie
    Response.Write "<TD ALIGN=CENTER> " &
               Request.Cookies(cookie)
    Response.Write "<TD ALIGN=CENTER> "
    Response.Write "<INPUT TYPE=CheckBox NAME='"
    Response.Write " cookie & "'>"
Next
Response.Write "</TABLE>"
Response.Write "<BR>"
Response.Write "<INPUT TYPE=Submit VALUE='Update Order'>"
Response.Write "</FORM>"
Response.Write "</HTML>"
%>
```

The UpdateOrder.asp script reads the parameters submitted by the SelectISBNs.asp script. The parameters of the Form on the SelectISBNs.asp page are the values of the check boxes. Each check box is named as the ISBN of a selected book (in effect, the name of a cookie), and its value is "On" if the corresponding box is checked.

The script iterates through the Cookies collection with a For Each ... Next loop. At each iteration it examines the status of the corresponding check box. If the box is checked, it removes the cookie from the client by setting its expiration date to a past date. If not, it renews the cookie by setting its expiration date three days ahead. The UpdateOrder.asp script is shown in following listing.

▶ *Listing 5.4: The UpdateOrder.asp Script*

```
<%
Response.Write "<HTML><FONT FACE='Comic Sans MS'>"
Response.Write "<CENTER>"
Response.Write "<H3>Your order was updated<BR><BR>"
Response.Write "<TABLE>"
Set AllCookies = Request.Cookies
For Each cookie in AllCookies
    Response.Write "<TR>"
    Response.Write "<TD ALIGN=CENTER> " & cookie
    If Not Request.Form(cookie)="on" Then
        Qty = AllCookies(cookie)
        Response.Write "<TD ALIGN=CENTER> " & Qty
        Response.Cookies(cookie) = Qty
        Response.Cookies(cookie).Expires = Now + 3
    Else
        Response.Cookies(cookie).Expires = Now - 1
        Response.Write "<TD ALIGN=CENTER> " & "(removed)"
    End If
Next
Response.Write "</TABLE></FORM>"
Response.Write "</HTML>"
%>
```

To test the two scripts that manipulate the cookies on the client computer, open the SelectISBNs page and mark a few of the cookies for deletion. Then click the Update Order button and you will see the cookies currently on the client computer. You can open the OrderBooks.asp page to reload all three cookies.

The `UpdateOrder.asp` script displays the names of the deleted cookies as well. If you refresh the page, then the deleted cookies will disappear, because they no longer exist on the client computer.

Cookies have a few more properties, which will be discussed in Chapters 6, *The Response Object,* and 7, *The Request Object.*

Maintaining State

Cookies are the primary mechanism for maintaining state in Web applications. The state of an application is a set of variables. The various modules of a desktop application, for example, maintain state because they can exchange and share variables. The same is not true for Web applications. A Web application runs over the HTTP protocol, which is a stateless protocol. Web pages can't exchange information with one another, and this is a fundamental problem in developing Web applications.

Web developers deal with this inherent problem with cookies. Cookies are central in maintaining state in Web applications. Shopping baskets are probably the most important aspect of commercial Web sites. That is why I devoted the last few sections of the chapter to the topic. Cookies, however, are used for other purposes too. Since a page can't communicate directly with any other page, it can use the client as a repository for temporarily storing the application's status.

Any page of the application can create cookies. The cookies left by the pages of an application to the client are transmitted automatically to the server by the client, along with each request. IIS creates a special cookie, which identifies each session. This cookie is sent to the client when the viewer opens the first page. The same cookie is sent back to the server every time the client requests another page. The server reads the value of the cookie and associates the viewer with a session. This cookie expires at the end of the session, and it can't be used to maintain state across sessions; just across the pages of the same session.

The problem with this approach is that some users turn off the cookies—not to mention that some older browsers don't even support cookies. For the purposes of this book we'll ignore the antiquated browsers, but we can't ignore the users who turn off the cookies. The only technique for maintaining state when clients don't accept cookies is to exchange a unique string with the client. You can create a unique string the first time a new client connects to the application. If all the pages of the site are generated by scripts, you can embed this string into every hyperlink on the page. A hyperlink of the form:

```
<A HREF="someScript.asp">Show</A>
```

would be encoded as:

```
<A HREF="someScript.asp?ID=xxx">Show</A>
```

This technique will work with all clients, as long as all pages are built on the fly with VBScript. Alternatively, you can include a hidden Text control on every page of the application and set its value to the string that identifies the current session. The scripts of the application can read this value and identify the session.

Per-Session Cookies

Ending the chapter on cookies, I would like to mention that Internet Explorer 5 supports two types of cookies. The first type of cookies are the ones that are stored on the client computer. These are the usual cookies, which are supported by all browsers that accept cookies. They are used to maintain state not only among the pages of a site, but among sessions as well.

The other type of cookies are the per-session cookies. These cookies are exchanged between the client and the server during a session, but they are not stored on the client computer.

Internet Explorer allows you to disable either type of cookies, even though the per-session cookies can't be used to monitor the viewers' habits. The per-session cookies are a tradeoff between privacy and functionality. Using regular cookies, a site can maintain a shopping basket, customize its pages according to the viewer's preferences, and provide a better interface. These cookies are also being used by advertisers to monitor viewer habits (sites they visit, products they buy, and so on), so more and more viewers disable them.

chapter 6

The Request Object

T he Request object represents the request from the client and allows you to retrieve information submitted by the client. The Request and Response objects are the basic ingredients for building interactive Web applications. The properties of the Request object allow you to retrieve the information passed from the client to the server, and they correspond to the fields of the HTTP Request header. This information includes cookies, the values of the HTML controls on the Form, and the values of several server variables. You can even probe the browser running on the client for specific capabilities and tune your pages for the target browser.

The first section of this chapter is an overview of the mechanisms for passing parameter values from the browser to the client and how the server intercepts these values. Then you'll find a detailed reference section on each of the Request object's members.

Reading Parameter Values

The single most important function of the Request object is to retrieve the parameter values passed by the client. This is done through the QueryString and Form properties, which are collections. Their elements are the values of the HTML controls on the Form of the page that submitted the data to the server. Which property you use to retrieve the parameter values submitted to your script by the client depends on the method used by the client to submit these values. Clients can submit data to the server with either of the GET and POST methods, which are described in the following section.

The GET and POST Methods

As you recall from Chapter 1, *Web Applications and ASP,* the HTML controls allow your Web application to interact with the client. The values entered on these controls by the viewer can be transmitted to the server in two ways: with the GET method or the POST method. The exact method is specified with the FORM tag's METHOD attribute. If a page contains the following Form, the values of the controls will be transmitted with the GET method:

```
<FORM NAME=Form1 ACTION=Scripts/script.asp" METHOD=GET>
Enter your ID <INPUT TYPE=Text NAME=ID>
<BR>
and your name <INPUT TYPE=Text NAME=UName>
</FORM>
```

The GET method is the default, and the values of the controls are appended to the URL of the destination page. The URL of the script that will process the Form is something like:

```
http://myserver.com/Scripts/script.asp?ID=4430&UName=Evans
```

Here, the Form on the page that called the script has two Text controls on it—the ID and UName controls—and the user entered the values "4430" and "Evans" in them.

The value of the ACTION attribute is the name of the script that will process the values of the controls. It is the `Script.asp` script and resides in the `Scripts` folder under the application's root folder on the server. The URL of the script is followed by a question mark, and the values of the controls are appended to the URL after the question mark. All parameter values are transmitted to the server as strings, even if they represent numeric values.

The complete URL of the requested script on the server is constructed automatically by the browser. The browser reads the value of the ACTION attribute of the <FORM> tag and appends to it the values of all the controls on the Form. The values of the controls are called parameters and are encoded in the form `parameter=value`. Multiple parameters are encoded as follows:

```
Parameter1=value1&parameter2=value2&parameter3=value3
```

In addition, the browser will also encode the values in a format suitable for transmission over the HTTP protocol. Spaces are replaced by plus (+) signs, while special symbols are encoded with the percent sign followed by the hex value of the special symbol. The plus sign, for example, is encoded as %2B; the forward slash is encoded as %2F. The dollar sign is also considered a special symbol in HTML, so the string "$40.25" will be encoded as %2440.25. We'll come back to the topic of parameter encoding in the following chapter, in the discussion of the HTMLEncode method of the Response object.

The URL of the requested script along with the parameter values appears in the browser's Address box when the viewer clicks the Submit button on the Form. The name of the button may be different, but it's the single button on the Form that sends the data entered on the Form to the client. The obvious drawback of the GET method is that all the information passed to the server appears in the browser's Address box. Yet viewers don't seem to object to this.

The other method for submitting parameter values to the server is the POST method. The POST method sends all the data to the server as part of the Request HTTP header. The advantages of the POST method are that it doesn't append any data to the URL of the requested page, and you can send more data with the POST method. The exact number of the bytes you can send with the POST method depends on the client and the server, but it's much more than the 2Kbytes limit of the GET method.

The viewer-supplied values are encoded in the same format as with the GET method, but the viewer can't see them. All the information is embedded into the request's header and not in the URL of the requested script.

To read the values entered by the viewer on a Form from within your script, you must use the appropriate property of the Request object:

- To read the parameter values passed to the server with the GET method, use the QueryString collection. The QueryString collection contains one member for each parameter. To extract the values of the parameters ID and UName from the QueryString collection, use the following statements in your script:

  ```
  UserID = Request.QueryString("ID")
  UserName = Request.QueryString("UName")
  ```

- To read the parameter values passed to the server with the POST method, use the Form collection. The Form collection contains one member for each control on the Form. To extract the values of the controls named ID and UName, use the following statements in your script:

  ```
  UserID = Request.Form("ID")
  UserName = Request.Form("UName")
  ```

I've described QueryString and Form both as properties and collections. The QueryString and Form collections contain a member for each parameter. The Request object exposes two properties with the same exact names as these collection names: the QueryString property and the Form property. These properties contain the entire string passed to the server. If you use the QueryString and Form properties, you must supply the code to extract the parameter names and values from the corresponding property.

The Request.QueryString property for the last example will be the following, provided you have used the GET method to submit the data to the client:

```
ID=443020&UName=Evans
```

The same string will be returned by the Request.Form property if the data was submitted to the server with the POST method.

As you can see from the examples, ASP differentiates between the Form (or QueryString) property and collection by the syntax. If the expression Request.Form (or the expression Request.QueryString) is followed by a parameter name enclosed in a pair of parentheses, then it's treated as a collection. If not, it's a property (a string with all parameter names and values).

Submitting Parameters without Forms

It is possible to call a script on the server and pass one or more parameter values to it from within an HTML page without a Form. A typical example is a list of products, where each product name (or model) is a hyperlink to the product's page. A list with the best-selling titles, where each title in the list is a hyperlink to the book's page, is a typical example. The following is a plain list of titles:

```
Database Design
SQL for Cobol Programmers
Introducing Microsoft Access
```

To convert the titles to hyperlinks pointing to the matching book's page, you must enclose the title in a pair of hyperlink tags (<A> and </A>). The destination of each hyperlink will be the name of a script that looks up the desired title in the database and builds the appropriate page on the fly. This script must be called with a parameter value, which is the ID of the selected book. Viewers need not enter any information on a Form in order to view the selected titles; all they have to do is click the appropriate title's hyperlink. This means that the HTML page must contain all the information needed by the script on the server to construct the selected title's page.

For the purposes of this example, I'll consider the book's ISBN (International Standard Book Number) to also be the book's ID. Assuming that the name of the script that looks up a book in the database and generates the book's page is ShowTitle.asp, and it expects the ISBN of a book, we can turn the titles into hyperlinks by enclosing them into a pair of <A> tags, as shown here:

```
<A HREF="ShowTitle.asp?ID=nnnn">Book_Title</A>
```

Book_Title is the book's title and *nnnn* is the book's ISBN. The ShowTitle.asp script must extract the value of the parameter ID, use it to look up the book's details in the database, and display a page with the book's complete description.

As you can see, the script that will build the list of the books must construct a URL identical to the one the browser would build, had we asked the viewer to enter the desired book's ISBN. The following code segment is the core of a script that builds a list of titles (like the best-selling titles, or the titles offered at a heavy discount). In Chapter 9, *ADO 2.5 For Web Developers*, I'll describe in detail the code that retrieves the information from the database.

```
<%
'CREATE A RECORDSET WITH THE ISBN AND TITLES
' OF THE BOOKS IN THE LIST.
' THEN SCAN EACH ROW IN THE RECORDSET WITH
' THE FOLLOWING LOOP:
While Not Titles.EOF
    HString = "<A HREF='" & Titles.Fields("ISBN") & "'>"
    HString = HString & Fields("Title") & "</A>"
    HString = HString & "<BR>"
    Response.Write HString
    Titles.MoveNext
Wend
%>
```

If the first row in the Recordset contains the title "Mastering C" from the BIBLIO database, the script will produce the following line:

```
<A HREF='0-4716082-0-3'>Mastering C</A>
```

This page could be static, although it's too much work to build all the hyperlinks and embed ISBNs manually. Let's say you have the ISBNs of the best-selling books stored in a text file, one item per line. We need a script that will read the text file (this file resides on the server and you can change it whenever you want), look up the actual book's title and author(s), and generate the list with the best sellers. Alternatively, you could execute a query against the database and retrieve the ISBNs of the titles with the largest sales. Once the text file with the ISBNs is in place, you can use the same script to build the list with the titles. We'll return to this example in Chapter 15, *The File Access Component*, where you'll see how to open a text file from within your script and read its lines. The same script will combine data access operations as well.

In the following sections we'll discuss the members of the Request object, starting with its collections. Strictly speaking, collections are properties, but the documentation differentiates between them, so we'll follow this distinction.

Collections

The Request object exposes five collections:

- The ClientCertificate collection, which contains information about the client certificate (if any)

- The Cookies collection, which contains the values of the cookies stored on the client computer

- The QueryString collection, which contains the values of the parameters passed by the client with the GET method

- The Form collection, which also contains the values of the parameters passed by the client with the POST method

- The ServerVariables collection, which contains the values of several environment variables with information about the server and the client

ClientCertificate

This collection gives you access to the fields of the client's digital certificate. Client certificates are automatically transmitted to the server every time a request through the Secure Sockets Layer (SSL) is made. To use SSL, set the protocol part of the request URL to "https". You can use the members of the ClientCertificate collection to validate the client (find out whether the certificate has expired, the certificate's issuer, and so on).

NOTE The ClientCertificate collection applies to client certificates only. If your company uses an intranet, you can require that clients be verified by a company like VeriSign before they're given access to a Web application. Alternatively, you can use the ClientCertificate collection in your script to verify the viewers before you allow them to access certain pages. Client certificates are independent of server certificates, and you don't need a server certificate in order to use the ClientCertificate collection.

Each element of the ClientCertificate collection can be accessed either by name or with an index value. To find out the name of the client certificate's issuer, use the following expression:

```
CAname = Request.ClientCertificate("ISSUER")
```

To access the name and value of the second field of the certificate, use the following expressions:

```
FName = Request.ClientCertificate.Key(2)
FValue = Request.ClientCertificate.Item(2)
```

The index of the first member in the collection is 1, and not 0. The Item property is the default property of the collection, so the second expression in the last example can be written as:

```
FValue = Request.ClientCertificate(2)
```

You can also iterate through the collection and retrieve names and values of its members with a loop like the following one:

```
For Each CertField In Request.ClientCertificate
    Response.Write "Certificate field name: " & CertField
    Response.Write "Value: " &
                    Request.ClientCertificate(CertField)
    Response.Write "<BR>"
Next
```

Each client certificate has the following fields:

Certificate   This is a string that represents the binary stream of the certificate content. This string is provided directly by the certificate authority.

Flags   This property is the combination of two flags that provide additional client certificate information.

The two flags are:

ceCertPresent   A client certificate is present.

ceUnrecognizedIssuer   The last certification in this chain is from an unknown issuer.

NOTE To use the preceding constants, you must include the client-certificate file in your ASP page. For VBScript, this is the cervbs.inc file in the \Inetpub\ASPSamp\Samples folder.

Issuer   This property is a string that contains information about the client certificate's issuer. The information is stored in a comma-delimited format, and the various fields of the Flags property are the Issuer property's subfields, which are discussed in the later section "Subkeys".

SerialNumber   This property is an ASCII representation of the hexadecimal bytes that make up the client certificate's serial numbers. The serial number is provided directly by the certificate authority.

Subject   This property is a comma-delimited string with information about the owner of the client certificate. The various fields of the Subject property are the Subject property's subkeys, which are discussed below.

ValidFrom   This property is the date on which the certificate becomes valid; it's a date/time value like 2/29/2000 11:59:50 PM.

ValidUntil   This property is the date on which the certificate becomes invalid; it's a date/time value like 1/1/2004 0:0:0 AM.

Subkeys

Some of the client certificate's keys have subkeys, too; the value of the Issuer key, for example, contains many values delimited with commas. You can extract the individual subkeys that make up the Issuer key with the following notation:

```
IssuerCountry = Request.ClientCertificate("IssuerC")
```

IssuerC is a subkey of the Issuer key and retrieves the country of origin of the certificate's issuer. This value is one of the fields in the comma-delimited fields returned by the Issuer key.

To retrieve a specific subkey's value, append one of the following digit(s) to the key:

C   The country of origin for the Subject or Issuer field

CN   The common name for the Subject field

GN   The given name for the Subject and Issuer fields

I   The initials for the Subject and Issuer fields

L   The locality for the Subject and Issuer fields

O   The organization or company name for the Subject and Issuer fields

OU   The name of a unit within the organization that issued the certificate for the Subject and Issuer fields

S   The state for the Subject and Issuer fields

T   The title for the Subject and Issuer fields

Cookies

The Cookies property is a collection that exposes the members discussed in Chapter 5, *The Cookies Collection*. The Cookies collection of the Request object lets you retrieve cookies from the client through the HTTP request header. Each time the viewer connects to a URL, the browser looks for cookies left on the client computer by the same site. If any cookies are found, they're transmitted to the server along with the request, in this form:

```
Cookie:name1=value1;name2=value2;...
```

where *nameX* is a cookie's name and *valueX* its value.

Your script can read the cookies through the Request object and use them in the application. The Cookies collection of the Response object allows you to create new cookies or change the values of existing cookies.

Cookies can be accessed either through an index value or a key value. The same notation applies to both the Request collection, which is used to read the values of the cookies, and the Response collection, which is used to create new cookies.

The Request.Cookies collection exposes the following properties.

Count

The Count property of the Cookies collection returns the number of cookies stored on the client computer. Use this property to iterate through the members of the Cookies collection with a For ... Next loop. An even better technique to iterate through the members of the collection is the For Each ... Next loop. Both techniques are demonstrated with examples in Chapter 5.

If a member of the Cookies collection is a dictionary, it's considered as another element of the collection and it contributes another item to the Count property, regardless of the number of members it contains. The same is true for arrays. If a cookie holds an array, it's considered a single cookie, regardless of how many elements make up the array. You will find information on creating and reading array cookies in Chapter 5.

Item

The Item property is the value of a specific cookie in the collection. You can specify the desired cookie either with an index value or with a key. If you iterate through the Cookies collection with a For ... Next loop, use the expressions Request.Cookies.Key(i) and Request.Cookies.Item(i) to read each cookie's key and value respectively:

```
<%
For i=1 to Request.Cookies.Count
    Response.Write Request.Cookies.Key(i)
    Response.Write " = "
    Response.write Request.Cookies.Item(i)
    Response.Write "<BR>"
Next
%>
```

Key

The Key property is the name of a cookie. If you know the key of a cookie, you can use it to request the cookie's value:

```
<%
Name = Request.Cookies("UserName")
%>
```

If you don't know the name of the cookie, you can use an index, as in the following statement:

```
<%
cookie1Name = Request.Cookies.Key(1)
cookie2Name = Request.Cookies.Key(2)
%>
```

Of course, if you don't know the names of the cookies, chances are you don't know the order of a specific cookie in the collection either. Consider an online store that stores the IDs of the selected products to the client as cookies (a client-side basket). If the server script doesn't know the names of the cookies (and you can't count on the order of the cookies retrieved from the client computer), it must scan the entire collection and retrieve the names and values of the cookies with a loop like the following one:

```
<%
For Each cookie In Request.Cookies
    Response.Write "Cookie: " & cookie
```

```
          Response.Write "Value: " & Request.Cookies(cookie)
          Response.Write "<BR>"
    Next
    %>
```

The variable *cookie* is the name of the current cookie and is equivalent to the expression `Request.Cookies.Key(cookie)`.

NOTE As you recall from Chapter 5, the Cookies collection exposes more properties, but these properties are write-only and apply to the Cookies collection of the Response object. The Request.Cookies collection doesn't expose the write-only properties, like the Path, Domain, and other properties available through the Response.Cookies collection.

Form

The Form collection contains one member for each control on the Form of the page that requested the script. The members of the Form collection can be accessed either by name or with an index value. If the first and second controls on the Form are named FirstName and LastName, you can retrieve their values with the following statements:

```
FName = Request.Form("FirstName")
LName = Request.Form("LastName")
```

You can also retrieve the values of the same controls with a numeric index:

```
FName = Request.Form(1)
LName = Request.Form(2)
```

Notice that the index of the first element in the Form collection is 1 and not 0.

The number of parameter values passed by the client is returned by the Form.Count property. You can use this property to set up a For ... Next loop to iterate through the members of the Form collection. (A better method to iterate through the Form collection is described in the following section.)

The Form collection is used when the data is submitted to the server with the POST method. If you attempt to call a member of the Form collection on a request that was submitted with the GET method, you will not get an error message. Instead, all the parameter values will be empty.

Navigating the Form Collection

To iterate through the Form collection, use a For Each ... Next loop, as shown in the following code segment:

```
For Each item In Request.Form
    Response.Write item & " = " &
                        Request.Form(item) & "<BR>"
Next
```

(The second line was broken to fit on the printed page, but you must enter it on a single line.) In the code above, *item* is the name of the current parameter and the expression Request.Form(item) reads the value of the current parameter. This loop accesses the values of the parameters by name, but it doesn't require that you know the names of the parameters; it reads both the names and values of the parameters. If you want to access the same parameters with an index, you can set up a For ... Next loop like the following:

```
For prmIndex = 1 To Request.Form.Count
    Response.Write Request.Form(prmIndex)
Next prmIndex
```

The Form collection does not expose a Name property that would allow you to access the name of the parameter. This loop can only read the values of the parameters, and you should prefer the For Each ... Next structure in your scripts.

The Form shown in Figure 6.1 contains all HTML controls. The HTML code for this page was presented in Chapter 1, *Web Applications and ASP*. In this section we'll explore the code for extracting the values of the controls on this Form from within a server-side script.

The FORM tag of the page shown in Figure 6.1 is:

```
<FORM ACTION=ParamsPost.asp METHOD=POST>
```

The name of the script on the server is ParamsPost.asp, and it must use the Request.Form collection to read the values of the controls. First, the script displays the number of members in the Form collection with the following statement:

```
Response.Write "<HR>"
Response.Write "There are " & Request.Form.Count &
                " items in the Form collection"
Response.Write "<HR>"
```

FIGURE 6.1: A FORM that contains all HTML controls

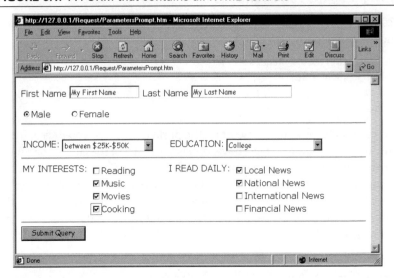

Then the script displays the value of the Request.Form property. For the values shown in Figure 6.1, the Request.Form property returns the following string (you will see all parameter values on a single line on the browser):

```
FirstName=My+First+Name&LastName=My+Last+Name&
Sex=Male&IncomeRange=Med&Education=College&Music=on&
Movies=on&Cooking=on&Local=on&National=on
```

Then, the values of the individual parameters are displayed with a For Each ... Next loop, as shown next:

```
For Each item In Request.Form
     Response.Write item & " = " &
                    Request.Form(item) & "<BR>"
Next
```

Finally, the script reads the values of all parameters by name and displays them in the browser (see Figure 6.2). Here are the lines that display the first few parameters:

```
Response.Write Request.Form("FirstName")
Response.Write "<BR>"
Response.Write Request.Form("LastName")
Response.Write "<BR>"
Response.Write "Local=" & Request.Form("Local")
Response.Write "<BR>"
```

```
Response.Write "International=" &
              Request.Form("International")
Response.Write "<BR>"
```

Listing 6.1 shows the ParamsPost.asp script. (Some of the lines were broken to fit on the page. These lines are properly indented in the listing.)

▶ *Listing 6.1: The ParamsPost.asp Script*

```
<%
Response.Write "There are " & Request.Form.Count &
              " items in the Form collection"
Response.Write "<BR>"
For Each item In Request.Form
    Response.Write item & " = " &
                  Request.Form(item) & "<BR>"
Next
Response.Write "<BR>"
Response.Write Request.Form
Response.Write "<HR>"
Response.Write Request.Form("FirstName")
Response.write "<BR>"
Response.Write Request.Form("LastName")
Response.write "<BR>"
Response.write "Local=" & Request.Form("Local")
Response.write "<BR>"
Response.write "IncomeRange=" & Request.Form("IncomeRange")
Response.write "<BR>"
Response.write "International=" &
              Request.Form("International")
Response.write "<BR>"
Response.write "Financial=" & Request.Form("Financial")
Response.write "<BR>"
Response.write "Sex=" & Request.Form("Sex")
Response.write "<BR>"
Response.write "HSchool=" & Request.Form("HSchool")
Response.write "<BR>"
Response.write "College=" & Request.Form("College")
Response.write "<BR>"
Response.write "University=" & Request.Form("University")
Response.write "<BR>"
%>
```

The first list on the Form is called *IncomeRange,* and all the items in the list have their own names. The selected item's name becomes the *IncomeRange* control's value. The same is true for the second list on the Form. This happens because only one item in the list can be selected.

FIGURE 6.2: The output of the ParamsPost.asp script for the data shown on the Form of Figure 6.1

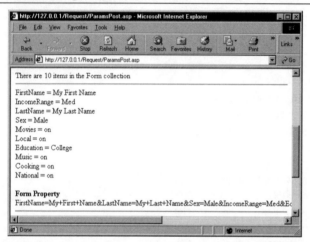

The items in the *IncomeRange* control are named Invalid, Low, Med, and High. The Invalid item is set to an invalid choice, to force the viewer to make a selection. If you display a valid default choice on the control, many viewers will not change it. Here's the HTML code for placing the *IncomeRange* control on the Form:

```
<SELECT NAME="IncomeRange">
<OPTION VALUE="invalid">Select your income range
<BR>
<OPTION VALUE="Low">less than $25K
<BR>
<OPTION VALUE="Med">between $25K-$50K
<BR>
<OPTION VALUE="High">more than $50K
```

The CheckBox control's value is "On" if the control is checked and an empty string ("") if the control is cleared. You should *not* use a statement like the following to determine whether a CheckBox control is checked:

```
'    THE FOLLOWING STATEMENTS WILL NOT WORK !
     <%
```

```
If Request.Form("Financial") Then
    ...
Else
    ...
End If
%>
```

Instead, you must compare the control's value to "On" but not to "Off." The following statement is valid:

```
<%
If Request.Form("Financial") = "On" Then
    ...
Else
    ...
End If
%>
```

Notice that a cleared CheckBox control's value is neither "Off" nor empty; it's a zero-length string. Notice also that the browser doesn't transmit (as parameter) the value of a cleared CheckBox control. If the Financial box on the page of Figure 6.1 is cleared, the control name "Financial" doesn't appear anywhere in the Form property.

If the CheckBox controls on the Form had the same name and the viewer checked more than one of them, the Form collection would contain two, or more, elements with the same name and different values. If all the Check-Boxes on the Form of Figure 6.1 (next to the header I READ DAILY) were named "News", and the viewer checked the items Local News and Financial News, then the Form collection would contain two members named "News". To access the value of the first CheckBox, you must use an index value, as shown here:

```
News1 = Request.Form("News")(1)
News2 = Request.Form("News")(2)
```

The value of the variable *News1* would be "Local" and the value of *News2* would be "Financial". If you request the value of the News parameter, it will return both values separated with a comma. The expression:

```
Request.Form("News")
```

will return the string:

```
Local, Financial
```

QueryString

The QueryString collection is equivalent to the Form collection. It should
be used when the parameters are submitted to the server with the GET
method. The QueryString collection contains one member for each control
on the Form of the page that requested the script. The members of the
QueryString collection can be accessed either by name or with an index
value. If the first and second controls on the Form are named FirstName
and LastName, you can retrieve their values with the following statements:

```
FName = Request.RequestString ("FirstName")
LName = Request.RequestString ("LastName")
```

You can also retrieve the values of the same controls with a numeric
index:

```
FName = Request.RequestString(1)
LName = Request.RequestString (2)
```

Notice that the index of the first element in the QueryString collection is 1
and not 0.

The number of parameter values passed by the client is returned by the
QueryString.Count property. You can use this property to set up a For ...
Next loop to iterate through the members of the QueryString collection,
but a better method to iterate through this collection is described in the
following section.

The QueryString collection is used when the data is submitted to the
server with the GET method. If you attempt to call a member of the Query-
String collection on a request that was submitted with the POST method, you
will not get an error message. Instead, all the parameter values will be empty.

Navigating the QueryString Collection

To iterate through the QueryString collection, use a For Each ... Next
loop, as shown in the following code segment:

```
For Each item In Request.QueryString
    Response.Write item & " = " &
                    Request.QueryString(item) & "<BR>"
Next
```

(The second line was broken to fit on the printed page, but you must enter
it on a single line.)

In the code above, *item* is the name of the current parameter and the expression `Request.QueryString(item)` reads the value of the current parameter. This loop accesses the values of the parameters by name, but it doesn't require that you know the names of the parameters; it reads both the names and values of the parameters. If you want to access the same parameters with an index, you can set up a `For ... Next` loop like the following:

```
For prmIndex = 1 To Request.QueryString.Count
    Response.Write Request.QueryString(prmIndex)
Next prmIndex
```

The QueryString collection does not expose a Name property that would allow you to access the name of the parameter. This loop can only read the values of the parameters, and you should prefer the `For Each ... Next` structure in your scripts.

We'll revise the `ParamsPost.asp` script of the previous section to submit the values of the same controls to the server with the GET method. In this section we'll explore the code for extracting the values of the controls on a Form from within a server-side script with the QueryString collection.

The FORM tag of the page shown in Figure 6.1 is:

```
<FORM ACTION=PARAMSGET.ASP METHOD=GET>
```

The name of the script on the server is `ParamsGet.asp`, and it must use the Request.QueryString collection to read the values of the controls. First, the script displays the number of members in the QueryString collection with the following statements:

```
Response.Write "<HR>"
Response.Write "There are " & Request.QueryString.Count &
               " items in the QueryString collection"
Response.Write "<HR>"
```

Then the script displays the value of the Request.QueryString property. For the values shown back in Figure 6.1, the Request.QueryString property returns the following string:

```
FirstName = My+First+Name&LastName=My+Last+Name&
National=on&International=on&IncomeRange=Low&
Education=College&Sex=Female
```

(You will see all parameter values on a single line on the browser.) Then, the values of the individual parameters are displayed with a For Each ... Next loop, as shown next:

```
For Each item In Request.QueryString
     Response.Write item & " = " &
                    Request.QueryString(item) & "<BR>"
Next
```

Finally, the script reads the values of all parameters by name and displays them on the browser (see Figure 6.3). Here are the lines that display the first few parameters:

```
Response.Write Request.QueryString("FirstName")
Response.Write "<BR>"
Response.Write Request.QueryString("LastName")
Response.Write "<BR>"
Response.Write "Local=" & Request.QueryString("Local")
Response.Write "<BR>"
Response.Write "International=" &
               Request.QueryString("International")
Response.Write "<BR>"
```

The following listing shows the ParamsGet.asp script. These lines are properly indented in the listing. (Some of the lines were broken to fit on the page.)

▶ *Listing 6.2: The ParamsGet.asp Script*

```
<%
Response.Write "There are " & Request.QueryString.Count &
               " items in the QueryString collection"
Response.Write "<BR>"
For Each item In Request.QueryString
    Response.Write item & " = " &
                   Request.QueryString(item) & "<BR>"
Next
Response.Write "<BR>"
Response.Write Request.QueryString
Response.Write "<HR>"
Response.Write Request.QueryString("FirstName")
Response.Write "<BR>"
Response.Write Request.QueryString("LastName")
```

```
Response.Write "<BR>"
Response.Write "Local=" & Request.QueryString("Local")
Response.Write "<BR>"
Response.Write "International=" &
              Request.QueryString("International")
Response.Write "<BR>"
Response.Write "Financial=" &
              Request. QueryString ("Financial")
Response.Write "<BR>"
Response.Write "Sex=" & Request.QueryString("Sex")
Response.Write "<BR>"
Response.Write "HSchool=" & Request.QueryString("HSchool")
Response.Write "<BR>"
Response.Write "College=" & Request.QueryString("College")
Response.Write "<BR>"
Response.Write "University=" &
              Request.QueryString("University")
Response.Write "<BR>"
Response.Write "<B>The QueryString Property</B><BR>"
Response.Write Request.QueryString
%>
```

FIGURE 6.3: The output of the ParamsPost.asp script for the data shown on the Form of Figure 6.1

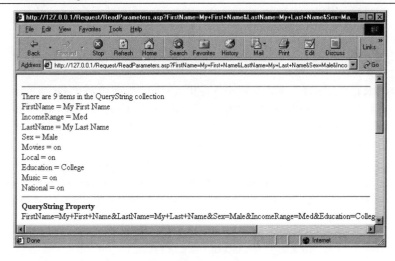

ServerVariables

The ServerVariables collection contains several environment variables, which you can access by name or with an index value. These are the names of the predefined server variables:

ALL_HTTP   This property is a string that contains all the HTTP headers sent by the browser. All of the following elements are part of the ALL_HTTP variable.

ALL_RAW   This is another string similar to the ALL_HTTP variable; it contains the same information as ALL_HTTP, but in the original form, as sent by the client. The elements of the ALL_HTTP variable are prefixed with HTTP, while the elements of ALL_RAW aren't.

APPL_MD_PATH   This string holds the path of the ISAPI DLL. Its value is /LM/W3SVC/1/ROOT, both for Personal Web Server (Windows 98) and IIS (Windows 2000).

APPL_PHYSICAL_PATH   This is the physical path of the APPL_MD_PATH item, and its value is the physical path to the server's root folder (in most systems it will be C:\INETPUB\WWWROOT\).

AUTH_PASSWORD   When IIS security is set to Basic Authentication, AUTH_PASSWORD is the password required to log into the Web server. For Web applications without strict security requirements it's an empty string.

AUTH_TYPE   This is the method used to validate users on Windows NT and Windows 2000.

AUTH_USER   This is the user name after the client has been authenticated by the Web server.

CERT_COOKIE   This is a unique ID for the client digital certificate, and it's an empty string for the HTTP protocol. It's used only with the HTTPS protocol. As you can guess by its name, this element is stored on the client computer as an encrypted cookie.

CERT_FLAGS   This is a two-bit value. The least significant bit is set to 1 if a client certificate is present. The second least significant bit is set to 1 if the Certifying Authority of the client certificate is invalid (i.e., if the issuer is not in the list of recognized certificate authorities on the server). These two values correspond to the *ceCertPresent* and *ceUnrecognizedIssuer* constants for the Flags element of the ClientCertificate collection.

CERT_ISSUER   This property returns the certificate's issuer. It is a comma-delimited string, which was described in the discussion of the ClientCertificate collection.

CERT_KEYSIZE   The number of bits in the SSL connection key size.

CERT_SECRETKEYSIZE   The number of bits in the server certificate private key.

CERT_SERIALNUMBER   The client's certificate serial number.

CERT_SERVER_ISSUER   The issuer of the server certificate.

CERT_SERVER_SUBJECT   This property returns the subject field of the server certificate. It is a comma-delimited string, whose fields were described in the discussion of the ClientCertificate collection earlier in this chapter.

CERT_SUBJECT   This property returns the subject field of the client certificate. It is a comma-delimited string, whose fields were described in the discussion of the ClientCertificate collection earlier in this chapter.

CONTENT_LENGTH   This is the total length of the body of the HTTP request sent by the client. This value does not include the length of data sent with the GET method.

CONTENT_TYPE   This is the MIME type of the information sent by he client. Most clients don't transmit anything but the values of the parameters entered by the user on a form: the type of this information is application/x-www-form/urlencoded. If the form includes a file, set the CONTENT_TYPE to multipart/form-data. You'll probably have to set the ENCTYPE parameter.

GATEWAY_INTERFACE   This variable is a string of the form "CGI/ revision #", where # is the version number. For the Personal Web Server, as well as for IIS, this variable is "CGI/1.1".

HTTP_header   In addition to the predefined server variables, you can add custom headers to the HTTP header. The custom headers can be accessed through the ServerVariables collection by their name prefixed with the string "HTTP_". If you have added the custom header "Warning" to the HTTP header, you can retrieve its value with the expression:

```
Request.ServerVariables("HTTP_Warning")
```

Among custom headers, the HTTP_ACCEPT header, for example, returns a string with all the file types the server can download to the client. The HTTP_ACCEPT header on most computers running Internet Explorer or Netscape Communicator is something like:

```
image/gif, image/x-xbitmap, image/jpeg, image/pjpeg,
application/vnd.ms-excel, application/msword,
application/vnd.ms-powerpoint, */*
```

Other custom headers are the HTTP_ACCEPT_LANGUAGE, HTTP_USER_AGENT, HTTP_COOKIE, and HTTP_REFERER.

HTTPS   The value of this variable is "On" if the client's request was sent using the SSL protocol. This happens when you want to transmit secure information and the destination URL starts with the prefix "https" instead of the usual "http".

HTTPS_KEYSIZE   This server variable is the same as the CERT_KEY-SIZE server variable, which was discussed briefly in the section "The ClientCertificate Collection," earlier in this chapter. If the script was called with the HTTPS protocol, then you must look up the HTTPS_KEY-SIZE property.

HTTPS_SECRETKEYSIZE   This server variable is the same as the CERT_SECRETKEYSIZE server variable discussed earlier. If the script was called with the HTTPS protocol, then you must look up the HTTPS_ SECRETKEYSIZE property.

HTTPS_SERVER_ISSUER   This server variable is the same as the CERT_SERVER_ISSUER server variable discussed earlier. If the script was called with the HTTPS protocol, then you must look up the HTTPS_ SERVER_ISSUER property.

HTTPS_SERVER_SUBJECT   This server variable is the same as the CERT_SERVER_SUBJECT server variable discussed earlier. If the script was called with the HTTPS protocol, then you must look up the HTTPS_ SERVER_SUBJECT property.

INSTANCE_ID   This is the ID of the IIS instance. You can use this variable to retrieve the ID of the Web-server instance to which the request belongs.

INSTANCE_META_PATH   This property holds the metabase path for the instance of IIS that responds to the request.

LOCAL_ADDR   This is the IP address of the Web server that accepted the request. This variable is used with Web servers that are part of a server farm, where each machine has a different IP address but they all belongs to the same domain. The IP address 127.0.0.1 is the local host (the address of your machine on the network).

LOGON_USER   This is the Windows NT account that the remote viewer is logged into.

PATH_INFO   This is the virtual path of the page that made the request. If this information comes from a URL, it is decoded by the server before it is passed to the requested script.

PATH_TRANSLATED   This property returns the physical path of the virtual path returned by the PATH_INFO server variable. If you're using the default installation of IIS, the path of a script in the root folder is C:\Inetpub\wwwroot\ServerVariables.asp.

QUERY_STRING   This property returns the same value as the Response .QueryString property. Its value is the string following the question mark (?) in the HTTP request.

REMOTE_ADDR   This is the IP address of the machine that made the request. You can't use this address to identify viewers between sessions, or monitor viewers that return to the site, because each time the typical user connects to the Internet, this address is assigned automatically by the server and it's different.

REMOTE_HOST   This variable returns the name of the client that made the request, and its value is usually the same as the REMOTE_ADDR.

REMOTE_USER   This is the name sent by the user for authentication purposes. If the user isn't required to log into the server, then this property is an empty string.

REQUEST_METHOD   This is the method used to pass the request data (GET, POST).

SCRIPT_NAME   This is the virtual path to the current script. You can use it to record the name of the script along with other information to a log file, or to build self-referencing URLs.

SERVER_NAME   This is the server's host name, DNS alias, or IP address as it would appear in self-referencing URLs. If you're using the local computer, then the SERVER_NAME server variable will be 127.0.0.1. If you have connected to the server using its IP address, then the SERVER_NAME variable's value will be that address. If the server has its own domain name, then the SERVER_NAME server variable will return the server's domain name.

SERVER_PORT The port number to which the request was sent. For HTTP requests this is port 80.

SERVER_PORT_SECURE If the request was submitted to the secure port (with the HTTPS protocol), this variable is 1; otherwise, it's 0.

SERVER_PROTOCOL The name and version of the protocol used by the Web server to handle the request. Its value is usually "HTTP/1.1".

SERVER_SOFTWARE The name and version of the server software that handles the request. Its value is "Microsoft-IIS/5.0" for both IIS 5.0 and the Personal Web Server.

URL This variable is the base portion of the requested page's URL. If your application resides in the MyApp virtual folder and the scripts reside in the MyApps/Scripts folder, the value of the URL property is: "/MyApps/Scripts/MyScript.asp", where MyScript.asp is the name of the requested script.

The following loop will iterate through the members of the Server-Variables collection (see Figure 6.4). It uses a For Each ... Next loop to access each member's name and value. At each iteration of the loop, the *key* variable is the variable's name and "Request.ServerVariables(key)" is the variable's value.

▶ *Listing 6.3: The ServerVariables.asp Script*

```
<HTML>
<TABLE FRAME=BOX>
<TR><TD><B>KEY</B><TD><B>VALUE</B>
<%
For Each key in Request.ServerVariables
    Response.Write "<TR><TD>" & key
    Response.Write "<TD>" & Request.ServerVariables(key)
Next
%>
</TABLE>
</HTML>
```

FIGURE 6.4: A segment of the page produced by the ServerVariables script

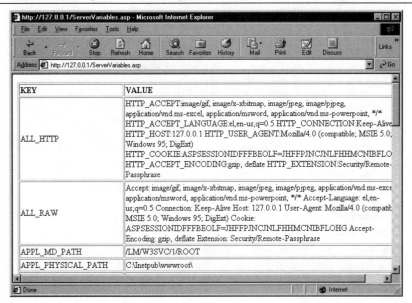

Properties

The Request object supports two of the most important properties of the ASP object model, ones that allow you to retrieve the information submitted to the server by the client. They are the Form and QueryString properties, which are functionally equivalent to the Form and QueryString collections.

Form

The Form property returns a string with all the parameters passed to the server with the POST method. If the data shown on the Form of Figure 6.1 are submitted to the server with the POST method and you retrieve the value of the Form property, that value will be:

```
FirstName=My+First+Name&LastName=My+Last+Name&
Sex=Male&IncomeRange=Med&Education=College&Music=on&
Movies=on&Cooking=on&Local=on&National=on
```

The Form property will return an empty string if the data were submitted with the GET method.

TIP You can use the Form property to extract the values of the parameters, although this is rarely done. If you do, however, you must first extract each parameter/value pair and then convert the URL-encoded characters to their original form. The parameter/value pairs can be extracted with the Split function, which parses a string and extracts the parts that are delimited with a character you specify. This character in the case of the Form property is the "&" character. Do not convert the special symbols to the matching characters before you split the string, because some of the URL-encoded symbols may be ampersands (&) or equal signs (=). Both characters will throw off the code that extracts the parameter/value pairs. The same comments apply to the QueryString property as well.

The Form property is URL-encoded: spaces are replaced with the plus sign, and all special symbols are replaced by the percent sign followed by the hexadecimal value of the corresponding character. The value of the Last Name control in the Form of Figure 6.1 is encoded as:

```
LastName=My+Last+Name
```

The search argument:

```
+pie -chart
```

will be encoded as

```
SearchArgument=%2Bpie+-chart
```

Notice that minus is not a special symbol in HTML. The following string contains quite a few HTML symbols

```
<<Mike & Maggy>>
```

and it will be encoded as follows:

```
%3C%3CMike+%26+Maggy%3E%3E
```

If the CheckBox controls on the Form had the same name and the viewer checked more than one of them, the Form collection would contain two, or more, elements with the same name and different values. If all the Check-Boxes on the Form of Figure 6.1 were named "News" and the viewer checked the items Local News and Financial News, then the Form property would contain the following string:

```
News=Local&News=Financial
```

This string corresponds to the values of the Checkbox controls shown in Figure 6.1.

QueryString

The QueryString property returns a string with all the parameters passed to the server with the GET method. If the data shown on the Form of Figure 6.1 were submitted to the server with the GET method, the retrieved value of the QueryString property will be:

```
FirstName=My+First+Name&LastName=My+Last+Name&
Sex=Male&IncomeRange=Med&Education=College&Music=on&
Movies=on&Cooking=on&Local=on&National=on
```

The QueryString property will return an empty string if the data were submitted with the POST method. The QueryString property is URL-encoded: spaces are replaced with the plus sign, and all special symbols are replaced by the percent sign followed by the hexadecimal value of the corresponding character. The value of the Last Name control in the Form of Figure 6.1 is encoded as:

```
LastName=My+Last+Name
```

The search argument:

```
+pie -chart
```

will be encoded as:

```
SearchArgument=%2Bpie+-chart
```

Notice that minus is not a special symbol in HTML. The following string contains quite a few HTML symbols:

```
<<Mike & Maggy>>
```

and it will be encoded as follows:

```
%3C%3CMike+%26+Maggy%3E%3E
```

The QueryString property's value is the same as the value of the QUERY_STRING server variable (see the discussion of the ServerVariables collection, earlier in this chapter).

TotalBytes

This is a read-only property that returns the number of bytes posted to the server with an HTTP request. There are other, simpler, methods to read the values of the parameters submitted by the client and the cookies, so the TotalBytes property is rarely used in ASP. However, it's an invaluable property when you want to retrieve binary data from a client. Because this is done with the BinaryRead method, the TotalBytes property is used exclusively with the BinaryRead method. The TotalBytes property and the BinaryRead method allow you to read files uploaded by the client with the File HTML control (this control is described in the section BinaryRead).

The TotalBytes property is the total number of bytes sent by the client and not just the length of the attached file. To ignore the HTTP headers and read the bytes of the uploaded file, you must parse the data posted by the client. However, this can't be done with VBScript and the ASP objects. You will have to develop a custom component to parse the data posted by the client. See the section describing the BinaryRead method for more information on posting binary data to the server and an example on using the TotalBytes property.

Method

The Request object supports a single method, the BinaryRead method, which is used along with the TotalBytes property to extract binary information posted to the server by the client.

BinaryRead

The BinaryRead method reads a specified number of bytes from the HTTP request body. These bytes are posted to the server with the POST method.

Syntax

The syntax of BinaryRead is:

```
SArray = Request.BinaryRead(nbytes)
```

nbytes is the number of bytes to be read. They are stored in a data structure known as SafeArray. SafeArray is a special structure that can be accessed from within Visual C++ applications. You can't read or process the contents of a safe array from within a script. You will find a simple example of retrieving arbitrary data from the client with the BinaryRead method in this chapter.

Why Post Binary Data to the Server?

A typical Web page need not post data to the server, and there aren't many sites that can accept files or binary information in general. There are a few sites, however, that allow viewers to upload binary files. The Yahoo mail page is a typical example. Yahoo allows you to set up an e-mail account and receive your mail through the Web.

It's fairly straightforward to build a site where viewers can identify themselves with a user name and a password, compose a message, and send it to another user. It's also fairly easy to implement features like carbon copies, message forwarding, and so on. But how would you implement attachments? You should be able to build a page that uploads binary files (using the File HTML control), reads the attachments on the server, and sends them to the message's recipient. There's only one method to read binary data embedded in the message's request header: the Request.BinaryRead method. Similarly, there's only one method to send binary data to the client, the Response.BinaryWrite method. This is how Web mail works.

However, you can use the same techniques to develop Web applications that can upload all types of data to the server. The viewer needn't do anything more than select the name of the file(s) to be posted and click a Submit button. The file's contents will be transmitted to the server along with the POST request, and a script can read the data on the server and act accordingly. This technique is not used widely on the Web today, but the need to enhance client-server communication will become more and more pressing in the near future, and you should expect to see more tools to simplify the interception of binary data on the server.

Example

The following statements retrieve the number of bytes sent by the client and return all the data in the request with the BinaryWrite method.

▶ *Listing 6.4: The BREAD.ASP Script*

```
<%
NBytes = Request.TotalBytes
Response.Write "The header contains " & NBytes & " bytes"
Response.Write "<BR>"
ClientData = Request.BinaryRead(Nbytes)
Response.BinaryWrite ClientData
%>
```

The Response.BinaryWrite method writes the binary data read with the BinaryRead method as is. To test the BREAD.ASP script, you must submit a file (text or binary) to the server. This can be done with the File HTML control, with an HTML page like the following one:

▶ *Listing 6.5: The SendFile.htm Page*

```
<HTML>
<H1>File Upload Demo</H1>
<FONT FACE="Comic Sans MS">
<FORM ENCTYPE="multipart/form-data"
      ACTION="BREAD.ASP" METHOD=POST>
Select the file to upload
<INPUT TYPE=FILE SIZE=40 NAME=Fname VALUE=Send File>
<BR>
and click here to
<INPUT TYPE=SUBMIT VALUE="Send File">
</FORM>
</HTML>
```

The File HTML control is supported by both Netscape Communicator and Internet Explorer. The page produced by the SendFile.htm script is shown in Figure 6.5. The Browse button on the Form is part of the File control, and so is the Text control where the name of the selected file will appear.

FIGURE 6.5: The SendFile.htm page

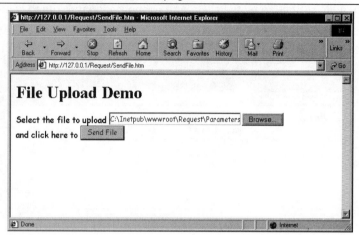

After you have selected a file through the File Open dialog box, you can click the Send File button to submit the Form to the server. The browser will submit the file's contents, not just its name. The script on the server can read the data with the BinaryRead method and process them accordingly.

As mentioned already, the BinaryRead method reads all the data submitted by the client, not just the file's contents. In other words, the ClientData variable includes the request header as well. Moreover, you can't process the data retrieved by the BinaryRead method with VBScript's string manipulation functions. Therefore, it's not easy to test the BinaryRead method. To test the BREAD.ASP script by submitting HTML documents to the server, open the SendFile.htm page on the server, select an HTML file, and submit it to the server. The script will display a new page with the request's header, followed by the file's contents. Because the file is HTML, it will be rendered on the browser's window.

Figure 6.6 shows the output of the BREAD.ASP script when the client submits the HTML document shown on the File control of Figure 6.5 (it is the HTML document shown in Figure 6.1). Notice that you can't enter the name of the file to be submitted in the Text control of Figure 6.5. You must click the Browse button and select the name of the file through the File Open dialog box.

FIGURE 6.6: The BREAD.ASP script uses Request.BinaryRead to read the contents of a file submitted by the client and Response.BinaryWrite to send them back.

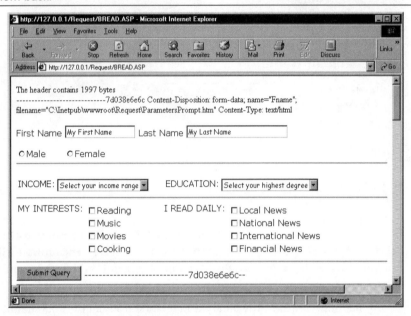

The first hundred bytes or so (or several thousand bytes, if the page contains a Form) are part of the HTTP request header. Following the request's header, there's a string beginning with many dashes. This string is a delimiter for the file's contents, which were embedded into the request. For the example shown in Figure 6.6, it's the string ending with the characters 7d038e6e6c--. The same string appears at the end of the request (it appears again right after the Form). If the client has submitted several files with the same request, there will be one delimiter for each file.

chapter 7

The Response Object

T he Response object represents your server's HTTP response to the client. It allows you to transmit information to the client, as well as to determine when this information will be transmitted. You can think of the Response object as a stream: every bit of information you want to transmit to the client in response to a request must be written to this stream with the Response.Write method. The server's response is not limited to an HTML document and the images or other binary information that's part of the document. It includes additional information such as cookies or custom headers.

Writing Responses

The most important member of the Response object is the Write method, which allows you to place data to the response buffer and build HTML documents on the fly. Every line in an HTML file could become the parameter to a call to the Response.Write method. Here's a simple HTML file:

```
<HTML>
<H1>Brief Overview of ASP</H1>
some text
</HTML>
```

This document could also be transmitted to the client with the following script:

```
<%
Response.Write "<HTML>"
Response.Write "<H1>Brief Overview of ASP</H1>"
Response.Write "some text"
Response.Write "</HTML>"
%>
```

As you recall from Chapter 1, any file that contains the <% and %> tags must be stored with extension ASP, and it must be opened through the browser, not by double-clicking its icon, as you would do with an HTML file. The script will be executed only if you request the page from a Web server. Notice that any VBScript statements in an HTML file will be completely ignored.

The data written to the Response object is actually stored in a buffer, and the buffer's contents are transmitted to the client after the script has completed its execution. (This is the default behavior of ASP 3, and it's the opposite of the behavior of the buffer in ASP 2.) In ASP 2, the buffer's contents are transmitted to the client little by little. In other words, the server doesn't wait for the script to end before it starts transmitting information to the client. You can change this behavior with the Response.Buffer property and Response.Flush method, which are discussed later in this chapter.

Of course, there's no reason to use the Response object to transmit straight HTML documents. The real advantage of the Response object is that you can mix HTML statements with scripting statements, so that you can prepare different responses for different clients. For example, you can insert different messages depending on date and/or time, retrieve information like stock prices from a database or another server, and insert them into the page and so on. Here's a script that displays the date and time on the server:

```
<%
Response.Write "The date on the server is " & Date()
Response.Write "<BR>"
Response.Write "and the time on the server is " & Time()
%>
```

Here's an alternate coding of the previous VBScript segment:

```
<HTML>
The date on the server is <% =Date() %>
<BR>
and the time is <% =Time() %>
</HTML>
```

The following script outlines the statements that will create a new page with information about items on sale:

```
' EXTRACT SALE ITEM FROM DATABASE
' INTO THE SALES RECORDSET
Response.Write "<TABLE>"

While Not Sales.EOF
   Response.Write "<TR><TD>"
   Response.Write "<TD>" & .Fields("ID") & "</TD>"
   Response.Write "<TD>" & .Fields("Descr") & "</TD>"
```

```
      Response.Write "<TD>" & .Fields("Price") & "</TD>"
      Response.Write "<TD>" & .Fields("SalePrice") & "</TD>"
      Sales.MoveNext
   Wend
   Response.Write "</TR></TABLE>"
```

This script can't be tested as is. In Chapter 9, *ADO 2.5 for Web Developers*, you will see the methods of the ADO object that allow you to query a database and display the results on a new page.

As with any programming language, a script may end without executing all of its statements. An unusual condition may force you to end the processing. To do so, call the method Response.End, which is equivalent to terminating a VB application with the End statement.

The next section shows a typical example of using the Response object to create an HTML page on the fly, with a server-side script. The members of the Response object are discussed in detail in the following sections.

The Calendar Example

Most of the time we use the Response object to create pages on the fly and send them to the client. Pages that contain information retrieved from a database in response to a user action are typical examples of pages that must be built on the fly. A page with products within a user-specified price range, or products that meet other user-supplied criteria, can't exist as static HTML files on the server. These pages must be built as requested and transmitted to the client. A dictionary, for example, is stored in a database, and you can write scripts to retrieve the definitions requested by the viewer, place them on a page, and transmit it to the client.

A calendar is another typical example of a page built on the fly. Figure 7.1 shows a form that prompts the user to specify a month and a year. The names of the SELECT controls with the months and years are Month and Year respectively. The script on the server uses the Request object to retrieve the values of the two controls. (The Request object and the methods for reading the values of the controls on a Form are discussed in detail in the following chapter.) When this information is transmitted to the server, a script (Listing 7.1) prepares a page with the selected month's calendar and sends it to the client. The page with the calendar shown in Figure 7.2 does not reside on the server; it's created by a server-side script as needed and transmitted to the client.

FIGURE 7.1: The `PromptMonth.html` page

FIGURE 7.2: The output of the `Calendar.asp` script

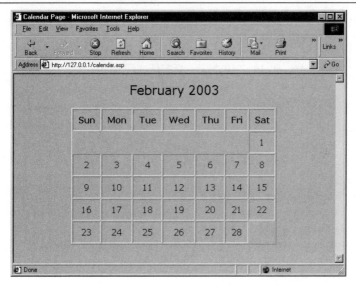

▶ *Listing 7.1: The Calendar.asp script*

```
<HTML>
<HEAD>
<TITLE>Calendar Page</TITLE>
<BODY BGCOLOR=#C0C0C0>
```

```
<CENTER>
<FONT FACE='Verdana' SIZE=5>
<%
iMonth=Request.Form("Month")
iYear=Request.Form("Year")
Response.Write MonthName(imonth) & " " & iYear
Response.Write "<P>"
Response.Write "<TABLE CELLPADDING=10 BORDER><TR>"
Response.Write
        "<TD><B>Sun<TD><B>Mon<TD><B>Tue<TD><B>Wed<TD>
        <B>Thu<TD><B>Fri<TD><B>Sat"
Response.Write "<TR>" & VBCRLF
thisdate=DateSerial(iYear, iMonth, 1)
nextday=1
' The following statements display the days
' of the first week in the month
For cday=1 to 7
    If WeekDay(thisdate)>cday Then
        Response.Write "<TD></TD>" & VBCRLF
    Else
        Response.Write "<TD ALIGN=CENTER><FONT SIZE=3>" & _
                    nextday & "</TD>" & VBCRLF
        nextday=nextday+1
        thisdate=DateSerial(iYear, iMonth, nextday)
    End If
Next
Response.Write "</TR><TR>"
weekDays=1
' The following lines display the days
' of the remaining weeks
While Month(thisdate)=CInt(iMonth)
    Response.Write "<TD ALIGN=CENTER><FONT SIZE=3>" & _
                nextday & "</TD>" & VBCRLF
    nextday=nextday+1
    weekDays=weekDays+1
    If weekDays>7 then
        WeekDays=1
        Response.Write "<TR>" & VBCRLF
    End If
    Thisdate=DateSerial(CInt(iYear), CInt(iMonth), nextday)
```

```
Wend
%>
</TABLE>
</CENTER>
</BODY>
</HTML>
```

As you can see, the script contains VBScript statements that prepare the appropriate HTML code to produce the calendar. Readers familiar with Visual Basic will see the similarities between VB and VBScript.

TIP Most clients will request the current month's calendar, so it will be easier for the server to transmit a static HTML page with the current month's calendar. If the user requests the calendar of another month, then you can use this script to create it on the fly.

The Cookies Collection

The Cookies property is a collection that exposes the members discussed in Chapter 5, *The Cookies Collection*. The Cookies collection of the Response object allows you to create new cookies or change the values of existing cookies. Individual cookies can be specified either through an index value or a key value. The same notation applies to the Response.Cookies collection, which is used to create new cookies (or modify the values of existing cookies), and the Request.Cookies collection, which is used to retrieve the values of the cookies.

The Response.Cookies collection exposes the following properties.

Item

The Item property is the value of a specific cookie in the collection. You can specify the desired cookie either with an index value or with a key. Chances are you'll never specify a cookie with an index value, because this means that your application must know the order of the cookies on the client computer. We always use a key value to specify cookies.

Key

The Key property is the name of a cookie, and each cookie has a unique name (key). To create the cookie *UserName* and set it to "Richard", use the following statement:

```
<%
Response.Cookies("UserName") = "Richard"
%>
```

Consider an on-line store that stores the IDs of the selected products to the client as cookies (a client-side basket). Each time the viewer selects another product, your script must create a new cookie, name it after the product's ID (a value that uniquely identifies the product), and set its value to the quantity ordered. If the product ID is stored in the variable *ProdID* and the quantity ordered is stored in the variable *qty*, you can use a statement like the following one to create a new cookie:

```
Response.Cookies(ProdID) = qty
```

If the specific cookie exists, its value will be set to *qty*. If not, a new cookie will be created.

Domain

The Domain property is write-only and specifies the domain to which the cookies will be sent. Cookies are sent by default to all the pages that belong to the same domain as the page that placed the cookies on the client computer. If you want certain cookies of your application to be viewed from another domain, set the Domain property of the individual cookies to the appropriate value.

Let's assume your application is running on the domain www.GreatBooks .com. Let's also assume you have an agreement with another site, www .GreatMusic.com, to exchange ads. Each site places a banner of the other site on the application's main page. You may be interested in recognizing viewers who have already been to the GreatMusic site, and the GreatMusic site also wants to recognize the viewers who have been to your site. The simplest method to exchange information with another site is to leave a cookie on the client and set its Domain property to the other site's domain name.

The GreatBooks site could leave the *VisitedBooks* cookie to indicate that the viewer has already visited the site. The GreatMusic site could leave the

VisitedMusic cookie to indicate that the viewer has already visited the site. Here's how the two cookies will be created by the two applications:

- The GreatBooks site must create the *VisitedBooks* cookie with the statements:

```
<%
Response.Cookies("VisitedBooks") = "Yes"
Response.Cookies("VisitedBooks").Domain = _
        http://www.GreatMusic.com
%>
```

- The GreatMusic site must create the *VisitedMusic* cookie with the statements:

```
<%
Response.Cookies("VisitedMusic") = "Yes"
Response.Cookies("VisitedMusic").Domain = _
        http://www.GreatBooks.com
%>
```

Any script of the application that runs on the GreatBooks site can read the *VisitedMusic* cookie to find out if a viewer has been to the GreatMusic site. Likewise, any script of the application that runs on the GreatMusic site can read the *VisitedBooks* cookie to find out if a viewer has been to the GreatBooks site. As you can understand, this technique is used widely (a better word would be wildly) in advertising.

Expires

By default, cookies expire at the end of the session. If you want cookies to remain on the client and be accessed in a later session, you must set an expiration date. The cookies will remain on the client computer until the specified expiration date, and your application can read their values. This is how shopping baskets are implemented, as discussed in Chapter 5, *The Cookies Collection*.

To set the expiration date of a cookie, use the following expression:

```
Response.Cookies(key).Expires = expDate
```

expDate is a date or date/time value. To specify that a cookie will expire at midnight of December 31, 2004, use one of the following statements:

```
Response.Cookies(key).Expires = #12/31/2004#
```

or

```
Response.Cookies(key).Expires = "December 31, 2004"
```

Of course, you can use any valid VBScript date function. The following cookie will expire one month from now:

```
Response.Cookies(key).Expires = DateAdd("m", 1, Now)
```

Notice that the cookies created by your site on the client computer need not have the same expiration date. Each cookie can have its own expiration date, which you can change at will by setting its Expire property. Since this property is read-only, you can't find out when a cookie will expire, so you should plan carefully what you use cookies for and avoid changing their usage after you have created them.

Path

The Path property determines which virtual path in the ASP application can accept the cookie. If you want a few scripts to have access to a specific cookie, create a virtual folder and set the cookie's Path property to this folder's virtual name. This cookie will be sent only to scripts in the specified folder. You must also place all the scripts you want to be able to access the cookie in the same virtual folder set with the Path property.

Secure

The Secure property determines whether the cookie will be sent to the server at all times (if False), or only if the client uses the Secure Sockets Layer (SSL). If a cookie contains sensitive information, you must set its Secure property to True. However, you should never store extremely sensitive information, such as credit card numbers, in the form of cookies.

The value of this cookie will be transmitted to the server only if the request uses the HTTPS protocol. These requests use a URL of the following form: https://www.yourserver.com/SecureData.asp

To specify that a specific cookie must be transmitted to the server only through the HTTPS protocol, set it Secure property to True, as shown here:

```
<%
Response.Cookies("AccountNumber")="240-2034345-1034"
Response.Cookies("AccountNumber").Expires = #12/31/2003#
Response.Cookies("AccountNumber").Secure = True
%>
```

Properties

The Response object exposes its functionality mostly through a set of properties, which are described in the following sections. Notice that the Buffer property behaves differently in ASP 3 than it did in ASP 2.

Buffer

The Buffer property determines whether the output of the script is transmitted to the client immediately and in parts, as it becomes available, or as a whole after the completion of the script. If you set this property to True (which is the property's default value), all the output generated by the script will be buffered on the server and transmitted to the client as soon as the scripts completes its execution.

The default value of the Buffer property in ASP 3 is True. All the output produced by the script is buffered. It's then transmitted to the client after the entire page has become available. The exact opposite happens with ASP 2. It doesn't hurt to set the Buffer property to True in a new script, but if an existing script replies on the default value of the Buffer property, you must set it explicitly to False before running it under ASP 3.

In terms of how the script works and how the information is delivered to the client, this change is a minor one. It's not going to seriously affect any existing scripts. The reason for changing the default value of the Buffer property is efficiency. IIS 5 can deliver data to the client much more efficiently when the Buffer property is set to True.

Syntax

The syntax of the Buffer property is:

```
Response.Buffer = True | False
```

When the Buffer property is set to True, you can still send the buffered output to the client in pieces by calling the *Flush* method (which is discussed later in this chapter). This method transmits the output of the script buffered so far to the client. Notice that the script's output will be sent to the client when the script is terminated with the Response.End method, when the script comes to an end, or it times out.

Notes

The Buffer property must be set before sending any data to the client. If the Buffer property is initially False and you have called the Response.Write method, you can't change the value of the property, because the header has already been transmitted. Also, you can't change the value of the Buffer property after calling the Flush method (discussed later in this chapter). If you attempt to set the Buffer property (or any other property that's transmitted to the client as part of the response header), an error message will appear on the browser indicating that you have modified the header after having sent some output to the client.

The Buffer property shouldn't be set to True (which is the default value for ASP 3) in scripts that take more than a few seconds to execute. Viewers may think that the server is not responding and either move to another page or resubmit the request by clicking the same button (or hyperlink) again. If you have a script that takes an unusually long time to execute, display a "Please wait" page, as described in the following section. This is the case with scripts that access multiple tables and create long pages.

The "Please Wait..." Page

Some sites warn you that an operation may take a while by displaying a "Please wait" page. When the operation on the server (a complicated query or some calculations) may take more than 5 or 10 seconds, the page with the results is transmitted automatically to the client. The "Please wait" page is displayed with a client-side script written either in VBScript or JavaScript. Let's say the name of the script that takes a while to execute is LongScript.asp. Instead of calling the LongScript.asp directly, you can call the PlsWait.asp script (Listing 7.2).

▶ *Listing 7.2: The PlsWait.htm Page (VBScript)*

```
<HTML>
<HEAD>
<SCRIPT LANGUAGE = "VBScript">
Sub Window_Onload
    Document.Location.HREF = "LongScript.asp"
End Sub
</SCRIPT>
```

```
<H3>Your Request is Being Processed</H3>
<H4>Please wait . . . </H4>
</HTML>
```

The script on this page is executed on the client. It consists of a sub-routine that's executed when the document is loaded on the client's window (this is when the Window_OnLoad event is fired). This script redirects the browser to the script that takes a while to execute. In the meantime, a message is displayed on the client, so that viewers know that the page they've requested will take a while to execute.

Document is an object that represents the document displayed on the browser. The HREF property of the Document object is the URL of the doc-ument being displayed. By setting this property we're in effect redirecting the client to another document, which will replace the current document on the browser's window.

The browser will attempt to load the new page (the script's output), but the server can't supply it before the script has completed. As long as the browser doesn't receive any data from the Web server, the page with the message will remain visible. As you realize, your script shouldn't send any output to the client before it has completed the time-consuming operation(s). If you display a few lines of text and then start executing the complicated code, the client will switch to the new page, display the information trans-mitted by the server, and then wait for a minute or two. To keep the page with the "Please wait" message on the browser window, you must either not call the Response.Write method before the calculations have completed, or buffer the script's output.

Not all browsers support VBScript, so this script may not work on all clients. Both Netscape Communicator and Internet Explorer support JavaScript, so the JavaScript implementation of the same script is shown in Listing 7.3:

▶ *Listing 7.3: The PlsWait.htm Page (JavaScript)*

```
<HTML>
<BODY onLoad="window.location='LongScript.asp'">
<H3>Your Request is Being Processed</H3>
</HTML>
```

This technique will work, but you don't have to use it with every script that takes a little longer to execute. If your page consists of two or more distinct sections, you can call the Flush method to send any buffered output to the client, as shown here:

```
<%
' CODE TO PREPARE THE FIRST PART OF THE PAGE
Response.Flush
' CODE TO PREPARE THE SECOND PART OF THE PAGE
Response.Flush
' MORE CODE MAY FOLLOW
%>
```

NOTE When coding a script that performs complicated operations, especially data access operations, you should examine the value of the IsClientConnected property from within your script to find out whether the client is still waiting for the page or has jumped to another page (or another site). If that's the case, you can terminate the script whose output will not be viewed anyway. See the description of the IsClientConnected property, later in this chapter, for more information.

CacheControl

This property lets you determine whether proxy servers can cache your pages. By default, ASP generated pages can't be cached. You can allow proxy servers to cache pages that are static and don't change frequently, so clients can access them faster.

Syntax

The syntax of the CacheControl property is:

```
Response.CacheControl = Private | Public
```

To allow proxy servers to cache the page, set the CacheControl property to Public. The default value of this property is Private. Private and Public are keywords, not constants.

Notes

Setting the CacheControl property to Public doesn't mean that it will be necessarily cached. This property determines whether proxy servers are allowed to cache the page, not whether the proxy server will actually cache it.

Like the Cookies and other properties, the CacheControl property must be set before sending the <HTML> tag to the client. If not, a runtime error will be generated and it will appear on the client's window.

Charset

This property sets or returns the name of the character set in effect. This information in embedded into the HTTP response header and remains in effect for the current page. As such, it must be set before sending any other output to the client. The default character set is "ISO-LATIN-1".

Syntax

The syntax of the Charset property is:

```
Response.Charset "ISO-LATIN-7"
```

As you can see, the syntax indicates that Charset is a method, rather than a property, but it's referred to in the documentation as a property. The same it True for the PICS property, described later in this chapter. If the value assigned to the Charset property is invalid, it will be ignored, but no runtime error will be generated.

ContentType

This property represents the Content-Type field of the HTTP response header. It specifies the type of data in the response's body. This information is required by the browser to determine how it will interpret the downloaded information.

Syntax

The syntax of the ContentType property is:

```
Response.ContentType = strType
```

strType is a string in the form type/subtype. The type part of the setting determines the *type* of data being sent to the client (text, audio, image, and so on), while the *subtype* part of the setting determines the specific type of the contents (the type of image or audio file, for example). The most common values of this property are shown in Table 7.1.

TABLE 7.1: The HTTP Content Types

Type	Description
Text	Plain text
Multipart	Multiple types of data
Message	Encapsulated message
Image	Image data
Audio	Audio data
Video	Video data
Application	Binary data

The list of HTTP content types keeps growing, as new types and subtypes are specified by the industry. The ContentType setting is transmitted to the client as part of the response header, so it must be sent before the <HTML> tag—unless you're buffering the output.

The default content type is text/plain and you need not set it if you're transmitting straight HTML code. For an example of how to use the ContentType property, see the discussion of the BinaryWrite method, later in this chapter.

Expires

The Expires property specifies the time interval (in minutes) that the client is allowed to cache the page. If the user refreshes the page within the specified interval, the cached page will be displayed. After that interval, the page is reloaded from the server.

Syntax

The syntax of the Expires property is:

```
Response.Expires = minInterval
```

The *minInterval* an optional parameter specifies the length of time (in minutes) that the page can be cached on the client. The default value is 24 hours.

Notes

If you set the Expires property to 0, you're actually forcing the browser to reload the page from the server every time the user connects to it. Do so with pages that contain information that changes constantly, like stock prices, bids, and so on.

The Expires property is encoded into the HTTP response header and must be set before sending the <HTML> tag to the client. If you set this property after the script has called the Write method, a runtime error will be generated. You can avoid the error by buffering the output and flushing the buffer after setting this property.

If the Expires property is set multiple times in the same script, then the shortest setting takes precedence, even if other (longer) settings are specified later in the script.

Finally, the Response.Expires property doesn't affect the expiration dates of the cookies set by the same script or another script of the same application. To change the Expiration date of a cookie, use the Response.Cookies.Expires property.

ExpiresAbsolute

The ExpiresAbsolute property is similar to the Expires property, only it specifies an absolute expiration date. Use the ExpiresAbsolute property to set an absolute expiration date if your pages change at midnight or another fixed time.

Syntax

The syntax of the ExpiresAbsolute property is:

```
Response.ExpiresAbsolute = #DateTime#
```

DateTime is a date or date/time value, in which the date is specified in the format "month, day, year." If you omit the time part, the browser will assume that the page expires at the midnight of the specified date. If you omit the date, the page will expire at the specified time of the current date. The pound signs that enclose the date/time value are mandatory. You can also set this property to a date value.

Example

To specify that your page expires at midnight, use the statement:

```
Response.ExpiresAbsolute = #24:00:00#
```

The statements in Listing 7.4 will force a page to expire by the end of the month.

▶ *Listing 7.4: Setting a Page's Expiration Date*

```
<%
Response.Buffer=True
LastDate =  Month(Now)+1 & "/1/" & Year(Now)
LastDate = CDate(LastDate) - 1
ExpDate =  FormatDateTime(LastDate, 0 )
Response.ExpiresAbsolute=ExpDate
Response.Write "The date on the server is " & Now()
Response.Write "This page will expire on " &
                Response.ExpiresAbsolute
%>
```

To calculate the last date of the current month, the script takes the first day of the following month and subtracts 1 (this saves us from calculating the number of days in the month). Then it formats the new date appropriately and assigns it to the Response.ExpiresAbsolute property.

IsClientConnected

This property is True if the client that requested an ASP page is still connected and waits for the script's output. If the client is no longer connected, you can terminate the processing of the script. Otherwise, you'll be wasting server resources to produce a page that will not end up on the browser.

Example

Listing 7.5 shows how IsClientConnected should be used in a script that takes a long time to execute. If the scripts find out that the client has disconnected, it terminates immediately with the Response.End method.

▶ *Listing 7.5: Aborting a Script When the Client Disconnects*

```
<%
' CODE TO RETRIEVE ROWS WITH A COMPLEX QUERY
If Not Response.IsClientConnected Then
    Response.End
End If
' CODE TO PREPARE A TABLE WITH THE QUERY RESULTS
```

```
If Response.IsClientConnected Then
    Response.Flush      ' SHOW TABLE
Else
    Response.End        ' ABORT EXECUTION OF SCRIPT
End If
' CODE TO DISPLAY MORE DATA
Response.Flush
%>
```

PICS

The PICS property is another HTTP header value that allows you to classify the contents of a page according to a number of subjects, such as language, violence, and so on. PICS (Platform for Internet Content System) is a rating method similar to the one used in the movie and television industry.

You can classify your page according to four categories: violence (V), sex (S), language (L), and nudity (N). Each category can be graded from 0 (lack of) to 3 (excess of the specific category). A page suitable for all types of viewers should be classified as:

```
Ratings (V 0 S 0 L 0 N 0)
```

You can assign this rating to the PICS property, so viewers with restricted access to the Web can view your pages.

Of course, this is only what you think about your own pages. Organizations that verify these settings are known as rating services; the most popular is the RSAC (Recreational Software Advisory Council). The PICS header is valid only if you include the URL of the rating service.

Here's a complete PICS header (the header is a single string, broken into several lines to fit on the page):

```
PICS-1.0 "http://www.rsac.org/ratingsv01.html" 1 gen true
comment "RSACi North America Server" for
http://www.yoursite.com on "2002.01.01T00:00-0700
r (v 0 s 0 l 0 n 1)
```

You must build this expression in your code and assign it to the Response.PICS property. You may have noticed that the string contains double quotes, which will complicate its coding a little. Use the expression Chr(34) to embed double quotes in your string:

```
DQ = Chr(34)
PICSVal = "PICS-1.0 " & DQ
```

```
PICSVal = PICSVal & "http://www.rsac.org/ratingsv01.html"
PICSVal = PICSVal & DQ & "1 gen true comment "
PICSVal = PICSVal & DQ & "RSACi North America Server"
PICSVal = PICSVal & DQ &
PICSVal = PICSVal & "http://www.yoursite.com  on "
PICSVal = PICSVal & DQ & "2002.01.01T00:00-0700"
PICSVal = PICSVal & DQ & "r (v 0 s 0 l 0 n 1)"
Response.PICS PICSVal
```

TIP Notice that the syntax of the PICS property is that of a method, but it's classified in the documentation as a property. Do not assign a value to the PICS property using the equal sign. In addition, the PICS property is write-only. If you want to view the value of the PICS header of the HTTP response, use an HTTP spy program.

NOTE For more information on using a rating service, visit the RSAC site at http://www.rsac.org.

Status

The Status property sends information about the status of the request to the client. Typical status messages are the "202 OK" (this status message is sent to the client when an HTML document is successfully transmitted) and "404 Not Found" (when the requested document does not exist on the server). You never see the Status messages, but they're transmitted to the client as part of the HTTP header. You can set the Status from within your code to force the browser to take some action, for example.

Syntax

The syntax of the Status property is:

```
Response.Status = NumDescription
```

numDescription is a string that starts with a numeric value (the number of the message), followed by a short description. The HTTP specification describes in detail all the three-digit numeric codes and their descriptions. The status messages can be categorized according to Table 7.2.

TABLE 7.2: The HTTP Status Codes

Error Code	Description
1XX	Status messages in this range send informational messages to the client (they don't correspond to unusual conditions). The HTTP Header status codes in the 1XX range are:
	100 Continue
	101 Switching Protocols
2XX	Status messages in this range indicate successful operations. The HTTP Header status codes in the 2XX range are:
	200 OK
	201 Created
	202 Accepted
2XX	203 Non-Authoritative Information
	204 No Content
	205 Reset Content
	206 Partial Content
3XX	Status messages in this range deal with redirection. The HTTP Header status codes in the 3XX range are:
	300 Multiple Choices
	301 Moved Permanently
	302 Moved Temporarily
	304 Not Modified
	305 Use Proxy
4XX	Status messages in this range indicate client errors (usually about documents that no longer exist on the server). The most common message in this category is the "404 Not Found" message. The HTTP Header status codes in the 4XX range are:
	400 Bad Request
	401 Unauthorized
	402 Payment Required
	403 Forbidden
	404 Not Found
	405 Method Not Allows

Continued on next page

TABLE 7.2 CONTINUED: The HTTP Status Codes

Error Code	Description
	406 Not Acceptable
	407 Proxy Authentication Required
	408 Request Time-out
	409 Conflict
	410 Gone
	411 Length Required
	412 Precondition Failed
	413 Request Entity Too Large
	414 Request-URI Too Large
	415 Unsupported Media Type
5XX	Status messages in this range indicate server errors. The most common message in this category is the "503 Service Not Available" message. The HTTP Header status codes in the 5XX range are:
	500 Internal Server Error
	501 Not Implemented
	502 Bad Gateway
	503 Service Unavailable
	504 Gateway Time-out
	505 HTTP Version Not Supported

NOTE You can't use the Status property on the client computer from within an HTML page. You can't access this property's value from within a client-side script, and you can't force the browser to take any special action based on the value of the Status property.

WARNING The Status property is set by the Web server and interpreted by the browser accordingly. Internet Explorer lets you set the Status property to any value. Netscape Communicator will not accept an invalid Status code (a code that's not part of the HTTP specification).

The Status property is used by applications that contact a Web server to download or upload information automatically. For example, you can write a Visual Basic application that contacts a Web server through the Internet Transfer control. To connect to a URL, use the OpenURL method of the Internet Transfer control, followed by the URL of an HTML document or an ASP script:

```
Inet1.OpenURL "http://127.0.0.1/Page1.asp"
```

(*Inet1* is the default name of the first instance of the Internet Transfer control on the Form).

If the script sets the Response.Status property, you can read this setting from within your application by examining the value returned by the Get-Header method of the Internet Transfer control. For example, if you set the Status property to the following string:

```
Response.Status = "190 Your account has expired"
```

the first line of the HTTP header will be:

```
HTTP/1.1 190 Your account has expired
```

Use the Status property to pass information to the client only if the client is using a custom application. Let's say you have an application that contacts a Web server and interacts with a script. You can pass information back to the client by setting the Status property. Even if a viewer connects to the same script, he or she won't be able to read the information passed to the client by the server.

The Status property is commonly used along with the AddHeader property to instruct the browser to take some special action. If you set the Status property to "401 Unauthorized" (a message we all have seen while surfing the Web) and then set the header "WWW-AUTHENTICATE" to "BASIC", as shown here, the browser will display the basic authentication dialog box, which prompts you for your user name and password.

```
Response.Status = "401 Unauthorized"
Response.AddHeader "WWW-AUTHENTICATE", "BASIC"
```

You can enter a valid user name and password in this dialog box and the Web server will authenticate your request. This technique will work only if you have enabled an authentication method (besides Anonymous authentication, of course) in your Web server. Only users with the appropriate rights will be authenticated by IIS.

Another common message is the "302 Object Moved" message, which tells the browser that the object it requested has been moved to a different URL. To automatically redirect the browser to the new URL, set the Status property to "302 Object Moved" and then set the LOCATION header to the new URL:

```
Response.Status = "302 Object Moved"
Response.AddHeader "LOCATION", newURL
```

Here *newURL* is the new address of the requested object (document or script). As you will see shortly, these two statements are equivalent to calling the Response.Redirect method, which redirects the request to the new site without an extra trip to the client. The difference between the two redirection methods is that when you use the Status and AddHeader members of the Response object, you're instructing the browser to request the new document. The Redirect method redirects the request itself, as if the browser had requested the new document.

Methods

The Response object exposes a number of methods, which are described in the following sections.

AddHeader

The AddHeader method lets you add custom headers to the HTTP response header. As with the Status property, the AddHeader method is not used commonly with Web applications. Adding a custom header doesn't mean that the browser will take a special action. Only applications written to contact Web servers can read the custom headers and process them.

As you will see in the next chapter, custom headers can be read through the Request.ServerVariables collection.

Syntax

The syntax of the AddHeader method is:

```
Response.AddHeader hName, hValue
```

hName is the name of the HTTP header you want to add to the response header, and *hValue* is its value. If the *hName* custom header exists already, it will not be overwritten. A second custom header with the same name will be added. Notice that once a header is added to the HTTP response header, you can't remove it.

Example

To add a new header to the response header, use the statement:

```
<%
Response.AddHeader "SendingTo", "GetPage"
%>
```

This statement will create a new header, the *SendingTo* header, and assign it to the value "GetPage". *GetPage* could be the name of an application that reads a special page with data. This page is probably a straight text file, but you can also send binary data to the client with the Binary-Write method, which is described later in this chapter.

To read the value of the *SendingTo* header, use the ServerVariables method of the Request object (the Request object is discussed in the following chapter):

```
<%
hdrSendingTo = Request.ServerVariables("SendingTo")
%>
```

Add a new header to your pages only if you're going to process the documents stored on the Web server with a custom application.

AppendToLog

This method adds an entry to the Web server's log for the current session. The server logs various entries in the log file on its own, but you can add your own entries to better monitor what's going on. For example, you can log the IP of the current user, the duration of the session, and so on.

Syntax

The syntax of the AddToLog method is:

```
Response.AddToLog logEntry
```

logEntry is the string you want to append to the log file. It can't exceed 80 characters in length and it must not contain commas, because the comma delimits the log entries. You can, however, add multiple entries by calling the AppendToLog method repeatedly from within your script.

Notes

The AppendToLog method will fail if the URI Stem option is not checked. To check this property open the Default Web Site Properties dialog box and select the Extended Logging Properties tab, as shown in Figure 7.3.

FIGURE 7.3: The URI Stem option must be set for IIS to log custom messages to the log file.

Example

Let's say you want to keep track of the number of rows retrieved by each query. The Web server doesn't log this information on its own. You can add custom entries to the log file with the AppendToLog method, as shown in the following example:

```
<%
' CODE TO SET UP THE CONN CONNECTION OBJECT
' CODE TO SET UP THE CMD COMMAND OBJECT
SQLstring = "SELECT * FROM TITLES WHERE PUBID=45"
CMD.CommandText = SQLString
Set RS = CMD.Execute(records)
LogEntry = "RETRIEVED " & records & " rows " & Now()
```

```
Response.AppendToLog LogEntry
' CODE TO DISPLAY THE QUERY RESULTS
%>
```

In Chapter 9, *ADO 2.5 For Web Developers*, you will find out how to access databases with the ADO component. *CMD* is a Command object that executes a SQL statement against a database and returns a Recordset with the selected rows. The resulting Recordset is assigned to the *RS* Recordset variable, which is later used to create the HTML page with the results.

The Execute method's *records* argument returns the number of rows selected by the query. This value is appended to the log file, along with the date and time of the request. Later, you can scan the log file and retrieve all the lines that contain the string "RETRIEVED" to find out the number of rows retrieved by each query.

In Chapter 15, *The File Access Component*, you will learn how to store the type of information discussed in this chapter to a text file.

BinaryWrite

This method writes binary information directly to the response stream without any character conversion. Use it to transmit binary information (sound, images, and so on) directly from within your script, as opposed to creating a file with the binary information and then placing the file on an HTML page.

Syntax

The syntax of the BinaryWrite method is:

```
Response.BinaryWrite binData
```

binData is an array of bytes. This method is used in conjunction with the Field.GetChunk method of the ADO component, which is described in Chapter 9, *ADO 2.5 for Web Developers*. See the description of the GetChunk method of the Field object in Chapter 9.

Notes

The type of information transmitted to the client is determined by the Response.ContentType property; its default value is "text/html". When you use the BinaryWrite method, make sure you set the value of the Content-Type property appropriately. If you want the browser to treat the data as a

JPEG image, set the ContentType property to "image/JPEG". For an example of how to use the BinaryWrite method, see the section "The BinaryRead Method" in Chapter 6, *The Response Object.*

Clear

The Clear method clears the Response buffer but doesn't send any information to the client. The Flush method empties the buffer too, but it also sends the data to the client. Call the Clear method (the syntax is simply `Response .Clear`) if the script encounters an unusual situation that necessitates the generation of a new page. Notice that like the Flush method, it will work only if the Buffer property is already set to True. If not, a runtime error will be generated.

Example

During the course of the script, you may discover an unusual condition that necessitates the interruption of the script. At this point, it may not make sense to send the partial output of the script to the client. If that's the case, you will probably build a new page with a short description of the problem and send this page to the client, instead of the original page. Or you may choose to redirect the viewer to another page. No matter how you decide to handle this situation, you must also clear the response buffer with the Clear method. Listing 7.6 is the outline of a script that clears the response buffer from within the script:

▶ *Listing 7.6: Clearing the Response Buffer*

```
<%
' STATEMENTS THAT PRODUCE OUTPUT
' THIS SECTION CONTAINS CALLS TO THE
' WRITE.RESPONSE METHOD
On Error Resume Next
' MORE VBSCRIPT STATEMENTS
If Err.Number <> 0 Then
    Response.Clear
    Response.Write "An unexpected error occurred!"
    Response.End
End If
' MORE STATEMETNS FOLLOW
%>
```

Notes

The Clear method does not reset any HTTP response header values you may have set from within your script. When the script's execution completes, the modified header will be sent to the client, even if the document's body is blank. In general, you should not set any HTTP headers in a script that may call the Clear method.

End

The End method terminates the script and sends any data in the Response buffer to the client. Any statements following the call of the Response.End method will not be executed.

Syntax

The syntax of the End method is:

```
Response.End
```

You may have multiple instances of the Response.End statement in a script. The first one that will be executed will terminate the script. The following script (Listing 7.7) will print a message and terminate if a user attempts to place an order but the basket on the client computer is empty:

▶ *Listing 7.7: Ending a Script*

```
<%
items = Request.Cookies("ID").Count
If items = 0 Then
    Response.Write "<HTML>"
    Response.Write "<H1>Your basket is empty!</H1> "
    Response.Write "Return to the home page to select "
    Response.Write "one or more products to order"
    Response.End
End If
    '  HERE COMES THE CODE TO PROCESS THE ORDER
%>
```

Flush

The Flush method sends the output buffered so far to the client. Use the Flush method together with the Buffer property to control the flow of information from the server to the client. The Flush method requires that the Buffer property is True; otherwise, it will generate a runtime error.

Syntax

The syntax of the Flush method is:

```
Response.Flush
```

The Flush method ends the current request, and a new connection must be established for each segment of data sent to the client with the Flush method. Use the Flush method in scripts that take an unusually long time to execute, so that the script can send sections of the output to the client as soon as they're ready. See the example of the IsClientConnected property, earlier in this chapter.

Redirect

This method redirects the client request to another URL. This method is commonly used when a site is moved to a new address. The old site is replaced by an ASP file that simply redirects the client to the new URL. You can also use the Redirect method to control what parts each client can see.

Syntax

The syntax of the Redirect method is:

```
Response.Redirect newURL
```

newURL is the URL of the site where the request will be redirected. This parameter can be an absolute URL or a virtual folder on the same site followed by the name of an HTML page or the name of a script.

Notes

Calling the Redirect method is equivalent to setting the Status property to 302 and using the Location HTTP header to redirect the viewer to another URL.

Any output generated by the script before it hits the Redirect method will be ignored, unless it's already been sent to the client, of course. The following script displays a message informing users that their request is being redirected to a different URL:

```
<HTML>
<H1>
You're being redirected to our new site ...
<% Response.Redirect http://www.yoursite.com/welcome.htm %>
</HTML>
```

Write

This is the most commonly used method of the Response object, and it writes information directly to the Response buffer. You can use the Write method to send straight HTML code to the client. The Response method is used to intersperse HTML statements with data retrieved from a database, or other information that changes from request to request.

Syntax

The syntax of the Write method is:

```
Response.Write chData
```

chData is the string that will be placed in the Response buffer. If the Buffer property is False, the string will be transmitted immediately to the client (or as soon as the Web server gets a chance to empty the Response buffer).

Notes

The *chData* parameter of the Write method is a double quote–delimited string. If you want to embed double quotes in this string, you must use the Chr(34) expression. You can also use two consecutive double quotes. The following statements are equivalent:

```
Response.Write "Welcome to ""the"" Bookstore"
Response.Write "Welcome to "  & Chr(34) & "the" & _
              Chr(34) & " Bookstore"
```

Unless you take some action, the output of each call to the Write method is appended to the output of the previous calls of the same method without any line feeds. As a result, the output becomes very difficult to read. To separate consecutive lines, use the carriage return/line feed combination (the vbCrLf constant). If you omit the vbCrLf constants from Listing 7.1, all the

HTML that displays the calendar on the browser's window will appear on the same line. You can view the code sent to the client (use the View ➤ Source Code command of Internet Explorer, or the View ➤ Page Source command of Netscape Communicator).

You can avoid many calls to the Response.Write method if the output is mostly HTML code. Instead of placing all the data to the response buffer with the Response.Write method, you can embed VBScript expressions in the HTML code. The VBScript expressions will be evaluated on the server and only the output they produce will be placed in the response buffer:

```
<HTML>
<FONT SIZE=+1>
The time is <% =Time() %> and the date is <% =Date() %>.
</FONT>
</HTML>
```

These are scripting statements and they must appear in an ASP file, not an HTML file. If you place them in an HTML file, they will be printed without being processed. It's worth mentioning that ASP 3 can process ASP files that contain straight HTML code as fast as HTML files. In other words, the HTML code in an ASP file does not slow the processing of the file, as was the case with ASP 2.

chapter **8**

The Server Object

T he Server object exposes a few members that simplify certain scripting operations. As its name implies, it represents the Web server and part of its functionality. The methods of the Server object are actually the same ones used by the Web server when it serves straight HTML documents to the clients.

The most important method of the Server object is the CreateObject method, which is equivalent to the CreateObject function of Visual Basic: it creates an instance of a component on the server. You can then use the properties and methods of the component from within your scripts. VBScript is the core of a programming language; it provides the basic statements to manipulate variables, control flow statements, and perform other useful functions. It doesn't include statements to access databases, or even text files. For these operations, VBScript must contact other components; this is done through the CreateObject method of the Server object.

In the third part of the book you will see the basic components you need to develop ASP applications. They include the File Access component (it gives you access to the server computer's file system), the ADO component (it gives you access to databases), and more. To include any of these objects in your script, you must call the CreateObject method and pass the name of the component as argument. The CreateObject method will return an object variable that represents the component, and you can access the properties and methods of the component from within your script through this object variable.

Your applications may require functionality that is not available through any of the available components. You can build your own custom components, install them on the server, and use them from within your script. To use the properties and methods of the custom component, you must first create an instance of the component with the CreateObject method. The process of building custom components for use with ASP is described in Appendix B, *Building ASP Script Components*.

If you have programmed with ASP 2, you'll welcome two new members of the Server object introduced with version 3 of ASP. They are the Execute and Transfer methods, which allow you to call another script. These methods will help you break long scripts into smaller modules and develop more robust and reusable scripts.

Properties

The Server object is designed to help you carry out various tasks on the server; it exposes its functionality with methods. It has a single property, ScriptTimeout.

ScriptTimeout

This is the Server object's single property and it specifies the amount of time for which the server will process the script. If this time interval is exceeded and the script is still executing, the server will abort the execution of the script.

Syntax

The syntax of the ScriptTimeout property is:

```
Server.ScriptTimeout = nSeconds
```

nSeconds is the maximum number of seconds you allocate to the execution of the script. Its default value is 90 seconds, which is plenty of time for a typical script. If your script is unusually complicated or it executes very complicated queries against a database, you may have to increase the value of this property.

You will rarely have to increase the value of this property. If the application's scripts take longer to execute, increasing the ScriptTimeout property isn't going to solve any problems. You should consider deploying multiple Web servers and balance the load among them. Change the default value of this property only for scripts that take unusually long to execute, even when the Web server isn't serving many requests.

Before increasing the ScriptTimeout property, you should consider the fact that there aren't many viewers willing to wait for a minute and a half for a page to arrive. Most of them will actually press the Submit button on the Form (or the browser's Refresh button) again. If your Web application runs on an intranet and users know they have to wait for the processing, they will. No Web page, however, should force viewers to wait for more than a few seconds.

If you absolutely have to display a page that takes long to be processed, you should display a "Please wait" page. At the very least, you should warn users about the delay. This is done with a client-side script (see the section "The 'Please Wait'... Page" in Chapter 7, *The Request Object.*

Methods

The Server object exposes several methods, the most important of them being the CreateObject and GetLastError methods. The CreateObject lets you call external components. The GetLastError retrieves information about the last error. The GetLastMethod returns an ASPError object, which is described in the last section of this chapter.

CreateObject

The CreateObject method creates an instance of an object (a component like a Class, an application, or a scripting object like the File Access component) and returns an object variable that represents the object. If you're a VB programmer, you already know how to use the Server.CreateObject method, which is equivalent to the CreateObject function of Visual Basic or VBA. You use the CreateObject method to instantiate an object and use the variable returned by the method to access the members exposed by the object.

Syntax

The syntax of the CreateObject method is:

```
Set objectName = Server.CreateObject(progID)
```

objectName is the name of the object variable that will reference the object instantiated with the CreateObject method. *progID* is the programmatic ID of the class that implements the object. One of the simpler components discussed in the second part of the book is the File Access component, which lets you access the file system on the server. To create an instance of the File Access component in your application, use the following statement:

```
Set FSYS =
        Server.CreateObject("Scripting.FileSystemObject")
```

(This is a single line but was broken to fit on the printed page.) "Scripting .FileSystemObject" is the programmatic ID of the Class that exposes the functionality of the File Access component. To access the functionality of the Ad Rotator component, which manages the banners you want to display on your pages, create an object variable with the following statement:

```
Set objAds = Server.CreateObject("MSWC.AdRotator")
```

You can use the methods and properties of the *FSYS* object variable in your scripts to access the server computer's file system, and the methods and properties of the *objAds* object variable to display banners on your site's pages. The FileExists method, for example, returns True if the specified file exists, False otherwise:

```
If FSYS.FileExists("C:\INETPUB\WWWROOT\SAMPLE.TXT") Then
    ' PROCESS FILE
Else
    ' CREATE FILE
End If
```

Examples

If you're not familiar with the CreateObject method of Visual Basic (or the Server.CreateObject method), here's a simple example of the flexibility this method can bring to your script. The following statement creates an object variable that represents Microsoft Word:

```
Set objWord=Server.CreateObject("Word.Application")
```

Using the *objWord* variable you can access all of Word's functionality from within your script. You can take advantage of Word's spell-checking capabilities to spell check some text entered by the viewer on a Form. You'll see how you can spell check a single word and retrieve the alternate spellings of the misspelled word, similar to the list of alternate words suggested by Word itself when you press Shift F7. You can repeat the same process for all words in a document.

To retrieve the alternate spellings of a word, call the GetSpelling-Suggestions method and pass the word to be checked as argument. If the spelling is correct, the GetSpellingSuggestions will return nothing. If the word was misspelled, the GetSpellingSuggestions method will return a collection of alternate spellings. This collection is called SpellingSuggestions and contains as many items as there are alternate spellings.

```
Set Suggestions = objWord.GetSpellingSuggestions("Antroid")
```

Now we can scan the collection with the spelling errors and retrieve the suggested spelling(s):

```
If Suggestions.Count > 0 Then
    Response.Write "The correct spelling for " &
                "<I>antroid</I> is <B><I>" &
                Suggestions(1) & </I></B>"
End If
```

If the *Suggestions* collection contains many members, they are the suggested spellings. We select the first alternate spelling in the collection and display it on the client's browser. Normally, you should display all suggested alternatives, present them to the viewer and let them choose the desired spelling. The following loop displays all the alternate spellings:

```
If Suggestions.Count > 0 Then
    Response.Write "Alternate spellings for <I>antroid</I>"
    For Each suggestion In Suggestions
        Response.Write "<BR><B><I>" &
                        suggestion & "</I></B>"
    Next
End If
```

Finally, we must terminate Word and release the *objWord* variable. If you skip these steps, a new instance of Word will be created every time this page is opened.

```
objWord.Quit False
Set objWord = Nothing
```

The output shown in Figure 8.1 was produced by the Word.asp script (as seen in Listing 8.1 below).

FIGURE 8.1: The output of the Word.asp script

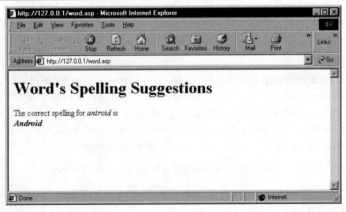

▶ *Listing 8.1: The Word.asp Script*

```
<HTML>
<H1>Word's Spelling Suggestions</H1>
```

```
<%
Set objWord=Server.CreateObject("Word.Application")
objWord.Documents.Add
Set Suggestions = objWord.GetSpellingSuggestions("Antroid")
If Suggestions.Count > 0 Then
    Response.Write "Alternate spellings for <I>antroid</I>"
    For Each suggestion In Suggestions
        Response.Write "<BR><B><I>" &
                        suggestion & "</I></B>"
    Next
End If
objWord.Quit False
Set objWord = Nothing
%>
</HTML>
```

This is a simple example, but it demonstrates the functionality you can incorporate in your scripts by creating instances of components that exist on the server computer. If the functionality you need is not available, you can write your own component and create an instance of it in your script with the CreateObject method.

You will find many examples of the CreateObject method in the second part of the book, where I discuss the installable components of ASP. All these components must be instantiated in your scripts with a call to the CreateObject method with the appropriate argument.

The scope of the object variable you create with the CreateObject method is limited to the module in which it was created. If you create the object variable in a script, the variable will be automatically destroyed when the script completes its execution. If you call the CreateObject method in the Session_OnStart event handler, then all the scripts of the current session will be able to access this variable. In general, you should avoid creating object variables with Session scope, because they will remain active for the duration of the session (and they may not be used by more than a couple of scripts). Certain components, however, will be used by all (or most) of the scripts that make up a Web application. In this case, it behooves you to create an object variable in the Session, or even at Application level, and use it from within your scripts. The Ad Rotator component is such an example. The Ad Rotator component can rotate banners on the pages of your application, and all the pages will access this component. To reserve resources, you can create an instance of the Ad Rotator component in the Application level and all the scripts, in all sessions, will use the same instance of the variable that represents the Ad Rotator component.

Execute

The Execute method interrupts the execution of the current script and temporarily transfers control to another script. After the script being called completes its execution, control is automatically returned to the calling script, which resumes with the statement following the call of the Execute method.

NOTE The Execute method of the Server object is new to ASP 3.

Syntax

The syntax of the Execute method is simply Server.Execute url. *url* is the address of the page to which you want to transfer control.

Example

A script that authenticates registered users should create a welcome message for returning customers and a registration Form for new customers. The two types of customers can be handled by two different scripts, as shown in the code segment of Listing 8.2. After its execution, either script will return control to the script that called it:

▶ Listing 8.2: Using the Execute Method

```
'     PAGE HEADER
<%
UserID = Request.QueryString("UID")
' LOOK UP USER'S ID IN A TABLE AND SET
' THE NewCustomer VARIABLE ACCORDINGLY
If NewCustomer Then
    Server.Execute "RegisterCustomer.asp"
    Else
    Server.Execute "ReturningCustomer.asp"
End If
%>
'     MORE HTML commands to complete the page
```

This script's code will call one of the `RegisterCustomer.asp` or the `ReturningCustomer.asp` scripts. The RegisterCustomer script will display instructions about registration, while the ReturningCustomer script will display a welcome message. Upon their execution both scripts will return control to the script that placed the call.

Notes

The viewer's environment (which consists of the session variables) is carried over to the new page. In other words, the page to which you transfer control can access all the variables set in the calling page. It can also complete transactions that were initiated in the calling page that were not completed.

The Execute method doesn't allow you to pass parameters to the script you call. The proper method to break a script into smaller modules is to implement the basic operations as functions. If you want to create two totally different pages, as in this section's example, use the Execute method. To pass data between scripts, set up the proper Session variables.

HTMLEncode

Have you ever tried to display HTML code on a Web page? It's a very complicated process, because all HTML tags must be carefully coded in hexadecimal notation. If not, the browser will interpret them, instead of displaying them. To transfer a string with HTML tags to the client and prevent the browser from processing them, you must encode all HTML tags. You can either do so by hand or use the *HTMLEncode* method.

Syntax

The syntax of the HTMLEncode method is:

```
Server.HTMLEncode HTMLstring
```

HTMLstring is the string to be HTML encoded and, presumably, it contains HTML tags. Use the HTMLEncode method to display the source code of HTML pages, or the results of queries that may contain special symbols.

Example

If you attempt to display the following sentence on the browser, and you place the text in an HTML document, you will actually see the word "and" in bold:

```
To display words in bold use the <B> and </B> tags.
```

In the days before ASP, HTML authors had to encode the sentence as:

```
To display words in bold use the
                &lt;B&gt; and &lt;/B&gt; tags.
```

(The line was arbitrarily broken to fit on the printed page.) The HTMLEncode method will replace all HTML tags in a string with the appropriate codes, so that they can be displayed, rather than processed, by the browser:

```
<%
Response.Write Server.HTMLEncode("To display words
                in bold use the <B> and </B> tags.")
%>
```

GetLastError

ASP 3 provides better error-handling capabilities, but it still can't trap errors with a statement like On Error Goto. The only way to trap an error is to insert the On Error Resume Next statement in the code and test the Err.Number property after each statement that may fail. The problem with this approach is that you must read the error information immediately after the error has occurred. If another statement is executed successfully, the Err object is reset to reflect the successful execution of the statement.

NOTE The GetLastError method of the Application object is new to ASP 3.

The GetLastError method allows you to retrieve information about the last error that occurred in a script and process it accordingly. This method is called from within the script, which is invoked automatically when an error occurs. The GetLastError method returns an ASPError object, which contains error information: the error's number, its description, the script name, line number where it occurred, and so on. You can use the properties of the ASP-Error object to take some action from within your script or at least display a descriptive error message to the viewer. For more information on ASP error handling and using the ASPError object, see the last section of this chapter.

WARNING The GetLastError method can't be used in any ASP page. With ASP 2 you could use the statement On Error Resume Next and examine the value of the Err object after certain statements to find out whether they executed successfully. You can still do this, but you can't call the GetLastError method to retrieve an ASPError object. Instead, the GetLastError method can be called only from within ASP custom error pages. You will see in the last section of this chapter how to specify custom error pages.

Syntax

The syntax of the GetLastError method is:

```
Set objError = Server.GetLastError()
```

objError is an ASPError object variable that exposes a number of properties with information about the last error. To find out the description of the error, use the Description property of the *objError* variable:

```
Response.Write objError.Description
```

MapPath

In processing a script on the server, you may need to know the absolute path of a virtual directory. The FileSystemObject component, for example, doesn't recognize the virtual folders. To retrieve the absolute path of a file in a virtual directory, use the MapPath method.

Syntax

The syntax of the MapPath method is:

```
absPath = Server.MapPath(relPath)
```

relPath is the relative path of a file and the MapPath method returns the file's absolute path. If you call the MapPath method from within the ProcessFiles.asp script, which resides in the SCRIPTS folder under the Web's root folder, the method will return the SCRIPTS folder's absolute path:

```
<%
Response.Write Server.MapPath("ProcessFiles.asp")
%>
```

This statement will display a string like "C:\INETPUB\EXAMPLES\ SCRIPTS\PROCESSFILES.ASP" on the browser. Once you have the absolute path, you can access any file and its properties in the same folder, through the FileSystemObject object, which is discussed in Chapter 14, *The File Access Component*. Let's say you want to modify one of the ASP files in the application or an auxiliary file used by the application. In the third part of the book you'll learn about the Ad Rotator component, which allows you to automatically insert banners on the pages of your application. The information about the banners is stored in a text file and, among other attributes, you can set the relative frequency of the ads. You can change the relative frequencies of the ads from within a script, using the FileSystemObject object. The Ad Rotator component uses a path relative to the Web's root folder to

access this file. To access this file through the methods of the FileSystem-
Object, however, you must supply the absolute path to the file. To convert a
path name from relative to absolute notation, use the MapPath method.

NOTE The MapPath method doesn't recognize the DOS relative notation (..) for the parent directory. If you need the parent folder of the
SCRIPTS folder, use the ParentFolder property of the Folder object
(described under the FileSystemObject component, in Chapter 14).

Transfer

This method interrupts the execution of the current script and transfers
control to another script. Control will not be returned to the script that
made the call after the processing of the script being called. This is roughly
similar to the infamous GOTO statement in all versions of BASIC.

NOTE The Transfer method of the Application object is new to ASP 3.

Syntax

The syntax of the Transfer method is simply `Server.Transfer url`, where
url is the address of the page to which you want to transfer control. After
the script at *url* has been processed, the response buffer is transmitted to
the client.

Example

Let's say you have a script that handles on-line payments. If the user pays by
credit card, the application must prompt them for billing and shipping information. Viewers will probably have to fill out several Forms. You can call
another script that does exactly that. If they haven't specified a valid payment
method, you can display a message and terminate the script. Listing 8.3
shows a script that calls the GetCardInfo.asp script to collect credit card information. If you later add another payment method, like COD, you can replace
the lines that display a message on the browser with a call to another script.

▶ *Listing 8.3: Using the Transfer Method*

```
<%
PayMethod = Request.QueryString("Payment")
If PayMethod="VISA" Or PayMethod="MASTER" Then
    Server.Transfer "GetCardInfo.asp"
```

```
Else
    Response.Write "Sorry, we don't ship COD"
    Response.Write "Please go to the previous page"
    Response.Write "and enter a credit card"
End If
%>
```

The GetCardInfo.asp script will display a Form where the viewer can enter information about his credit card. When either script completes its execution, the control will not return to the original script and any statements following the code segment shown above will never be executed.

Notes

The viewer's environment (which consists of the session variables) is carried over to the new page. In other words, the page to which you transfer control can access all the variables set in the calling page. It can also complete transaction that were initiated in the calling page, but not completed.

The Transfer method is used internally by the IIS to transfer control to a script when an error occurs in the application. IIS provides a default error page for each error type (it also lets you specify custom error pages), and it uses the Transfer method to transfer control to the error-handling script.

URLEncode

This method is similar to the HTMLEncode method, only it encodes URLs. Use it to build a URL string in your script, and use it as parameter in a <FORM> tag or <A> tag.

Syntax

The syntax of the URLEncode method is:

```
newURL = Server.URLEncode(strURL)
```

strURL is the URL you want to encode, and newURL is the encoded version of it.

Example

Use the URLEncode method to prepare a destination URL before embedding it in your code. If you're building a Form on the fly with a script on the server and you need to include URLs, encode the addresses with the URLEncode before passing them to the output stream. The statements:

```
<%
viewerID = Session("ViewerID")
vURL = "http://www.proto.com/scripts/welcome?" & viewerID
vURL = Server.URLEncode(vURL)
Response.Write vURL
%>
```

will produce the following output on the browser:

```
http%3A%2F%2Fwww%2Eproto%2Ecom%2Fscripts%2Fwelcome%3F
```

This is how the browser encodes a URL before transmitting it to the server. If the *vURL* string were the destination of a hyperlink on a page and you clicked this hyperlink, you'd see the URL-encoded version of the destination URL in the address box of the browser.

The ASPError Object

This section discusses the ASPError object, which contains information about the most recent error and is returned by the GetLastError method. To use the ASPError object, you must understand how ASP and IIS handle errors.

You're certainly familiar with certain pages that describe common errors, such as the "Page Not Found" error page. The error pages are displayed automatically by IIS when the client requests a page that doesn't exist or a page that the client isn't allowed to view. These are static HTML pages, which you can customize in the Custom Errors tab of the Server Properties window. To access this window, which is shown in Figure 8.2, right-click the Web Server icon in the IIS Manager window and select properties.

On the window of Figure 8.2, you see the HTTP error codes and the file that's automatically displayed by IIS when the specific error occurs. You can change the default pages and specify your own, custom error pages. If you are familiar with VB and its error-handling mechanisms, notice that you can't handle the error from within a custom error page and resume the execution of the script that caused the error. The script's execution will terminate as soon as an error occurs, and you must instruct the viewer as to how to handle the error.

FIGURE 8.2: The pages displayed for each error by IIS

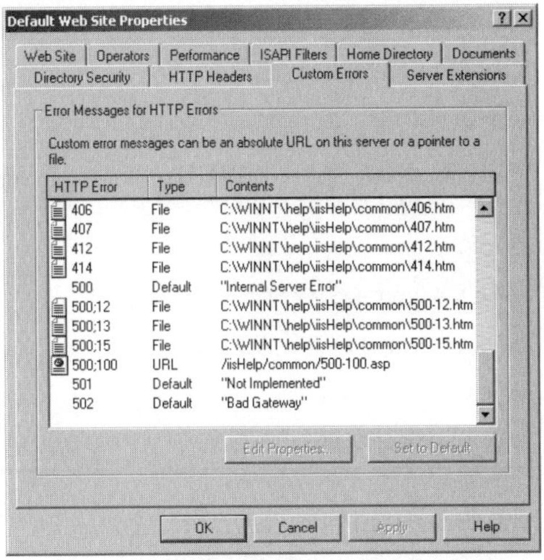

To specify a custom error page, select the error number in the window of Figure 8.2, then click the Edit Properties button. A dialog box will pop up, where you can specify the URL of the page you want to display when an error occurs. This is how IIS can display custom error pages.

Let's see how you can use the GetLastError method from within your custom error page and how to retrieve additional information about the error through the ASPError object. First, you must call the GetLastError method and assign its value to an object variable:

```
Set objASPError = Server.GetLastError
```

The objASPError variable represents an ASPError object, which provides additional information about the error that caused the script to terminate through the properties in Table 8.1.

TABLE 8.1: Properties of the ASPError Object

Property	Description
ASPCode	The error number generated by ASP or IIS. This is a long hex value of the form: 0x800A0???, where the last three digits correspond to the VBScript error code. The codes of the VBScript runtime errors can be found in Appendix B.

Continued on next page

1

TABLE 8.1 CONTINUED: Properties of the ASPError Object

Property	Description
ASPDescription	The detailed description of ASP errors.
Category	The source of the error (ASP, the scripting language, or an object error).
Column	The character position where the error occurred in the ASP file.
Description	A short description of the error.
File	The ASP file in which the error occurred.
Line	The line where the error occurred in the ASP file.
Number	The standard COM error code.
Source	The statement that caused the error.

Because IIS internally uses the Transfer method to transfer control to the custom error script, you can access the Session variables of the script that was running. For example, you can still access the ServerVariables collection to find out the URL from which the page with the error was called (in most cases this will be another page of the same application).

The SCRIPT_NAME server variable will return the name of the page that contained the error, and not the name of the custom error page. Only the values of the script's local variables will no longer be available.

Example

The following statements will display all the information about the error that invoked the custom error page that contains them:

```
Set objASPError = Server.GetLastError
Response.Write "ASPCODE " & objASPError.ASPCode & "<BR>"
Response.Write "DESCRIPTION " &
                        objASPError.ASPDescription & "<BR>"
Response.Write "Category " & objASPError.Category & "<BR>"
Response.Write "LINE IN ERROR " & objASPError.Line & "<BR>"
Response.Write "ERROR COLUMN " & _
                objASPError.Column & "<BR>"
Response.Write "IN FILE " & objASPError.File & "<BR>"
Response.Write "SOURCE " & objASPError.Source & "<BR>"
```

chapter 9

ADO 2.5
For Web Developers

The most important, and most complicated, of the installable components is ActiveX Data Objects (ADO), which enables your scripts to access databases. The ADO object model is the simplest data-access model yet, consisting of just a few objects and collections. Most objects expose several members, which are discussed in the following sections. This chapter discusses ADO 2.5 from a Web developer's point of view. ADO supports features you can't harvest from within ASP scripts, such as asynchronous execution of commands, as well as other features that are very useful in building interactive desktop applications, but are not used in Web development.

As far as Web applications go, most developers use ADO to:

1. Query a database and format the results of the query as HTML documents. If a query returns too many rows, you'll probably want to display them on multiple pages with the usual Next/Previous buttons at the bottom of the Form.

2. Update tables by adding new rows or editing and deleting existing rows.

Web applications are not nearly as interactive as desktop applications. Usually, we don't allow users to view records on their browser, edit them, and then commit the changes to the database. A typical Web application isn't concerned with concurrency issues, either; a customer can't edit another customer's fields, and two customers are not allowed to edit (or even view) the same order. Any changes made to the database through the browser overwrite the existing data. This assumption is much more reasonable in Web applications than in desktop applications. The material in this chapter addresses the needs of a typical Web application that maintains a list of customers (each customer can view and edit their own data), sales and delivery information, and so on. If you want to allow the editing of the products table, for example, from within a browser, you should look into other technologies, like RDS (Remote Data Services).

Using the ADO Objects

The objects exposed by ADO 2.5 are shown next. The Record and Stream objects are new to ADO 2.5 and are used in accessing semi-structured data stores such as e-mail and file systems. They're not commonly used in developing Web applications, but they're covered in this guide for the sake of completeness.

- **Connection object**
  - Errors collection
- **Command object**
  - Parameters collection
- **Recordset object**
  - Fields collection
- **Record object**
  - Fields collection
- **Stream object**

The Connection object represents a connection from your script to the database. All the actions you want to perform on the database must use this object to access the database. Usually, we set up a Connection object at the beginning of the script and release it when we're done. Most of the scripts in a Web application will probably connect to the same database, and you may be tempted to create a Connection variable in the Session level so that all scripts can use the same Connection object. You should never create Connection objects in the Session level. None of these objects will be released before the end of the session, and you may have hundreds or thousands of concurrent sessions. Moreover, any object involved in a transaction is automatically released at the end of the transaction (see Chapter 10, *The ObjectContext Object*, for more information on transactions).

The Command object represents a command to be executed against the database. This object contains the SQL statement or the name of the stored procedure to be executed and the values of any parameters expected by the stored procedure. The parameters of a stored procedure are stored in the Parameters collection of the Command object, each in a different Parameter object. You assign values to input parameters before calling the procedure, and you read the values of output parameters after the execution of the stored procedure. If the stored procedure returns a cursor, you can assign it to a Recordset variable through the Command.Execute method.

The ADO object you'll be using most often in your ASP scripts is the Recordset object, which contains the cursor returned by a stored procedure or SQL statement, and it exposes the functionality you need to read and edit the rows of the cursor. For example, you can scan the rows of the cursor through the navigational methods of the Recordset object, or edit the fields of a row, and commit the changes to the database. All the functionality for accessing the cursor is exposed by the Recordset object. A Record object represents an item in a Recordset of semi-structured rows. A Recordset that contains rows from one or more tables in a database is not made up of Record objects. Record objects are used to represent files or directories, messages, or other information that's not as rigidly structured as a table row. The Stream object, finally, lets you access the contents of a Record. If the Record represents a text file, for example, the Stream object lets you read (or edit) the file. If the Record object represents an e-mail message, the corresponding Stream object gives you access to the actual message (its body, attachments, and so on). The Record and Stream objects are part of Microsoft's Universal Data Access. I'm not going to discuss them in detail here but rather, I'll discuss only the methods of these objects needed to support data access operations in Web development. If you're familiar with ADO, you will notice that a few members are missing. The methods used to perform asynchronous operations, for example, are not discussed here; asynchronous operations are not used in scripts. Some of the ADO objects raise events, which are also not discussed here, because scripts can't handle events.

The Properties Collection

Most objects support the Properties collection, which is made up of Property objects. This collection contains provider-specific information, through properties that are not part of ADO. We use this property to query the provider about specifics, such as the maximum number of columns it can return in a cursor, whether it supports outer joins, and so on. Most developers never use the Properties collection—you may have to query a provider if you're writing applications that might contact several providers, or if you want to take advantage of a specific feature of a provider. For example, Access doesn't support the outer join operation, while SQL Server does.

ADO objects expose a number of properties and methods, which all providers must support. Because ADO is designed to handle different databases, it should be able to cope with features that are specific to a provider. The Properties collection is the mechanism to determine the features that are specific to a provider. The Properties collection contains a very large number of members. Please consult the ADO documentation for more information on the members of the Properties collection.

In the following sections you will find detailed descriptions of each ADO object's methods and properties. The most important members are demonstrated with examples. However, this is reference material, and if you're totally unfamiliar with database programming, you should probably read a book with a tutorial structure, such as the *Visual Basic Developer's Guide to ADO*, or *Mastering Database Programming with Visual Basic 6*, both published by Sybex. Please keep in mind that certain members that can't be used in Web applications were omitted here.

NOTE Most of the arguments of the ADO objects' methods have a limited set of possible values, which are called enumerated types. The members of the various enumerated types are listed in the ADO documentation.

The Connection Object

The Connection object represents a connection to a data source. The Connection object is used to indicate the database against which a command will be executed, or the database from which the rows of a Recordset object will come; it contains all the information needed to establish a connection to the database server and access the specified database.

You usually set up a Connection object and then use it as an argument to the methods of the Command and Recordset objects that access the database. However, you can use the Connection object's Execute method to execute a Command object directly against the database, as long as the command doesn't pass any parameters to the query or stored procedure. In addition, you must use the Connection object to execute multiple commands in a transaction—only the Connection object supports transactions.

Finally, you can use the Connection object's OpenSchema method to retrieve schema information about your database. This operation isn't common in Web applications, however, and database schemas are only discussed briefly in this guide.

To execute a command through the Connection object, declare a Connection object and a Recordset object where the result of the query will be stored. Then, call the Connection object's Execute method to execute a SQL statement or a stored procedure against the database. The following statement retrieves the ISBN and Title columns of all the rows in the Titles table of the Pubs database:

```
<%
Dim CN
Dim RS
Set CN=Server.CreateObject("ADODB.Connection")
CN.Open "Provider=SQLOLEDB.1;uid=sa;
        password=;Initial Catalog=Pubs"
Set RS = CN.Execute("SELECT Title_ID, Title FROM Titles")
%>
```

If you're using Access, use the following statements to retrieve a few fields of the Titles table of the BIBLIO database:

```
<%
Dim CN
Dim RS
Set CN=Server.CreateObject("ADODB.Connection")
CN.Open "DSN=BIBLIO"
Set RS = CN.Execute("SELECT ISBN, Title, Notes FROM Titles")
%>
```

To execute the "Ten Most Expensive Products" stored procedure of the NorthWind database through the Connection object, use the following statements in your script:

```
<%
Dim CN
Dim RS
Set CN=Server.CreateObject("ADODB.Connection")
CN.Open "provider=SQLOLEDB.1;uid=sa;
        password=;Initial Catalog=NorthWind"
Set RS = CN.Execute("[Ten Most Expensive Products]")
%>
```

Notice that the CN object variable must be created explicitly. The RS object variable is declared, but not created. ASP knows that the Connection.Execute method returns a Recordset and it automatically creates a Recordset object to accept the cursor returned by the Execute method.

The last example opens the NorthWind database, retrieves the specified rows, and stores them. To iterate through the rows of the Recordset, use a loop like this:

```
While Not RS.EOF
    Response.Write "<TR>"
    Response.Write "<TD>" & RS.Fields("ProductName") & "</TD>"
    Response.Write "<TD>" & RS.Fields("UnitPrice") & "</TD>"
    Response.Write "</TR>"
    RS.MoveNext
Wend
```

You will find more information on manipulating the rows of a Recordset in the section "The Recordset Object." In the following sections you'll find detailed information on the members of the Connection object.

Properties

Attributes

This property represents the characteristics of a Connection object. For example, you can use Attributes to find out whether the Connection object can perform "retaining commits" and "retaining aborts."

CommandTimeout

This property indicates how long to wait for a command to be executed on the Connection object. This value is expressed in seconds, and its default value is 30 seconds. This property is different from the ConnectionTimeout property, which determines how long to wait for a connection to be established. The CommandTimeout property applies to open connections.

ConnectionString

This property contains the information required to establish a connection to a data source. The information is stored in a string, and it consists of a series of *argument = value* statements, separated by semicolons, as in the following example:

```
CN.ConnectionString = "Provider=Microsoft.Jet.OLEDB.4.0;" & _
                       "Data Source=C:\VB\NWind.mdb"
```

You must pass some or all of the following five items to a Connection object to establish a connection to the database:

Provider = <provider name>   This is the name of a provider: "OLEDB-SQL" for SQL Server, "Microsoft.Jet.OLEDB" for the OLE DB driver for Access databases, and so on.

File Name = <file name>   This item is used for Recordsets that have been persisted to the file *<file name>*.

Remote Provider = <remote provider name>   This item specifies the name of a provider to be used with a client-side connection (Remote Data Source only).

Remote Server = <remote server name>   This specifies the path name of the server to use when opening a client-side connection (Remote Data Service only).

URL=<absolute URL>   This item specifies the connection string as an absolute URL identifying a resource, such as a file or directory.

The ConnectionString property automatically inherits the value used for the *ConnectionString* argument of the Open method, and you can override the current ConnectionString property during the Open method call.

If you specify the *File Name* item in the ConnectionString, ADO will load the associated provider and will ignore the *Provider* setting. You can't pass both the *Provider* and *File Name* items in the connection string.

Most developers set up a Data Source Name (DSN) for the database and assign the following value to the ConnectionString property:

```
CN.ConnectionString = "DSN=AllBooks"
```

where *AllBooks* is the database's DSN. To set up a DSN for a database, use the ODBC Data Sources tool in the Control Panel. This tool is a wizard that lets you specify the provider (OLEDB drivers for SQL Server, for instance) and the database. If you set up a DSN for a SQL Server database, you must also provide a username and password, as in the following example:

```
CN.Open "DSN=SQLNWIND;uid=sa;password=;"
```

ConnectionTimeout

This property indicates how long to wait while establishing a connection before terminating the attempt and generating an error. The default value is 15 seconds.

CursorLocation

This property sets or returns the location of the cursor. Any Recordset created through a Connection object inherits the CursorLocation setting of the Connection object.

ADO supports server-side and client-side cursors. Server-side cursors reside on the server and with them, every time your application requests another row of the Recordset, the row has to be fetched from the server. Server-side cursors are used by applications that need access to "live" data. When the cursor resides on the server, changes to the underlying tables can be posted immediately to the cursor. Client-side cursors are transmitted to the client at once and, as a result, any changes made to the underlying tables are not automatically reflected to the client cursor. Server-side cursors are much more flexible than client-side cursors, but this flexibility comes with a price. Moreover, not all applications need "live" cursors. A client-side cursor is quite adequate for a typical Web application. Web applications use small cursors, and it makes sense to move the entire cursor to the client before processing it. Notice that the "client" here is the Web server (the machine that executes the script) and not the Web client (the machine on which the browser runs). For small sites, the Web server and the database server may run on the same computer.

The most common operation for Web applications is to fetch data from the server, format them as HTML pages, and send them to the client. Not only that, these applications limit the number of rows sent to the client at a time. If the user has requested more than a few dozen rows, the application will usually generate HTML pages with only 10 or 20 rows, and the usual Next/Previous buttons. See the section "Implementing Paged Recordsets," later in this chapter, for more information on this technique.

DefaultDatabase

This is the default database for a Connection object. If there is a default database, SQL strings may use an unqualified syntax to access objects in that database (i.e., you can omit the database name). If you have not defined a default database, you must prefix the database object names with the name of the database.

Errors Collection

Any errors that may occur during the execution of a command against a database are stored in the Errors collection of the Connection object. The members of the collection are Error objects, and the Error object's members are described in the last section of this chapter.

IsolationLevel

This property indicates the level of isolation for a Connection object. This property is set to an IsolationLevelEnum constant and its default type is adXactChaos. The isolation level determines how other transactions interact with yours, whether your application is allowed to see changes made by other transactions, and whether other transactions can see changes made by your transaction. If your script needs such fine control over transactions, you should implement the transactions with stored procedures, or develop custom components with Visual Basic, or Visual C++.

Mode

The Mode property indicates the available permissions for modifying data in a Connection, Record, or Stream object; its setting is one of the Connect-ModeEnum constants. The default value for a Record object is adModeRead. The default value for a Stream associated with an underlying source (opened with a URL as the source or as the default Stream of a Record) is adReadOnly. The default value for a Stream not associated with an underlying source (instantiated in memory) is adReadWrite.

Properties Collection

This is a collection of Property objects that contain provider-specific information about the Connection object. See the section "The Properties Collection," at the beginning of the chapter for more information.

Provider

The Provider property returns the name of the provider used with the Connection object. When you set the ConnectionString property, or the *connectionString* argument of the Connection object's Open method, the Provider property is set automatically. The default provider is MSDASQL. This is the OLE DB provider for ODBC, and you use it to access all ODBC-compliant databases that don't have a native OLE DB provider. The value of the provider is

MSDASQL for ODBC

Microsoft.Jet.OLEDB.4.0 for Access

SQLOLEDB for SQL Server

MSDAORA for Oracle

MSDataShape for the Microsoft Data Shape driver, which returns hierarchical Recordsets

State

This read-only property indicates whether a Connection object is open, and the property's value is an ObjectStateEnum constant. If a Connection is open, you can't call its Open method again to establish a connection to a different database. You must first close it, and then open it with a new connection string.

Version

This read-only property returns the version of ADO in use.

Methods

BeginTrans, CommitTrans, RollbackTrans

These methods manage transactions. To initiate a transaction, use the BeginTrans method. Then, code all the actions involved in the transaction. Finally, call the CommitTrans method to complete the transaction, or call the RollbackTrans method to abandon the transaction and undo the changes made so far in the transaction. The syntax of the BeginTrans method is level = BeginTrans. The other two methods don't accept any arguments and they don't return a value either.

The BeginTrans method returns a value that indicates the nesting level of the transaction. The top transaction's level is 1. If you're executing nested transactions by initiating a new transaction before another one has completed, then the BeginTrans method that initiates the nested transaction will return the value 2, and so on.

Not all providers support transactions. Verify that the provider-defined property "Transaction DDL" appears in the Connection object's Properties collection, indicating that the provider supports transactions. If the provider does not support transactions, calling one of these methods will return an error. Both Access and SQL Server support transactions.

The statements in Listing 9.1 add an order to the NorthWind database. First, a new row is added to the Orders table. Then a few rows are added to the Order Details table. The ID of the order added to the Orders table is assigned automatically by the database. This value is stored in the OrderID variable and is used in the new rows of the Order Details table. All actions take place in a transaction, so if one of them fails, the transaction is aborted and any changes made to the database are rolled back.

▶ *Listing 9.1: The Transact1.asp Script*

```
<!-- #include file="adovbs.inc" -->
<%
Dim CN
Dim RSOrders
Dim RSDetails

Set CN=Server.CreateObject("ADODB.Connection")
CN.Open "DSN=SQLNWIND;uid=sa;password=;"

On Error Resume Next
CN.BeginTrans
Set RSOrders = Server.CreateObject("ADODB.Recordset")
Set RSOrders.ActiveConnection = CN
RSOrders.LockType = adLockOptimistic
RSOrders.CursorLocation = adUseServer
RSOrders.CursorType = adOpenKeyset
RSOrders.Open "Orders"

RSOrders.AddNew
RSOrders.Fields("CustomerID")="ALFKI"
```

```
RSOrders.Fields("OrderDate")=Date
RSOrders.Update

OrderID = RSOrders.Fields("OrderID")
Response.write "Order " & OrderID & " added successfully"
RSOrders.Close
Set RSOrders = Nothing

Set RSDetails = Server.CreateObject("ADODB.Recordset")
Set RSDetails.ActiveConnection = CN
RSDetails.LockType = adLockOptimistic
RSDetails.CursorLocation = adUseServer
RSDetails.CursorType = adOpenKeyset
RSDetails.Open "[Order Details]"
RSDetails.AddNew
RSDetails.Fields("OrderID") = OrderID
RSDetails.Fields("ProductID") = 14
RSDetails.Fields("Quantity") = 2
RSDetails.Fields("UnitPrice") = 23.25
RSDetails.Update
Response.Write "<BR>Item 14 added to order"
RSDetails.AddNew
RSDetails.Fields("OrderID") = OrderID
RSDetails.Fields("ProductID") = 18
RSDetails.Fields("Quantity") = 5
RSDetails.Fields("UnitPrice") = 14
RSDetails.Update
Response.Write "<BR>Item 18 added to order"
Response.Write "<B>Transaction committed successfully</B>"
CN.CommitTrans
Response.End
%>
```

Notice that the CN.AbortTrans method is not called explicitly. If an error occurs in the script, the script's execution will be terminated and the transaction will be aborted automatically. To make the transaction fail, comment out the line that sets the ProductID field of the second detail line. The database requires that each row added to the Order Details table have a valid

ProductID field (it won't accept Null values in this field). If you execute the script again, the following message will appear:

```
Order 11107 added successfully
    Item 14 added to order
Microsoft OLE DB Provider for ODBC Drivers error '80040e2f'
[Microsoft][ODBC SQL Server Driver][SQL Server]Cannot insert
    the value NULL into column 'ProductID', table
    'Northwind.dbo.Order Details'; column does not allow nulls.
    INSERT fails.
/ado/transact.asp, line 62
```

This page informs you initially that a new row was added to the Orders table and that a new row was added to the Order Details row. The insertion of the second row failed, as expected. If you open the Orders and the Order Details tables, you'll see that the rows reported as being added successfully cannot be found in the corresponding tables. The transaction failed, and any changes made to the database were rolled back automatically.

This method for handling transactions works, but the output it produces isn't quite user-friendly. This message isn't what you want your viewers to see. In a high-level language like VB, you could intercept the error and display your own message. With VBScript, you can't use the statement On Error GoTo TransactionError. Listing 9.2 is a revised version of the same script that handles each error as it occurs. This script uses the On Error Resume Next statement to handle errors. After each call that may fail, the code examines the value of the Err.Number property. If an error has occurred, the script displays the appropriate message, calls the RollbackTrans method, and terminates.

▶ *Listing 9.2: The Transact2.asp Script*

```
<!-- #include file="adovbs.inc" -->
<%
Dim CN
Dim RSOrders
Dim RSDetails

Set CN=Server.CreateObject("ADODB.Connection")
CN.Open "DSN=SQLNWIND;uid=sa;password=;"
```

```
On Error Resume Next
CN.BeginTrans
Set RSOrders = Server.CreateObject("ADODB.Recordset")
Set RSOrders.ActiveConnection = CN
RSOrders.LockType = adLockOptimistic
RSOrders.CursorLocation = adUseServer
RSOrders.CursorType = adOpenKeyset
RSOrders.Open "Orders"

RSOrders.AddNew
RSOrders.Fields("CustomerID")="ALFKI"
RSOrders.Fields("OrderDate")=Date
RSOrders.Update
If Err.Number <> 0 Then
    Response.Clear
    Response.Write "Could not add order. Transaction aborted."
    CN.RollBackTrans
    Response.End
End If

OrderID = RSOrders.Fields("OrderID")
Response.write "Order " & OrderID & " added successfully."
RSOrders.Close
Set RSOrders = Nothing

Set RSDetails = Server.CreateObject("ADODB.Recordset")
Set RSDetails.ActiveConnection = CN
RSDetails.LockType = adLockOptimistic
RSDetails.CursorLocation = adUseServer
RSDetails.CursorType = adOpenKeyset
RSDetails.Open "[Order Details]"
RSDetails.AddNew
RSDetails.Fields("OrderID") = OrderID
RSDetails.Fields("ProductID") = 14
RSDetails.Fields("Quantity") = 2
RSDetails.Fields("UnitPrice") = 23.25
RSDetails.Update
If Err.Number <> 0 Then
    Response.Clear
```

```
        Response.Write "Could not add item (1). Transaction aborted."
        CN.RollBackTrans
        Response.End
    Else
        Response.Write "<BR>Item 14 added to order."
    End If


    RSDetails.AddNew
    RSDetails.Fields("OrderID") = OrderID
    'RSDetails.Fields("ProductID") = 18
    RSDetails.Fields("Quantity") = 5
    RSDetails.Fields("UnitPrice") = 14
    RSDetails.Update
    If Err.Number <> 0 Then
        Response.Clear
        Response.Write
            "<BR>Could not add item (2). <B>Transaction aborted</B>."
        CN.RollBackTrans
        Response.End
    Else
        Response.Write "<BR>Item 18 added to order."
    End If
    Response.Write "<B>Transaction committed successfully.</B>"
    CN.CommitTrans
    Response.End
%>
```

To test the revised script, comment out the line that adds the ID of the second detail line and run it. This time the revised script will display a more descriptive message, as shown below:

```
Order 11108 added successfully.
Item 14 added to order.
Could not add item (2). Transaction aborted.
```

You can also implement transactions through the ObjectContext object, described in the following chapter. The best method of implementing transactions is to write middle-tier components that accept the appropriate arguments, attempt to update the database, and return a True/False result, indicating the success or failure of the transaction. This topic is beyond the scope of a reference book like this, but you can find more information on implementing transactions with middle-tier components in Sybex's *Visual Basic Developer's Guide to SQL Server.*

Close

This method closes an open Recordset (or Connection, Record, or Stream) object. Closing an object does not remove it from memory, but it frees the resource allocated to it by the system. You can change the object's properties and open it again later. To completely eliminate an object from memory, set the object variable to *Nothing.*

When you close a Connection object, any active Recordset objects associated with the connection will also be closed. When you close a Recordset, Record, or Stream object, the system releases the associated data. One of the most common runtime errors is that the requested operation can't be performed on a closed object. You may have forgotten to open a connection for a Recordset, or call a method of the Recordset object before opening it. See the discussion of the Open method for more information on opening and closing objects.

Execute

This method executes the specified SQL statement or stored procedure. If the command returns a Recordset, then use the following syntax

```
Set RS = CN.Execute (commandText, recordsAffected, options)
```

where *CN* is a Connection object. *commandText* is a string holding the name of the SQL statement, table name, or stored procedure; *recordsAffected* is a variable that returns the number of rows affected by the action queries. The *options* argument indicates how the provider will interpret the *commandText* argument. Its value is the CommandTypeEnum constant.

The Recordset returned by the Connection.Execute method is a server-side, read-only, forward-only Recordset. This cursor is quite flexible for typical Web applications, which scan the rows of a cursor forward-only, but you can't use its RecordCount property to find the number of qualifying rows. If you want to know the number of rows before processing the rows of the cursor, use the Recordset object's Open method to set up a static client-side cursor.

To execute a SQL statement against a database through the Connection object's Execute method, pass the statement to be executed as an argument:

```
<%
Set CN = Server.CreateObject("ADODB.Connection")
Set RS = Server.CreateObject("ADODB.Recordset")
CN.ConnectionString = "DSN=BIBLIO"
CN.Open
SQL = "SELECT Title FROM Titles WHERE ISBN LIKE '0-672%'"
Set RS = CN.Execute(SQL)
%>
```

This statement retrieves the titles with the specified digits at the beginning of their ISBN and stores the qualifying titles in the *RS* Recordset object variable.

To retrieve an entire table, use the table's name as argument to the Execute method. Likewise, to execute a stored procedure, pass the procedure's name as an argument. If the procedure expects any arguments or returns values other than a cursor, you can't use the Connection object's Execute method; use the Command.Execute method instead.

Open

This method opens a connection to a data source and its syntax is:

```
Open [connectionString, userID, password, options]
```

The *connectionString* argument contains connection information. *userID* and *password* will be used to verify the user against the database; these arguments overwrite the equivalent settings in the *connectionString* argument. The last argument, *options*, is a ConnectOptionEnum constant that determines whether this method runs synchronously or asynchronously. You can't use asynchronous operations in scripts, so you can ignore this argument.

When you no longer need the connection, call its Close method to free any associated system resources. Closing an object does not remove it from memory. To completely eliminate an object from memory, set the object variable to *Nothing*.

The following statements establish a connection to the BIBLIO database, through the *CN* object variable. This object variable is assigned to a

Recordset's ActiveConnection property, so that you can execute SQL statements against the database through the Recordset's Open method:

```
<%
Set CN = Server.CreateObject("ADODB.Connection")
Set RS = Server.CreateObject("ADODB.Recordset")
CN.ConnectionString = "DSN=BIBLIO"
CN.Open
' MORE STATEMENTS
Set RS.ActiveConnection = CN
%>
```

BIBLIO is an access database and you don't need a user ID and password to log on. To connect to a SQL Server database with a DSN, specify the additional arguments, inserting your user ID and password:

```
"DSN=BIBLIO;uid=;password=;"
```

OpenSchema

The OpenSchema method returns database schema information from the provider—information such as the tables in the database: their columns, data types, and so on. It is called as follows:

```
Set Recordset = _
        Connection.OpenSchema (queryType [, criteria, schemaID])
```

The information is returned in a Recordset object, and the exact contents of the Recordset depend on the *queryType* argument, which is a SchemaEnum constant. The *criteria* optional argument is an array of query constraints. The constraints for each *queryType* constant are listed in the same table with the SchemaEnum constants.

The *schemaID* argument is used with providers that support schema queries not defined in the OLE DB specification. This argument is ignored if the *queryType* is set to a value other than adSchemaProviderSpecific. Use the adSchemaProviderSpecific constant if the provider defines its own nonstandard schema queries.

The code in Listing 9.3 will display the names of all the tables in a database on a new page. Notice that the script uses the Access version of the BIBLIO database, but you can change the value of the ConnectionString property accordingly to make it work with a SQL Server database. This script doesn't refer implicitly to any of the tables in the database; it simply maps the structure of the database.

▶ *Listing 9.3: The ShowTables.asp Script*

```
<%
Const adSchemaTables = 20
Set CN = Server.CreateObject("ADODB.Connection")
CN.ConnectionString = "DSN=BIBLIO"
CN.Open
Set RSTables = CN.OpenSchema(adSchemaTables)
Response.Write "<B>The database contains the following tables</B>"
While Not RSTables.EOF
    If RSTables.Fields("TABLE_TYPE") <> "SYSTEM TABLE" Then
        Response.Write "<BR>     "
        Response.Write RSTables.Fields("TABLE_NAME")
    End If
    RSTables.MoveNext
Wend
%>
```

To retrieve the names of the *columns* of all tables, use the statements in Listing 9.4:

▶ *Listing 9.4: The ShowColumns.asp Script*

```
<%
Const adSchemaColumns = 4
Set CN = Server.CreateObject("ADODB.Connection")
CN.ConnectionString = "DSN=BIBLIO"
CN.Open
Set RSCols = _
    CN.OpenSchema(adSchemaColumns)
currCatalog = RSCols.Fields("TABLE_NAME")
Response.Write "<TABLE>"
Response.Write "<TR><TD COLSPAN=2>TABLE NAME " & currCatalog
RSCols.MoveNext
Do While RSCols.Fields("TABLE_NAME") = currCatalog
    Response.Write "<TR><TD WIDTH=50></TD><TD>"
```

```
    Response.Write "<B>" & RSCols.Fields("COLUMN_NAME") & "</B>"
    Response.Write "</TD></TR>"
    RSCols.MoveNext
    If RSCols.EOF Then Exit Do
    If currCatalog <> RSCols.Fields("TABLE_NAME") Then
        currCatalog = RSCols.Fields("TABLE_NAME")
        Response.Write "<TR><TD COLSPAN=2>TABLE<B> " & _
                        currCatalog & "</B>"
        Response.Write "<TR><TD></TD><TD>"
        Response.Write RSCols.Fields("COLUMN_NAME")
        Response.Write "</TD></TR>"
    End If
Loop
Set RSCols = Nothing
%>
```

Part of the output produced by the ShowColumns.asp script is shown
next. Notice that this script will display the structure of the views too. You
can edit the code to view the columns of selected tables.

```
TABLE Orders
        OrderID
        OrderID
        UserID
        OrderDate
        BookISBN
        BookQTY
TABLE Publishers
        PubID
        PubID
        Name
        Company Name
        Address
        City
        State
        Zip
        Telephone
        Fax
        Comments
```

The Command Object

A Command object is a definition of a specific command that you intend to execute against a data source. The commands can be SQL statements or stored procedures, which either retrieve rows from a database or update it.

To execute a command, you must set up a Connection object and a Command object. If the Command object invokes a stored procedure, you may have to create a Parameters collection and add Parameter objects to this collection. Each Parameter object corresponds to a different parameter of the stored procedure.

The following statements execute a simple SQL statement against the NorthWind database through a Command object:

```
Set CMD = Server.CreateObject("ADODB.Command")
Set CMD.ActiveConnection = CN
CMD.CommandText = "SELECT CompanyName FROM Publishers"
CMD.CommandType = adCmdStoredProc
Set RS = CMD.Execute
```

The *CN* Connection object represents an existing connection to the database. You have already seen how to establish connections to databases.

The following statements execute the "Ten Most Expensive Products" stored procedure. Again, *CN* is the name of an existing Connection object:

```
Set CMD = Server.CreateObject("ADODB.Command")
Set CMD.ActiveConnection = CN
CMD.CommandText = "[Ten Most Expensive Products]"
CMD.CommandType = adCmdText
Set RS = CMD.Execute
```

The cursor with the rows returned by the Command.Execute method is a forward-only cursor. Even if you set the properties of the *RS* object variable in your code differently, the Command.Execute method will reset the Recordset object's properties.

Finally, you can use the Command object to execute a stored procedure with parameters. The simplest form to pass parameters to the Command.Execute method is the following:

```
Set CMD = Server.CreateObject("ADODB.Command")
```

```
Set CMD.ActiveConnection = CN
CMD.CommandText = "[Sales By Year]"
CMD.CommandType = adCmdStoredProc
Set RS = CMD.Execute (, Array("1/1/1996", "31/1/1996")
```

The first, optional, argument is the number of rows affected by action queries, as you will see in the description of the Execute method. You can also set up Parameter objects and append them to the Parameters collection of the Command object before calling the Execute method. See the section "The Parameter Object" for more information.

Properties

ActiveConnection

This property indicates the Connection to which the Command object belongs. You can assign to this property either a Connection object or a string that contains the connection's ConnectionString property. You should prefer the first method, if a Connection object is available, because it allows you to reuse an existing connection. When you specify the connection's properties with a connection string, ADO creates a new Connection object.

```
<%
Dim CN
Dim CMD
Set CN = Server.CreateObject("ADODB.Connection")
CN.ConnectionString = "DSN=BIBLIO"
Set CMD = Server.CreateObject("ADODB.Command")
Set CMD.ActiveConnection = CN
Set RS = CMD.Execute "SELECT CompanyName FROM Publishers"
' Insert here the statements to process the Recordset
%>
```

CommandText

This property contains a string with the text of a command that you want to issue against a database. The value of this property is a string that contains an SQL statement, a table name, a relative URL, or a stored procedure name. See the section "The Command Object" above for an example.

CommandTimeout

CommandTimeout indicates how long to wait while executing a command before terminating the attempt and generating an error. Its default value is 30 seconds. Notice that the Connection object's Timeout property has no effect on the CommandTimeout property of the Command objects on this connection. Moreover, the CommandTimeout property shouldn't be longer than the script's timeout interval.

CommandType

This property sets/returns the type of a Command object and is a CommandEnumType constant. Use the adExecuteNoRecords constant (this is an ExecuteOptionEnum constant) to specify that you don't care about the number of rows affected by the command. Although ADO will figure out the command's type, you can optimize the execution of the command by specifying its type (this minimizes the internal processing). If you don't set this property or set it to adCmdUnknown (the default value), ADO will attempt to execute it first as a SQL statement, then as a stored procedure, and finally as a table name. In other words, ADO uses a trial-and-error technique to resolve the command's type.

Name

This is the name of the Command object. The Name property is rarely used in programming, and certainly not in ASP programming.

Parameters Collection

This collection is made up of Parameter objects. Each Parameter object contains information about a parameter of the query or stored procedure you will execute through the Command object. For a discussion of the members of a Parameter object, see the description of the Parameters collection.

The following loop (Listing 9.5) reads the definition of the Sales By Year stored procedure from the database, goes through the Parameters collection, and displays each parameter's name, type, and direction. The script calls the Refresh method of the Parameters collection to retrieve information about the parameters.

► *Listing 9.5: The Params.asp Script*

```
<!-- #include file="adovbs.inc" -->
<%
Set RS = Server.CreateObject("ADODB.Recordset")
Rs.CursorLocation=adUseClient
RS.CursorType=adOpenStatic
Set CMD = Server.CreateObject("ADODB.Command")
Set CN=Server.CreateObject("ADODB.Connection")
CN.Open "DSN=SQLNWIND;uid=sa;password=;"

CMD.ActiveConnection=CN
CMD.CommandType = adCmdStoredProc
CMD.CommandText = "Sales by year"

CMD.Parameters.Refresh
Response.Write "<TABLE BORDER><TR>"
Response.Write "<TD><B>Name</B></TD>"
Response.Write "<TD><B>Type</B></TD>"
Response.Write "<TD><B>Direction</B></TD><TR>"
For Each param In CMD.Parameters
    Response.Write "<TD>" & param.Name
    Select Case param.Direction
        Case adParamInput:
            Response.Write "<TD>Input"
        Case adParamOutput:
            Response.Write "<TD>Output"
    ' INSERT CODE FOR MORE CASES HERE
    End Select
    Select Case param.Type
        Case adCurrency:
            Response.Write "<TD>Currency</TD>"
        Case adDate, adTime, adDBDate, adDBTime, adDBTimeStamp:
            Response.Write "<TD>Date/Time</TD>"
    ' INSERT CODE FROM MORE CASES HERE
    End Select
    Response.Write "</TR>"
Next
Response.Write "</TABLE>"
%>
```

The output produced by the ShowParams.asp script is a table, like the following one:

Name	Type	Direction
RETURN_VALUE	Return Value	Other
@Beginning_Date	Input	Date/Time
@Ending_Date	Input	Date/Time

Prepared

This property returns a Boolean value that determines whether to save a compiled version of a command before executing it. If you save the compiled version of the command before executing it (by setting its Prepared option to True), the command will take longer to execute the first time. Subsequent calls to the same command will return sooner, however, because the compiled version is already available. If the property is False, the provider will execute the Command object directly without creating a compiled version.

Properties Collection

This is a collection of Property objects that contain provider-specific information about the Command object.

State

This is a read-only property that returns an ObjectStateEnum constant. This constant specifies whether the object is executing a command, fetching rows, or attempting to connect.

For example, you can examine the State of a Recordset object before attempting to access its rows, to make sure the Recordset has been populated. If its State property is not adStateOpen, then any attempt to manipulate its rows will result in a runtime error. I mentioned scripts don't perform asynchronous operations.

The State property of the Command object is used to find out whether an asynchronous command has completed its execution. Technically, it is possible to initiate a connection or the execution of a command asynchronously from within a script, but then you'd have to constantly monitor the State of the object to find out whether the operation has completed. This defeats the purpose of asynchronous operations, and that's why we don't use asynchronous operations in scripting. Asynchronous operations are used in environments that can handle events. Only then can we initiate an asynchronous operation, continue with some other task, and be notified through an event about the completion of the operation.

Methods

Cancel

Call this method to cancel an asynchronous Open operation. A runtime error will be generated if the operation you're attempting to cancel is not asynchronous.

CreateParameter

Use this method to create a new Parameter object, passing the parameter's attributes as arguments to the method, as shown here:

```
Set parameter = _
        Command.CreateParameter ([name, type, direction, size,
        value])
```

The new Parameter object must be appended to a Command object's Parameters collection with the Append method. The *name* argument is the parameter's name, *type* is its data type, and its *size* is in bytes or characters. The *direction* argument is equivalent to the parameter's Direction property, and it specifies whether it's an input or output parameter. The last argument, *value*, is the parameter's value.

As you can see from the syntax of the method, all arguments are optional. You can create a Parameter object and then set all its properties as follows:

```
<%
Set oParam = CMD.CreateParameter
oParam.Name = "parameter1"
oParam.Type = adTypeInteger
oParam.Direction = adParameterDirectionInput
oParam.Value = 1001
%>
```

This code segment assumes you have set up a Command object (the CMD variable) and creates a new parameter for the Command object. The new parameter's name is *parameter1*, its type is integer, and it will be used to pass a value to the stored procedure. Since integers have a fixed size, you need not set the Parameter object's Size property. If you do, the setting will be ignored.

After setting up a Parameter object, you can add it to the Parameters collection with the following statement:

```
CMD.Parameters.Add oParam
```

After creating all necessary Parameter objects and attaching them to the Parameters collection, you can execute a stored procedure with the Execute method. The parameters you specified will be matched to the stored procedure's parameters automatically.

All stored procedures return a value, but you need not set up a Parameter object for this parameter, if you don't care about its value. If you want to specify a Parameter object for the procedure's return value, its Direction property must be set to adParamReturnValue. For more information on setting up and using parameters, see the section "The Parameter Object."

Execute

The Execute method executes a SQL statement or stored procedure, as specified by the CommandText property. If the command retrieves a cursor, the Execute command will return a Recordset object, using the following statement:

```
Set RS = Command.Execute ([recordsAffected, parameters, options])
```

The provider sets the *recordsAffected* optional argument; it's the number of rows affected by the command. This argument is set only for action queries or stored procedures. *recordsAffected* does not return the number of records returned by a result-returning query or stored procedure. The *parameters* argument is also optional, and it's an array of parameter values passed to a SQL statement. You can't retrieve output parameters when passing parameters with this method. Most developers set up a Parameters collection and attach it to the Command object. The last argument, *options*, is also optional and specifies how the provider should evaluate the CommandText property of the Command object. This property can be one or more CommandType-Enum constants.

If the CommandText property specifies a cursor-returning query, the results of the query are stored in a new Recordset object. If the command is not a cursor-returning query, the provider returns a closed Recordset object.

See the section "The Command Object" earlier in this chapter for an example of how to execute a command through the Command object.

The Recordset Object

A Recordset object represents a cursor retrieved from a database by executing a Command (usually a SELECT SQL statement). The Recordset has the structure of a grid. The columns map fields, and the rows map records. However, you can't access a row with an index; you must first move to the desired row, which is referred to as *current row*, and then access this row's fields.

Properties

AbsolutePage

This property specifies the page on which the current row resides. The size of the page can be set with the PageSize property. See the description of the PageSize property for an example of using the AbsolutePage property to display paged Recordsets.

AbsolutePosition

AbsolutePosition specifies the position of the current row in a Recordset object; it's an ordinal number between 1 and the number of rows in the Recordset (which is given by the RecordCount property). The Absolute-Position and the RecordCount properties are reported correctly with static, client cursors only. Do not use server-side cursors if you plan to use the AbsolutePosition property in your script.

ActiveCommand

This property returns the Command object that created the Recordset object. If the Recordset is not based on a command, the ActiveCommand property returns an empty string.

ActiveConnection

The ActiveConnection property sets or returns the Connection object used by a Recordset to connect to the database. The property applies to Command and Recordset objects as well. It does not return an object; instead, it returns a string with the definition of the connection (the Connection-String property). To set the ActiveConnection property, use a Connection object:

```
RS.ActiveConnection = CN
```

When you request the value of this property, a string like the following will be returned (all in one line):

```
Provider=SQLOLEDB.1;Persist Security Info=False;
        User ID=sa;Initial Catalog=Northwind
```

BOF, EOF

The BOF property returns True if the current row is ahead of the first row in the Recordset. The EOF property returns True if the current row is after the last row in the Recordset. If both BOF and EOF are True, then the Recordset is empty. The EOF property is also set to True by the Find and Seek operations to indicate that there's no matching row in the Recordset. Here's how you determine whether a row was located:

```
RS.Find "CompanyName LIKE 'SYBEX%'"
If RS.EOF Then
Response.Write "No rows were found"
Else
    {process row}
End If
```

The EOF property is used frequently in loops that iterate through the rows of a Recordset:

```
While Not RS.EOF
    ' process current row's fields
```

```
        RS.MoveNext
    Wend
```

Bookmark

This property returns a bookmark that uniquely identifies the current row in a Recordset. You can also set this property to move to another row. To bookmark a row, use the statement

```
    thisRow = RS.Bookmark
```

You can return to a bookmarked row by assigning an existing bookmark to the Recordset's Bookmark property:

```
    RS.Bookmark = thisRow
```

Do not compare bookmarks with the usual relational operators. Use the CompareBookmark method instead.

CacheSize

This property specifies how many rows are stored in the cache. If a row exists in the cache, ADO doesn't fetch it from the database. The CacheSize property is changed when we create paged Recordsets, to match the Page-Size property. See the section "Creating Paged Recordsets with PageSize," later in this chapter for more information.

CursorLocation

CursorLocation sets or returns the location of a cursor, which may reside either on the client or on the server; the property's value is one of the CursorLocationEnum constants. The client is not the remote machine; it's the machine on which the script is executing. The Web client can't access the database remotely. All it can do is request the execution of a script on the server. The script, in turn, will contact the database server (a machine running SQL Server, for example), retrieve the information, and send it to the client in HTML format. Client-side cursors are transmitted to the client. The advantage of client-side cursors is that they report the number of rows in the cursor and they allow your script to specify the absolute position in the Recordset. Server-side cursors don't report this value; their rows are moved to the client as needed. In Web applications, the size of the cursors is quite small, and we prefer to download them to the client, where they can be processed without further trips to the server. Again, these trips are between the database server and the Web server (and in many cases the two servers run on the same machine).

The CursorLocation, as well as the CursorType property, must be set before the Recordset is opened. Notice that you can't set the location and type of a cursor returned by the Command.Execute method; this cursor is always client-side and forward-only. Use the Recordset.Open method to specify the kind of cursor you want to open.

CursorType

This property sets or returns the type of a cursor, and its value is one of the CursorTypeEnum constants. The default value is adOpenForwardOnly. The various cursor types support the different features listed here, and you should use the Supports method to find out whether a Recordset supports a specific property. The cursor can be one of the following types:

Forward-Only   This is the simplest type of cursor, but also the least flexible cursor. It can only be scanned forward and its membership is fixed. This means that you can't see additions and changes made to the same rows by other users. Always use forward-only cursors in situations when you need to make only a single pass through a Recordset.

Static   The static cursor contains an image of the rows the moment it was created. Like the forward-only cursor, the static cursor doesn't allow you to see additions made by other users. However, you can see the changes made to the cursor's rows by other users (as long as it's a server-side cursor). Supports adBookmark, adHoldRecords, adMovePrevious, and adResync features.

KeySet   Changes and deletions made by other users are visible. All types of movement through the Recordset are allowed except for book-marks, if the provider doesn't support them. Supports adBookmark, adHoldRecords, adMovePrevious, and adResync features.

Dynamic   Dynamic cursors are the most flexible cursors. As their name implies, the membership is dynamic. You can see not only changes to the cursor's rows, but also to the rows added by other users (as long as they qualify for inclusion to the cursor). It supports all types of movement and it's the most expensive cursor in terms of server resources.

If the cursor resides on the client, its type is Static, regardless of the value you set in the code. If a provider does not support the requested cursor type, the provider may return another cursor type.

Fields Collection

This collection is made up of Field objects, and each Field object contains information about a column of the Recordset (the column's type, its value, and so on). For a discussion of the members of a Field object, see the section "The Field Object," later in this chapter.

Filter

This property specifies a filter for a Recordset. The rows that do not match the filter's specification are screened out. You can restore the original Recordset by setting its filter property to adFilterNone.

This property can be set to a FilterGroupEnum constant or a criterion that combines field names, values, and relational operators. In addition to the usual relational operators (<, <=, >, >=, =, and <>), you can use the LIKE operator, as well as the logical operators AND and OR. To use literals in a Filter expression, use single quotes. Use the pound sign (#) to delimit dates.

The filter constants allow you to identify the pending rows before a batch update or the conflicting rows after a batch update. Setting the Filter property to a zero-length string ("") has the same effect as using the adFilterNone constant.

Whenever the Filter property is set, the first row of the filtered Recordset becomes the current row. You can also create an array of bookmarks and use it to screen out undesired rows. This allows you to create groups that can't be declared with formal filter expressions. If no row matches the specified criteria, then the Recordset.EOF property is set to True.

The Filter property is used to implement multiple operations on the same Recordset. You can create a single Recordset with all the rows you need for a few operations (as long as all the operations will be performed in the context of the same page) and then isolate the rows you need for each operation and act on them. For example, you can retrieve the orders of all customers who have placed more than 10 orders in the last month. Then you can filter this Recordset to locate customers in certain states, or customers with a total sales

that exceed a certain amount, and so on. Without the Filter property, you'd
have to go through the entire Recordset, isolate the desired rows with an If
statement, and then act on these rows.

The following script (Listing 9.6) retrieves the order totals for each customer in the NorthWind database. The rows are stored in a client-side, static
Recordset. Then, the script filters the Recordset to display the number of
orders placed by customers in selected countries, applying a different filter
for each country. After that, it counts the number of orders in different
ranges; again, it applies three filters, one for each range. The output produced by the script is shown in Figure 9.1. Without the Filter property,
you'd have to execute six different SQL statements against the database, or
iterate through the Recordset at least once with a fairly complicated loop,
which should maintain several counters.

FIGURE 9.1: The output of the `Filter.asp` script

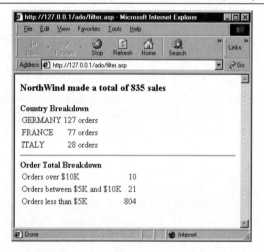

<hr />

▶ *Listing 9.6: The Filter.asp Script*

```
<!-- #include file="adovbs.inc" -->
<%
Dim CN
Dim RS
```

```
SQL="SELECT Customers.CompanyName, Customers.Region, " & _
    "Customers.Country, Orders.OrderID, " & _
    "SUM(Quantity*(1-Discount)*[Order Details].UnitPrice) " & _
    "As OrderTotal FROM Customers INNER JOIN Orders ON " & _
    "Customers.CustomerID=Orders.CustomerID " & _
    "     INNER JOIN [Order Details] ON " & _
    " [Order Details].OrderID=Orders.OrderID " & _
    "GROUP BY Customers.CompanyName, Customers.Region, " & _
    " Customers.Country, Orders.OrderID " & _
    "ORDER BY Customers.CompanyName, OrderTotal DESC "
Set CN=Server.CreateObject("ADODB.Connection")
CN.Open "DSN=SQLNWIND;uid=sa;password=;"
Set RS = Server.CreateObject("ADODB.Recordset")
RS.CursorLocation = adUseClient
RS.CursorLocation = adOpenStatic

Set RS.ActiveConnection = CN
RS.Open(SQL)
Response.Write "<H3>NorthWind made a total of " & _
                RS.RecordCount & " sales" & "</H3>"
Response.Write "<B>Country Breakdown</B>"
Response.Write "<TABLE>"
RS.Filter = "Country='Germany'"
Response.Write "<TR><TD>GERMANY</TD>"
Response.Write "<TD ALIGN=right>" & RS.RecordCount & _
                " orders</TD></TR>"

RS.Filter = "Country='France'"
Response.Write "<TR><TD>FRANCE</TD>"
Response.Write "<TD ALIGN=right>" & RS.RecordCount & _
                " orders</TD></TR>"

RS.Filter = "Country='Italy'"
Response.Write "<TR><TD>ITALY</TD>"
Response.Write "<TD ALIGN=right>" & RS.RecordCount & _
                " orders</TD></TR>"
Response.Write "</TABLE>"
```

```
Response.Write "<HR>"
Response.Write "<B>Order Total Breakdown</B>"
Response.Write "<TABLE>"
RS.Filter = "OrderTotal > 10000"
Response.Write "<TR><TD>Orders over $10K</TD>"
Response.Write "<TD ALIGN=right>" & RS.RecordCount & "</TD></TD>"

RS.Filter = "OrderTotal <= 10000 And OrderTotal > 5000"
Response.Write "<TR><TD>Orders between $5K and $10K</TD>"
Response.Write "<TD ALIGN=right>" & RS.RecordCount & "</TD></TR>"

RS.Filter = "OrderTotal <= 5000"
Response.Write "<TR><TD>Orders less than $5K</TD>"
Response.Write "<TD ALIGN=right>" & RS.RecordCount & "</TD></TR>"
Response.Write "</TABLE>"
%>
```

Index

The Index property sets or returns the name of the index currently in use and its syntax is:

```
Recordset.Index = indexName
```

where *indexName* is the name of an index. This property is used in conjunction with the Seek method, which locates rows instantly based on an existing index. The index is part of the database and you can't create an index on the fly for the needs of a specific script. If a table column is used frequently in searches, create an index based on this column's values and use it with the Seek method. See the Seek section for an example.

LockType

This property sets or returns the type of locks placed on the rows in a Recordset, and its value must be a LockTypeEnum constant. The default value is adLockReadOnly, which eliminates concurrency problems altogether by making the application unable to edit a row. This property must be set before you open the Recordset.

The most flexible locking mechanism is *optimistic locking*. This allows other programs to view the rows you're editing. As far as Web applications go, we don't allow viewers to edit rows in a highly interactive mode (not yet, at least). Web applications retrieve a very small number of rows from one or more tables, download them to the client, and return the edited rows to the server, where a script updates the database. Moreover, each viewer doesn't edit a large section of the database. Typically, viewers can edit their own orders or other information that doesn't apply to other viewers. So, use the read-only locking mechanism when you retrieve rows from the database and call a stored procedure to update the database.

MarshalOptions

This property is used with disconnected Recordsets. The user can edit a dis-connected Recordset for a long time before committing the changes to the database. The changes you make to a disconnected Recordset are not posted until you call the Recordset's UpdateBatch method. When the update method is called, you may not wish to send all the rows to the database. It is possible to send only the rows that have changed (including added and deleted rows) since the disconnected Recordset was opened. The MarshalOptions property determines which rows are sent to the client and it can have one of the values adMarshalAll (0) and adMarshalModifiedOnly (1).

MaxRecords

The MaxRecords property specifies the maximum number of records to be returned into a Recordset from a query. Use this property to limit the number of rows returned by the Recordset. This property is equivalent to including the TOP N clause in the SQL statement.

PageCount

PageCount indicates how many pages are contained in the Recordset object. The value of this property is set by the number of rows in the Recordset and the setting of the PageSize property. A page is a group of rows whose size equals the PageSize property setting.

PageSize

This property indicates how many records constitute one page in the Recordset. Use PageSize to determine how many records make up a logical page of data. Use the AbsolutePage, PageCount, and PageSize properties to create paged output for display on a browser.

Creating Paged Recordsets with PageSize

There are hardly any Web applications that use a database but *don't* have to display the rows of large cursors on multiple pages. When a viewer looks up information in a database, the search may return a few dozen or a few hundred rows. Obviously, you can't display all the information on a single page. Instead, you must display the rows in groups of 10 or 20 at a time and allow viewers to select any group in this cursor. Because each group is displayed on the same page, this technique is known as *paged cursors*, or *paged Recordsets*. Because paged Recordsets are so important in building Web applications, I present a rather lengthy example to demonstrate this technique.

Let's start with the core VBScript code for displaying, not all the rows in the entire Recordset that match specific requirements, but a specific group of these rows (the third group of 20 matching rows, for example). If you set the PageSize to 20, you can execute the following statements to display the third group of 20 matching rows (rows 41 through 60).

```
Set SelTitles=Server.CreateObject("adodb.Recordset")
SelTitles.CursorLocation = adUseClient
SelTitles.CursorType = adOpenStatic
SelTitles.CacheSize=20
SelTitles.PageSize=20
SelTitles.Open SQLArgument, connectString
SelTitles.AbsolutePage = 3
While Not SelTitles.EOF
    ' statements to display the fields
Wend
```

Figure 9.2 shows a Form that prompts the viewer to enter a part of a book's title. The script that processes this Form, TitleSearch.asp (Listing 9.8), searches the database to locate rows that contain this string in their title.

FIGURE 9.2: The `FindTitle.asp` script

▶ *Listing 9.7: The FindTitle.asp Script*

```
<HTML><FONT FACE='MS Sans Serif'>
<FORM ACTION="TitleSearch.ASP" METHOD="GET" NAME="SRCHFORM">
    <P>
    <FONT size="3" FACE="Comic Sans MS">Find it</FONT>
    <FONT FACE="Comic Sans MS"> </FONT>
    <INPUT TYPE="text" SIZE="35" NAME="SRCHARG">
    <INPUT TYPE="submit" NAME="Search" VALUE="NOW">
</FORM>
</FONT>
</BODY>
</HTML>
```

The FindTitle script includes a reference to a second script, `TitleSearch`
`.asp`. It's a fairly complicated script (Listing 9.8), so focus on its main operations, which are outlined after the listing. As you can see in Figure 9.3, the
`TitleSearch.asp` script displays the qualifying rows in groups of 20. Each
page contains 20 rows, while the user can select any group of 20 rows by
clicking the appropriate hyperlink at the bottom of the page. You can't see
the navigational hyperlinks in Figure 9.3, but you can see the total number
of rows that match the search criteria and the number of the pages on
which they're displayed.

FIGURE 9.3: Displaying paged Recordsets

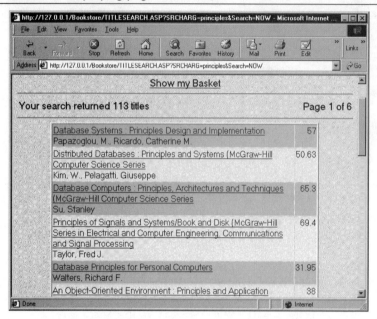

▶ *Listing 9.8: The TitleSearch.asp Script*

```
<!-- #include file="adovbs.inc" -->
<HTML><FONT FACE='MS Sans Serif'>
<body BGCOLOR="#F0F0B0">
<%
currentPage=Request.QueryString("whichpage")
If currentPage="" Then
    currentPage=1
End If
pageSize=Request.QueryString("pagesize")
If pageSize="" Then
    pageSize=20
End If

ReqTitle = Request.QueryString("SRCHARG")
```

```
SQLArgument = "SELECT Titles.ISBN, Titles.Title, " & _
              "Titles.Description As Price, Authors.Author " & _
              "FROM Titles, [Title Author], Authors " & _
              "WHERE Titles.Title LIKE '%" & _
              UCase(ReqTitle) & "%' " & _
              "AND Titles.ISBN = [Title Author].ISBN AND " & _
              "[Title Author].Au_ID = Authors.Au_ID "
connectString="DSN=BIBLIO"
Set SelTitles=Server.CreateObject("adodb.Recordset")
SelTitles.CursorLocation = adUseServer
SelTitles.CursorType = adOpenStatic
SelTitles.CacheSize=pageSize
SelTitles.PageSize=pageSize
SelTitles.Open SQLArgument, connectString
If SelTitles.EOF Then
    Response.Write "Sorry, no title matches your " & _
                   "search criteria (" & ReqTitle & ")."
    Response.Write "<BR>"
    Response.Write "Please press Back to return to the main page."
    Response.End
End If
SelTitles.MoveFirst
PageCount = CInt(SelTitles.PageCount)
maxCount=20
maxRecordsAllowed=200
If PageCount > Int(maxRecordsAllowed / PageSize) Then
    maxCount = Int(maxRecordsAllowed / PageSize + 0.5)
Else
    maxCount = PageCount
End If
SelTitles.AbsolutePage=currentPage
totRecords=0
BooksTotal=SelTitles.RecordCount
Response.Write "<BR>" & BooksTotal
Response.Write "<CENTER ALIGN=LEFT BGCOLOR=cyan>" & _
               "<FONT SIZE=+1><A HREF=BASKET.ASP>" & _
               "Show my Basket</A></FONT></CENTER>"
Response.Write "<HR>"
Response.Write "<TABLE WIDTH=100% ><TR><TD ALIGN=LEFT>"
```

```
Response.Write "<FONT SIZE=4>Your search returned " & _
               booksTotal & " titles</FONT>"
Response.Write "<TD ALIGN=RIGHT>"
Response.Write "<FONT SIZE=4> Page " & currentPage & _
               " of " & maxcount & "<br>"
Response.Write "</TABLE>"
Response.Write "<HR>"
%>
<CENTER>
<TABLE RULES=none WIDTH=80%>
<%
   BooksFound = False
   bcolor = "lightyellow"
   Do While Not SelTitles.EOF And totRecords < SelTitles.PageSize
     If bcolor = "lightyellow" Then
        bcolor = "lightgrey"
      Else
        bcolor = "lightyellow"
      End If
%>
<TR BGCOLOR = <% =bcolor %>>
<TD> <A HREF="BookISBN.asp?ISBN=<% =SelTitles("ISBN") %>">
     <% =SelTitles("Title") %></A>
<%
currentISBN=SelTitles.Fields("ISBN")
currentPrice=SelTitles.Fields("Price")
BookISBN=SelTitles.Fields("ISBN")
Authors=""
Do
   If Not IsNull(SelTitles.Fields("Author")) Then _
        Authors=Authors & SelTitles.Fields("Author") & ", "
   SelTitles.MoveNext
   If SelTitles.EOF Then
       currentISBN=""
   Else
       currentISBN = SelTitles.Fields("ISBN")
   End If
Loop While currentISBN = BookISBN
Authors = Left(Authors, Len(Authors)-2)
%>
```

```
<BR> <% =Authors %>
<TD ALIGN=RIGHT VALIGN=TOP> <% =currentPrice %>
<%
     BooksFound = True
     If Not SelTitles.EOF Then SelTitles.MoveNext
     totRecords = totRecords + 1
  Loop
%>
</TABLE>
<%
  If BooksFound=False Then
     Response.Write "No books were found."
  End If
  Set SelTitles = Nothing
%>
<P>
<%
  pad = "0"
  Scriptname = Request.ServerVariables("script_name")
  For pgCounter=1 to maxcount
     If pgCounter>=10 then pad=""
     ref="<a href='" & Scriptname & "?whichpage=" & _
        pgCounter & "&SRCHARG=" & ReqTitle & "&pagesize=" & _
        pageSize & "'>" & pad & pgcounter & "</a>  "
     response.write ref & " "
  Next
  If PageCount > maxCount Then
     Response.Write "<HR>"
     Response.Write "<FONT SIZE=3>Your search for [" & _
                   ReqTitle & "] returned " & _
                   booksTotal & " titles, "
     Response.Write "but you will see only the first " & _
                   maxRecordsAllowed & " of them. "
     Response.Write "Please specify better the titles " & _
                   "you're interested in, or"
     Response.Write "use the Detailed Search Form.</FONT>"
     Response.Write "<HR>"
  End If
%>
</HTML>
```

The TitleSearch script selects the rows to be displayed by setting the AbsolutePage property of the Recordset object. The PageSize property is set to 20 (the number of rows per page), and the CacheSize property is also set to the same value. There's no reason to keep more rows in the cache, and keeping fewer rows in the cache means more trips to the server.

After displaying the current group of 20 rows, the script prepares hyperlinks at the bottom of the page. Each hyperlink corresponds to another page, and its destination is something like:

```
<A HREF='TitleSearch.asp'?whichpage=4&
SRCHARG='principles'&pageSize=20>04</A>
```

The destination of the hyperlink 04 (which leads to the fourth group of 20 rows) calls the same script, passing as parameters the desired group's number, the search argument (because it can no longer be retrieved from the Request collection), and the size of the page.

RecordCount

This property returns the number of rows in a Recordset. The property returns –1 when ADO cannot determine the number of records, or if the provider or cursor type does not support RecordCount. Only client-side Recordsets (which are static by definition) and keyset cursors return the correct number of rows.

Sort

The Sort property allows you to sort the rows of a Recordset. Its value is one or more field names on which the Recordset is sorted. You can also specify whether the Recordset will be sorted in ascending or descending order. Multiple field names are separated by a comma. A space and the keyword ASC, which sorts the field in ascending order, or DESC (descending order), optionally follow them. By default, the field is sorted in ascending order. Use the following syntax:

```
Sort fieldname [ASC|DESC] [, fieldname [ASC|DESC]]
```

The Sort operation is quite fast because the rows are not physically rearranged; they're simply accessed in the specified order. If the Recordset resides on the client, a temporary index will be created for each field specified in the Sort property. To reset the rows to their original order and delete temporary indexes, set the Sort property to an empty string.

The *fieldname* argument cannot be named "ASC" or "DESC" because those names conflict with the keywords ASC and DESC. Give a field with a conflicting name an alias by using the AS keyword in the query that returns the Recordset.

Source

Source indicates the source for the data in a Recordset object (Command object, SQL statement, table name, or stored procedure). To set this property, assign a string value with the name of the Command object or the Command object itself.

State

The State property indicates whether a Recordset object is open. If a Recordset is open, you can't call its Open method again to populate it with a different cursor. You must first close it and then open it with a new SQL statement or stored procedure.

You can also use the same property with asynchronous operations to find out whether the Recordset is fetching rows or whether it has read the entire cursor. The State property applies to Connection objects (it indicates whether a connection has been established) and to Command objects (it indicates whether the command is still executing or whether it has completed its execution).

The State property is read-only and returns an ObjectStateEnum constant. Because this property may return multiple constants, you must use the AND operator to find out a specific state. While a Recordset is being opened, the State property will return the constant adStateOpen + adStateExecuting.

Status

The Status property of the Recordset object is a read-only value that indicates the status of the current row, and its value is a RecordStatusEnum type. The value adRecModified (2), for example, indicates that the current row has been modified. If you're on a new row, added with the AddNew method, the Status property is adRecNew (1).

StayInSync

The StayInSync property is read-only and it applies to hierarchical Recordsets. It indicates whether a change in one or more child rows implies a change in the parent row. If so, you must refresh the hierarchical Recordset by calling the Resync method.

Methods

AddNew

This method creates a new row and appends it to the Recordset (provided that the Recordset is updateable). The syntax of the AddNew method is:

```
AddNew [fieldList, values]
```

You can edit the fields and then commit the changes to the database with the Update method or by moving to another row. Alternatively, you can specify a list of field names and values to be inserted into the new row, similar to the INSERT SQL statement. If you use the second form of the method, be sure that the order of field names matches the order of field values.

Here's how to add a new row with the AddNew/Update methods:

```
RS.AddNew
RS.Fields(0) = <value>
RS.Fields(1) = <value>
   . . .
RS.Update
```

Here's how to add a new row with a single statement:

```
RS.AddNew Array("field1", "field2", …, "fieldN"), _
          Array(value1, value2, …, valueN)
```

When you use the second method, ADO submits the changes immediately to the database; there's no need to call the Update method.

Cancel

Call this method to cancel an asynchronous Open operation. A runtime error will be generated if the operation you're attempting to cancel is not asynchronous.

CancelBatch

Call this method to cancel a pending batch update and its syntax is:

```
CancelBatch [affectRecords]
```

The *affectRecords* optional argument determines which records will be affected and can be an AffectEnumType constant. Batch updates are not used commonly in Web applications.

CancelUpdate

This method cancels an AddNew operation, as well as any changes made to the current row. You call this method to restore the original field values of a row in data-editing applications. This method isn't used commonly in Web applications; use stored procedures to update rows in the database from within your script.

Clone

The Clone method creates a copy of a Recordset object, through the syntax

```
Set RS2 = RS1.Clone (lockType)
```

The *lockType* argument specifies whether the clone is read-only and must be a LockTypeEnum constant.

Clone Recordsets are used when you want to maintain two identical Recordsets (usually when you need two current rows at once). The Clone method is more efficient than creating and opening a new Recordset object with the same definition. Changes you make to one Recordset object are visible in all of its clones, regardless of cursor type. However, once you execute Requery on the original Recordset, the clones will no longer be synchronized to the original.

You can only clone a Recordset object that supports bookmarks. Bookmarks are identical in the original and the cloned Recordset, so you can locate a row in any Recordset. Cloned Recordsets can be sorted differently, and this is a good reason to clone a Recordset.

Close

This method closes an open Recordset (or Connection, Record, or Stream) object. Closing an object does not remove it from memory, but it frees the resources allocated to it by the system. You can change the object's properties and open it again later. To completely eliminate an object from memory, set the object variable to *Nothing*.

When you close a Connection object, any active Recordset objects associated with the connection will also be closed. When you close a Recordset, Record, or Stream object, the system releases the associated data. One of the most common runtime errors is that the requested operation can't be performed on a closed object. You may have forgotten to open a connection for a Recordset or even the Recordset itself. See the discussion of the Open method for more information on opening and closing objects.

CompareBookmarks

This method compares two bookmarks and returns an indication of their relative values. The syntax of the CompareBookmarks property is:

```
CompareBookmarks (bookmark1, bookmark2)
```

The value returned is a CompareEnum constant, which indicates the relative order of the two rows in the Recordset.

Delete

This method deletes the current record or a group of records; its syntax is:

```
Delete [affectRecords]
```

The *affectRecords* optional argument determines which records will be affected and can be an AffectEnumType constant.

After deleting the current record, the deleted record remains current until you move to a different record. If you attempt to access the value of these fields, however, an error will be generated. Once you move away from the deleted record, it is no longer accessible.

If the attempt to delete records fails because of a conflict with the underlying data (for example, if a record has already been deleted by another user), ADO will set the Error object, but it will not set the Err object (the two objects are different). As a consequence, it will not halt the execution of the script. You can set the Filter property to adFilterConflictingRecords to isolate the conflicting rows.

Find

The Find method searches a Recordset to locate the first row that matches the specified criteria. Its syntax is:

```
Find criteria [, skipRows, searchDirection, start]
```

If no row matches the criteria, the Find method sets the EOF property to True (or the BOF property, if you're searching backward). The *criteria* argument is a string that contains a column name, a comparison operator, and a value to be used in the search. Notice that you can't combine multiple criteria with the logical operators (AND/OR). The second argument, *skipRows,* specifies an offset from the current row (or the *start* bookmark) where the search will begin. By default, the search starts on the current row. Most applications call the MoveFirst method before calling the Find method. The *searchDirection* argument specifies whether the search should begin on the current row or the next available row in the direction of the search, and its value can be a DirectionEnumType constant. The last argument, *start,* is the bookmark of the row that will be used as the starting position for the search.

The *criteria* argument may contain relational operators (<, <=, >, >=, =, <>) as well as the LIKE operator.

GetRows

The GetRows method retrieves multiple records of a Recordset object into an array. The method returns a variant that evaluates to a two-dimensional array when called as:

```
array = RS.GetRows ([rows, start, fields])
```

The *rows* optional argument is a GetRowsOptionEnum constant that indicates the number of records to retrieve. The *start* optional argument is a string or variant value that evaluates to the bookmark of the record from which the GetRows operation should begin. You can also use a BookmarkEnum constant. The last argument, *fields,* is the name of a field (or an array of field names) that specifies which columns will be retrieved. If you omit the *fields* argument, then all columns will be returned.

To manipulate the array from within your code, keep in mind that the first subscript corresponds to the columns of the Recordset (fields), and the second index corresponds to the rows of the Recordset. The array is dimensioned automatically to fit the size of the Recordset.

To specify which fields you want the GetRows method to return, you can pass either a single field name (or ordinal position) or an array of field names (or ordinal numbers) in the *fields* argument.

GetString

This method returns the Recordset as a string. Call it as:

```
Set Variant = RS.GetString _
    ([stringFormat, numRows, columnDelimiter, _
    rowDelimiter, nullExpr])
```

The *stringFormat* argument specifies how the Recordset will be converted to a string, and its value is a *StringFormat* constant. The *rowDelimiter, columnDelimiter,* and *nullExpr* parameters are used only when the stringFormat is adClipString. The *numRows* argument is also optional, and you can use it to specify the number of rows to be converted. If you omit this argument, all the rows in the Recordset are converted. The last argument is the delimiter that will be used between columns. The default delimiter is the TAB character. The *nullExpr* parameter is a value to be used in the place of Null fields.

The GetString method is a very convenient method to convert a cursor into an HTML table. All you have to do is define the <TR><TD> tag as row delimiter and the <TD> tag as column delimiter. The Cursor2Table script (Listing 9.9) displays a table with the first 20 ISBN and Title fields of the Titles table of the BIBLIO database.

▶ *Listing 9.9: The Cursor2Table.asp Script*

```
<%
Set CN = Server.CreateObject("ADODB.Connection")
Set RS = Server.CreateObject("ADODB.Recordset")
CN.ConnectionString = "DSN=BIBLIO"
CN.Open
Set RS.ActiveConnection = CN
RS.Open "SELECT TOP 20 ISBN, Title FROM Titles"
TBL = RS.GetString(, , "<TD>", "<TR><TD>" & vbCrLf)
Response.Write "<TABLE>" & TBL & "</TABLE>"
%>
```

Move

The Move method moves *numRecords* rows ahead of the current row or of the row number specified by the *start* argument. If the *numRecords* argument is negative, the Move method moves toward the beginning of the Recordset. The syntax of the Move method is:

```
Move numRecords [, start])
```

If your code attempts to move to a row before the first record, ADO sets the current record to the position before the first record in the Recordset and sets the BOF property to True. An attempt to move backward when the BOF property is already True generates an error. Likewise, with an attempt to move to a row after the last row, ADO sets the current record to the position after the last record in the Recordset and sets the EOF property to True. Calling the Move method from an empty Recordset object generates an error.

This is the only navigational method supported by forward-only Recordsets. You can specify a negative value for the *numRecords* argument to move backward, provided that the destination row is in the cache. Use a large value for the CacheSize property to support full scrolling with a forward-only cursor.

MoveFirst, MoveLast, MoveNext, and MovePrevious

These are the Recordset object navigational methods: they move to the first, last, next, or previous row in a Recordset, respectively. Forward-only cursors support the MoveFirst and MoveNext methods only.

NextRecordset

The statement Set RS2 = RS1.NextRecordset returns the next Recordset. Some SQL statements may return multiple Recordsets (a T-SQL batch with multiple SELECT statements, for example). After you have iterated through the rows of the first Recordset, you can call the NextRecordset method to move to the next Recordset. At any given time, you can see only one Recordset.

Multiple Recordsets are generated by compound statements, which must be executed with the Execute method of the Command object or the Open method of the Recordset object. The NextRecordset method can be called many times; as long as there are Recordsets, NextRecordset returns a new one. When it runs out of Recordsets, it will return an empty Recordset. To test empty Recordsets, examine the EOF and BOF properties. If they're both True, then the Recordset is empty.

If one of the statements in the compound command does not return a Recordset, the NextRecordset method will be closed. You can examine its State property to test for this case.

When you call the NextRecordset method, ADO executes only the next command in the statement. If you explicitly close the Recordset object before stepping through the entire command statement, ADO never executes the remaining commands.

The NextRecordset method is used with non-uniform Recordsets, which are usually the result of SQL statements that include COMPUTE clauses. The following SQL statement returns each order's details followed by their totals. The customer total follows the customer's orders.

```
SELECT CompanyName, Orders.OrderID, ProductName,
       UnitPrice=ROUND([Order Details].UnitPrice, 2),
       Quantity, Discount=CONVERT(int, Discount * 100),
       ExtendedPrice=ROUND(CONVERT(money, Quantity * (1-Discount)*
                     [Order Details].UnitPrice), 2)
FROM Products, [Order Details], Customers, Orders
WHERE [Order Details].ProductID=Products.ProductID And
      [Order Details].OrderID=Orders.OrderID And
      Orders.CustomerID=Customers.CustomerID
ORDER BY Customers.CustomerID, Orders.OrderID
COMPUTE SUM(ROUND(CONVERT(money, Quantity * (1 - Discount) *
        [Order Details].UnitPrice), 2))
        BY Customers.CustomerID, Orders.OrderID
COMPUTE SUM(ROUND(CONVERT(money, Quantity * (1 - Discount) *
        [Order Details].UnitPrice), 2))
        BY Customers.CustomerID
```

The structure of this Recordset is not uniform. The first few lines contain the details of the first order, followed by the order's total. The other orders of the same customer follow and after the last order for each customer, the customer's total appears, as shown in Figure 9.5 (this is how a script renders the information in the Recordset on a Web page, but you get an idea of the Recordset's structure). This statement returns a peculiar

Recordset: its rows do not have the same structure. Some rows contain many columns, some rows contain a single value. Technically, this isn't a single Recordset. It's a set of Recordset objects and each one of them has the same structure. To scan this Recordset, you must start as usual, but the first Recordset will be exhausted as soon as you hit the first row with a different structure. This marks the beginning of a new Recordset, and you must call the NextRecordset method to retrieve the next Recordset and scan its rows.

The script in Listing 9.10 scans the multiple Recordsets returned by the previous SQL statement. The output it produces is shown in Figure 9.4.

FIGURE 9.4: Scanning multiple Recordsets

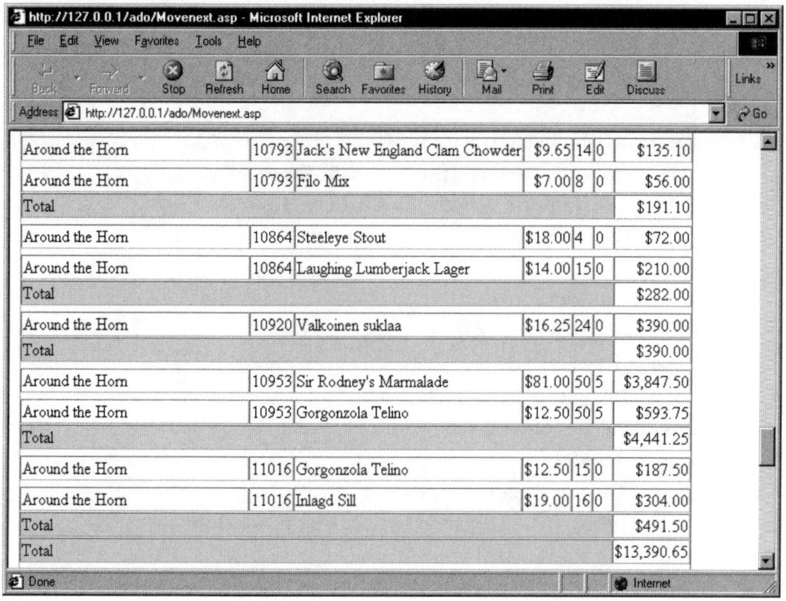

Around the Horn	10793	Jack's New England Clam Chowder	$9.65	14	0	$135.10
Around the Horn	10793	Filo Mix	$7.00	8	0	$56.00
Total						$191.10
Around the Horn	10864	Steeleye Stout	$18.00	4	0	$72.00
Around the Horn	10864	Laughing Lumberjack Lager	$14.00	15	0	$210.00
Total						$282.00
Around the Horn	10920	Valkoinen suklaa	$16.25	24	0	$390.00
Total						$390.00
Around the Horn	10953	Sir Rodney's Marmalade	$81.00	50	5	$3,847.50
Around the Horn	10953	Gorgonzola Telino	$12.50	50	5	$593.75
Total						$4,441.25
Around the Horn	11016	Gorgonzola Telino	$12.50	15	0	$187.50
Around the Horn	11016	Inlagd Sill	$19.00	16	0	$304.00
Total						$491.50
Total						$13,390.65

▶ *Listing 9.10: The MultiRecordset.asp Script*

```
<!-- #include file="adovbs.inc" -->
<%
SQL="SELECT TOP 100 " & _
    "CompanyName, Orders.OrderID, ProductName, " & _
```

```
        "UnitPrice=ROUND([Order Details].UnitPrice, 2), " & _
        "Quantity, Discount=CONVERT(int, Discount * 100), " & _
        "ExtendedPrice=ROUND(CONVERT(money, Quantity * " & _
        " (1-Discount)* [Order Details].UnitPrice), 2) " & _
        "FROM Products, [Order Details], Customers, Orders " & _
        "WHERE [Order Details].ProductID = " & _
        "Products.ProductID And " & _
        "[Order Details].OrderID=Orders.OrderID And " & _
        "Orders.CustomerID=Customers.CustomerID " & _
        "ORDER BY Customers.CustomerID, Orders.OrderID " & _
        "COMPUTE SUM(ROUND(CONVERT(money, Quantity * " & _
        "(1 - Discount) * [Order Details].UnitPrice), 2)) " & _
        "BY Customers.CustomerID, Orders.OrderID " & _
        "COMPUTE SUM(ROUND(CONVERT(money, Quantity * " & _
        " (1 - Discount) * " & _
        "[Order Details].UnitPrice), 2)) BY Customers.CustomerID"

Set RS = Server.CreateObject("ADODB.Recordset")
Set CMD = Server.CreateObject("ADODB.Command")
Set CN=Server.CreateObject("ADODB.Connection")
CN.Open "DSN=SQLNWIND;uid=sa;password=;"

CMD.ActiveConnection=CN
CMD.CommandType = adCmdText
CMD.CommandText = SQL
Set RS = CMD.Execute
Response.Write "<TABLE BORDER=Frame CELLSPACING=0>"
While Not RS.EOF
    If RS.Fields.Count=1 Then
        Line= "<TR><TD COLSPAN=6 BGColor=yellow>Total "
    End If
    For i=0 To RS.Fields.Count-1
        If RS.Fields(i).Type = adCurrency Then
            Line = Line & "<TD ALIGN=right>" & _
                    FormatCurrency(RS.Fields(i)) & "</TD>"
        Else
            Line = Line & "<TD>" & RS.Fields(i) & "</TD>"
        End If
        Response.Write "</TR><TR>"
```

```
        Next
        Response.Write Line
        Response.Write "</TR>"
        Line = ""
        RS.MoveNext
        If RS.EOF Then
            Set RS = RS.NextRecordset
            If RS Is Nothing Then
                Response.End
            End If
        End If
    Wend
    %>
```

Open

The Open method opens a Recordset by executing a cursor-returning command against the database or by opening a table, and its syntax is:

```
Open [source, activeConnection, cursorType, lockType, options]
```

The *source* argument is a Command object, a SQL statement, a table's name, or a stored procedure's name. It can also be a URL, the name of a file where a persisted Recordset has been stored (most likely with the Save method), or a Stream object. The *activeConnection* argument is a Connection object.

The *cursorType* argument (a CursorTypeEnum constant) specifies the type of the cursor, and the *lockType* argument (a LockTypeEnum constant) specifies the cursor's locking mechanism. The default cursor is forward-only and read-only. The *options* argument indicates how the *source* argument should be interpreted (i.e., whether it's something different from a Command object, or whether the Recordset should be read from a file, where it was previously stored with the Save method).

If the *source* argument is not a Command object, you can use the *options* argument to specify the type of the *source*. This will optimize performance because ADO will not have to figure on its own the type of command it must execute against the database.

If the data source returns no records, the data store returns an empty Recordset by setting both its BOF and EOF properties to True.

If you want to create a custom Recordset, you must first set its Fields (by populating the Fields collection with Field objects) and then call Open with no arguments.

The simplest method to create a Recordset is the Recordset object's Open method. The following statements create a Recordset with the rows of the Titles of the BIBLIO database. It also sets the cursor's location and type. The CursorLocation and CursorType properties must be set before the Recordset is opened:

```
<%
SQLArgument = "Titles"
connectString="DSN=BIBLIO"
Set SelTitles=Server.CreateObject("adodb.Recordset")
SelTitles.CursorLocation = adUseClient
SelTitles.CursorType = adOpenStatic
SelTitles.Open SQLArgument, connectString
Response.Write "The cursor contains " & _
               SelTitles.RecordCount & " rows"
%>
```

The *SQLArgument* argument is the name of a table. To retrieve selected rows, use a SQL statement instead. The following is a lengthy SQL statement that retrieves all the orders in the NorthWind database. This information isn't stored in any single table. Instead, we must calculate each order's total by summing the products of the units of each item times their prices:

```
SQL="SELECT Customers.CompanyName, Customers.Region, " & _
    "Customers.Country, Orders.OrderID, " & _
    "SUM(Quantity*(1-Discount)*[Order Details].UnitPrice) " & _
    "As OrderTotal FROM Customers INNER JOIN Orders ON " & _
    "Customers.CustomerID=Orders.CustomerID " & _
    "INNER JOIN [Order Details] ON "  & _
    "[Order Details].OrderID=Orders.OrderID "
    "GROUP BY Customers.CompanyName, Customers.Region, " & _
    "Customers.Country, Orders.OrderID " & _
    "ORDER BY Customers.CompanyName, OrderTotal DESC "
```

To retrieve the qualifying rows in a Recordset, use the following statements. This time we set the Recordset's ActiveConnection property to an existing Connection object:

```
<%
Set CN=Server.CreateObject("ADODB.Connection")
CN.Open "DSN=SQLNWIND;uid=sa;password=;"
Set RS = Server.CreateObject("ADODB.Recordset")
RS.CursorLocation = adUseClient
RS.CursorLocation = adOpenStatic
Set RS.ActiveConnection = CN
RS.Open(SQL)
%>
```

Requery

The Requery method updates the data in a Recordset object by executing the query on which the Recordset is based. In `Requery [options]`, the *options* argument is an ExecuteOptionEnum constant that affects how the operation is performed. The Requery method is equivalent to calling the Close method and then the Open method of the Recordset. The number of rows in the Recordset may change after calling the Requery method.

Resync

This method synchronizes the data in the Recordset with the underlying database, and it's called with the following syntax:

```
Resync [affectRecords, resyncValues]
```

The *affectRecords* argument is an AffectEnumType constant that specifies which records will be updated. The *resyncValues* argument is a ResyncEnum type that specifies whether the underlying values will be overwritten.

The Resync method does not execute the query on which the Recordset was based. As a result, the Resync method doesn't see any new rows inserted since the Recordset was created. If one or more of the underlying rows were deleted, ADO will return warnings in the Errors collection. You can set the Filter property to adFilterConflictingRecords to isolate the conflicting rows. The Resync property is not commonly used in Web development.

Save

This method saves (persists) the Recordset to a file or Stream object, using the syntax

```
Save destination [, persistFormat]
```

The *destination* argument is the path name of the file where the Recordset will be saved or a reference to a Stream object. The *persistFormat* argument specifies the format in which the Recordset will be saved, and its value can be a PersistFormatEnum constant. The Recordset can be saved either in a proprietary format (adPersistADTG) or in XML format (adPersistXML).

If a filter is in effect, only the rows accessible under the filter are saved. If the Recordset is hierarchical, then the current child Recordset and its children are saved, including the parent Recordset. If the Save method of a child Recordset is called, the child and all its children are saved, but the parent is not.

You must specify a destination argument only the first time you call the Save method. If you call the Save method with a different destination, then both destinations will remain open.

Seek

The Seek method searches the index of a Recordset to quickly locate the row that matches the specified values, and changes the current row position to that row. The Seek method works with server-side cursors only. Its syntax is:

```
Seek keyValues [, seekOption]
```

The *keyValues* argument is an array representing one or more columns; the array contains a value to compare against each corresponding column. The second argument specifies the comparison to be executed between the index columns and the corresponding *keyValues*.

If the Seek method does not find the desired row, no error occurs and the Recordset is positioned at EOF.

Supports

The method Supports (cursorOption) determines whether a specified Recordset object supports a particular cursor-related feature; it returns True if the feature is supported, False otherwise. The *cursorOption* argument is a CursorOptionEnum constant.

Usually, you know whether your Recordset object supports a feature at design time. If you want to find out whether an open Recordset supports a specific feature, call the Supports method with the appropriate argument.

Update

This method commits any changes made to the current row of a Recordset in the underlying tables. To commit all the fields, set their values first and then call the Update method without arguments. If you want to change the values of selected fields, use `Update [fields, values]`, passing the field names and their new values as two matched-order arrays.

You use the Update method to save a new row after calling the AddNew method or after the user makes changes on data-bound controls on a Form. If you move to another row with one of the Move methods, or if you close the Recordset with the Close method, any changes in the current row are committed to the database automatically.

To update selected fields of the current row, call the Update method, as follows:

```
RS.Update Array("Phone", "FAX"), Array("555-1234", "555-2233")
```

or

```
RS.Fields("Phone") = "555-1234"
RS.Fields("FAX") = "555-2233"
RS.Update
```

You don't have to call the Update method in the second code segment. The changes will be committed to the database once you move to a different row with one of the Move methods.

The following statements add a new row to the Recordset and set the values of a few of the fields of the new row through the Fields collection. Then, the Update method is called to commit the changes:

```
RS.AddNew
RS.Fields("CustomerID") = "NCMPY"
RS.Fields("CompanyName") = "New Company Name"
RS.Update
```

UpdateBatch

This method writes all pending updates to disk in batch mode and its syntax is:

```
UpdateBatch [affectRecords]
```

The optional argument determines which rows of the Recordset will be transmitted to the database server, and its value must be an adAffectEnumType constant. Batch updates are possible with keyset or static cursors only.

If the attempt to transmit changes fails for any or all records because of a conflict with the underlying data (for example, if a record has already been deleted by another user), the provider returns warnings to the Errors collection and a runtime error occurs. Set the Filter property to adFilterAffectedRecords to screen the conflicting rows.

The Record Object

The Record object represents a row in a semi-structured Recordset. A folder, for example, can be represented as a Recordset, and individual files are represented by Record objects. Notice that the Record object isn't the row of a typical Recordset, like the ones presented earlier in this chapter. The Stream and Record objects are used to access semi-structured data sources, but not databases.

The Record object also represents an alternative way to navigate hierarchically organized data. A folder may be represented with a Record, which has subordinate Records that represent its files and folders.

A folder is uniquely identified by an absolute URL, so you can open a Record object by specifying an absolute URL. A Connection object is implicitly created and set to the Record object when the Record is opened with an absolute URL (see the description of the Open method for more details).

Properties

ActiveConnection

This property identifies the Connection object to which the specified Record belongs.

Fields Collection

Each Record object has a Fields collection that contains information about the Record's fields. See the section "The Field Object" for more information on the members of the individual fields.

Mode

This property indicates the permissions for modifying data in a Record object; its value is a ConnectModeEnum constant.

ParentURL

The ParentURL property returns an absolute URL string that points to the parent Record of the current Record object. This property is Null if there is no parent for the current object (for example, if the Record object represents the root of a directory). It is also Null if the Record object represents an entity that cannot be specified with a URL.

RecordType

This property indicates the type of a Record and returns a RecordTypeEnum constant.

Source

This property indicates the entity represented by a Record object. The Source property returns the Source argument of the Record object's Open method. It can be a string with an absolute or relative URL, or a reference to an already open Recordset object.

State

The State property indicates whether a Record object is opened or closed, and it returns an ObjectStateEnum constant.

Methods

Cancel

This method cancels an asynchronous operation on a Record object. The asynchronous operation can be a call to the following methods: CopyRecord, DeleteRecord, MoveRecord, or Open.

Close

Use the Close method to close a Record object. All related data are released, and you must reopen the Record if you need it.

CopyRecord

The CopyRecord method copies a file or directory, and its contents, to another location. In the syntax

```
CopyRecord source, destination [, _
    userName, password, options, async]
```

source is a URL that identifies the file or directory to be copied. If the *source* argument is omitted (or if it's set to an empty string), the method will copy the file or directory represented by the Record object on which the method is applied. The *destination* argument is the URL of the destination (where the source will be copied), and it must be different from the *source* argument. The *userName* and *password* arguments may be needed to authorize the user's access to the destination.

The *options* argument is a CopyRecordOptionsEnum constant that specifies the behavior of this method. The last argument, *async*, determines whether the operation should take place asynchronously (if True) or synchronously (if False). All subdirectories in the source are copied recursively, unless the adCopyNonRecursive option is specified. In a recursive operation, *destination* must not be a subdirectory of *source*.

DeleteRecord

The DeleteRecord method deletes a file or directory, and all its subdirectories, using the syntax

```
DeleteRecord source [, async]
```

The *source* argument specifies a URL that identifies the object to be deleted (a file or directory). If the *source* argument is omitted, then the DeleteRecord method will remove the file or directory represented by the Record on which the method is applied. The *async* argument specifies whether the operation will take place synchronously (if False) or asynchronously (if True).

GetChildren

The statement

```
Set Recordset = Record.GetChildren
```

returns a Recordset whose rows represent the files and subfolders in the folder represented by the stated Record object.

MoveRecord

This method moves a file, or a directory and its contents, to another location. Call it with the syntax:

```
MoveRecord (source, destination _
               [, userName, password, options, async])
```

The *source* argument is a URL that identifies the Record object to be moved. This argument is usually omitted, and the operation is applied on the Record object on which the method is applied. The *destination* argument is the URL of the location where the Record will be moved. The *source* and *destination* arguments must be different, or else a runtime error is generated. The *userName* and *password* arguments are used to verify the user's rights.

The *options* argument is a MoveRecordOptionsEnum constant, which specifies the method's behavior. If the destination exists already, you can overwrite it by setting the adMoveOverWrite option. You can specify multiple options by combining the individual options with the OR operator.

The last argument, *async*, determines whether the operation will be executed asynchronously (if True) or synchronously (if False).

Open

The Open method opens a Record object. Its full structure is:

```
Open [source, ActiveConnection, mode, _
      createOptions, options, userName, password]
```

The *source* argument is the URL of the entity represented by the Record object. For the simplest type of Record, which represents a row, Record can be a row of an open Recordset object. For Recordset-related Records, the *ActiveConnection* argument is a connection string or a valid Connection object. If the Record is associated to a file system, then *source* can be a relative or an absolute URL. In the second case, it specifies the file or folder over which subsequent operations will apply. The mode argument is a Connect-ModeEnum constant that specifies the access mode for the Record object that will be opened.

The *createOptions* argument is a RecordCreateOptionsEnum constant that specifies whether an existing file or folder should be opened, or a new one should be created. The *options* argument is a RecordOpenOptionsEnum constant that specifies options for opening the Record. The last two arguments are used to validate the user's rights to the files or folders that will be accessed through the Record object.

The following statements open a Record from the URL of an existing folder.

```
Dim RecSet Rec = Server.ObjectVariable("ADODB.Record")
Rec.Open "http://127.0.0.1/PublicDocs/"
```

A relative URL is the URL of a document in the context of the Connection object:

```
Dim CN
Set CN = Server.CreateObject("ADODB.Connection")
Dim Rec
Set Rec = Server.CreateObject("ADODB.Record")
CN.Open "http://127.0.0.1/PublicDocs/"
Rec.Open "Resume.doc", aConnection
```

The Stream Object

A Stream object represents a stream of binary data or text. ADO can access semi-structured data stores, such as a file system or an e-mail system. A Stream object consists of Records that correspond to the contents of a file or the items in an e-mail system.

A Stream object can be obtained in these ways:

- From a URL pointing to an object (typically a file) containing binary or text data. This object can be a simple document, in which case a Record object represents a document or a folder. Accessing files and folders through a Stream object is similar to using the FileSystem-Object (this is an object of the Windows Scripting Host).

- From a Record object. After you have opened a Record object, you can obtain its default stream.

- By creating a Stream object with the appropriate declaration. This Stream can be used to store data, which you can manipulate from within your code.

You can use the Stream object's methods and properties to access its Records (the subfolder of a folder, the contents of a file, the messages stored in an e-mail system, and so on). You can also save information to a folder or file by using the Stream object. The Stream object allows you to access non-traditional data stores (non-relational databases) through the ADO object. This capacity of ADO doesn't apply to databases and their programming, and it's not discussed in this book.

Properties

Charset

This property specifies the character set into which the contents of a text Stream should be translated. The default value is "Unicode." Other values are the character set strings used in the HTML <META> tag (Windows-1252, etc.). For a list of the character sets available on your system, see the following branch of the Registry:

```
HKEY_CLASSES_ROOT\MIME\Database\Charset
```

EOS

The EOS (End Of Stream) property is the equivalent of the EOF property for Stream objects. It returns True if the current position is the end of the Stream. Unlike the EOF property, the EOS property can be set. When you set the EOS property to True, you specify that the current position becomes the end of the Stream. Any additional characters or bytes in the Stream are discarded.

LineSeparator

This property specifies the character to be used as the line separator in a text stream, and its value must be a LineSeparatorEnum constant. The default value is adCRLF. The LineSeparator must be used with text streams only; it's ignored if specified with a binary stream.

Mode

The Mode property indicates the permissions for modifying data in a Stream object. The same property applies to Connection objects and Record objects as well.

Position

This property identifies the current position in a Stream object. It sets a long integer value, which is the offset (in characters or bytes) of the current position from the beginning of the Stream. The value zero corresponds to the first byte in the Stream.

Size

This property returns the size of a Stream object in number of bytes. If the size of the Stream object is not known, the Size property will return the value –1, similar to the RecordCount property.

State

Like the State property of all other objects, the Stream.State property indicates whether the Stream object is open or closed, as well as the status of an asynchronous operation. Its value is an ObjectStateEnum constant. If the Stream object is open, the State property may also indicate the status of an asynchronous operation. If the operation hasn't completed, the value of the State property will be adStateOpen + adStateExecuting.

Type

The Type property identifies the type of the data stored in a Stream object, and it can be a StreamTypeEnum constant. The default value is adTypeText. This property can be set only while you're on the first byte of the Stream; at any other position, the Type property is read-only.

Methods

Cancel

Call this method to cancel an asynchronous Open operation. A runtime error will be generated if the operation you're attempting to cancel is not asynchronous.

Close

This method closes an open Stream object. Closing a Stream object does not remove it from memory. To remove the object from memory and release its resources, set it to *Nothing*. The Close method releases the data associated with the Stream object.

CopyTo

The CopyTo method copies *numChars* characters or bytes from one Stream object to another, and its syntax is:

```
CopyTo destStream [, numChars]
```

The *destStream* argument is a reference to an open Stream object, into which the characters or bytes will be copied. If you omit the *numChars* argument, the method will copy all the characters or bytes from the current location to the end of the Stream.

Flush

This method flushes the Stream to the object (a file, for example) to which the Stream object is associated. This method need not be called frequently because the Stream object flushes its buffer as frequently as possible in the background. When a Stream object is closed, its contents are automatically flushed.

LoadFromFile

This method loads the contents of an existing file into a Stream; its only argument is the source filename. The Stream object must be already open before its LoadFromFile method can be called. Any existing bytes in the Stream are overwritten by the contents of the file. Any existing bytes after the EOS created by LoadFromFile are truncated.

Open

The Open method opens a Stream object. Its syntax is:

```
Open [source, mode, openOptions, userName, password]
```

The *source* argument specifies the source of the Stream's data. It may be an absolute URL or a string pointing to a structured data source, such as a file system of an e-mail storage. Alternately, *source* may contain a reference to an already open Record object, which opens the default stream associated with the Record. The *mode* argument specifies the access mode for the Stream. The *openOptions* argument is a StreamOpenOptionsEnum constant and specifies whether the Stream's data will come from a URL or a file. The *userName* and *password* arguments contain information required to validate access to the Stream object.

Read

The Read method is called by

```
variant = Stream.Read (numBytes)
```

and reads *numBytes* bytes from a Stream object. The data read from the Stream are stored in a variant. The *numBytes* argument can be a StreamReadEnum constant; its default value is adReadAll.

ReadText

To read the beginning of a text stream, use

```
String = Stream.ReadText (numChars)
```

This method reads *numChars* characters from a text Stream object. The text read from the Stream is stored in a string variable. The *numChars* argument can be a StreamReadEnum constant, and its default value is adReadAll.

SaveToFile

This method saves the binary contents of a Stream to a file by means of

```
SaveToFile filename [, saveOptions]
```

The *filename* argument is the name of the file to which the contents of the Stream will be saved. The *saveOptions* argument is a SaveOptionsEnum constant that specifies whether a new file should be created by SaveToFile if it does not already exist. The default value is adSaveCreateNotExists.

SetEOS

This method defines the end of the stream. SetEOS updates the value of the EOS property by making the current Position the stream end; any bytes or characters following the current position are truncated.

SkipLine

This method skips one entire line when reading a text stream. The SkipLine method is used with text streams only.

Write

This method writes binary data to a Stream object. Its argument contains an array of bytes that will be written to the Stream. The current Position is set to the byte following the written data. The Write method does not truncate the rest of the data in a stream. If you want to truncate these bytes, call SetEOS.

WriteText

The WriteText method writes a specified text string to a Stream object when called as

```
WriteText data [, options]
```

The *data* argument contains the text to be written to the Stream. The *options* argument is a StreamWriteOptionsEnum constant, and it specifies whether a line separator must be written to the end of the string.

The WriteText method does not truncate the rest of the data in a stream. If you want to truncate these characters, call SetEOS. If you WriteText past the current EOS position, the size of the stream will be increased to contain any new characters, and EOS will move to the new last byte in the stream.

A simple example follows of using the Stream object in a Web application. The same functionality can be achieved through the FileAccess component, but I'll use the Stream object to demonstrate how you can access semi-structured information using the Stream object. The essence of Universal Access is a uniform set of tools for accessing not only databases, which are rigidly structured, but semi-structured data sources, like folders and files, inboxes, and so on.

The example displays the contents of a text file in a TextArea control on a Web page. The viewer can edit the information and submit the revised text to the server.

The EditText.htm file is shown in the following listing. Instead of placing some text between the two <TEXTAREA> tags, it uses a script to read the contents of a file from a Stream object. You could have used the FileSystem-Object object (described in Chapter 14, *The Content Rotator Component*) to read the file, but this is a simple example to demonstrate the use of the Stream object.

```
<HTML>
<FORM ACTION="GetText.asp" METHOD=GET>
<TEXTAREA NAME=MyText STYLE='WIDTH=90%; HEIGHT=250'>
<%
Const adOpenFromURL=8
Set objStream = Server.CreateObject("ADODB.Stream")
objStream.Open _
        "URL='http://127.0.0.1/ADO/test.txt', _
        adModeRead, adOpenStreamFromURL"
Response.Write objStream.ReadText
%>
</TEXTAREA>
<BR>
<INPUT TYPE=Submit>
</FORM>
</HTML>
```

The Submit button sends the contents of the TextArea control to the Web server, where it's processed by the GetText.asp script. This script overwrites the original file (test.txt), creates a new Web page with the revised text, and sends that back to the client as a confirmation. Here's the listing of the GetText.asp script:

```
<%
Const adOpenFromURL=8
Const adModeReadWrite = 4
Set objStream = Server.CreateObject("ADODB.Stream")
objStream.Open "URL='http://127.0.0.1/ADO/test.txt',
                adModeReadWrite, adOpenStreamFromURL"
objStream.Position=0
objStream.SetEOS
newText = Request.Form("MyText")
objStream.WriteText newText
objStream.Close
Response.Write "<HTML>"
```

```
Response.Write newText
Response.Write "</HTML>"
%>
```

By setting the Stream object's Position property to 0, the script moves to the beginning of the file, so that the write operation will overwrite the original file. The SetEOS method resets the file; it sets the end of the stream to the current location, which is the beginning of the file. Then the script writes the contents of the TextArea control to the file and closes the Stream object.

It's not the most exciting example, but it shows how you can use ADO to manipulate text files. In the second part of the book, you'll see how to access text files with the File Access component.

The Field Object

A Field object represents a column of a table in the database. Each table exposes the Fields collection, which contains a Field object for each column in the table. Use the items of the Fields collection to find out information about the table's columns. Most of the members of the Field object are the same as the properties of the Parameter object.

Properties

ActualSize

This property returns the actual length of the data stored in a field. Use ActualSize with variable length fields to find out the length of the data stored in the field. For fixed-length fields, the ActualSize property is the same as the DefinedSize property.

Attributes

This property indicates one or more characteristics of a Field object, and its value is a FieldAttributeEnum constant. To find out whether an attribute is set, AND the Attributes property value with the desired constant:

```
If (Field.Attribute And adFldLong) = adFldLong Then
    {can call the AppendChunk method on this field}
End If
```

DefinedSize

This property indicates the defined size of a Field object (the size that appears in the table's definition). You can set a size for only varchar and binary fields.

Name

This property returns or sets the field's name. You must set this property in a custom Recordset and read it in a Recordset, based on a query.

NumericScale

This property indicates the scale of a numeric field (the number of digits to the right of the decimal point).

OriginalValue

This is the value of a field the moment it was read from the database; it doesn't change when you edit the field.

Precision

This property specifies the precision of a field that holds a numeric value (the same property applies to the Parameter object as well). A numeric value's precision is the maximum number of digits used to represent the field's value.

Status

The Status property indicates whether a Field object has been added to the Fields collection, or whether an existing field has changed value. Its value is a FieldStatusEnum constant.

Type

This is the field's (column's) data type, and it can a DataTypeEnum constant.

UnderlyingValue

This is the value of a field in the database. If the user has edited the field, then the UnderlyingValue is different from the Value property. If another user has edited the field in the database, then the underlying value is different from the Value and OriginalValue properties.

Reading a field's UnderlyingValue property is similar to calling the Resync method for a specific field. The UnderlyingValue and OriginalValue properties are used to resolve conflicts in batch updates.

Value

This is the current value of a Field object. This value is different from the UnderlyingValue property if the field has been edited since it was read on the client. The Value is the default property of the Field object and you can omit its name. The following expressions are equivalent:

```
RS.Fields("Name").Value
RS.Fields("Name")
```

Because the Fields property is the default property of the Recordset object, the previous expressions are also equivalent to the following one:

```
RS("Name")
```

Methods

AppendChunk

The AppendChunk method appends data to a large text or binary field. Its only argument is a variant holding the data to be appended to the Field object. The first time you call the AppendChunk method, it overwrites any existing data. Subsequent calls to this method append to the data already written to the field. If you switch to another field, the Append-Chunk method assumes that you're done appending data. The next time you call the AppendChunk method on the same field, it will overwrite.

GetChunk

This method returns a large text or binary field, or part of it, via variable = GetChunk(size). The size argument is the number of characters or bytes you want to retrieve. In situations where system memory is limited, you can use the GetChunk method to manipulate long values in portions, rather than in their entirety.

The first call to the GetChunk method retrieves data from the beginning of the field. Each successive call of the GetChunk method retrieves data starting from where the previous call left off.

Fields Collection Methods

Append

This method appends a Field object to the Fields collection with the syntax

```
Append fieldname, type [, definedSize, Attributes]
```

fieldname is the field's name and *type* is its data type (a DataTypeEnum constant). The optional argument *definedSize* is used with character and binary fields to denote the maximum length of data that can be stored in the field. *Attributes* is another optional argument (a FieldAttributeEnum constant) that specifies additional field attributes.

Delete

This method deletes a Field object from the Fields collection. The sole argument is the name of the Field object to be deleted, and this cannot be the ordinal position of the object in the Fields collection. This method should be used with custom Recordsets. You can't manipulate the structure of a table by adding or deleting fields in the Fields collection.

Refresh

The Refresh method reads the field definitions in the Fields collection directly from the database.

The Parameter Object

A Parameter object represents a parameter or argument associated with a Command object, based on a parameterized query or stored procedure. To call a stored procedure with input/output parameters, you must create a Parameter object for each of the stored procedure's parameters, and then append it to the Command object's Parameters collection. After you have populated the Parameters collection, you can call the stored procedure with the Command object's Execute method. The members of the Parameter object described in the following section allow you to manipulate the parameters of the stored procedures, set the values of the input parameters, and read the values of the output parameters.

Properties

Attributes

This property sets or returns one or more characteristics of a Parameter object. It is a ParameterAttributesEnum constant, or a combination of two or more constants. To assign a new attribute, you must OR the appropriate constant with the existing attributes:

```
param.Attributes = param.Attributes OR adParamNullable
```

To find out whether an attribute is set, use a statement like the following:

```
If (param.Attributes AND adParamNullable) Then . . .
```

Direction

The Direction property represents an input parameter, an output parameter, or both. Its value is a ParameterDirectionEnum constant.

Name

The name of the Parameter object is used to identify the object in the Parameters collection. The Parameter object's Name property need not be the same as the name of the parameter in the stored procedure.

NumericScale

This property determines the numeric scale (the number of digits to the right of the decimal point) of the numeric value stored in the Parameter object.

Precision

This property specifies the precision of a parameter that holds a numeric value (the same property applies to the Field object as well). A numeric value's precision is the maximum number of digits used to represent the parameter's value.

Size

This property indicates the maximum size, in bytes or characters, of a Parameter object (or a Field object). This property must be used with variable-length data types (varchar and binary types). Fixed-length data types have a Size property, but setting it doesn't affect the parameter's actual size.

Type

This property indicates the data type of a Parameter, Field, or Property object; it's a DataEnumType constant.

Value

This property sets or returns the Parameter object's value. You set this value for input parameters before calling a stored procedure through the Command object, and read this value for output parameters to retrieve the values returned by the stored procedure.

Method

CreateParameter

The CreateParameter method creates a new Parameter object with the properties specified in the following syntax:

```
Set parameter = _
    Command.CreateParameter ([name, type, direction, size, value])
```

The new Parameter object must be appended to a Command object's Parameters collection with the Append method. The *name* argument is the parameter's name, *type* is its data type, and *size* is in bytes or characters (the last argument applies to variable-length fields only). The *direction* argument is equivalent to the parameter's Direction property and specifies whether the object is an input or output parameter. The last argument is the parameter's value.

As you can see from the syntax of the method, all arguments are optional. You can create a Parameter object and then set all its properties as follows:

```
Set oParam = CMD.CreateParameter
oParam.Name = "parameter1"
oParam.Type = adTypeInteger
oParam.Direction = adParameterDirectionInput
oParam.Value = 1001
```

Notice that the Size argument need not be set with data types of fixed size. Even if you set the Size property of an integer parameter, this setting will be ignored.

Parameters Collection

The Parameters collection supports three methods for adding and removing Parameter objects to the collection.

AppendChunk

AppendChunk appends a large section of text or binary data of the Value property of a Parameter object. It accepts a single argument, which is the text or the binary data to be appended.

Delete

This method deletes an object from the Parameters collection. Its argument is the name of the object you want to remove from the Parameters collection. You can also specify the parameter's order in the collection with an index value.

Append

The Append method appends a Parameter object to a Parameters collection. (The Fields collection supports the Append method too, only in this case it appends a Field object to the Fields collection). The Append method accepts a single argument, which is an object variable. It represents a Parameter object that will be appended to the Parameters collection. To append a Parameter object to the Parameters collection of a Command object, create a Parameter object and set its properties, as discussed in the section "The

Parameter Object." Then use the following statement to append the *oParam* object to the Parameters collection of the *CMD* object as follows:

```
CMD.Parameters.Apend oParam
```

The Error Object

The Error object holds information about an error returned by the OLE DB provider. As such it contains only data-access errors and provides additional information about an error to your application. The same condition may result in multiple errors, so you must scan the Errors collection of the Connection object to read them all.

Properties

Description

This property is a string with a short description of the error. The Description property is used to display additional information to the user when you can't handle the error from within your code.

HelpFile, HelpContext

These two properties determine the help file and the ContextID within this file, where the user can find additional information about the error. If you set these two properties, the corresponding help file will be opened automatically and the user will be positioned to the entry specified by the HelpContext property.

NativeError

This is an integer value that indicates the provider-specific error code for the current Error object.

Number

This property is a number that uniquely identifies an error. Use this property to find out which error occurred and handle it from within your code.

Source

This property is the name of the object (or application) that generated the error. The Source property is used in applications that make use of many different objects. For an ADO-generated error, for example, this property will be *ADODB.objName*, where objName is the name of the object that caused the error (Recordset, Command, and so on).

SQLState

This property indicates the SQL state for an Error object. This is a five-character string returned by the provider and identifies an error that occurred during the processing of an SQL statement. The error code S1109 means "invalid cursor location," and the error code 07001 means "wrong number of parameters." For a complete list of SQL Server's SQLState codes, consult SQL Server's Books Online.

Methods

The Error object does not support any methods.

chapter **10**

The ObjectContext Object

I n Chapter 9 we looked at the ADO object and how you use this object in your scripts to access databases. A major requirement in updating databases is that certain actions be implemented as transactions. You saw how to implement transactions with ADO, but there's a simpler method that doesn't require stored procedures or complicated scripts. Moreover, a transaction may involve non-database operations, which must also be rolled back if a database operation fails. A simple syntax error in a script may prevent the script from completing a transaction successfully. To handle these conditions, you can use the ObjectContext object, which lets you implement all the statements in a script as a transaction. Such a script is called transactional.

Using ObjectContext to Implement Transactions

A *transactional script* requires that all actions complete successfully or they all fail together. Ideally, we'd like to count on the ObjectContext object to roll back all the statements in a transactional script that failed. However, a script may contain actions besides database operations. All the actions performed against a database can be rolled back, but this isn't true for other actions, like the setting of Session and Application variables, file manipulation actions, and so on. A script could create or delete files depending on the success or failure of a database operation. If the file-copying operation fails, then you must declare the transaction a failure and reverse the effects of the previous statements. Changes in the database can be easily rolled back, but if the script has added a few lines to a text file, you must remove them from within your script.

The ObjectContext object is actually an object of the Microsoft Transaction Server (MTS). This object allows you to implement a series of operations as transactions and let a component commit the operations to the database (if they all succeed) or roll them back when one of them fails. If you write a component in a language like VB, for instance, you must use the ObjectContext object to make sure that the component can be used in transactions.

In short, MTS can roll back transactions that are Data Transaction Coordinator (DTC)–compliant. Currently, only database operations can participate in a transaction. To be more specific, the DTC can handle databases that support the XA protocol from the X/Open consortium (this includes SQL Server and Oracle). In the future, the DTC may be able to handle other types of operations, such as file operations.

The ObjectContext object of ASP allows you to write scripts that implement transactions. Of course, MTS should know about the operations that make up a transaction, because it may have to roll back some. If one of the operations is the insertion of a line in a text file, MTS won't be able to roll back the operation, because it doesn't know how to handle text files. Another example of a transaction might involve the deletion of multiple files. If one of the files can't be deleted (or copied or moved, for that matter), you may wish to restore the files already deleted and reverse any changes made to the database. Another type of action that can't be rolled back automatically is the editing of Session or Application variables. These actions aren't supported by MTS, and you can't count on the ObjectContext object to roll back the transaction. Yet you can undo these actions with some additional code, as you will see in the examples that follow.

A transaction must be initiated and completed within a single script. In other words, you can't initiate a transaction in one script and complete it (or abort it) in another script. The Server.Execute and Server.Transfer methods of ASP 3, however, allow transactions to span multiple pages. This is possible because an ASP page invoked with either method executes in the context of the calling page. So, it is possible to initiate a transaction in page StartTran.asp and abort it in the page AbortTran.asp, as long as Abort-Tran.asp is invoked from within StartTran.asp with the Execute or Transfer method. The AbortTran.asp page should never be called directly. When a transactional script ends, the transaction is also terminated successfully. (Since the script came to an end, there's no reason to assume that the transaction failed.)

Finally, the ObjectContext object exposes the SetComplete and SetAbort methods, which complete or abort a transaction explicitly. You will see when and how to call these methods later in the chapter.

Declaring Transactional Scripts

To use the MTS and the ObjectContext object in a script, you must declare that the actions of a script must be implemented as a transaction. To do so, insert the following line at the top of the script:

```
<%@ TRANSACTION = Required %>
```

This line must be the very first line in the script. If not, a runtime error will occur.

The TRANSACTION directive tells ASP to treat the entire script as a transaction. Every action performed by the script on a database will be rolled back as soon as an error occurs. Every error on the page that prevents the script from completing successfully will cause the transaction to abort. If your script performs a series of updates to a database, you don't have to do anything to ensure that the database won't be partially updated. The TRANSACTION directive is all you need.

Other types of errors will also cause MTS to abort the transaction. If the script attempts to create an object from a Class that hasn't been registered, for example, the script will roll back the operations. If the following statement appears in a transactional script, then any database operation that has already taken place will be rolled back:

```
Set someObject =
            Server.CreateObject("MyComponent.OfMyClass")
```

We rely on MTS to catch the types of errors we can't prevent. Let's say you're executing a statement that updates a row in the database. If, for any reason, the action can't be completed (because the row has been deleted in the meantime, or because the database server has stopped), then MTS will interpret this error as a condition that prevents the transaction from completing and will abort the transaction.

NOTE Before you execute a transactional script on the server, you must make sure that MTS is running. Open the SQL Server menu and select the MSDTC Administrative Console window. Then, click the Start button to start the DTC services. You must also start SQL Server, if it's not configured to start automatically when the computer is turned on. If you're using Windows 98, start the MSDTC service in the SQL Server Manager.

The TRANSACTION directive can have one of the values shown in Table 10.1.

TABLE 10.1: Values of the Transaction Directive

Value	Meaning
Disabled	The script isn't executed in the context of a transaction.
Required	The script requires a transaction, and a new transaction will be created if one doesn't exist already.
Requires_New	The script requires a new transaction.
Supported	The script will not initiate a new transaction, but it will be executed in the context of an existing transaction if one exists.
Not_Supported	The script will not be executed in the context of a transaction, even if one exists already.

These settings are used by COM+ components. As far as ASP pages go, the only setting you will need is the Required setting, which specifies that your page contains a transaction. If the script isn't transacted, then you can simply omit the TRANSACTION directive.

Methods

The ObjectContext object exposes two methods, which allow you to declare an operation as a success or failure. To declare the success of an operation, you must call the SetComplete method, while to declare the failure of an operation, you must call the SetAbort method.

If you count on MTS to commit or roll back a database transaction (or any transaction MTS will be able to handle on its own in the future), you don't need to call either method. If the script completes successfully, the operations are committed to the database. If not, the operations are rolled back. However, you may wish to abort a transaction from within your script if you detect an abnormal condition.

SetAbort

The SetAbort method declares the failure of a transaction, and MTS rolls back the transaction by reversing any operations already performed as part of the transaction.

Syntax

The syntax of the SetAbort method is `ObjectContext.SetAbort`. This method is called when a statement doesn't fail but returns some unreasonable or unexpected result. For example, you may have a component that verifies credit card numbers or ZIP codes. If this component returns False (to indicate that it wasn't able to verify the information you supplied), you can abort the transaction explicitly from within your script with a statement like the following:

```
If Not FinanceComponent.VerifyCard(CardNum) Then
    objectContext.SetAbort
End If
```

The execution of the script will terminate as soon as the statement that calls the SetAbort method is reached.

Normally, you shouldn't execute SQL statements directly against the database from within your scripts. You should implement the necessary stored procedures and call them with the appropriate arguments to act on the database. Then, you can examine the return value of stored procedures to find out whether they have completed successfully. If one of them fails, then you must call the SetAbort method to roll back the transaction.

You can also call the SetAbort method if a non-database operation fails. If you have already changed the database and another operation fails (like the deletion of a file), you must call the SetAbort method to undo the changes in the database.

Example

The following script updates a database by entering a new order. It involves many operations, and if any one fails, then the entire transaction will abort. The script is modeled after a database similar to the NorthWind sample database, which comes with SQL Server 7. First, it creates a new order for a specific customer by adding a row to the Orders table. Then it adds the order's details by appending one row per item to the Order Details table. All details contain the ID of the order they belong to, the ID of the item ordered, and the corresponding quantity. Finally, we charge the customer with the order's total. If the customer has no more credit, we abort the transaction by calling the SetAbort method. Here's the outline of the script:

```
<%@ TRANSACTION = Required LANGUAGE = "VBScript" %>
<%
'   other statements . . .
OrderID = Orders.PlaceNewOrder(custID)
If Not Orders.AddItem(orderID, item1, qty1) Then
                    objectContext.SetAbort
If Not Orders.AddItem(orderID, item2, qty2) Then
                    objectContext.SetAbort
If Not Orders.AddItem(orderID, item3, qty3) Then
                    objectContext.SetAbort
If Not Customers.GetCredit(custID) Then
    objectContext.SetAbort
Else
    Customers.ChargeCustomer(custID, orderTotal)
End If
%>
```

Presumably, you have built the Orders and Customers components, which expose the members shown in the code. The Orders.PlaceNewOrder method adds a new order for the specified customer and returns the ID of the new order. The Orders.AddItem method adds an item to an existing order. Both methods are implemented with simple SQL statements (they're action queries). If the AddItem method wasn't able to add the item to the order, then the entire order must be rolled back. The AddItem method may return False to indicate that it couldn't add a new item to the order because one of the items wasn't in stock or because the item's ID was invalid. When this happens, the script terminates by rolling back any operations that have already taken place and the OnTransactionAbort event handler is triggered.

If your application updates a database in transactional mode, you should implement the proper stored procedures, like the ones discussed in Chapter 9, *ADO 2.5 for Web Developers*. The stored procedure should return an error code indicating the success or failure of the transaction. In the case of a failed transaction, it should also report the reason that caused the transaction to fail, so that you can display a more meaningful message to the viewer. If you implement transactions either through a stored procedure or through a COM+ component, there's no reason to create transacted scripts, except to include actions that can't be rolled back automatically.

SetComplete

The SetComplete method declares the successful completion of a transaction, and MTS commits the transaction to the database.

Syntax

The syntax of the SetComplete method is `ObjectContext.SetComplete`. You need not call this method from within your scripts. When a transacted script terminates, the transaction is assumed to have completed. If the script times out, however, then the transaction is aborted.

Events

The ObjectContext object recognizes two events, which allow you to manually commit or roll back transactions that can't be handled automatically by the MTS. They are *OnTransactionCommit* and *OnTransactionAbort* events. Let's say you have renamed a file as part of a transaction and a later operation fails. You can insert the appropriate code in the TransactionAborted event handler to restore the file's original name.

OnTransactionAbort

The OnTransactionAbort event occurs after a script's transaction is aborted. A transaction may abort because the script timed out, because SQL Server isn't able to execute a SQL statement or because the script has called the SetAbort method. When the OnTransactionAbort event occurs, IIS will process the script's OnTransactionAbort subroutine, if it exists.

OnTransactionCommit

The OnTransactionCommit event occurs after the successful termination of a transactional script, or after a call to the SetComplete method. After the completion of a transaction, IIS executes the script's OnTransaction-Commit subroutine, if it exists. The OnTransactionCommit event is executed if the script calls the SetComplete method of the ObjectContext object, or if the script completes its execution successfully, but not if the script times out.

The OnTransactionCommit event handler is used to inform the viewer that the transaction completed successfully or to execute any code after the successful completion of a transaction. For example, you may wish to prepare and send a message when a transaction completes. If the transaction involves operations that are not critical (the update of auxiliary files, the addition of a few entries in a log file, and so on), you can code them in the OnTransactionCommit event handler. Should one of these operations fail, the transaction itself won't be affected.

Using the Events

The event handlers for both events are coded in the same script that handles the transaction. They're usually at the beginning of the file, following the TRANSACTION directive. Here's the structure of a transactional script:

```
<%@ TRANSACTION = Required LANGUAGE = "VBScript" %>
<%
Sub objContext_OnTransactionComplete
'    code for successful transactions
End Sub

Sub objContext_OnTransactionAbort
'    code for unsuccessful transactions
End Sub
'    the transactional script
'    call ObjectContext.SetComplete if transaction completes
'    or ObjectContext.SetAbort if transaction fails
%>
```

Example

The example of this section demonstrates how to use the two events of the ObjectContext object. The Transact.asp script creates a Recordset with all the products in the NorthWind database (the NorthWind sample database comes with both Access and SQL Server). Then it marks up the price of the first two products by 10 percent. The two actions are totally independent of one another, but for the sake of the example we'll treat them as a transaction.

Figure 10.1 shows the output of the Transact.asp script. The first two calls to the Response.Write method show the price of the first product before and after the 10 percent markup. The next two calls to the Response.Write method show the price of the second products before and after the same markup.

▶ *Listing 10.1: The Transact.asp Script*

```
<%@ TRANSACTION = Required LANGUAGE = "VBScript" %>
<!-- #include file="adovbs.inc" -->
<%
Response.Buffer = True
Response.Write "<FONT SIZE='4' FACE='Verdana'>"
Response.Write "<B>Simple Transactional Web Page</B>"
Response.Write "<FONT SIZE='2'>"
Response.Write "<HR>"

Sub OnTransactionCommit()
    Response.Write "<P><B>OnTransactionCommit " & _
                   "Handler</B><BR>"
    Response.Write "Transaction completed successfully"
End Sub

Sub OnTransactionAbort()
    Response.Clear
    Response.Write "<P><B>OnTransactionAbort " & _
                   "Handler</B><BR>"
    Response.Write "Transaction failed, " & _
                   " no changes made to the database"
End Sub

    Set objConn = Server.CreateObject("ADODB.Connection")
    Set objRs   = Server.CreateObject("ADODB.Recordset")
    objConn.Open "Provider=SQLOLEDB;User ID=sa;" & _
                 "Initial Catalog=NorthWind; " & _
                 "Data Source=PROTOSERVER"
    Set objRs.ActiveConnection = objConn
```

```
' Uncomment the following statement to generate
' a runtime error
' Set someObject = Server.CreateObject("MyComponent.OfMyClass")
    objRs.Source = "SELECT ProductID, UnitPrice " & _
                   "FROM Products"
    objRs.CursorType = adOpenForwardOnly
    objRs.LockType = adLockOptimistic
    objRs.Open
    If (Not objRs.EOF) Then
        strProdID=objRs("ProductID").Value
        Response.Write "Product ID=" & strProdID & _
             " PRICE=" & objRS.Fields("UnitPrice") & _
             "<BR>"
        objRS.Fields("UnitPrice") = _
                1.1 * objRS.Fields("UnitPrice")
        objRS.Update
        Response.Write "Product ID=" & strProdID & _
                " PRICE=" & objRS.Fields("UnitPrice") & _
                "<BR>"
    End If

    objRs.MoveNext
'''''''''''''''''''''''''''''''''''''''''''''''''''''''
' Uncomment the following line to generate
' a different type of runtime error
'    objRs.MovePrevious
    If (Not objRs.EOF) Then
        strProdID=objRs("ProductID").Value
        Response.Write "Product ID=" & strProdID & _
             " PRICE="  & objRS.Fields("UnitPrice") & _
             "<BR>"
        objRS.Fields("UnitPrice") = _
                1.1 * objRS.Fields("UnitPrice")
        objRS.Update
        Response.Write "Product ID=" & strProdID & _
                " PRICE=" & objRS.Fields("UnitPrice") & _
                "<BR>"
    End If
%>
```

FIGURE 10.1: The output of the TRANSACT.ASP script

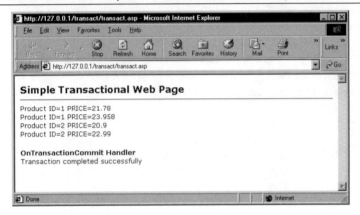

Notice that the script doesn't even use the ObjectContext object. The TRANSACTION directive informs ASP that all the statements of the script must be executed as a transaction. If one of them fails, then the transaction is aborted and the OnTransactionAbort event is triggered automatically. Database operations are rolled back automatically by MTS, and we don't have to undo any changes in our code.

There are many ways to make the transaction fail. You can change the Recordset object's locking mechanism from optimistic to read-only. In this case, the script won't be able to update the rows of the Recordset and the transaction will fail immediately.

The script will fail if you insert a call to the MovePrevious method of the Recordset object. Since its type is forward-only, the MovePrevious method will cause an error. This error will take place after the successful completion of the first operation, and the DTC will undo the changes to the database made by the first UPDATE statement.

Finally, any VBScript statement that can't be executed will cause the transaction to fail. If you attempt to create an object variable with the CreateObject method by calling a component that doesn't exist, the transaction will fail.

When the transaction aborts, the OnTransactionAbort event handler is activated. The code in this event handler clears any output buffered so far and creates a new page with the appropriate message. The script generates output as each operation completes. If the transaction aborts, any output is invalid (the operations are rolled back) and must be cleared. If the transaction completes successfully, then the output generated by the script is displayed, along with a message confirming the successful completion of the transaction.

Here's a last interesting note about the script. At the beginning of the script, we set the Buffer property of the Response property to True. We want to be able to display different messages on the client and suppress the error message returned by the database, in case one of the operations fails. If you omit the OnTransactionAbort event handler and the transaction fails, you will see on your browser the message returned by SQL Server. This isn't the most appropriate message to display to the viewer. Instead, if the transaction fails, we clear the output and display a message to the effect that the transaction failed.

chapter 11

The Ad Rotator Component

Many sites on the Web today do not generate income by selling products, but by advertising other sites, companies, or products. If you succeed in creating substantial traffic to your site, then why not take advantage of it and advertise other sites? Indeed, advertising on the Web is a fast-growing business. Even commercial sites advertise other sites.

Maintaining ads in your site is quite a challenge. For one thing, you can't keep showing the same banner. If viewers don't follow the link to an advertised site from the first few pages where they see it, chances are that they aren't interested in the specific company or product. Not only that, but they may be bored seeing the same ad over and over. It's very important that you change the banner not from session to session, but from page to page within the same session.

If you require your viewers to register, or you allow them to customize their pages, you probably know what their interests are and you can tune the banners you display on their custom pages to the products and services they're interested in. If a viewer buys computer books frequently, you can make the most of your banner space by displaying related ads. You can even keep track of the viewer's search keywords and base the ad selection on these keywords (or keep track of specific keywords, if your site provides a list of options). AltaVista is an example of a site that tunes its banners to the interests of the viewers by matching the supplied keywords to the banners.

The bottom line is that you want to make the most of the ads you display on your pages. The corporations advertised in the pages of your site will keep track of the customers you send to them, and so should you. You will see later in this chapter how you can count the viewers who have clicked on each banner.

Displaying Banners with the Ad Rotator

Maintaining banners without specialized software is a nightmare. You must edit static pages all the time, change hyperlinks, test the pages, and then move them to the production server. To simplify the display of banners on the pages of a site, Microsoft has designed the Ad Rotator component. The Ad Rotator component allows Web developers to put together a list of banners and special placeholders on their pages for these banners.

Then, the Ad Rotator component randomly selects a banner and places it in the appropriate placeholder. The selection isn't quite random, as you can specify the relative frequency of each banner—one banner may be displayed twice as often as another, and so on.

Finally, viewers that click a specific banner aren't taken to the advertised site immediately. Instead, their request is processed by another script at your site, which can keep track of who has clicked, the banner clicked, and the destination of the banner. After recording all this information, your script can redirect the viewer to the banner's site.

The drawback of the Ad Rotator component is that it wasn't designed to tune the ads to the viewers. You can't replace the ad selection algorithm with one that takes into consideration the time of the day, the viewer's domain, and so on. You will see how you can use the component to tune the banners to groups of viewers with similar interests—provided that this information is available to you.

To use the Ad Rotator component, you must create the following:

1. **The Banner's Placeholder**   A placeholder (or multiple placeholders) for the banner on your page. This placeholder is a rectangle of specific dimensions, and all banners must fit in these dimensions. The banners themselves are images, usually animated GIFs. If they're not all the same dimensions, they'll be resized to fit the placeholder and be distorted in the process.

2. **The Schedule File**   A text file with the banners you want to display. This file contains the names of the image files with the banners, the destination of each banner (if any) and the relative frequency of each banner. The syntax of this file is straightforward (one item per line), but it must be absolutely correct. Miss a line in this file and the Ad Rotator component will be totally confused. This file is the Ad Rotator's Schedule file.

3. **The Redirection Script**   A script that processes each request on your server before redirecting the viewer to the site of the selected banner. This script could store information about the traffic generated by your site to the advertised sites. The information can be stored in a text file or to the server's log file. This is the Redirection script; its last line calls the Response.Redirect method to redirect the viewer to the site associated with this banner in the Schedule file. The Redirection

script is optional; if you omit it, the viewer will be taken directly to the site associated with the specific banner in the Ad Rotator's Schedule file.

Figure 11.1 shows how these items work together. When a viewer requests a page with a banner placeholder, the Ad Rotator component consults the Schedule file and picks an ad (1). It places the banner's bitmap into the placeholder and sets the image's destination to the URL of the site associated with this ad (2). Then the page is transmitted to the client (3).

FIGURE 11.1: How the Ad Rotator works

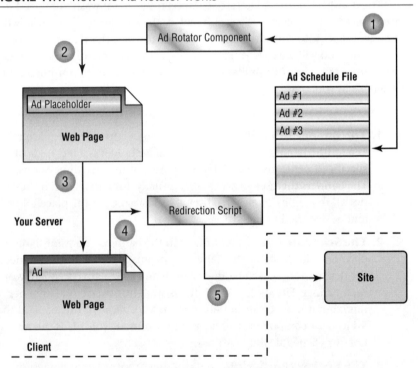

If the user clicks on the banner (4), the Redirection script is called automatically with two parameter values: the URL of the banner's destination and the name of the image file used to display the banner. The Redirection script can examine the values of these parameters, take some action, and finally send the viewer to the destination (5).

The Ad Schedule File

Before we discuss the properties and methods of the Ad Rotator component, let's look at the structure of the Ad Schedule file. This is a text file, and each line holds a separate item. The first few lines apply to all banners; they are the following:

```
REDIRECT    RedirectionScript
WIDTH       ww
HEIGHT      hh
BORDER      nn
```

RedirectionScript is the path and name of the Redirection script on your server. If this script is stored in the Ads subfolder of the Web's root folder and is named BannerRedirect.asp, then the value of the RedirectionScript item should be /Ads/BannerRedirect.asp.

ww and *hh* are the dimensions of the banner's placeholder. The banner's bitmap will be resized to fill this space, so it must be designed to exactly fit in this space. One of the shortcomings of the Ad Rotator component is that it doesn't allow you to specify different dimensions for each banner. Moreover, you shouldn't count on the browser to resize the banner to fit the available space. The results will be unacceptable; ask the advertised party to design a banner that fits exactly the space provided. Large banners are usually 468×60, and small banners are usually 234×60 (the dimensions are in pixels). The BORDER line specifies the width of the border (*nn*), in pixels, that will be drawn around the banner. Set it to 0 (or omit the BORDER line) to skip the border around the banner.

The next line in the Ad Schedule File contains an asterisk, which separates the initial section of the file from the banner details. Following the line with the asterisk, you specify each banner's details with four lines:

1. The URL of the banner's image.

2. The URL of the destination of the banner (this is the advertiser's home page address).

3. A short string about the ad (something like "The largest shoe store in the planet," or "Faster Internet Connections). This string will appear in a tip box when the viewer hovers the pointer over the banner.

4. The relative frequency of the banner. If the Schedule File contains three banners and their relative frequencies are 2, 1, and 1, the first banner will be displayed twice as frequently as either of the others.

All of the items in each banner's section are optional. If you omit them, however, you must insert a line with a hyphen in its place. Listing 11.1 presents a typical Ad Schedule file.

▶ *Listing 11.1: A Typical Ad Schedule File*

```
REDIRECT /ADROTATOR/AdCounter.asp
WIDTH 457
HEIGHT 34
BORDER 2
*
http://www.sybex.com/images/top_banner/header_sybex.gif
http://www.sybex.com
Check out Sybex books
100
http://www.amazon.com/g/post-holiday/logo-2000-nav/
     product-type-books.gif
http://www.amazon.com
Order books at Amazon
50
http://www.borders.com//web_images/2/head/gnav-none.gif
http://www.borders.com
Order books at Borders
50
```

(The indented lines were broken to fit on the printed page, but they should appear on a single line in the text file.) Notice that the images used in the banners are not local to the Web server; instead, they're read from the corresponding sites (or a depository of banners on some server). You'll probably want to store the bitmaps of the banners on your server to make sure they have the proper dimensions. The three banners of the example are displayed randomly on the pages of the site with the specified frequencies.

Omitting the banner's bitmap is rather unusual. How will people notice the ad in the first place without an image? Not to mention that if the banner's image is missing, the usual X sign will appear in the placeholder on the page. However, you can safely omit any of the other parameters.

Adding a Banner to Your Pages

To add a banner to any of your pages, you must create an instance of the Ad Rotator component with the following statement:

```
Set AdObj = Server.CreateObject("MSWC.AdRotator")
```

This line is always the same; you can only change the name of the object variable, *AdObj*. The *AdObj* variable will be used from within many of your site's pages (possibly all of them). Instead of creating an instance of this object from within each page, you should instantiate this object at the Application or Session level. If you create the *AdObj* variable in the Application_OnStart event, then all the scripts will use this object to retrieve a banner. If you create the *AdObj* variable in the Session_OnStart event, then each time a new session is established, a new instance of the *AdObj* object variable will be created; all the scripts of the current Session will use this object to retrieve a banner.

Once the *AdObj* object variable has been instantiated, you can call its *GetAdvertisement* method to retrieve a banner. This method returns HTML code, which is inserted at the current point in the HTML file. To place a banner on a page, insert a call to the GetAdvertisement method where you want to place the banner, as if it was another HTML tag. To place the selected ad's banner in a table's cell, use a statement like the following one:

```
<TD>
<% = AdObj.GetAdvertisement("Ads/ScheduleFile.txt") %>
</TD>
```

To center the banner at the current location on the page and place two lines above and below it, use the following statements:

```
<CENTER>
<HR>
<% = AdObj.GetAdvertisement("Ads/ScheduleFile.txt") %>
</HR>
</CENTER>
```

Redirecting the Viewer

The last step is to write the script that will be called when the banner is clicked. This will redirect the viewer to the site advertised in the banner. As you will see shortly, the banner's destination URL is not the address of the

advertised site, but the address of the Redirection script, as specified in the
Ad Schedule file. The URL of the advertised site and the name of the file
with the banner's bitmap are passed to the Redirection script as parameters:

```
www.yourserver.com/AdScript.asp?url=adURL&image=imgName
```

The AdScript.asp file usually contains a few statements to keep track of
the number of viewers redirected from the current site to each one of the
advertised sites. Listing 11.2 is a simple Redirection script.

▶ *Listing 11.2: The AdScript.asp Script*

```
<%
adURL = Request.QueryString("url")
Application(adURL)=Application(adURL)+1
strLog = "ADCOUNTER " & Application(adURL) & _
         " visits to site " & adURL
strLog = strLog & " originating IP=" & _
         Request.ServerVariables("REMOTE_ADDR")
Response.AppendToLog strLog
Response.Redirect adURL
%>
```

(Again, the indented lines were broken to fit on the printed page, but
they should appear on a single line in the text file.) The Redirection script
logs the number of visitors generated by the banner, as well as the visitors'
addresses.

Testing a Page with Banners

Once you have created the Ad Schedule file and the Redirection script, you
can build a simple site that displays a banner randomly selected from the Ad
Schedule file. To test the files, create a simple page with a banner. Figure 11.2
shows a page with the Sybex banner. It was created with the script shown in
Listing 11.3.

▶ *Listing 11.3: The AdRotator.asp Script*

```
<%
Set AdObj = Server.CreateObject("MSWC.AdRotator")
RotScheduleFile = "AdRotator/AdSchedule.txt"
```

```
adString = AdObj.GetAdvertisement(RotScheduleFile)
%>
<HTML>
<CENTER>
<H1>Active Server Pages</H1>
<H3>Instant Reference</H3>
<HR>
<% = adString %>
<%
Set AdObj = Nothing
%>
<BR>
Click on the banner above to visit our sponsors.
<HR>
<H1>Welcome to the ASP 3.0 Instant Reference</H1>
</CENTER>
<FONT SIZE=+1>
Select an object from the list below
to view its methods and properties:
<BR>
' MORE HTML STATEMENT FOLLOW
</HTML>
```

FIGURE 11.2: The output of the AdRotator.asp script

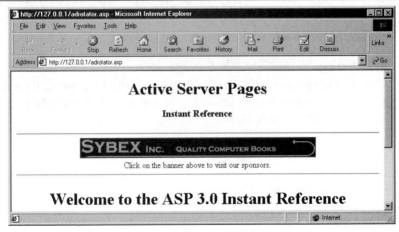

To test the page with the rotating ads, do the following:

1. Create the AdSchedule.txt and AdScript.asp files and store them in the AdRotator folder under the Web's root folder.

2. Create the AdRotator.asp script and store it in the Web's root folder. If you store the AdRotator.asp script in a subfolder of the root folder, make sure the AdRotator folder is created under the virtual folder.

3. Start your browser and connect to AdRotator.asp file. As you refresh the page by pressing F5, the two banners will alternate.

Now that you have seen how the Ad Rotator component works at large, let's examine its members in detail.

Properties

The Ad Rotator component exposes a few properties that control the appearance and placement of the banners on the page. These properties are explained in the following sections.

Border

Use the Border property to specify the width of the border to be placed around the banner. Its value is an integer that represents the width of the banner's border in pixels. The syntax is:

```
objAdRotator.Border = border_width
```

border_width is the border's width in pixels.

The following statements select a banner from the Ad Schedule file and set the border of the selected banner to 2 pixels, regardless of the BORDER setting in the Ad Schedule file:

```
<%
Set objAdRotator = Server.CreateObject("MSWC.AdRotator")
ObjAdRotator.Border = 2
Response.Write "<HR>"
Response.Write
 objAdRotator.GetAdvertisement("Ads/ScheduleFile.txt")
Response.Write "</HR>"
%>
```

> **NOTE** If you don't set the Ad Rotator component's Border property, the default border width specified with the BORDER keyword in the Ad Schedule file will be used. If you set the Border property, the new value will overwrite the default border width for the current page.

Clickable

Some of the banners may not take the viewer to another site. They could simply be non-clickable graphics that advertise a product or service. The Clickable property determines whether the banner graphic is a clickable image (a hyperlink, in essence). The syntax for Clickable is:

```
objAdRotator.Clickable = True | False
```

If you want to display a graphic that doesn't act as a hyperlink on the page, set the Ad Rotator object's Clickable property to False. If this property is False, the destination URL in the Ad Scheduler file is ignored, even if it's specified. If it's True (which is the property's default value), then you must either specify a valid destination URL in the Ad Schedule file, or make sure that the Redirection script sends the viewer to the proper page.

If the user is in the process of filling out a Form, for example, you shouldn't let them interrupt the process by visiting another site. The following statements display a banner selected from the Ad Schedule file and make it non-clickable:

```
<%
Set objAdRotator = Server.CreateObject("MSWC.AdRotator")
objAdRotator.Clickable = False
Response.Write "<HR>"
Response.Write
    objAdRotator.GetAdvertisement("Ads/ScheduleFile.txt")
Response.Write "</HR>"
%>
' THE STATEMENTS TO DISPLAY THE FORM FOLLOW
```

TargetFrame

If your page contains frames, you can display the banner's destination page in a frame. This is a trick many developers use to prevent users from leaving their sites altogether. You may still display the header of your page in a small frame at the top and the advertised site in the main frame.

The syntax for TargetFrame is:

```
objAdRotator.TargetFrame = frameName
```

frameName is the name of the frame on which the banner's destination page will be loaded. As a reminder, the following are special frame names: _BLANK, _CHILD, _PARENT, _NEW, and _TOP.

Methods

The Ad Rotator component exposes a single method, GetAdvertisement, which reads a banner from the schedule file and inserts it at the current location on the page.

GetAdvertisement

This is the method that actually reads the banner from the Ad Schedule file and generates the appropriate HTML code to insert the banner on the current page. The GetAdvertisement method takes into consideration the relative frequencies of the various banners and may select a different one, even when the page is refreshed. Its syntax is:

```
objAdRotator.GetAdvertisement(schedFileName)
```

schedFileName is the path and name of the Ad Schedule File. The path is relative to the current virtual folder.

Assuming that:

- Your scripts are in the Scripts folder under the Web's root folder,

- The Ad Schedule file is called Sched.txt, and

- Sched.txt resides in the AdFiles folder under the Web's root folder,

the following statement will select a banner from the Ad Schedule file and place it at the current location on the page:

```
<%
Set objAdRotator = Server.CreateObject("MSWC.AdRotator")
```

```
%>
<HTML>
<HR>
<% = objAdRotator.GetAdvertisement("AdFiles/Sched.txt") %>
</HR>
```

If you open the page displayed on the browser, you will see that the following HTML statements replace the line calling the GetAdvertisement method:

```
<A HREF="/ADROTATOR/AdCounter.asp?
    url=http://www.sybex.com&
    image=http://www.sybex.com/images/
    top_banner/header_sybex.gif" >
<IMG SRC="http://www.sybex.com/images/
    top_banner/header_sybex.gif"
    ALT="Check out the Sybex books"
    WIDTH=457 HEIGHT=34 BORDER=2>
</A>
```

(The indented lines indicate that they're broken to fit on the printed page.) The entire segment shown above will appear on a single line. Notice that the banner's destination isn't the URL of the advertised site. Instead, it points to the Redirection script on your server and passes two parameter values to it: the URL of the destination and the name of the image file with the banner's graphic. You can use the URL in your script to redirect the viewer to the advertised site.

NOTE If you omit the Redirection script, the destination of the hyperlink will be the advertised site's URL and viewers will be redirected to this site automatically. Your application will not get a chance to record any information about viewers redirected to another site through a banner.

Tuning Ads to Target Groups

If you keep track of the viewers' interests, you can tune the banners to specific viewer groups and make the best use of your site's advertising capacity.

If you ask your viewers to select product types they're interested in, you can use this information to redirect them to appropriate sites. For example, you can create different Ad Schedule files for each type of viewers and display the appropriate file's banners to each group.

Let's say the Session variable "Favorite" can have one of the following values: Books, Computers, and Gadgets. You can create three Ad Schedule files, name them Books.txt, Computers.txt, and Gadgets.txt, and populate them with the most suitable banners. Notice that the products addressed to each group need not be mutually exclusive. Then, each time you display a page, you can select a banner from the file that best describes the group's interests:

```
<%
Select Case Session("Favorite")
    Case "Books": schedFile = "Books.txt"
    Case "Computers": schedFile = "Computers.txt"
    Case "Toys.txt": schedFile = "Toys.txt"
    Case Else: schedFile = "AllBanners.txt"
End Select
Set objAdRotator = Server.CreateObject("MSWC.AdRotator")
<% = objAdRotator.GetAdvertisement(schedFile) %>
```

chapter 12

The Browser Capabilities
Component

HTML is a pretty limited formatting language for generating static pages. One of the most obvious limitations of HTML is that it doesn't allow you to adjust your pages to the client's window. A common dilemma among Web developers is how much information to put on a page and how to arrange it. Most developers design long pages with a width that doesn't exceed 800 pixels. These pages can become quite long: The vertical scroll bar on the right side of the browser's window allows viewers to quickly locate any section of the page. Having to scroll the page vertically to read is no inconvenience either. If there's a mismatch in the page's width and the width of the browser, however, the page becomes practically unreadable. The horizontal scrolling is simply unacceptable.

The browser rearranges the elements of the page, so that they'll fit in the browser's window. A page that looks great at a resolution of 800 × 600, however, may look odd when viewed on a monitor with a different resolution. Web developers are trying to design pages that will look good at all resolutions, and this isn't a simple task. The simple approach is to design pages for viewing at a low resolution, like 800 × 600 (and this is what most sites do today). A more complicated approach is to take into consideration the resolution of the client, and adjust the placement of the elements on the page.

Other design issues are the use of cookies, even frames. How will you handle clients that don't support cookies, or clients that have turned off cookies? Browsers that don't support cookies or frames are rather antiquated, but the more information you can get about the browser, the more you can adjust your site and make it work with all browsers out there.

The Browser Capabilities component provides information to your scripts about the capabilities of the client's Web browser. This information is sent to the Web server through an HTTP header, the HTTP_USER_AGENT header. Internet Explorer 5 transmits the following HTTP_USER_AGENT header to the server:

```
Mozilla/4.0 (compatible; MSIE 5.0; Windows 95; DigExt)
```

This string contains hardly any information about the browser's capabilities, but the Browser Capabilities component compares the header to the entries in the Browscap.ini file. If it finds a match, it returns the values of the various properties of the browser listed in the corresponding section of Browscap.ini. If no match is found, then it uses the default browser properties.

The Browscap.ini file contains information about various browsers. Each browser has its own section in the Browscap.ini file and each line corresponds to a specific feature of the browser. When new capabilities are added to an existing browser (or a new one is introduced), the Browscap.ini file must be updated. You can locate the latest version of the Browscap.ini file at www.cyscape.com. This is the site Microsoft recommends for the latest updates to the Browscaps.ini file.

Using the Browser Capabilities Component

To use the Browser Capabilities component in your scripts, you must create an object variable with the following statement:

```
Set objBrowser = Server.CreateObject("MSWC.BrowserType")
```

The Browser Capabilities component consults the Browscap.ini file, which maps browser capabilities to the HTTP User Agent header. To find out whether the client that requested the current page supports frames, use a statement like the following one:

```
If objBrowser.frames = TRUE Then
    ' display page with frames
Else
    ' display a single page without frames
End If
```

The browser features reported by the Browser Capabilities component are exposed as properties of the *objBrowser* object variable and they're summarized in Table 12.1.

TABLE 12.1: The browser features reported by the Browser Capabilities component

Property Name	Description
ActiveXControls	Specifies whether the browser supports ActiveX controls.
backgroundsounds	Specifies whether the browser supports background sounds.
beta	Specifies whether the browser is beta software.
browser	Specifies the name of the browser.
cdf	Specifies whether the browser supports the Channel Definition Format for webcasting.
cookies	Specifies whether the browser supports cookies. Notice that the client may have turned off the cookies. This will not affect the setting of the cookies property, which will be True.
frames	Specifies whether the browser supports frames.
Javaapplets	Specifies whether the browser supports Java applets.
javascript	Specifies whether the browser supports JavaScript.
platform	Specifies the platform that the browser runs on.
tables	Specifies whether the browser supports tables.
vbscript	Specifies whether the browser supports VBScript.
version	Specifies the version number of the browser (5.01, for example).
majorver	Specifies the major version number of the browser (5, for example).
minorver	Specifies the minor version number of the browser (0.01, for example).

The *Browscap.ini* File

The Browscap.ini file must reside in the same folder as the BROWSCAP.DLL file (which implements the Browser Capabilities component) and it has the following structure:

```
[; comments]
[HTTPUserAgentHeader]
[parent = browserDefinition]
[property1 = value1]

...
```

```
[propertyN = valueN]
; Default Browser Capability Settings
[defaultProperty1 = defaultValue1]
...
[defaultPropertyN = defaultValueN]
HTTPUserAgentHeader
...
```

You can insert comments anywhere in the Browscap.ini file as long as you prefix the comment lines with a semicolon. The HTTPUserAgentHeader is the HTTP User Agent header, as transmitted by the client. Each browser sends a different header. The Browscap.ini file contains multiple browser definitions, each one starting with a unique HTTPUserAgentHeader value. The Browser Capabilities component uses this header to locate the appropriate section in the file. If the HTTP header matches more than one section in the Browscap.ini file, the first matching section will be used.

You can use the asterisk (*) character as a wildcard character in the HTTPUserAgentHeader to replace zero or more characters. For example, if you specified the following string for HTTPUserAgentHeader:

```
[Mozilla/2.0 (compatible; MSIE 3.0;* Windows 95)]
```

it would match all of the following User Agent headers:

```
[Mozilla/2.0 (compatible; MSIE 3.0; Windows 95)]
[Mozilla/2.0 (compatible; MSIE 3.0; AK; Windows 95)]
[Mozilla/2.0 (compatible; MSIE 3.0; SK; Windows 95)]
[Mozilla/2.0 (compatible; MSIE 3.0; AOL; Windows 95)]
```

The *objBrowser* object will attempt to match exactly the User Agent header to a value of HTTPUserAgentHeader. If that fails, it will make a match that uses wildcard characters.

browserDefinition is an optional parameter specifying the HTTP User Agent header of a browser's parent browser. The parent browser is usually an earlier version of the same browser and the child browser inherits all the entries of the parent browser in the file. This way, we don't have to repeat all the property settings, just the ones that are different and the new ones. The inherited property values can be overwritten by explicitly setting a new value for the property using the syntax propertyN = valueN.

The pairs *propertyN* = *valueN* specify the name of a browser property and its value. Property names must start with an alphabetic character and cannot be longer than 255 characters. By definition, property values are strings. To specify an integer value, prefix the value with a number sign (#). To specify a Boolean value, use TRUE or FALSE.

Each browser definition in the Browscap.ini file can contain as many property values as needed. For example, if your application only needs to know whether or not the client browser supports cookies and VBScript, you would only need two property entries for each browser definition. They would be the pairs:

```
Cookies = TRUE
VBScript = TRUE
```

The pairs *defaultPropertyN* = *defaultValueN* specify the name of a browser property and its default value. This value is used if none of the HTTPUser-AgentHeader values matches the one supplied by the client.

Example

The VBScript statements in Listing 12.1 use the Browser Capabilities component to display a table with information about the current browser.

▶ *Listing 12.1: Reading the Browser's Capabilities*

```
<%
Set objBrowser = Server.CreateObject("MSWC.BrowserType")
Response.Write "<TABLE>"
Response.Write "<TR><TD>Your Browser's Capabilities"
Response.Write "</TD></TR>"
Response.Write "<TR><TD>Version</TD>"
Response.Write "<TD>" & objBrowser.version
Response.Write "</TD></TR>"
Response.Write "<TR><TD>Frames</TD>"
If objBrowser.frames = TRUE then
    Response.Write "<TD>Supported</TD>"
Else
    Response.Write "<TD>Not Supported</TD>"
End If
Response.Write "<TR><TD>VBScript</TD>"
```

```
If objBrowser.vbscript = TRUE then
    Response.Write "<TD>Supported</TD>"
Else
    Response.Write "<TD>Not Supported</TD>"
End If
Response.Write "<TR><TD>BackgroundSounds</TD>"
If objBrowser.BackgroundSounds = TRUE Then
    Response.Write "<TD>Supported</TD>"
Else
    Response.Write "<TD>Not Supported</TD>"
End If
%>
```

Examining the *Browscap.ini* File

You can open the Browscap.ini file in your computer and examine its contents. You'll see, for example, that the section for the final release of IE 4 for Windows 95 and Windows NT are quite short. It inherits all the properties of the last beta of the IE 4 browser and overwrites the properties "platform" and "beta":

```
;;ie 4 final release
[Mozilla/4.0 (compatible; MSIE 4.0; Windows 95)]
parent=IE 4.0
platform=Win95
beta=False

[Mozilla/4.0 (compatible; MSIE 4.0; Windows NT)]
parent=IE 4.0
platform=WinNT
beta=False
```

These lines correspond to the default browser properties. The following property values will be used if the HTTPUserAgentHeader sent by the client doesn't match any of the headers in the Browscap.ini file:

```
;;;;;;;;;;;;;;;;;;;;;;;;;;;;
;;; Default Browser    ;;;
;;;;;;;;;;;;;;;;;;;;;;;;;;;;
[Default Browser Capability Settings]
browser=Default
```

```
Version=0.0
majorver=#0
minorver=#0
frames=False
tables=True
cookies=False
backgroundsounds=False
vbscript=False
javascript=False
javaapplets=False
activexcontrols=False
AK=False
SK=False
AOL=False
beta=False
Win16=False
Crawler=False
CDF=False
AuthenticodeUpdate=
```

Using the clientCaps Behavior

To design really elaborate pages that take into consideration the display capabilities of the browser, you can use the clientCaps behavior, which is built into Internet Explorer 5. The technique described here applies to IE 5 only, but since this is the dominant browser out there you may find it useful.

The property definitions in the Browscap.ini file are static, in a way. This file is updated from time to time to reflect the capabilities of the latest versions of each browser, but the information in the Browscap.ini file doesn't take into consideration the configuration of specific clients. The Browscap.ini file, for instance, will tell you whether the browser supports cookies, but it will not tell you whether the client has disabled cookies. The technique described here is much more flexible because it gets the property definitions directly from the browser. The clientCaps behavior can query the actual browser and return the resolution of the monitor and the color depth. This immediate feedback allows you to build pages that will exploit the capabilities of the client computer, and generate pages that look best for any given client configuration. If the client computer can't display more than 256 colors, you need not include true color images on your pages. Prepare versions of the pictures that use the "safe-palette" (the 236 colors any browser can display) and include them in your pages.

If you knew the type of connection used by a specific client, you could choose different images to download to the client. Users connected to the server through a LAN can afford to download large images and video clips. Users connected to the server through a dial-up connection shouldn't have to wait forever for a page to arrive. Alternatively, you can provide hyperlinks on your pages that lead to the large images and video clips and warn the users about the time it will take to download the optional content.

To insert a behavior on a page, you must use the <STYLE> tag. The clientCaps behavior is specific to IE 5 and the page that queries the client about additional browser capabilities is shown in Listing 12.2:

▶ *Listing 12.2: The QueryBrowser.htm Page*

```
<HTML XMLNS:IE>
<HEAD>

<STYLE>
IE\:clientCaps {behavior:url(#default#clientCaps)}

</STYLE>
</HEAD>

<BODY>
<IE:clientCaps ID="oClientCaps" />

<SCRIPT LANGUAGE = VBScript>
Sub window_onload()
    sCookieStr = "availHeight=" & oClientCaps.availHeight
    Document.Cookie = sCookieStr
    sCookieStr = "availWidth=" & oClientCaps.availWidth
    Document.Cookie = sCookieStr
```

```
    sCookieStr = "bufferDepth=" & oClientCaps.bufferDepth
    Document.Cookie = sCookieStr
    sCookieStr = "colorDepth=" & oClientCaps.colorDepth
    Document.Cookie = sCookieStr
    sCookieStr = "connectionType=" & _
                    oClientCaps.connectionType
    Document.Cookie = sCookieStr
    sCookieStr = "cookieEnabled=" & _
                    oClientCaps.cookieEnabled
    Document.Cookie = sCookieStr
    sCookieStr = "cpuClass=" & oClientCaps.cpuClass
    Document.Cookie = sCookieStr
    sCookieStr = "height=" & oClientCaps.height
    Document.Cookie = sCookieStr
    sCookieStr = "javaEnabled=" & oClientCaps.javaEnabled
    Document.Cookie = sCookieStr
    sCookieStr = "platform=" & oClientCaps.platform
    Document.Cookie = sCookieStr
    sCookieStr = "systemLanguage=" & _
                    oClientCaps.systemLanguage
    Document.Cookie = sCookieStr
    sCookieStr = "userLanguage=" & oClientCaps.userLanguage
    Document.Cookie = sCookieStr
    sCookieStr = "width=" & oClientCaps.width
    Document.Cookie = sCookieStr
End Sub
</SCRIPT>
</BODY>
</HTML>
```

The script leaves a number of cookies on the client computer. Each cookie corresponds to one of the browser capabilities listed in Table 12.2. If you send this script to the client as part of the main page (or another page all viewers are requested to visit the first time they connect), these cookies will be created on their computer. Because the cookies have no expiration date, they're not saved on the client computer. They are per-session cookies and they expire at the end of the current session.

TABLE 12.2: The browser capabilities reported by the clientCaps behavior of IE 5

Client Capability	Description
availHeight	Sets or returns the height of the working area of the system's screen, excluding the Windows taskbar at the bottom of the screen.
availWidth	Sets or returns the width of the working area of the system's screen, excluding the Windows taskbar.
bufferDepth	Sets or returns the number of bits per pixel used for colors in the off-screen bitmap buffer.
colorDepth	Returns the number of bits per pixel used for colors on the destination device or buffer.
cookieEnabled	Returns True if client-side cookies are enabled in the browser.
cpuClass	Returns a string identifying the CPU class.
height	Returns the vertical resolution of the screen.
javaEnabled	Returns True if Java is enabled.
platform	Returns the name of the operating system on the client computer.
systemLanguage	Returns the default language used by the system.
userLanguage	Returns the current user language.
width	Returns the horizontal resolution of the screen.

To access the value of the cookie with the additional browser properties, you can read the values of the cookies from within any script. The following statements retrieve the values of the cookiesEnabled and Width capabilities:

```
ClientCookies = Request.Cookies("cookiesEnabled")
BrowserWidth = Request.Cookies("Width")
If Not ClientCookies Then
    Response.Write
        "We have detected that you have disabled cookies."
    ' more statemetns
Else
    Response.Cookies("LastVisit") = Now()
End If
```

```
If BrowserWidth < 1000 Then
    ' show a low resolution page
Else
    ' show a high resolution page
End If
```

The clientCaps behavior is an invaluable tool, but not all browsers support it. It would be nice if we could query every browser for specific capabilities, but you can't count on this tool for browsers other than Internet Explorer. (The good news is that 80 percent of the viewers are using Internet Explorer, but you must still take into consideration the other 20 percent.)

chapter 13

The Content Linking Component

One of the most challenging problems Web developers face is the organization of the information on a site. The information should be broken into small, easy-to-digest parts. Each part, or topic, is encoded as a separate page. These pages should be enhanced with navigational hyperlinks, so that viewers can jump to the next/previous topic. Another common navigational paradigm is that of the navigational frame, which contains a vertical list of all topics, and viewers can jump to any page by clicking the appropriate navigational hyperlink. Figure 13.1 is an example of the first navigational model, which is more suitable for tutorials, where topics are structured according to the degree of difficulty or they build on previous topics. Use this model if you expect that most readers will go through the topics in sequence, as when reading a book.

FIGURE 13.1: The Next/Previous navigational model

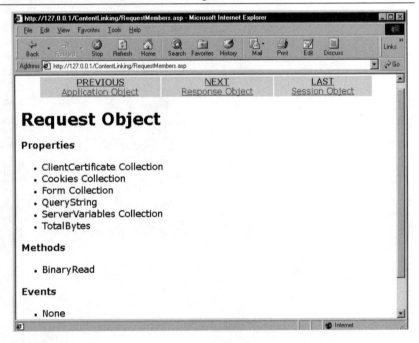

The second navigational model, illustrated in Figure 13.2, is more suitable for unrelated topics, like the sections of a newspaper or a list of products. The frame on the left contains a list of all topics, and the selected topic is displayed in the large frame.

FIGURE 13.2: This navigational model allows viewers to jump to any topic they wish to view.

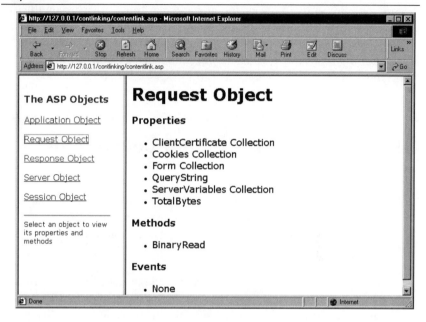

Breaking up the site's content into smaller sections is a question of design. Maintaining a list of topics, however, is a tedious, error-prone procedure. You must keep a copy of the site, make all the changes, verify the hyperlinks, and then move the new site to the production server. Inserting one or more pages to a site that use the Next/Previous navigational model entails changes in the existing pages. Changing the order of certain pages is even more difficult, because you must change several hyperlinks both in the pages you move around and in the pages before and after the ones you have moved.

To simplify the maintenance of such sites, use the Content Linking component. This component is similar to the Ad Rotator component, in that it expects to find all the information in a text file. This text file contains the available topics, in the order they should appear, and the URLs of the individual documents. All you have to do is add some VBScript code to each page to insert the usual First/Previous/Next/Last hyperlinks. This code is common to all pages. You can then manipulate the topics through the text file, which is the Content Linking list file. You can change the order of the topics by rearranging the lines in the list file, remove topics by deleting the corresponding entry in the list file, and add new topics anywhere in the list file. The site will be automatically organized, and you don't have to edit the pages. The Content Linking component will insert the appropriate hyperlinks on each page; your site will be updated as soon as you edit the list file.

Using the Content Linking Component

To use the Content Linking component, you must do the following:

1. **The Table of Contents**   Create a list of all the topics making up the site (or a section of it). The topics must be entered in a text file, each one on its own line. Each line in this file has the following structure:

   ```
   DocumentURL    Description    Comments
   ```

   Successive items on a line are separated by a tab character, which makes the file a bit difficult to read. The *DocumentURL* item is the URL of a page, and *Description* is a descriptive title for the same page. When you write the code to insert the usual navigational hyperlinks, *DocumentURL* will become the destination address of a hyperlink and *Description* will become the hyperlink's title. The last item, Comments, is optional; it's included as an aid to the developer and is ignored by the Content Linking component.

   Every time the user selects the First/Next/Previous/Last hyperlink, the appropriate document will be displayed. Exactly which document will appear depends on the list file's contents and the document being displayed at the moment.

2. **The Page Navigational Section**   Write some VBScript code that uses the Content Linking component to insert the proper hyperlinks at the top or bottom of each page. You must create an instance of the Content Linking component on your page, program it to read the URLs and descriptions of the next and previous pages, and then display the corresponding descriptions as hyperlinks. Their destinations will be the matching URLs.

All pages will use the same piece of code, so you must handle some special cases, such as not displaying the Previous hyperlink when the viewer is on the first page. The Content Linking component exposes all the functionality you need with several methods, which are described in the following sections.

The Content Linking List File

To demonstrate how to use the Content Linking component, we'll build a small site with reference material on the ASP objects. It's a very simple example, but it demonstrates just about any method exposed by the Content Linking component.

The material is organized into separate pages, and each page contains reference information about a specific object. The various objects, which are the topics of our site, are arranged alphabetically; each page is named after the object it describes (`ApplicationMembers.asp`, `ResponseMembers.asp`, and so on). The first page of the site is the `ApplicationMembers.asp` page. This page describes the members of the Application object and contains hyperlinks to the next and last topic. The `RequestMembers.asp` page, shown back in Figure 13.1, contains three of the four hyperlinks because the previous document, the `ApplicationMembers.asp` page, happens to be the first one as well

Let's start with the list file, because its structure is very simple and it can be used as a guide for building the site. This will force you to lay out the site before you start developing it. Here's the Content Linking list file for the sample site:

▶ *Listing 13.1: A Typical Content Linking List File*

```
ApplicationMembers.asp      Application Object
RequestMembers.asp          Request Object
ResponseMembers.asp         Response Object
ServerMembers.asp           Server Object
SessionMembers.asp          Session Object
```

Name this file `ASPObjectsTOC.txt` and save it in the virtual folder of the application. For this example, we'll use the Linking virtual folder.

Next you must design the individual pages. Break up the information you want to present into smaller sections, design the pages of your site, and place them in the Linking virtual folder. As you recall from the previous section, we must also insert the code that appends the hyperlinks on each page. Because this code is common to all pages, you don't have to include it on every page.

Adding Navigational Buttons to Your Pages

The navigational buttons are added at the top or bottom of the page and are the usual First/Previous/Next/Last hyperlinks. The destinations of these hyperlinks are read from the Content Linking list file and inserted on each page with a short script. The same script must be inserted on each page, so you should place all statements in an Include file. Insert an #INCLUDE FILE directive, like the following one, in each page at the place where the hyperlinks should appear:

```
<!-- #INCLUDE FILE = NavigationCode.INC-->
```

Since the same code will be inserted in each page, you must make sure the code takes into consideration the order of the current page in the list file. For example, you shouldn't insert a Previous or First hyperlink on the page of the first topic. Here's the page with the Response object's description (actually, it only lists the names of the methods, but it's quite adequate for our purposes):

▶ *Listing 13.2: The RequestMembers.asp Page*

```
<HTML>
<FONT FACE=Verdana>
<!-- #INCLUDE FILE = NavigationCode.INC-->
<H1>Request Object</H1>
<H3>Properties</H3>
<FONT SIZE=+1>
<UL>
<LI>ClientCertificate Collection
<LI>Cookies Collection
<LI>Form Collection
<LI>QueryString
```

```
<LI>ServerVariables Collection
<LI>TotalBytes
</UL>
<H3>Methods</H3>
<UL>
<LI>BinaryRead
</UL>
<H3>Events</H3>
<UL>
<LI>None
</UL>
</FONT>
<!-- #INCLUDE FILE = NavigationCode.INC-->
</HTML>
```

The INCLUDE FILE directive is inserted twice, so that the hyperlinks will appear both at the top and the bottom of the page.

The code that inserts the navigational hyperlinks of the site of Figure 13.1 is shown in Listing 13.3. Notice that the code doesn't change from page to page; that's why I had to include several If statements to create the proper hyperlinks for all pages. This file contains a script, but it has the extension INC. Because the same code must be inserted in multiple pages, we'll use an Include file (with extension INC) and include this file in every page.

▶ Listing 13.3: The NavigationCode.inc File

```
<%
Set objContents = Server.CreateObject("MSWC.NextLink")
PageCount = objContents.GetListCount("ASPObjectsTOC.txt")
currPage = objContents.GetListIndex("ASPObjectsTOC.txt")

Response.Write "<CENTER>"
Response.Write "<TABLE WIDTH=90% ><TR>"
If currPage > 2 Then
  firstURL = objContents.GetNthURL("ASPObjectsTOC.txt", 1)
  firstDescription = _
    objContents.GetNthDescription("ASPObjectsTOC.txt", 1)
  Response.Write "<TD ALIGN=center BGColor=yellow>"
```

```
      Response.Write "<A HREF='" & firstURL & _
                     "'><B>FIRST</B></A><BR>"
    Response.Write "<A HREF='" & firstURL & "'>" & _
                   firstDescription & "</A>"
      Response.Write "</TD>"
  End If


  If currPage > 1 Then
    prevURL = objContents.GetPreviousURL("ASPObjectsTOC.txt")
    prevDescription =
      objContents.GetPreviousDescription("ASPObjectsTOC.txt")
    Response.Write "<TD ALIGN=center BGColor=yellow>"
    Response.Write "<A HREF='" & prevURL & _
                   "'><B>PREVIOUS</B></A><BR>"
    Response.Write "<A HREF='" & prevURL & "'>" & _
                   prevDescription & "</A>"
    Response.Write "</TD>"
  End If


  If currPage < PageCount Then
    nextURL = objContents.GetNextURL("ASPObjectsTOC.txt")
    nextDescription =
      objContents.GetNextDescription("ASPObjectsTOC.txt")
    Response.Write "<TD ALIGN=center BGColor=yellow>"
    Response.Write "<A HREF='" & nextURL &
                   "'><B>NEXT</B></A><BR>"
    Response.Write "<A HREF='" & nextURL & "'>" & _
                   nextDescription & "</A>"
    Response.Write "</TD>"
  End If


  If currPage < PageCount Then
    lastURL =
      objContents.GetNthURL("ASPObjectsTOC.txt", PageCount)
    lastDescription =
      objContents.GetNthDescription("ASPObjectsTOC.txt",
      PageCount)
    Response.Write "<TD ALIGN=center BGColor=yellow>"
    Response.Write "<A HREF='" & lastURL & _
                   "'><B>LAST</B></A><BR>"
```

```
    Response.Write "<A HREF='" & lastURL & "'>" & _
                    lastDescription & "</A>"
    Response.Write "</TD>"
End If
Response.Write "</TABLE>"
Response.Write "</CENTER>"

Set objContent = Nothing
%>
```

Create a text file with the lines of Listing 13.3, name it Navigation-Code.inc, and store it in the site's virtual folder. You can now test the site by connecting to the first page (which is the ApplicationMembers.asp script). The NavigationCode.inc file must be included in every page of the site with the following statement:

```
<!-- #include file="NavigationCode.inc" -->
```

The statement will be replaced by the code that displays the navigational hyperlinks. The code will be executed and the viewer will see the hyperlinks, as shown in Figure 13.1.

The ApplicationMembers.asp script displays the members of the Application object, similar to the RequestMembers.asp script, shown in Listing 13.2. At the end of the script is the statement that inserts the navigational hyperlinks. All the pages of the site have the same structure.

The code segment of Listing 13.3 demonstrates the basic members of the Content Linking component. The GetNextURL/GetPreviousURL retrieve the next/previous URLs from the list file. The GetNextDescription/ GetPreviousDescription retrieve the next/previous descriptions from the same file. Finally, the GetNthURL and GetNthDescription retrieve an arbitrary item from the list file, which is then used in the code to retrieve the URL and description of the first and last items in the file. The GetListCount method retrieves the total number of lines in the list file, and the GetList-Index method retrieves the index of the current page in the list file (the index of the first page is 1, not 0). Even if you've never used the Content Linking component, you should be able to follow the listing. The names of the component's properties and methods are intuitive, and the code's structure is fairly simple.

Methods

The Content Linking component exposes its functionality through several methods and doesn't provide any properties. Before you can call a method of the component, you must create an instance of it on your page with the following statement:

```
<%
Set objContents = Server.CreateObject("MSWC.NextLink")
%>
```

When you no longer need the *objContents* object in your script, release the memory associated with it by setting it to Nothing:

```
<%
Set objContents = Nothing
%>
```

GetListCount

This method returns the number of topics (URLs and descriptions) in a Content Linking list file. The syntax of GetListCount is:

```
objContents.GetListCount(contentFileName)
```

contentFileName is the path and name of the Content Linking list file. The path is relative to the current virtual folder, and it can't be a physical or absolute URL.The objContents variable must be instantiated with the CreateObject method, as shown in the previous section.

Assuming that your Content Linking list file is called ASPObjectsTOC.txt and it resides in the Content folder under the Web's root folder, the following statements retrieve the number of topics, which is the number of lines in the file, and display this value on a new page:

```
<%
Set objContents = Server.CreateObject("MSWC.NextLink")
TopicCount = objContents.GetListCount("ASPObjectsTOC.txt")
Set objContents = Nothing
%>
<HTML>
<HR>
```

```
<H1>Content Linking Component</H1>
There are <% = TopicCount %> topics in your Content
Linking file.
</HTML>
```

GetListIndex

The GetListIndex method returns an integer, which is the order of the current page in the content list. Use this method to find out from within your code which page is displayed on the client, in the following syntax:

```
objContents.GetListIndex(contentFileName)
```

contentFileName is the path and name of the Content Linking list file. The path is relative to the current virtual folder, and it can't be a physical or absolute URL.

If the current page is not in the content list file, the GetListIndex method will return 0. This will happen when you jump to the first page of the list from within another page.

The following statements display the index of the current page. You could insert this statement at the top of every page for debugging purposes:

```
Response.Write "You're viewing page # " & _
    ObjContents.GetListIndex(contentFileName)
```

GetNextDescription

This method returns the description of the next item in the Content Linking list file. If the current item is the last one in the file, then the GetNextDescription method returns the description of the first item in the list file. Use this syntax:

```
objContents.GetNextDescription(contentFileName)
```

contentFileName is the path and name of the Content Linking list file. The path is relative to the current virtual folder, and it can't be a physical or absolute URL. See the NavigationalCode.inc file (Listing 13.3) for an example of using this method to retrieve the next page's description.

GetNextURL

This method returns the URL of the next item in the Content Linking list file. Use the value returned by this method as the Next hyperlink on the page. If the current item is the last one in the file, then the GetNextURL method returns the URL of the first item in the list file when called as follows:

```
objContents.GetNextURL(contentFileName)
```

contentFileName is the path and name of the Content Linking list file. The path is relative to the current virtual folder and can't be a physical or absolute URL. If an item doesn't have a URL (this shouldn't really happen in a well-designed site), then an empty string will be returned. See the Nav-igationalCode.inc file (Listing 13.3) for an example of using this method to retrieve the next page's URL.

GetNthDescription

This method returns the description of an arbitrary item in the Content Linking list file. Use the value returned by this method as the description of an item (hyperlink) in a navigational frame. Its syntax is:

```
objContents.GetNthDescription(contentFileName, itemIndex)
```

contentFileName is the path and name of the Content Linking list file, and *itemIndex* is the index of the item whose description you want to retrieve. Notice that the index of the first item is 1, not 0. If an item doesn't have a URL (this shouldn't really happen in a well-designed site), then an empty string will be returned.

If the *itemIndex* argument's value exceeds the number of items in the Content Linking list file, a runtime error will be generated. To avoid this error, you must make sure that the argument *itemIndex* doesn't exceed the value returned by the GetListCount method. The example in the following section (Listing 13.4) shows how to retrieve the number of topics in a content file and iterate through them with a For ... Next loop.

GetNthURL

This method returns the URL of an arbitrary item in the Content Linking list file. Use the value returned by this method as the destination of an item (hyperlink) in a navigational frame. The syntax of GetNthURL is:

```
objContents.GetNthURL(contentFileName, itemIndex)
```

contentFileName is the path and name of the Content Linking list file, and *itemIndex* is the index of the item whose URL you want to retrieve. Notice that the index of the first item is 1, and not 0. If the *itemIndex* argument's value exceeds the number of items in the Content Linking list file, a run-time error will be generated. To avoid this error, you must make sure that the argument *itemIndex* doesn't exceed the value returned by the GetList-Count method.

The statements in Listing 13.4 read the URLs and descriptions of the content list file and display them on a table. A similar technique will be used later to build a navigational frame with all the topics:

▶ *Listing 13.4: Scanning the Items of the List File*

```
<HTML>
<FONT FACE=Verdana COLOR=Red>
<BR>
<H3>The Contents of the List File</H3>
<FONT COLOR=Black>
<TABLE>
<TR>
<TD><B>Description</B></TD>
<TD><B>URL</B></TD></TR>
<TR>
<%
Set objContents = Server.CreateObject("MSWC.NextLink")
TopicCount = objContents.GetListCount("ASPObjectsTOC.txt")
For i = 1 To TopicCount
    strURL = objContents.GetNthURL _
            ("/ContLinking/ASPObjectsTOC.txt", i)
    strTopic = objContents.GetNthDescription _
            ("/ContLinking/ASPObjectsTOC.txt", i)
    Response.Write "<TD>" & strTopic & "</TD><TD>" & _
            strURL & "</TD>" & vbCrLf
    Response.Write "</TR>"
Next
%>
</TABLE>
</HTML>
```

Some of these lines were arbitrarily broken to fit on the printed page. The continued lines are indented to the right and are easy to spot in the listing. In your scripts you must enter them on a single line.

GetPreviousDescription

This method returns the description of the previous item in the Content Linking list file. Use the value returned by this method as the description of the Previous hyperlink on your page. The syntax for GetPreviousDescription is as follows:

```
objContents.GetPreviousDescription(contentFileName)
```

contentFileName is the path and name of the Content Linking list file. If the current page isn't in the Content Linking list file, then the description of the first item in the file is returned. If the current page is the first one in the file, then the GetPreviousDescription returns the description of the first item in the file.

GetPreviousURL

This method returns the URL of the previous item in the Content Linking list file. Use the value returned by this method as the destination of the Previous hyperlink on your page. The syntax you need is:

```
objContents.GetPreviousURL(contentFileName)
```

contentFileName is the path and name of the Content Linking list file. If the current page isn't in the Content Linking list file, then the URL of the first item in the file is returned. If the current page is the first one in the file, then the GetPreviousURL returns the URL of the first item in the list file.

Building Navigational Frames

The final example combines many of the methods of the Content Linking component to build a page with two vertical frames, as shown in Figure 13.2. The frame on the left is a navigational frame; all the topics are displayed in this frame as hyperlinks. When a topic name in the navigational frame is clicked, the corresponding document is displayed in the larger frame to the right.

Every Web developer has built pages with navigational frames, but in this example you'll see how the Content Linking component can automate the design of similar pages. As you update the content file with additional topics, the new topics are added automatically to the navigational frame and the site's structure is updated. This means that you won't have to edit HTML code manually, test the site, and then copy the HTML file to the production server. All you have to do is supply the titles of the topics and their URLs in the content file, and the script will do the rest.

The code for building the navigational frame based on the content list file is very similar to the example in the section "GetNthURL." It reads the descriptions and URLs of each item in the file and formats them as hyperlinks.

▶ Listing 13.5: Building a Navigational Frame with the Content Linking Component

```
<HTML>
<FONT FACE=Verdana COLOR=Red>
<BR>
<H3>The ASP Objects</H3>
<FONT COLOR=Black>
<%
Set objContents = Server.CreateObject("MSWC.NextLink")
For i = 1 To objContents.GetListCount("ASPObjectsTOC.txt")
    strTopic = "<A TARGET='Frame2' HREF='" & _
            objContents.GetNthURL _
            ("ASPObjectsTOC.txt", i) & "'>"
    strTopic = strTopic & _
            objContents.GetNthDescription _
            ("ASPObjectsTOC.txt", i)
    strTopic = strTopic & "</A>"
    Response.Write strTopic & "<BR><BR>" & vbCrLf
Next
%>
<HR>
<FONT SIZE=-1>
```

```
Select an object to view
<BR>
its properties and methods
</HTML>
```

Building a navigational frame is straightforward, but rearranging the hyperlinks can be a hassle. The Content Linking component reduces the complexity of maintaining the topic titles and their hyperlinks in the navigational frame to maintaining a text file. To insert new topics, you need only add new lines to this file. To rearrange the topics, you simply move the lines of the Content Linking list file up and down.

To complete the example, you must build a home page with two vertical frames, a narrow one for the list of topics and a wider one for the description of each topic. The main page is called ContentLink.htm and is shown in Listing 13.6.

▶ *Listing 13.6: The ContentLink.htm Page*

```
<HTML>
<FRAMESET COLS="20%, 80%">
    <FRAME NAME="Frame1" SRC="TOC.ASP">
    <FRAME NAME="Frame2" SRC="APPLICATIONMEMBERS.ASP">
</FRAMESET>
</HTML>
```

The two frames are called Frame1 and Frame2. Notice that all hyperlinks in the navigational frame use the attribute TARGET='Frame2' to display the destination document in the second frame. To test the example, copy all the files with the descriptions of the ASP objects to the application's virtual folder. Notice that these files are plain HTML files; they contain no server-side scripts. This is because the navigation takes place from within the navigational frame, and not the pages themselves. You must also copy the TOC .asp script and the ContentLink.htm page in the same folder, and then connect to the ContentLink.htm page by entering its URL in the browser's address box.

chapter 14

The Content Rotator Component

Whether you design and maintain commercial sites, or a site with rich content that generates income by selling ads, one of the challenges you'll face is how to constantly update the site's content. In most situations, you don't have to redesign entire pages. All you have to do is change a few sections on the main page, or the most popular pages of your site. A few changes in strategically selected sections could make viewers return to the site to view the new content. A site with tutorials on programming, for example, could display a new tip every day. If the tip is nontrivial it will keep some readers coming back for more tips. If you spread the tips in several pages of the same sections, you will probably keep viewers in your site long enough to notice an ad, or order an item.

Changing the content manually entails quite a bit of editing and testing. In addition, the revised pages will remain the same until you decide to change them again. *The Content Rotator component* is a tool that allows you to change content constantly, with the same ease as changing banners with the Ad Rotator component. Adjusting the content of your site, however, requires more careful planning, because the sections of the page that change must fit nicely into the corresponding pages. A tip will not cause any problems, because it's not directly related to the page's content. I have used this technique to present different titles to visitors on the main page of an electronic bookstore. The file with the new/noteworthy titles is prepared ahead of time and is used for an entire week. To revise the file with the rotating content, the Web manager replaces some of the titles and adds new ones. All we have to do is make sure that the size of this file increases as the traffic of the site increases, to avoid displaying the same title too many times (which isn't necessarily bad).

As you can guess, the Content Rotator component is very similar to the Ad Rotator component. They're both based on a file that contains the rotating content (HTML code or banners) and a few VBScript statements in the page that randomly select a banner or an HTML section of the page.

If you require your viewers to register, or you allow them to customize their pages, you probably know what their interests are and can tune the rotating section on their custom pages to the products and services they're interested in. If a viewer buys computer books frequently, you can display reviews of recently released computer books. You can even keep track of the viewer's search keywords and base the content selection they see on these keywords. The rotating HTML sections are selected randomly from a text file, but you can have multiple files, one for each interest or buying pattern.

Using the Content Rotator

To use the Content Rotator component, you must do and have the following:

1. **Content Placeholders**   Create a placeholder (or multiple place-holders) on one or more pages for the rotating HTML section. This placeholder need not be a rectangle of specific dimensions (as is the case with the Ad Rotator component), but you must make sure that all rotating sections fit in the placeholder. In most cases you'll build a table and change the content of its cells dynamically with the Content Rotator component.

2. **The Rotating Content File**   Create a text file with the HTML sections you want to display. This file contains text and HTML tags, including <IMG> tags for inserting images in the rotating section. The structure of this file is straightforward and you must follow the specifications described later in this chapter precisely.

The Rotating Content File

Before we discuss the properties and methods of the Content Rotator component, let's look at the structure of the rotating content file. This is a text file that contains the following few lines for each of the rotating sections. Consecutive sections are delimited with a blank line. Each section's structure is shown next:

```
%% #weight  //comments
HTML Content

%% #weight  //comments
HTML Content
```

The first two lines correspond to the first rotating section. Then comes an empty line followed by the second rotating section. Notice that the first line of each section must begin with two percent signs. The *weight* and *//comments* items are optional. The *weight* argument is prefixed by a pound sign and is an integer in the range of 1 through 10000. This is the relative weight of the corresponding HTML section. The Content Rotator component selects an HTML section randomly using these weights. The probability of a specific section to be selected is its own weight divided by the sum of the weights of all sections.

The last item on the first line of each section is a comment describing the section and is not used by the Content Rotator component. If you want to insert multiple comment lines, start each one after the first line with two percent signs followed by two forward slashes, as in the following example:

```
%% #weight  //comments
%%// more comments
HTML Content
```

Insert the HTML section following the line(s) with the weight and the comments. This section contains text and HTML code. Just make sure the section can fit in its placeholder and it will not throw off the entire page. (For example, avoid too much text and many images if the placeholder is the first cell in a table's row and the other cells contain a few lines of text.)

The next section is identified by the double percent line, so you can have as many lines of HTML code as you wish; you can even insert empty lines in the HTML section. Here's a typical rotating content file:

▶ *Listing 14.1: A Typical Rotating Content File*

```
%% #33  //The first section
<B>1st Book's Title</B>
<I>Author Name</I>
<TABLE>
<TR>
<TD><IMG SRC="001-345-990-X"></TD>
<TD>The book's short description</TD>
</TR>
</TABLE>

%% #66  //The second section
<B>2nd Book's Title</B>
<I>Author Name</I>
<TABLE>
<TR>
<TD><IMG SRC="001-345-991-3"></TD>
<TD>The book's short description</TD>
</TR>
</TABLE>
```

The second book's section will appear twice as frequently as the first book's section on the viewer's page. The rotating content file is usually very long, because our goal is to make viewers come back to view more content.

You may have noticed that there's a chance that the same HTML section will appear twice on the same page! You can minimize the chances of having the Content Rotator component grab the same section twice by making the rotating content file very long, but there's always a chance that a few pages will repeat information. The only method to avoid this situation is to use a different Rotating Content file for each section on the page. If you provide two placeholders, at the top and the bottom of the page, for rotating content, you can grab the top HTML section from one file, and the bottom HTML section from another file. If you see that there's no overlap in the HTML sections of the two files, then no page will contain identical HTML sections.

Adding Rotating Content to Your Pages

To add a rotating HTML section to a page, you must create an instance of the Content Rotator component with the following statement:

```
Set objCRotator = Server.CreateObject("MSWC.ContentRotator")
```

This line is always the same; you can only change the name of the object variable, *objCRotator*. The *objCRotator* variable will be used from within many of your site's pages (possibly all of them). Instead of creating an instance of this object from within each page, you should instantiate this object in the Application or Session level. You will see the advantages and disadvantages of both approaches shortly.

Once the *objCRotator* object variable has been instantiated, you can call its ChooseContent method to retrieve a section. This method returns HTML code, which is inserted at the current point in the HTML file. To place an HTML section in a table's cell, place a call to the ChooseContent method between the cell's <TD> and </TD> tags, as if it was another HTML tag. To place the selected section in a table's cell, use a statement like the following one:

```
<TD>
<% = objCRotator.ChooseContent("Contents/ContentFile.txt") %>
</TD>
```

To center the HTML section at the current location on the page and place two lines above and below it, use the following statements:

```
<CENTER>
<HR>
<% = objCRotator.ChooseContent("Contents/ContentFile.txt") %>
</HR>
</CENTER>
```

Testing a Simple Page with Rotating Content

Once you have created the rotating content file, you can build a simple page with fixed content (headers, a navigational frame, and so on) and a few sections with rotating content. The rotating content is selected randomly from the text file with the rotating content. To test the files, create a simple page with a single-cell table, centered horizontally on the page. Figure 14.1 shows a page with information on the ASP objects. The tip below the page's header is selected randomly from a text file that contains many tips.

FIGURE 14.1: The output of the ContentRotator.asp script

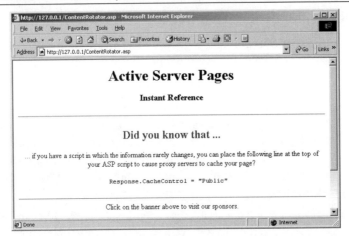

The page of Figure 14.1 was created with the following script:

▶ *Listing 14.2: The ContentRotator.asp Script*

```
<%
Set objCRotator = Server.CreateObject("MSWC.ContentRotator")
RotContentFile = "Contents/ContentFile.txt"
HTMLString = objCRotator.ChooseContent(RotContentFile)
%>
<HTML>
<CENTER>
<H1>Active Server Pages</H1>
<H3>Instant Reference</H3>
<HR>
<H2><FONT COLOR=red>Did you know that ...</FONT></H2>
<% = HTMLString %>
<%
```

```
Set objCRotator = Nothing
%>
<BR>
Click on the banner above to visit our sponsors.
<HR>
<H1>Welcome to the ASP 3.0 Instant Reference</H1>
</CENTER>
<FONT SIZE=+1>
Select an object from the list below to view its methods and prop-
erties:
<BR>
' MORE HTML STATEMENT FOLLOW
</HTML>
```

The tips are retrieved from a text file like the following one:

▶ *Listing 14.3: The CONTENTFILE.TXT File*

```
%% #25 //the first tip
... if you have a script in which the information
rarely changes, you can place the following line
at the top of your ASP script to cause
proxy servers to cache your page?
<BR>
<PRE>Response.CacheControl = "Public"
%% #50 // the second tip
... cookies are small files that live in the
Temporary Internet Files folder and they're a great
way to personalize your Active Server web pages?
%% #25 //the third tip
... your server-side (SSI) include files shouldn't include
too many functions if the Web page in question uses only
two of those functions?
```

To test the example with the rotating tips, follow these steps:

1. Create the ContentFile.txt and store it in the ContentRotator folder under the Web's root folder.

2. Then create the ContentRotator.asp script and store it in the Web's root folder. If you store the ContentRotator.asp script in a subfolder of the root folder, make sure the ContentRotator folder is created under the virtual folder.

3. Start your browser and connect to ContentRotator.asp file. As you refresh the page by pressing F5, the tips will alternate.

Now that you have seen how the Content Rotator component works at large, let's examine its members in detail.

Methods

The Content Rotator component exposes two methods, one for grabbing an HTML section randomly (similar to the GetAdvertisement method of the Ad Rotator component) and another one for grabbing the entire rotating HTML sections from a file.

ChooseContent

This is the method that reads an HTML code segment from the Rotating Content file and inserts it on the current page. The ChooseContent method takes into consideration the relative frequencies of the various sections, but you shouldn't display two sections from the same rotating content file on the same page. There's a chance that the ChooseContent method will select the same section. To avoid this situation you can use a very large file with many different sections, or retrieve the sections that will end up on the same page from two or more different files.

Syntax

```
objCRotator.ChooseContent(contentFileName)
```

contentFileName is the path and name of the rotating content file. The path is relative to the current virtual folder.

Example

Assuming that your scripts are in the Scripts folder and the rotating content file is called ContentFile.txt (both residing in the Contents folder under the Web's root folder), the following statement will select a section from the rotating content file and place it at the current location on the page:

```
<%
Set objCRotator = Server.CreateObject("MSWC.ContentRotator")
%>
<HTML>
```

```
<HR>
<% =
  objCRotator.ChooseContent("Contents/ContentFile.txt")
%>
</HR>
```

If you open the page displayed on the browser, you will see that the line calling the ChooseContent method is replaced by the HTML code of the selected section.

Tuning Content to Target Groups

It is possible to tune rotating content to the preferences and/or buying patterns of your site's viewers. To do so, you must maintain a number of Rotating Content files. If you ask your viewers to select a type of products they're interested in, you can rotate the appropriate content for each viewer group. For example, you can create different content files for each type of viewers and display the appropriate file's content to each group.

Let's say the Session variable "Language" can have one of the following values: VBScript, Vbasic, and HTML. You can create three content files, name them VBSCRIPT.TXT, VBASIC.TXT, and HTML.TXT, and populate them with the appropriate tips, hyperlinks, and so on. Notice that the rotating sections addressed to each group need not be mutually exclusive. Then, each time you display a page, you can select an HTML section from the file that best describes the group's interests:

```
<%
Select Case Session("Language")
    Case "VBScript": cntFile = "VBSCRIPT.TXT"
    Case "VBASIC": cntFile = "VBASIC.TXT"
    Case "HTML": cntFile = "HTML.TXT"
    Case Else: cntFile = "ALLCONTENT.TXT"
End Select
Set objCRotator =
        Server.CreateObject("MSWC.ContentRotator")
Response.Write "<H1>The ASP Tutorials</H1>"
Response.Write "<BR>"
<% = objCRotator.ChooseContent(cntFile") %>
'    more content follows the randomly selected tip
%>
```

GetAllContent

The GetAllContent method retrieves all the sections of the rotating content file and places them on the current page. The sections are listed with a horizontal line between them. The GetAllContent method is a debugging tool that allows the developer to proofread the contents of the rotating content file. If the sections of this file are tips, for example, you can display all the tips on the same page.

Syntax

```
objCRotator.GetAllContent(contentFileName)
```

contentFileName is the path and name of the rotating content file. The path is relative to the current virtual folder.

Example

The following statements display all the tips in the ContentFile.txt file. The output they produce is shown in Figure 14.2.

```
<H1>The Ultimate Tips List</H1>
<%
Set objCRotator = Server.CreateObject("MSWC.ContentRotator")
objCRotator.GetAllContent "Contents/ContentFile.txt"
%>
```

FIGURE 14.2: Displaying all the entries in the rotating content file on the same page.

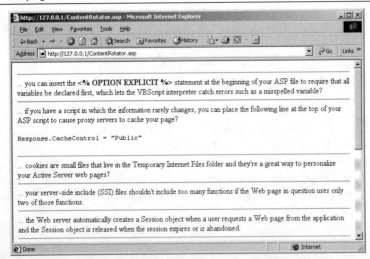

chapter 15

The File Access Component

A common operation in developing Web applications is the access of files on the server. You have seen how to access databases from within your scripts, but not all the information you need in your Web applications resides in databases. As with any other programming language, you should be able to access the host computer's file system and manipulate its files. This functionality can be incorporated in your Web applications with the help of the *File Access component*.

Granted, a typical Web application doesn't move files around, but there are many operations that require input from text files. A list of popular products, for example, is usually derived from the database with the sales. This list, however, doesn't change frequently. Querying the database every time a viewer requests the page(s) with the most popular products is a waste of CPU time. I would much rather extract the information from the database once, create the appropriate HTML file(s), and serve them to the viewers as static pages. This page can be updated every few hours for a system with very heavy traffic, or every few days for a typical store.

Other applications may create text files and leave them to specific folders to identify unusual conditions. For example, you may create a text file with a query that failed, or you may record all the information about viewers that attempt to access files they're not authorized to view. The same information could be stored in the site's log file, but text files are convenient alternatives, especially if you plan to process them with auxiliary applications.

The File Access Component consists of two separate objects, the *FileSystemObject* and the *TextStream* objects. The FileSystemObject object gives you access to the file system: you use its methods to manipulate files and folders (copy, move, rename files and folders, see their properties, and so on). The TextStream object lets you access text files: you use the TextStream object to connect your application to a text file and read from, or write to, the text file. In addition to these two objects, there's a Drive, a File and a Folder object, which represent drives, folders and files respectively.

To gain access to the server computer's file system, you must create a FileSystemObject object variable with the CreateObject() function:

```
Set FSYS = _
          Server.CreateObject("Scripting.FileSystemObject")
```

The variable *FSYS* represents the file system, and you can use this variable to access the file system of the Web server. This variable's members are described in detail in the following sections.

Manipulating Files

Let's exercise the FileSystemObject object. Create a new script and enter the following lines:

```
<%
Set FSYS = CreateObject("Scripting.FileSystemObject")
Response.Write FSYS.FileExists("C:\AUTOEXEC.BAT")
Set FSYS = Nothing
%>
```

If the file C:\AUTOEXEC.BAT exists, the string "True" will appear in the browser's window. FileExists is a method of the *FSYS* object and it returns True if the specified file exists; otherwise, it returns, False.

The FileSystemObject object provides a number of properties and methods for manipulating files and folders, as well as for creating new text files (and opening existing ones), to read from or write to. Unlike Visual Basic, VBScript doesn't provide its own statements for accessing text files (or binary files, for that matter), so the File Access component is particularly useful to Web developers.

For Example, to create a copy of the AUTOEXEC.BAT file in the BACKUP folder and rename it to AUTOEXEC.OLD at the same time, use the *CopyFile* method of the *FSYS* object variable, as shown in the following statements:

```
<%
Set FSYS = CreateObject("Scripting.FileSystemObject")
FSYS.CopyFile "C:\AUTOEXEC.BAT", _
                "C:\BACKUP\AUTOEXEC.OLD", True
Set FSYS = Nothing
%>
```

The last argument of the CopyFile method tells the FileSystemObject to overwrite the AUTOEXEC.OLD file in the BACKUP folder, should such a file exist.

Accessing Text Files

Being able to write information to text files, and read from them, is a basic operation in scripting. Many scripts save their results to text files, and read information from the same files. To establish a connection to a text file, you must obtain a reference to the second File Access component, the TextStream object. There are two methods of the FileSystemObject object that return a TextStream object, and they are the OpenTextFile and CreateTextFile, which open and create a text file respectively. The following statements show how to connect to an existing or new file. If the file MyFile.txt exists, the script displays its lines on a new page. If the file doesn't exist, then the script creates a new one and adds a few lines of text with the WriteLine method of the TextStream object. The next time you'll run the script, it will find the MyFile.txt file and display its lines.

▶ *Listing 15.1: The ReadWrite.asp Script*

```
<%
Set FSYS = _
        Server.CreateObject("Scripting.FileSystemObject")
FileName = "C:\Web\Scripts\MyFile.txt"
If FSYS.FileExists(FileName) Then
    Set TStream = FSYS.OpenTextFile(FileName)
    While Not TStream.AtEndOfStream
        Response.Write TStream.ReadLine
    Wend
Else
    Set TStream = FSYS.CreateTextFile(FileName)
    TStream.WriteLine "The is a new file created with "
    TStream.WriteLine "the CreateTextFile method of the"
    TStream.WriteLine "FileSystemObject object."
    TStream.WriteLine "You can use the same script to"
    TStream.WriteLine "read this file."
End If
Set TStream = Nothing
Set FSYS = Nothing
%>
```

The FileSystemObject object is a major scripting component, not only for developing Web applications, but also in Windows programming and scripting. The Windows Scripting Host (WSH) allows you to automate many tasks through scripting. You can use VBScript to write small programs that are equivalent to the batch files of DOS and, as you can understand, the File Access component is a major ingredient of these scripts.

The FileSystemObject Object

The FileSystemObject object exposes its functionality through a large number of methods, which are described later. It also exposes a single property, the *Drives* property, which is a collection that contains a member for each drive in the server computer's file system. Under the Drives collection there's a *Folders* collection, which contains a member for each folder in the selected drive. Under the Folders collection, in turn, there's a *Files* collection, which contains a member for each file in the selected folder. We'll start with the methods of the FileSystemObject object. The Drives, Folders and Files collections are discussed in three separate sections toward the end of the chapter.

Methods

The FileSystemObject object exposes a number of methods, which are described in the following sections. These methods let you access the attributes of the files and folders on the server's file system, as well as manipulate files and folders similar to the DOS commands (create and delete files and folders, copy or move them around, and so on).

BuildPath

The *BuildPath* method appends a file name to a path and returns a file's path name.The syntax for BuildPath is: `pathName = FSYS.BuildPath(path, name)`. *path* is an existing path name, to which the second argument, *name*, is appended. The path argument need not be an existing path, since the BuildPath method doesn't check the specified path against the file system.

The BuildPath method performs a simple concatenation operation, but it includes the necessary logic to determine whether it must insert a path separator between the two arguments or not. Without the BuildPath method, you'd have to examine the path argument and insert the path separator only if it's required. The following calls to the BuildPath method will return the same path name, which is `"C:\myFolder\Test.txt"`.

```
pName = FSYS.BuildPath("c:\myFolder", "test.txt")
pName = FSYS.BuildPath("c:\myFolder\", "test.txt")
```

The same path name will be returned by the following, rather unusual, call to the BuildPath method:

```
pName = FSYS.BuildPath("c:\myFolder", "\test.txt")
```

CopyFile

The *CopyFile* method copies one or more files from one location to another.

Syntax

```
FSYS.CopyFile source, destination [,overwrite]
```

source is the specification of the file(s) to be copied. If you want to specify multiple files, you must use wildcard characters. *destination* is the specification of the destination (the file or folder name where the files will be copied). The last argument, *overwrite*, is optional and it determines whether the destination files will be overwritten (if they exist). If True, the files are overwritten.

TIP If the destination file exists, but it's read-only, it will not be overwritten, even if you set the overwrite argument to True. You must use the Attributes property of the destination file to reset the file's read-only attribute and then copy the file. See the discussion of the File object's Attributes property for an example of how to overwrite read-only files.

Example

The following statement copies the file Sales.xls from its original folder to the folder OldFiles:

```
FSYS.CopyFile "C:\Current\Sales.xls", "C:\OldFiles\Sales.xls", True
```

If you're copying multiple files, the second argument must be a folder name, as shown in the following statement:

```
FSYS.CopyFile "C:\Current\*.xls", "C:\OldFiles\", True
```

If the destination doesn't end with the path separator, it is assumed to be a file name. If you're copying a single file, it will be copied and renamed accordingly. If you're copying multiple files, and the destination argument doesn't end with the path separator, then an error occurs.

CopyFolder

This method copies a folder from one location to another, including the subfolders (this is called *recursive copying*).

Syntax

```
FSYS.CopyFolder source, destination [, overwrite]
```

source is the path of the source folder (where files will be copied from) and may include wildcard characters, in case you want to copy selected files. The *destination* argument is the path of the destination folder (where the files will be copied to), and it may not contain wildcard characters. The last argument, *overwrite*, is optional, and it's a Boolean value that indicates whether existing folders can be overwritten. If it's True, the destination files can be overwritten, if they exist. To protect existing files in the destination folder, set it to False.

Example

To copy all the files from the folder MyDocuments to the folder Work-Docs\February, use the following statement:

```
FSYS.CopyFolder "C:\MyDocuments\", "C:\WorkDocs\Feb\"
```

in which *FSYS* is a properly declared FileSystemObject object variable. This statement will copy all files in the c:\MyDocuments folder, but it will ignore any subfolders. To copy a folder recursively (including the files in its subfolders), use a wildcard character, as in the following statement:

```
FSYS.CopyFolder "C:\MyDocuments\*", "C:\WorkDocs\Feb\"
```

Only the last component of the *source* path can be wildcard character. A *source* specification like "C:\MyFiles**" is invalid.

NOTE The CopyFolder method stops on the first error it encounters. This means that when the error occurs, some files have been copied already, and some have not. The CopyFolder method isn't going to move the copied files back to their source folder, nor will it continue with the remaining files.

CreateFolder

The CreateFolder method creates a new folder, whose path name is passed as an argument. This method creates a folder under an existing folder—you can't create nested new folders with a single call of the CreateFolder method.

Syntax

```
FSYS.CreateFolder folderName
```

folderName is the path of the folder to be created. If the folder exists already, a run-time error will be generated.

Example

The CreateFolder method doesn't create nested folders. If you call it with the argument shown in the following statement, the Folder1\Folder2 folder must exist:

```
FSYS.CreateFolder "c:\Folder1\Folder2\newFolder"
```

If the specified folder exists, an error will occur. You must call the FolderExists method to find out whether a folder by that name exists and call the CreateFolder method only if the folder doesn't exist. The following VBScript statements create a new folder, but only if it doesn't exist already.

▶ *Listing 15.2: Creating a New Folder*

```
<%
newFolderName = "C:\Store\SalesData\"
Set FSYS = _
         Server.CreateObject("Scripting.FileSystemObject")
If Not FSYS.FolderExists(newFolderName) Then
    FSYS.CreateFolder newFolderName
    Response.Write "Folder " & newFolderName & _
                   " created successfully"
Else
    Response.Write "Folder " & newFolderName & _
                   " exists already"
End If
Set FSYS = Nothing
%>
```

This code will work whether the folder C:\Store exists or not. If not, the FileSystemObject component isn't going to create nested folders. You should probably add the code to verify that the parent folder of the new folder (Store) exists already, before attempting to create the nested folder (SalesData). The safest method to do this is to use the Split() function to extract the component of the path and verify that all the components of the path up to the last one exist.

While working with nested folders (not necessarily creating new ones), you may find useful the following code segment that extracts the components of a path and stores them into an array.

▶ *Listing 15.3: Extracting a Path Name's Parts*

```
<%
pName = "c:\Folder1\Folder2\My Folder\My New Folder"
PathParts = Split(pName, "\")
Parts = UBound(PathParts)
For i=0 To Parts
    Response.Write PathParts(i)
    Response.Write "<BR>"
Next
%>
```

The array `PathParts()` contains all the components of the path, which are:

```
Parts(0) = "c:"
Parts(1) = "Folder1"
Parts(2) = "Folder2"
Parts(3) = "My Folder"
Parts(4) = "My New Folder"
```

CreateTextFile

This method creates a new text file and returns a reference to a TextStream object that can be used to read from or write to the file.

Syntax

```
Set TStream =
    FSYS.CreateTextFile(filename[, overwrite[, unicode]])
```

filename specifies the name of the file to be created and is the only required argument. *overwrite* is a Boolean value that indicates whether you can overwrite an existing file (if True) or not (if False). If you omit the *overwrite* argument, existing files are not overwritten. The last argument, *unicode*, indicates whether the file is created as a Unicode or an ASCII file. If the *unicode* argument is True, the new file will be created as a Unicode file; otherwise, it will be created as an ASCII file. If you omit the *unicode* argument, an ASCII file is assumed.

To create a new text file, create a FileSystemObject object variable, *FSYS*, and then call its CreateTextFile method as follows:

```
Set TStream = FSYS.CreateTextFile("c:\testfile.txt")
```

The *TStream* variable represents a TextStream object, whose methods are discussed later in this chapter. The WriteLine method, for example, writes a line to the text file and the ReadAll method returns a string with all the lines of the text file.

DeleteFile

The DeleteFile method deletes one or more files.

Syntax

```
FSYS.DeleteFile filespec [, force]
```

filespec is the name of the file(s) to delete and may contain wildcard characters. The *force* argument is optional, and it's a Boolean value that indicates whether read-only files will be deleted (if True) or not (if False).

The following statements delete a single file; all the TMP files and all files in the C:\MyDocuments\Site folder respectively:

```
FSYS.DeleteFile "C:\MyDocuments\Site\100399TMP.TXT"
FSYS.DeleteFile "C:\MyDocuments\Site\*.TMP"
FSYS.DeleteFile "C:\MyDocuments\Site\*.*"
```

Like the CopyFile method, the DeleteFile method stops on the first error it encounters. It's your responsibility to delete the remaining files, or restore the files already deleted. It's safer to iterate through the files you want to delete and call the Delete method for each one. This way you can handle errors as you encounter them.

DeleteFolder

This method deletes a specific folder and its contents, including its sub-folders and their files.

Syntax

```
FSYS.DeleteFolder folderspec[, force]
```

folderspec is the name of the folder to delete. The specified folder is deleted, regardless of whether it contains files or not (unlike the RMDIR command of DOS command). The *force* argument has the same meaning as it has with the DeleteFile method.

DriveExists, FileExists, FolderExists

These three methods return True if the specified drive, file or folder exists respectively. Use them to make sure a drive, folder or file exists before attempting to access it from within your script.

Syntax

```
FSYS.DriveExists(driveSpec)
FSYS.FileExists(fileSpec)
FSYS.FolderExists(folderSpec)
```

driveSpec is a drive specification, *fileSpec* is a file specification, and *folderSpec* is a folder specification. The *driveSpec* argument is always absolute, but the *fileSpec* and *folderSpec* arguments can be either absolute or relative to the current path.

Example

The following code segment processes the text file BestProducts.txt. If the file doesn't exist, the script displays a page with a message.

```
<%
Set FSYS = _
        Server.CreateObject("Scripting.FileSystemObject")
If FSYS.FileExists("C:\Web\Store\BestProducts.txt") Then
'     process text file
Else
    Response.Write "File BestProducts.txt not found"
End If
Set FSYS = Nothing
%>
```

Usually, scripts are not aware of absolute path names; they locate all the auxiliary files they need with relative references, so that they will function even when the Web application is moved to another folder. It's common to translate path names relative to the application's root folder to absolute path names with the Server.MapPath method. Assuming that Store is a folder under the Web application's root folder, the previous script could be written as follows:

```
<%
Set FSYS = _
        Server.CreateObject("Scripting.FileSystemObject")
```

```
absPathName = Server.MapPath("Store\Products.txt")
If FSYS.FileExists(absPathName) Then
'    process text file
Else
    Response.Write "File BestProducts.txt not found"
End If
Set FSYS = Nothing
%>
```

This script will work even after you move the application to another virtual folder. The sample code that uses absolute path names won't work. If this script resides in the default IIS folder, the *absPathName* variable will be `"C:\Inetpub\wwwroot\Store\Products.txt"`.

GetAbsolutePathName

This method returns the absolute path name of a file or folder.

Syntax

```
FSYS.GetAbsolutePathame pathSpec
```

PathSpec is the relative specification of the path to be changed to a complete (absolute), unambiguous path name. A path is complete and unambiguous if it can reference a file or folder from any other folder. A complete path ends with a path separator character (\) if it specifies the root folder of a mapped drive.

Example

Assuming the current directory is C:\Web\Store\, the GetAbsolutePathName method with different arguments returns the path shown on the following intended, bold line:

```
FSYS.GetAbsolutePathName("c:")
        c:\Web\Store
FSYS.GetAbsolutePathName("c:...")
        c:\Web
FSYS.GetAbsolutePathName("c:\\\")
        c:\
FSYS.GetAbsolutePathName("Images")
        c:\Web\Store\Images
FSYS.GetAbsolutePathName("c:\..\..\newProducts.txt")
        c:\newProducts.txt
```

GetBaseName

The GetBaseName method returns the name of the last component in a path. If the path name is that of a file, the extension is omitted.

Syntax

The syntax for GetBaseName is: FSYS.GetBaseName(path). *path* is the path specification of the component whose base name is returned. The GetBase-Name method returns a zero-length string if no component matches the path argument. Notice also that the *path* argument need not exist. The Get-BaseName method will return the base name of the last component in any path specification.

Example

If you call the GetBaseName method with the argument shown in the following statement, it will return the name of the file "My File.txt" without the extension.

```
pName = "c:\Folder1\Folder2\My Folder\My File.txt"
Response.Write FSYS.GetBaseName(pName)
```

The file name returned by the GetBaseName method need not exist on the server's file system. The GetBaseName simply extracts the last component in the path name. To retrieve the file's extension call the GetExtension method, discussed later in this chapter.

GetDrive

The GetDrive method returns a Drive object, which represents the drive specified with an argument. The Drive object exposes the attributes of the drive (such as its file system, the free space) with a number of properties, which are described in the section "The Drive Object," later in this chapter.

Syntax

```
objDrive = FSYS.GetDrive(driveSpec)
```

driveSpec is a drive specification and it can have one of the following formats:

- a drive letter (c)
- a drive letter followed by a colon (c:)
- a drive letter followed by a colon and a path separator (c:\)
- a network share specification (\\Toolkit\driveD)

To make sure that you're using the proper format, call the GetAbsolutePathName method, as shown next:

```
objDrive = FSYS.GetDrive(FSYS.GetAbsolutePathName(drvSpec))
```

GetDriveName

The GetDriveName returns a string containing the name of the drive of a specified path.

Syntax

```
drvName = FSYS.GetDriveName(driveSpec)
```

The *GetDriveName* method returns a string, which you can use as an argument to other methods, but you can't use it to retrieve information about the drive. The GetDriveName method works on the supplied argument; it doesn't check the *driveSpec* to make sure the drive exists and can be accessed.

GetExtensionName

The GetExtensionName returns the extension of the last component in a path.

Syntax

```
extName = FSYS.GetExtensionName(path)
```

path is the path specification for the component whose extension name is returned. The GetExtensionName method returns a zero-length string ("") if the path does not correspond to a file.

Example

If you call the GetExtensionName method with the argument shown in the following statement, it will return the string "txt":

```
<%
Set FSYS = _
        Server.CreateObject("Scripting.FileSystemObject")
pName = "c:\Folder1\Folder2\My Folder\My New Folder.txt"
Response.Write FSYS.GetExtensionName(pName)
Set FSYS = Nothing
%>
```

GetFile

The GetFile method returns a File object, which represents a specific file. It doesn't return the entire file, nor does it return the name of the file. It returns an object that references a file, and you can use this variable to access the file's properties. The File object and the members it exposes are discussed in the section "The File Object," later in this chapter.

Syntax

```
objFile = FSYS.GetFile(fileSpec)
```

fileSpec is a file's path and *objFile* is a File object. If the specified file doesn't exist, a run-time error occurs.

Example

To create a File object variable with the GetFile method, you must first create a FileSystemObject object variable and then call its GetFile method:

```
<%
Set FSYS = Server.CreateObject("Scripting.FileSystemObject")
Set thisFile = FSYS.GetFile("c:\autoexec.bat")
Set FSYS = Nothing
%>
```

The variable *thisFile* represents the file AUTOEXEC.BAT, and you can use its properties and methods to manipulate the file. For example, you can use its Size property (thisFile.Size) to find out the file's size, its DateCreated (this-File.DateCreated) property to find out when the file was created, and so on.

GetFileName

This method returns the last component of a path, which is a filename with its extension. Without the GetFileName method, you'd have to provide your own routine for parsing the path name.

Syntax

```
fileName=FSYS.GetFileName(fileSpec)
```

filename is the last component in the *fileSpec* argument.

Example

If you call the GetFileName method with the following argument:

```
fName = FSYS.GetFileName("c:\Web\Store\Images\OnSale.gif")
```

the variable *fName* will be "OnSale.gif".

Notice that, like many other methods of the FileSystemObject component, the GetFileName method works on its argument, regardless of whether such a path exists or not.

GetFolder

The GetFolder method returns a Folder object, which represents a specific folder. The GetFolder method doesn't return the name of the folder. It returns a reference to a folder, through which you can access the folder's properties. The Folder object and the members it exposes are discussed in the section "The Folder Object," later in this chapter.

Syntax

```
ObjFolder = FSYS.GetFolder(folderSpec)
```

folderSpec is a folder's path and *objFolder* is a Folder object. If the specified folder doesn't exist, a run-time error occurs.

Example

To create a Folder object variable with the GetFolder method, you must first create a FileSystemObject object variable and then call its GetFolder method:

```
Set thisFolder = FSYS.GetFolder("c:\windows\desktop")
```

The variable *thisFolder* represents the Desktop folder and you can use its properties and methods to manipulate the folder. For example, you can use its Size property (thisFolder.Size) to find out the folder's total size, its Date-Created (thisFolder.DateCreated) property to find out when the folder was created, and so on.

GetParentFolderName

This method returns a string with the name of the parent folder of the last component in a path.

Syntax

```
parentName = FSYS.GetParentFolder(pathSpec)
```

pathSpec is a path name, whose parent folder name you want to retrieve. Like many other methods, the GetParentFolder method doesn't resolve the pathSpec argument; it simply returns its parent folder's name, regardless of whether the path exists or not.

Example

The following statements will display the strings shown in bold, below the statements:

```
<%
Set FSYS = _
         Server.CreateObject("Scripting.FileSystemObject")
pathSpec="c:\Folder1\Folder2\My Folder\My TextFile.txt"
Response.Write FSYS.GetParentFolderName(pathspec)
Response.Write FSYS.GetBaseName(pathspec)
Response.Write FSYS.GetExtensionName(pathspec) Set FSYS = Nothing
%>
```

C:\Folder1\Folder2\My FolderMy
My TextFile
txt

GetSpecialFolder

Every Windows installation has a few special folders, which are located in different paths on different machines. The WindowsFolder is such an example. The GetSpecialFolder method returns a Folder object variable that represents the specified special folders on the host machine. In effect, it's identical to the GetFolder method when you call it with the path of the special folder.

Syntax

```
FSYS.GetSpecialFolder(folderspec)
```

folderSpec is the name of the special folder to be returned and it can have one of the following values as shown in Table 15.1.

TABLE 15.1: The special folders recognized by the GetSpecialFolder method

Constant	Value	Description
WindowsFolder	0	The Windows folder (it contains the files installed by the operating system).
SystemFolder	1	The Windows\System folder (it contains libraries, fonts, and device drivers).
TemporaryFolder	2	The Temp folder is used to store temporary files.

Example

The following statement returns True if the MyComponent.dll file exists in the System folder:

```
DLLName = _
    FSYS.BuildPath(FSYS.GetSpecialFolder(1) ,
    "MyComponent.dll")
If FSYS.FileExists(DLLName) Then
    ' perform an operation
Else
    Response.Write "Could not locate a library file"
End If
```

To retrieve the files on the host machine's desktop use the statement:

```
DTopFolderName = _
        FSYS.BuildPath(FSYS.GetSpecialFolder(0), "Desktop")
Set DTopFolder = FSYS.GetFolder(DTopFolderName)
Set DTopFiles = DtopFolder.GetFiles
```

GetTempName

This is a very useful method for creating random file and folder names. These components are used during operations that store intermediate results to the disk and are deleted after the completion of the operation.

Syntax

```
tmpName = FSYS.GetTempName
```

tmpName is a random file or folder name. The GetTempName won't create the file or folder for you; it simply returns a unique (and meaningless) name. Besides, the method doesn't know whether you'll use the name it returns as a file or folder name.

Example

The following script segment outlines an operation that creates temporary files and deletes them upon completion:

▶ *Listing 15.4: Using Temporary Files in a Script*

```
tmpFolder = FSYS.GetTempName
FSYS.CreateFolder tmpFolder
tmpFile1 = FSYS.BuildPath(tmpFolder, FSYS.GetTempName)
tmpFile2 = FSYS.BuildPath(tmpFolder, FSYS.GetTempName)
```

```
Set TStream1 = FSYS.CreateTextFile tmpFile1
Set TStream2 = FSYS.CreateTextFile tmpFile2
' statements to populate the files tmpFile1 and tmpFile2
TStream1.Close
TStream2.Close
FSYS.DeleteFolder tmpFolder
Set TStream1 = Nothing
Set TStream2 = Nothing
Set FSYS = Nothing
```

Notice that the script doesn't delete the individual files. By removing the parent folder, the temporary files are deleted as well.

MoveFile

The MoveFile method moves one or more files from one folder to another. You can use this method to rename a file as well (simply move it to a different file name in the same folder), or move the file to another folder and rename it at the same time.

Syntax

```
FSYS.MoveFile source, destination
```

source is the path of the file(s) to be moved and *destination* is the path to which the file(s) will be moved. The MoveFile method works identically to the Copy method, but the original files are deleted after they are copied. The *source* argument string can contain wildcard characters to move multiple files, but the destination argument can't contain wildcard characters. If you're copying a single file, the destination argument can be either a file name, or a folder name (in which case, the file is moved to the specified folder). If you're copying multiple files, then the *destination* must be a folder's path, to which the files will be moved. If the destination is an existing file's name, an error occurs.

MoveFolder

The MoveFolder method moves a folder to another location.

Syntax

```
FSYS.MoveFolder source, destination
```

source and *destination* are the specifications of the source and destination folders.

OpenTextFile

In addition to creating new text files, you can open existing files with the OpenTextFile method. Like the CreateTextFile method, the OpenTextFile method returns a TextStream object, whose methods you use to write to, or read from, an existing text file.

Syntax

```
Set TStream = FSYS.OpenTextFile(filename[, _
                    iomode[, create[, format]]])
```

The *filename* argument is the only required one. The value of the *iomode* argument is one of the constants shown, as you can see in Table 15.2.

TABLE 15.2: The Values of the OpenTextFile Method's iomode Argument

Constant	Value	Description
ForReading	1	The file is opened for reading existing data.
ForAppending	8	The file is opened for appending new data.
ForWriting	2	The file is opened for writing.

The optional *create* argument is a Boolean value that indicates whether a new file can be created if the specified filename doesn't exist. If it's True, then a new file is created. The last argument, *format*, is also optional and can be True (the file is opened in Unicode mode) or False (the file is opened in ASCII mode). If you omit the *format* argument, the file is opened using the system default (ASCII).

Example

To open a TextStream object for reading the lines of a text file, use the following statements:

```
Set TStream = _
    FSYS.OpenTextFile("c:\testfile.txt", ForReading)
```

Now that you have seen how the FileSystemObject object is used to open and create files, we are ready to discuss the TextStream object, which connects your application to text files. The FileSystemObject object has more methods, which allow you to access the various drives, copy and delete files or entire folders, and more. I'll come back to the methods of the FileSystemObject object, but first let's see how you can manipulate text files through the TextStream object.

The TextStream Object

This is the object that allows you to manipulate the contents of text files from within your Web applications. The TextStream object exposes a few properties that allow you to find out where exactly you are in the text files, as well as a number of methods for manipulating the contents of the file represented by the TextStream object.

Properties

The TextStream object's properties allow your code to know where the pointer is in the current TextStream and they're described in the following sections.

AtEndOfLine

This is a read-only property that returns True if the file pointer is at the end of a line in the TextStream object; otherwise, it returns, and is False.

Example

The AtEndOfLine property applies to files that are open for reading. You can use this property to read a line of characters, one at a time, with a loop similar to the following one:

```
Do While TStream.AtEndOfLine = False
    newChar = TStream.Read(1)
    {process character newChar}
Loop
```

This loop scans the file represented by the *TStream* object, and while it hasn't reached the end of the current line, it reads and processes another character. It's actually faster to read an entire line and process it, rather than read one character at a time.

AtEndOfStream

This is another read-only property that returns True if the file pointer is at the end of the TextStream object. The AtEndOfStream property applies only to TextStream files that are open for reading. You can use this property to read an entire file, one line at a time, with a loop such as the following one:

```
Do While TStream.AtEndOfStream = False
    newLine = TStream.ReadLine
    {process line}
Loop
```

Column

This read-only property returns the column number of the current character in a TextStream line. The first character in a line is in column 1. Use this property to read data arranged in columns, without tabs or other delimiters between them.

Line

Line is a read-only property that returns the current line number in the TextStream. The Line property of the first line in a TextStream object is 1. We use this property when writing data to a file and not when we read data from the file. After a file has been opened and before anything is written to it, the Line property is 1.

Methods

After you have created a TextStream object with the CreateTextFile or the OpenTextFile method of the FileSystemObject object, you can use the following methods to read from and write to the file. Notice that the TextStream object applies only to text files only, as its name implies.

Close

The Close method closes a TextStream object (in effect, it closes an open file). You should close all files when you no longer need them to conserve resources.

Syntax

```
TStream.Close
```

The Close method doesn't require any arguments and you can only close one file at a time by applying the Close method to the TStream object you want to close.

Read

The Read method reads a specified number of characters from a text file represented by a TextStream object.

Syntax

```
lineText = TStream.Read(characters)
```

characters is the number of characters to be read from the text file and *TStream* is a TextStream variable. The Read method returns a string with the specified number of characters.

Assuming that you have a text file with fields that start at specified locations, you can use the following loop to read them into an array.

```
<%
Set FSYS= _
        Server.CreateObject("Scripting.FileSystemObject")
pName = "c:\Site\Data\SampleData.txt"
Set pFile = FSYS.OpenTextFile(pName)
Response.Write "<TABLE>"
While Not pFile.AtEndOfStream
    ProdID = pFile.Read(18)
    ProdPrice = CCurr(pFile.Read(11))
    ProdUnits = CLng(pFile.Read(6))
    Response.Write "<TR>"
    Response.Write "<TD>" & ProdID & "</TD>"
    Response.Write "<TD>" & ProdPrice & "</TD>"
    Response.Write "<TD>" & ProdUnits & "</TD>"
    Response.Write "</TR>"
Wend
Response.Write "</TABLE>"
Set FSYS = Nothing
%>
```

The text file's structure is something like this:

```
12345678901234567890123456789012345
Product001      99.95       45
002             19.4        5
someproduct     9.34        314
```

The first line is there to help you locate the starting column of each field, and it's not part of the file; if it is, you must skip it. The values shown here could be product names, prices, and units in stock. Notice that numeric values are read as strings and converted to numeric values.

ReadAll

The ReadAll method reads the entire stream (the text file) and returns the text as a string variable.

Syntax

```
fileText = TStream.ReadAll
```

The *ReadAll* method returns a string that contains all the characters in the file. Successive lines are separated by a carriage return/line feed combination (vbCrLf).

Example

The following script reads all the lines of the text file Sales2000.txt, and then extracts all the individual lines and stores them into the Sales2000() array.

```
<%
Set FSYS = _
          Server.CreateObject("Scripting.FileSystemObject")
pName = "c:\Site\Data\SampleData.txt"
Set pFile = FSYS.OpenTextFile(pName)
allText = pFile.ReadAll
Sales2000 = Split(allText, vbCrLf)
Response.Write "There are " & Ubound(Sales2000) & " lines"
Set FSYS = Nothing
%>
```

ReadLine

The ReadLine method reads one line of text at a time (up to, but not including, the newline character) from the text file represented by a TextStream object and returns them in a string. The syntax is:

```
fileText = TStream.ReadLine
```

Example

In most situations you will iterate through the lines of the text file, reading and processing one line at a time, with a loop like the following one:

```
While Not TStream.AtEndOfStream
    Newline = TStream.ReadLine
    ' process NewLine
Wend
```

Skip

The Skip method skips a specified number of characters when reading a text file.

Syntax

```
TStream.Skip(characters)
```

characters is the number of characters to be skipped. The Skip method is used when we read data from a text file with the Read method. If you're reading the file's contents with the ReadLine method, then use the SkipLine method to skip a line.

SkipLine Method

The SkipLine method skips the next line of the text file. The syntax for Skip Line is: `TStream.SkipLine`. The characters of the skipped line are discarded, up to and including the next newline character.

Write

The Write method writes the specified string to the file represented by the TextStream object. The syntax for Write is: `TStream.Write(string)`. *string* is the string (literal or variable) to be written to the file. Strings are written to the file with no intervening spaces or characters between each string.

Example

The statements:

```
Write "This is a string"
Write "This is another string"
Write "And this is the last string"
```

are equivalent to the following call:

```
Write "This is a string" & _
     "This is another string" & _
     "And this is the last string"
```

(This is a single statement broken into multiple lines to fit on the printed page.) Use the WriteLine method to append multiple lines to the text file.

WriteBlankLines

The WriteBlankLines method writes a specified number of blank lines (newline characters) to the file. The syntax for Write BlankLines is: `TStream .WriteBlankLines(lines)`. *lines* is the number of blank lines to be inserted into the file.

WriteLine

The WriteLine method writes the specified string followed by a newline character to the file.

Syntax

```
TStream.WriteLine(string)
```

string is the text you want to write to the file. If you call the WriteLine method without an argument, a newline character (an empty line) is written to the file.

The following statements will write three lines to the text file. Notice that with the WriteLine method you don't have to specify the newline character.

```
WriteLine "This is a string"
WriteLine "This is another string"
WriteLine "And this is the last string"
```

The File Object

The File object represents a file and provides properties, which represent the various properties of the actual file. It also provides methods, which let you copy, move, and delete files.

To obtain a File object and examine its properties, use the following steps:

1. Create a FileSystemObject variable by declaring it as follows:

```
Set FSYS =
CreateObject("Scripting.FileSystemObject")
```

2. Use the *FSYS* variable to obtain an object that represents a specific file:

```
Set file = FSYS.GetFile(fileName)
```

where *fileName* is the desired file's path name (c:\Images\Sky.bmp, for example).

3. Then access the file's properties through the *file* object variable:

```
FName = file.Name
FDate = file.DateCreated
FSize = file.Size
```
and so on.

Properties

The File object provides the following properties. Many of these properties apply to the Folder object as well, which is discussed in the section "The Folder Object," later in this chapter.

Attributes

You use the Attributes property to read or set a file's attributes, such as read-only, archive, hidden, and so on). The attributes of a file are numeric values and a file can have multiple attributes. In this case, the file's attribute is the numeric sum of the values of the individual attributes.

Syntax

```
fileAttributes = thisFile.Attributes
```

fileAttributes is a numeric value that contains information about the file's attributes. You can also set selected attributes using the syntax:

```
thisFile.Attributes =
thisFile.Attributes Or attribute
```

The *attribute* variable can have any of the values shown in Table 15.2. To change multiple attributes, combine the corresponding values with the logical OR operator. Notice that the statement:

```
thisFile.Attributes = attribute
```

will turn on a specific attribute, but it will clear all other attributes. If a file is read-only and hidden, its Attributes property is 3 (1+2 according to Table 15.3). If you attempt to turn on the Archive attribute by setting its Attributes property to 32, the other two attributes will be cleared. By combining the new attribute (32) and the existing attributes with the OR operator, the file will be Read-only, Hidden, and Archive (its actual Attributes property will be 35).

TABLE 15.3: The attributes are read-write, except for the Volume, Directory, Alias, and Compressed, which are read-only.

Constant	Value	Description
Hidden	2	Hidden file
System	4	System file

Continued on next page

TABLE 15.3 CONTINUED: The attributes are read-write, except for the Volume, Directory, Alias, and Compressed, which are read-only.

Constant	Value	Description
Volume	8	Disk drive volume label (It's listed in the Object browser in VB when you select the FileSystem object.)
Directory	16	Folder or directory
Archive	32	File has changed since last backup
Alias	64	Link or shortcut
Compressed	2048	Compressed file

To find out whether a file is read-only, use this statement:

```
If thisFile.Attributes and 1 Then
     ' THE FILE IS READ-ONLY
End If
```

To delete the file, you must first change the read-only attribute of the file with a statement like the following one:

```
If thisFile.Attributes And 1 Then
    thisFile.Attributes = thisFile.Attributes + 1
End If
```

Normally, when we set a file's attributes, we don't reset the existing ones. For example, you may choose to add the hidden attribute from a file that has its read-only attribute set. To turn on the hidden attribute without affecting the other ones, use a statement such as:

```
thisFile.Attributes = thisFile.Attributes + 2
```

or

```
thisFile.Attributes = thisFile.Attributes Or 2
```

To remove a specific attribute, first find out whether this attribute is already set, and then subtract its value for the Attributes property's value. To remove the Hidden attribute, use a structure like the following one:

```
If thisFile.Attributes And 2 Then
    thisFile.Attributes = thisFile.Attributes - 2
End If
```

DateCreated

The DateCreated property is read-only and returns the date and time that the specified file or folder was created.

Syntax

```
crDate = thisFile.DateCreated
```

crDate is the date of creation of the file represented by the *thisFile* object variable.

Example

The following code segment calculates the age of a file in days. You can calculate the file's age in any other time interval by multiplying or dividing the file's age in days by the appropriate constant.

```
Set thisFile = FSYS.GetFile("c:\windows\Explorer.exe")
DateCreated = thisFile.DateCreated
Response.Write "The file is " & _
    Int(Now() - DateCreated) & _
    " days old"
```

To express this difference in hours, multiply the difference by 24.

DateLastAccessed

This property returns the date and time that the specified file or folder was last accessed. The DateLastAccessed property is identical in its use to the DateCreated property.

DateLastModified

This property returns the date and time that the specified file or folder was last modified. The DateLastModified property is identical in its use to the DateCreated property.

TIP The DateCreated, DateLastAccessed, and DateLastModified properties are read-only. Sometimes, we need to "touch" the files in a folder (change the DateLastAccessed property, for example). If you are using scripts or another automated mechanism for deleting or moving old files, touching them will enable you to exclude certain files from an automatic deletion operation. It would be convenient to touch a file by changing the value of its DateLastAccessed property, but this is impossible. To change the DateLastAccessed property, you should copy the file, delete the original, and then rename the copied file back to the name of the original file.

Drive

The Drive property returns the drive letter of the drive on which the specified file or folder resides. It's a read-only property and it applies to the File and Folder objects.

Name

The Name property returns or sets the name of a file or folder (the last part of the path). To find out the name of a file, use the statement:

```
FileObject.Name
```

To rename an existing file (or folder), use the following syntax:

```
FileObject.Name = new_name
```

where *newname* is the new name of the file represented by the FileObject variable (or the corresponding Folder object variable).

ParentFolder

The ParentFolder property returns a Folder object, which represents the parent folder of the specified file or folder. The ParentFolderis property is read-only. The syntax for this is: `thisFolder = objFolder.ParentFolder`.

Path

The Path property returns the path for a specified file or folder. If the file resides in the root folder, the backslash character (\) is not included. In other words, the path for the file `C:\Autoexec.bat` is "C:", not "C:\".

Example

If the *objFile* variable represents the file `c:\windows\desktop\TOC.doc`, then the expressions `FileObject.Path` returns the string "c:\windows\ desktop", and the expression `FileObject.Name` returns the string "TOC.doc" respectively.

ShortName

This property is similar to the Name property, but it returns the short name (eight-dot-three convention) of the specified file or folder.

Size

When applied to the File object, this property returns the size, in bytes, of the specified file. When applied to the Folder object, it returns the size, in bytes, of all files and subfolders contained in the folder.

Syntax

The syntax for Size is:

```
fileSize = objFolder.Size
```

fileSize is size of the file represented by the *objFolder* object variable in bytes.

Example

The following loop scans a folder and returns the names of the files, along with the Name, size, and property type of each file.

▶ *Listing 15.5: Displaying File Properties*

```
folderName="d:\ASP Book\ASP Samples\"
Set FSYS = _
        Server.CreateObject("Scripting.FileSystemObject")
Set ThisFolder = FSYS.GetFolder(folderName)
Set AllFiles = ThisFolder.Files
Response.Write "<TABLE>"
For Each file in AllFiles
    Response.Write "<TR>"
    Response.Write "<TD>" & file.Name & "</TD>"
    Response.Write "<TD>" & file.Type & "</TD>"
    Response.Write "<TD>" & file.Size & "</TD>"
    Response.Write "</TR>"
    totSize=totSize+file.size
Next
Response.Write "</TABLE>"
Response.write totSize
```

Type

The Type property returns information about a file's type. This information is the string associated with the file's extension ("Text Document" for files ending in .TXT, "Microsoft Word Document" for files ending in .DOC, and so on).

Syntax

The syntax for Type is as follows:

```
fileType = objFile.Type
```

fileType is the string describing the files type.

Methods

The File object provides a number of methods for moving files around, and they are very similar to the methods of the FileSystemObject object. They are described in the following sections. The difference between the methods of the FileSystemObject object and those of the File object is that with the File object's methods you can't operate on multiple files at once with the File object's methods. Each method applies to a specific file only.

Copy

This method copies a file (or folder) from one location to another. The syntax of the Copy method is:

```
FileObject.Copy destination [, overwrite]
```

destination is the new name of the file and may not contain wildcard characters. The second argument, *overwrite*, is optional, and it's a Boolean value that indicates whether existing files or folders are to be overwritten (if True) or not (if False).

Delete

This method deletes a file (or folder) it applies to. If applied to a Folder object, it will remove all the files in the folder represented by the Folder object, as well any subfolders, and all files in them.

Syntax

The syntax for delete is as follows:

```
FileObject.Delete force
```

The *force* argument is optional and indicates whether files with their read-only attributes should be deleted anyway (if True) or not (if False). Unlike the DOS RMDIR command, the Delete method removes a folder regardless of whether it contains files or subfolders.

Move

The Move method moves a file to a new location (it's equivalent to copying the file to a new location and then deleting the original file).

Syntax

```
FileObject.Move destination
```

destination is the path to which the file is moved. If the destination argument is a folder name, the file is moved to the specified folder with the same name. If the destination argument also contains a filename, too, the file is moved and renamed. You can call the Move method with a different filename to simply rename the original file.

OpenAsTextStream

This method opens a specified file and returns a TextStream object that can be used to read from or write to the file.

Syntax

```
FileObject.OpenAsTextStream(iomode, format)
```

Both arguments are optional. The *iomode* argument specifies whether the file will be opened for input, output, or appending, and it can have one of the values shown in Table 15.4.

TABLE 15.4: The Settings of the *iomode* Argument of the OpenAsTextStream Method

Constant	Value	Description
ForReading	1	Open a file for reading only. You can't write to this file.
ForWriting	2	Open a file for writing. If a file with the same name exists, its previous contents are overwritten.
ForAppending	8	Open a file and write to the end of the file.

The second argument, *format*, as shown in the syntax; indicates whether the file should be opened as the UnicCode or ASCII, and it can have one of the values shown in Table 15.5.

TABLE 15.5: The Settings of the *format* Argument of the OpenAsTextStream Method

Value	Description
-2	Opens the file using the system default
-1	Opens the file as Unicode
0	Opens the file as ASCII

The OpenAsTextStream method does the same thing as the OpenTextFile method of the FileSystemObject object. They both prepare a file for input or output. Use the OpenAsTextStream method when you have an object variable that represents the file you want to open. If you know the name of the file, use the OpenTextFile method of the FileSystemObject object.

The Files Collection

The Files Collection contains a File object for each file in a folder. To retrieve the Files collection of a folder, you must first create a Folder object and then call its Files method, as shown in the following example. The following script iterates through the files of a specific folder using the For Each...Next statement:

```
Set ThisFolder = FSYS.GetFolder(folderName)
Set AllFiles = ThisFolder.Files
For Each afile in AllFiles
    {process current file}
Next
```

In the loop's body, you can access the various properties of the current file, which is represented by the *afile* variable. The *afile* variable is a File object variable, whose properties and methods were discussed in the previous section. Its name is file.Name, its creation date is file.DateCreated, and so on.

The Drive Object

The Drive object represents a drive and it allows you to access the properties of a physical drive. To create a Drive object you must first create a

FileSystemObject object variable and then call its GetDrive method, using the drive's path as the argument:

```
Set FSYS = _
        Server.CreateObject("Scripting.FileSystemObject")
Set thisDrive = FSYS.GetDrive("C:")
```

After these lines are executed, the variable *thisDrive* represents the C: drive and you can access the drive's properties through the *thisDrive* variable's properties.

Properties

The Drive object exposes the following properties, which allow you to read a drive's attributes. Most of the properties are read-only, with the exception of the VolumeName property, which allows you to read or set the drive's volume name.

AvailableSpace

The AvailableSpace property returns the amount of space available to a user on the specified drive or network share. This is not always the same as the drive's FreeSpace property, which reports the total available space on the drive. The user may not be allowed to use all of it, so the AvailableSpace returns usually the same value as the FreeSpace property, but sometimes less.

Syntax

The syntax for nBytes is as follows:

```
nBytes = objFolder.AvailableSpace
```

nBytes is a long value and it's the number of available bytes. Divide it by 1024 to convert this number to KBytes, by (1024 * 1024) to convert it to MBytes and so on.

DriveLetter

DriveLetter is a read-only property that returns the drive letter of a physical drive or a network share. The syntax for Drive letter is: objDrive.Drive-Letter. If the drive is a network share that has not been mapped to a drive letter, the *DriveLetter* property returns an empty string.

DriveType

DriveType is a read-only property that returns a value indicating the type of a specified drive. The syntax for this is: drvType = obFolder.DriveType. *drvType* is an integer and it can be one of the values shown in Table 15.6.

TABLE 15.6: The types of drives

Value	Drive Type
0	Unknown
1	Removable
2	Fixed
3	Network Share
4	CD-ROM
5	RAM Disk

FileSystem

FileSystem is a read-only property that returns the type of file system in use for the specified drive. FileSystem has a syntax of:

```
FSYStemType = objFolder.FileSystem.
```

FsystemType is a string variable that can have one of the following values: FAT, NTFS, and CDFS. On other operating systems, the FileSystem return value may be include additional values.

FreeSpace

FreeSpace is a read-only property that returns the amount of free space available on the specified drive or network share.

Syntax

```
objDrive.FreeSpace
```

The value returned by the FreeSpace property is typically the same as that returned by the AvailableSpace property. Differences may occur between the two for computer systems that support quotas.

IsReady

IsReady is a read-only property that returns True if the specified drive is ready. This property applies to removable-media drives and CD-ROM drives It returns True only when the appropriate media is inserted and it's ready for access.

Syntax

```
status = objDrive.IsReady
```

status is a True/False value that indicates the status of the device (ready or not).

Path

This property returns the full path name of the Folder object to which it applies. The syntax for Path is: `pName = objFolder.Path`. *pName* is the path of the folder represented by the *objFolder* variable.

RootFolder

RootFolder is a read-only property that returns a Folder object representing the root folder of the specified drive.

Syntax

```
rootFolder = objDrive.RootFolder
```

rootFolder is a Folder object that corresponds to the root folder of the drive represented by the *objDrive* object variable. All the files and folders contained on the drive can be accessed using the returned Folder object. You can use the rootFolder.Folders collection to access the files in the drive's root folder, the rootFolder.Subfolders to access the subfolders under the root folder, and so on.

SerialNumber

SerialNumber is a read-only property that returns the decimal serial number used to uniquely identify a disk volume. The syntax is: `serialNum = objDrive.SerialNumber`. Use this property with removable drives to make sure that the correct disk is inserted in the drive.

ShareName

ShareName is a read-only property that returns the network share name for the specified drive.

353

Syntax

```
sharedDriveName = objDrive.ShareName
```

sharedDriveName the share name of the network drive represented by the *objDrive* object variable. If objDrive is not a network drive, the ShareName property returns an empty string.

TotalSize

TotalSize is a read-only property that returns the total space, in bytes, of a drive or network share.

Syntax

```
driveSize = objDrive.TotalSize
```

driveSize is the total capacity of the drive represented by the *objDrive* object variable, regardless of how much of the drive is available. The percentage of the free disk space is:

```
objDrive.FreeSpace / objDrive.TotalSize
```

VolumeName

The VolumeName property sets or returns the volume name of the specified drive.

Syntax

```
drvName = objDrive.VolumeName
objDrive.VolumeName = newname
```

Use the first form to retrieve the drive's volume name and the second one to set the drive's name.

The Folder Object

The Folder object represents a folder and allows you to manipulate the actual folders on the server's disk(s) through its properties and methods. To create a Folder object, you must first create a FileSystemObject object variable, and then call its GetFolder method, using the folder's path as the argument:

```
Set FSYS = _
        Server.CreateObject("Scripting.FileSystemObject")
Set thisFolder = FSYS.GetFolder("c:\windows\desktop")
```

After these lines are executed, the variable *thisFolder* represents the folder C:\Windows\Desktop, and you can manipulate the folder through the *thisFolder* variable's properties and methods.

Properties

The Folder object's properties are listed next. Since most of these properties are quite similar to corresponding properties of the File object, I'll just mention them briefly and focus on the unique properties of the Folder object.

Attributes

The Attributes property returns, or sets, the attributes of files or folders. See the discussion of the Attributes property of the File object for more information on using this property.

DateCreated

The DateCreated property returns the date and time that the specified file or folder was created, and it's read-only.

DateLastAccessed

The DateLastAccessed property returns the date and time that the specified file or folder was last accessed.

DateLastModified

The DateLastModified property returns the date and time that the specified file or folder was last modified.

Drive

The Drive property returns the letter of the drive on which the specified file or folder resides, and it's read-only. This property returns a Drive object variable, which you can use to access the drive's properties and/or its folder.

Files

The Files property returns a Files collection with one member for each file in the Folder object to which the property applies. The syntax for files is: `Files = objFolder.Files`. *Files* is a collection of File objects, one for each file in the folder referenced by the *objFolder* object.

Example

The statements in Listing 15.6 create a Files collection with the files in the Desktop folder of your system.

▶ Listing 15.6: Creating a Files Collection

```
<%
Set FSYS = _
        Server.CreateObject("Scripting.FileSystemObject")
Set aFolder = FSYS.GetFolder("C:\Windows\Desktop")
Set allFiles = aFolder.Files
For Each file In allFiles
    Response.Write file.Name & "<BR>"
Next
%>
```

IsRootFolder

This property returns True if the specified folder is the root folder; otherwise, it returns False. There is no equivalent property for the File object. You can use the IsRootFolder property to calculate the depth of a folder, with a subroutine such as the one in Listing 15.7.

▶ Listing 15.7: The GetDepth Function

```
Function GetDepth(FolderObject)
    If FolderObject.IsRootFolder Then
        Response.Write _
            "The specified folder is the root folder."
    Else
        Do Until FolderObject.IsRootFolder
            Set FolderObject = FolderObject.ParentFolder
            fdepth = fdepth + 1
        Loop
    GetDepth= fdepth
    End If
End Function
```

Notice that the GetDepth function expects a Folder object variable to be its argument. To call this function ,use a few statements like the following ones:

```
Set FSYS = Server.CreateObject("Scripting.FileSystemObject")
dpth = GetDepth(FSYS.GetFolder("c:\windows\desktop"))
Response.Write "The folder is " & dpth & " levels deep"
```

Name

This property returns the name of a specified file or folder (the last part of the folder's path name). See the Name property of the File object for details on using this property.

ParentFolder

This property returns the parent folder of a Folder object. See the discussion of the IsRootFolder property for an example.

Path

The Path property returns the path of a specified file or folder (the folder's path name without the last component). See the Path property of the File object for details on using this property.

ShortName

This property returns the short folder name (eight-dot-three convention) of a Folder or File object.

ShortPath

This property returns the short path name (eight-dot-three convention) of a Folder or File object.

Size

Size is a property of both files and folders, and it returns the size (in bytes) of a file, or it returns the total size of all the files in a folder and its sub-folders. To find out the size of a file or a folder, you must first create the appropriate File or Folder object variable and then read the variable's Size property:

```
Set FSYS = CreateObject("Scripting.FileSystemObject")
Set thisFile = _
        FSYS.GetFile("c:\windows\desktop\Message.doc")
```

```
Response.Write "The MESSAGE.DOC file is "
Response.Write thisFile.Size & " bytes long."
Set thisFolder = FSYS.GetFolder("c:\windows\")
Response.Write "The WINDOWS folder's size is " & _
Response.Write thisFolder.Size \ (1024*1024) & _
               " Mbytes."
```

SubFolders

The Subfolders property returns a Folders collection, which contains all the subfolders of a specific folder. To obtain the collection of subfolders in the folder C:\WINDOWS, create a FileSystemObject variable, then use its Get-Folder method to obtain a reference to the specific folder, and then create a Collection with its subfolders, using the SubFolders property, as shown in the following statements:

```
Set FSYS = CreateObject("Scripting.FileSystemObject")
Set thisFolder = FSYS.GetFolder("c:\windows")
Set allSubFolders = aFolder.SubFolders
For Each subFolder in allSubFolders
    {process folder subFolder}
Next
```

To scan the subfolder under the specified folder we use a For Each ... Next loop. To access the current folder's name in the loop's body use the expression subFolder.Name. The processing of the current folder could be to examine its files, and this is exactly what we are going to do in the last example of the chapter. The script in the section "Recursive Folder Scan" you'll see the script that scans a folder recursively.

Type

The type property returns a string with the description of the folder, if one is available. Only the special folders have a type (the Desktop and Recycle folders, for example).

The Folders Collection

The Folders collection contains a Folder object for each subfolder in a folder. The following script iterates through the subfolders of a specific folder using the For Each...Next statement.

▶ *Listing 15.8: Scanning a Folder's Subfolders*

```
Set FSYS = CreateObject("Scripting.FileSystemObject")
    FolderName = "C:\Site\Images"
Set ThisFolder = FSYS.GetFolder(folderName)
Set AllFolders = ThisFolder.SubFolders
For Each folder in AllFolders
    {process current folder}
Next
```

In the loop's body you can access the various properties of the current folder. Its name is folder.Name, its creation date is folder.DateCreated, and so on. The Folders collection exposes a method too, which is discussed next.

The Add Method

The Add method adds a new Folder object to a Folders collection. This method is similar to the CreateFolder method of the FileSystemObject object, but it doesn't require that you specify the complete path of the folder. The Add method of the Folder object creates a subfolder under the folder object to which it's applied.

Syntax

```
FolderObject.Add folderName
```

folderName is the name of the new folder to be added. If a folder by the same name exists already, a run-time error occurs.

Example

To add a new folder to the desktop, use the following statements:

```
Set dtopFolder=FSYS.GetFolder("C:\windows\Desktop")
Set dtopFolders=dtopFolder.SubFolders
dTopFolders.Add "Test Folder"
```

The *dtopFolder* variable represents the desktop folder. We call its SubFolders property to retrieve the list of folders under the Desktop folder and then we add a new folder with the Add method.

Recursive Folder Scan

Scanning a folder recursively (that is, scanning the folder's files and its sub-folders' files to any depth) is a very common operation in programming the file system. This section discusses the FolderScan script, which displays a tree-like structure with the files of a specified folder, including the files in its subfolders. Let's start with the actual script's listing, which is shown in Listing 15.9.

▶ *Listing 15.9: Scanning a folder recursively*

```
<%
Dim depth

Set FSYS = CreateObject("Scripting.FileSystemObject")
'    Specify here the folder you to map
folderSpec = "C:\InetPub\"
ScanFolder (folderSpec)
Response.Write "*** END OF DIRECTORY LISTING ***"
Response.End

Sub ScanFolder(folderSpec)
    depth = depth + 1
    Set thisFolder = FSYS.GetFolder(folderSpec)
    Set sFolders = thisFolder.SubFolders
    Set AllFiles = thisFolder.Files

    For i = 0 To depth
        indent = indent &
              "      "
    Next

    For Each fileItem In AllFiles
        Response.Write indent & FileItem.Name
        Response.Write "<BR>"
    Next

    For Each folderItem In sFolders
        indent = ""
        Response.Write "<B> " & folderItem.Path &
                    "</B><BR>"
        ScanFolder (folderItem.Path)
```

```
        Next
        depth=depth-1
End  Sub
%>
```

The script starts by calling the ScanFolder subroutine, passing the name of the folder to be scanned as argument. ScanFolder() creates an object variable, *thisFolder*, which represents the current folder. Then, the program creates a collection of the subfolders under the folder being scanned. This collection, *sFolders*, is scanned, and the names of the subfolders are displayed on the output page. After displaying each folder's name, the ScanFolder() subroutine displays the files in the current folder, by iterating through the AllFiles collection. Then it calls itself to scan the subfolders of the current folder. This process is repeated until all the folders immediately under the initial folder have been scanned (see Figure 15.1).

FIGURE 15.1: The output of the FolderScan script

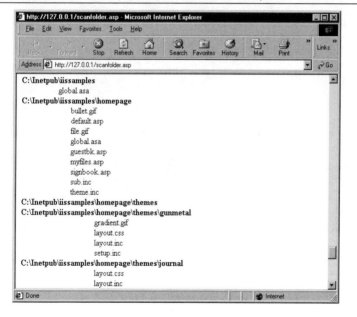

chapter 16

The Collaboration Data
Objects for NT Server

The Collaboration Data Objects for NT Server (CDONTS) is a component you can use to add e-mail capabilities to your Web applications. Very few Web sites offer e-mail capabilities to the viewers, but many sites use a mail server to send messages (and in many cases receive and process messages without user involvement). You could use the CDONTS component to send messages automatically—confirm orders, notify viewers about the status of their order, and so on.

The CDONTS component uses the SMTP (Simple Mail Transfer Protocol) server that comes with IIS. The SMTP server has its own message-storing mechanism, which is based on two folders: Inbox and Outbox. All incoming messages are gathered in the Inbox folder, but users can view their own messages only (the messages sent to the address specified when the user logs in). Outgoing messages are stored in the Outbox folder and delivered according to the delivery schedule.

The CDONTS deploys a fairly lengthy object model, certainly more complicated than the object models of most other components, which is shown in Figure 16.1. The Session object at the top of the object model represents the viewer's session in the mail server. By establishing a Session object that represents CDONTS, all of your scripts can access the current viewers' mailboxes.

The CDONTS component's functionality is more limited than that of Outlook or Exchange Server. For example, with CDONTS you don't have access to a folder with contacts or appointments. CDONTS doesn't even support methods to forward or reply to messages. You can perform these actions, but you must provide the code. CDONTS is a simple mail component, meant to send and receive messages from within Web applications, and it's not a complete mail system. You can add the missing functionality to your Web applications through the CDO component, which uses Exchange Server as the mail server and supports more advanced features, including appointments, discussions, message filtering, and so on.

In addition to CDONTS and CDO, there's a third version of the Collaboration Data Objects component, the CDO for Windows 2000. This version of CDO is functionally equivalent to CDONTS. Like CDONTS, CDO for Windows 2000 doesn't work with Exchange Server and doesn't support the MAPI protocols. This chapter focuses on CDONTS, because this is the simplest mail component and it's quite adequate for typical Web applications.

FIGURE 16.1: The CDONTS Object Model

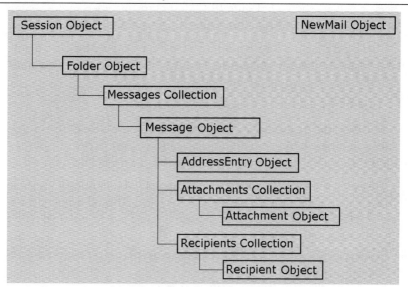

The CDONTS object model is presented in the following sections. We'll start with the Session object, which exposes nearly all of the component's functionality. The NewMail object encapsulates a little of the functionality of the Session object. Its purpose is to simplify the creation of new messages— something you can do through the Session object as well.

The Session Object

The Session object represents a user session and gives your script access to the current user's folders in the mail system. To access a user's messages, you must use the properties of the Session object, which are described next. But first, you must create a Session object variable with the following statement:

```
Set objSession = Server.CreateObject("CDONTS.Session")
```

The *objSession* variable represents a session; you can use it to access its members, which are shown in Figure 16.1. Most of the members of the Session object are objects, which in turn expose their own properties and methods.

To access their mailboxes, users must log in by supplying a username and an address. Before you can access any of the other objects, you must call the Session.LogonSMTP method as shown here:

```
objSession.LogonSMTP userName, userAddress
```

userName is the user's display name and *userAddress* is the address of the user. After the user has logged in successfully, you can access any of the objects shown in Figure 16.1 through the *objSession* variable.

To access the incoming messages, for example, you must open the Inbox folder and then retrieve the messages in the folder. The following statements create a Session variable, use it to access the Inbox folder, and then retrieve the messages in this folder:

```
Set objSession = Server.CreateObject("CDONTS.Session")
Set InFolder = _
    objSession.GetDefaultFolder(CdoDefaultFolderInbox)
Set InMessages = InFolder.Messages
```

InMessages is a collection and contains one member for each message. The constant CdoDefaultFolderInbox causes the GetDefaultFolder method to retrieve the Inbox folder.

> **TIP** There is no *include* file with the CDONTS constants. To use these constants, add a reference to the following type library to the GLOBAL.ASA file with the statement:
>
> ```
> <!--METADATA TYPE="TypeLib" NAME="Microsoft CDO"
> UUID="{0E064ADD-9D99-11D0-ABE5-00AA0064D470}"
> VERSION="1.2"-->
> ```

As you will see, it is possible to iterate through the incoming messages and examine their attributes, such as the message's sender and subject, the body of the message, and so on. *InFolder* is a Folder object that exposes its own properties and methods.

You can use the GetDefaultFolder method to retrieve the outgoing messages from the Outbox folder too. Moreover, you can create new messages by appending new members to the collection that represent the messages in the Outbox folder.

Common Properties

All the objects under the Session object in the object model shown in Figure 16.1 expose a few common properties, which are discussed in this section.

Application

This property returns the name of the current application. When you use the CDONTS component in ASP scripts, the Application object returns the following string:

```
"Collaboration Data Objects for NTS 1.2"
```

Class

The Class property returns the object's type; its value can be one of the constants shown in Table 16.1. Use the Class property to find out the object represented by a variable in your script.

TABLE 16.1: The Settings of the Class Property

Constant	Value	Object Type
CdoSession	0	Session
CdoFolder	2	Folder
CdoMsg	3	Message
CdoRecipient	4	Recipient
CdoAttachment	5	Attachment
CdoAddressEntry	8	AddressEntry
CdoMessages	16	Messages collection
CdoRecipients	17	Recipients collection
CdoAttachments	18	Attachments collection

Example   The following statements process the *objMsg* variable differently, depending on the type of object it represents:

```
Select Case objMsg.Class
    Case CdoMsg:
        ' PROCESS MESSAGE
    Case CdoMessages:
        ' PROCESS ALL MESSAGES IN FOLDER
End Select
```

Parent

The Parent property returns the parent of the object to which the method applies. The parent objects can be determined by looking at the object model of Figure 16.1. The parent of an AddressEntry object, for example, is a Message object, while the parent object of the Session object is Nothing.

Session

The Session property returns a reference to the Session object, to which any subordinate object belongs.

Collections

The two basic properties of the Session object are two collections, Inbox and Outbox, that contain the incoming and outgoing messages. Each collection returns a Folder object, and you can access the individual messages through the Folder object's members.

As collections, both the Inbox and Outbox objects expose the Item and Count properties. The Count property returns the number of messages in the folder, while Item lets you access a message in the folder based on its index.

Inbox

This property returns a Folder object that represents the user's Inbox folder and its syntax is:

```
Set iBox = objSession.Inbox
```

iBox is a Folder variable, which exposes the methods of the Folder object. See the section "The Folder Object," later in this chapter, for more details.

You can iterate through the messages of the selected folder with a For Each ... Next loop like the following one:

```
For Each msg In iBox
    ' STATEMENTS TO PROCESS CURRENT MESSAGE
Next
```

In the loop's body you can access the current message, which is represented by the *msg* object variable. The message's subject and text, for example can be read with the following expressions:

```
msg.Subject
msg.Text
```

Outbox

This property returns a Folder object that represents the user's Outbox folder. The syntax of the Outbox property is:

```
Set oBox = objSession.Outbox
```

oBox is a Folder variable, which exposes the methods of the Folder object. See the section "The Folder Object," later in this chapter, for more details. To iterate through the messages of the selected folder, use a For Each ... Next statement, as shown in previous discussion of the Inbox collection.

Properties

The Session object exposes three properties.

MessageFormat

This is a constant that specifies how the messages are encoded by default; it can have one of two values:

Constant	Value	Description
CdoMIME	0	Message is in MIME format.
CdoText	1	Message is in plain text.

You can overwrite the default encoding scheme for individual messages by setting the MessageFormat property of the Message object that represents the individual message.

Name

The Name property returns the display name that was used in the LogonSMTP method to log in to the current session. Use this property to find out the current user's display name and set the Sender field of a new message.

Version

This property returns the version number of the CDONTS component. The current version is 1.2.

Methods

The Session object exposes its functionality through the following four methods.

LogonSMTP

The LogonSMTP method allows your script to bind a Session object to a user's mailbox. This is the first statement you must call after creating the Session object. If you don't log in to the mail server, the script will not be able to access any of the objects subordinate to the Session object. Call the LogonSMTP method with the statement:

```
objSession.LogonSMTP userName, address
```

where *userName* is the user's name and *address* is their address.

To access your mailbox, use the following statements. After the execution of these statements, you'll be able to access all the objects of the CDONTS object model.

```
Set objSession = Server.CreateObject("CDONTS.Session")
objSession.LogonSMTP "Peter Evans", "evans@proto.net"
```

NOTE The LogonSMTP method does not authenticate users. If you specify a nonexisting address, a Session object will be created but it will not be bound to a mailbox.

LogOff

This method signals the end of the session and terminated the session. After calling the LogOff method, you should release the Session variable:

```
objSession.LogOff
Set objSession = Nothing
```

If you plan to reuse the *objSession* object, don't set it to Nothing. Just call its LogonSMTP method again to gain access to a different user's mailboxes.

GetDefaultFolder

The GetDefaultFolder method returns a Folder object, similar to the Inbox and Outbox properties, and it has the following syntax:

```
Set objFolder = objSession.GetDefaultFolder(folderType)
```

folderType is a constant that determines the folder to be retrieved, and its value can be one of these two constants:

Constant	Value	Description
CdoDefaultFolderInbox	1	Returns the Inbox folder
CdoDefaultFolderOutbox	2	Returns the Outbox folder

The *objFolder* variable is a Folder variable and contains all the messages in the selected folder. See the section "The Folder Object" for more information on accessing the messages in a folder.

SetLocaleIDs

The SetLocaleIDs method sets the user's locale. The locale determines the user's environment (language, date/time and currency formats, and so on). The default locale is the one you specify with the Regional Settings utility in the Control Panel. This information is stored in the Registry. To overwrite these settings for a specific session, use the SetLocaleIDs property, as shown:

```
objSession.SetLocaleIDs CodePageID
```

The value of the CodePageID argument is 1031 for German users, 1036 for French users, and so on.

The SetLocaleID method of the Session object must be called before the creation of a new Session object; it becomes the default locale for all new messages you will create through the Session object. The locale of all new messages you will create through the Messages collection's Add method will inherit the Session's locale. However, you can change the locale of a message created through the NewMail object by calling the NewMail object's SetLocaleIDs method. This method affects the locale of an individual message and not the locale of subsequent messages.

The Folder Object

The Folder object represents a folder in the mail system, such as the Inbox and Outbox folders. Incoming messages for the current user are stored in the Inbox folder, while outgoing messages are stored temporarily in the Outbox folder. Notice that SMTP doesn't support other folders, like the Sent and Deleted folders of other mail servers.

To access the messages in the Inbox folder, use the following statements. First, you must instantiate a Session object and then call the GetDefault-Folder method, or the Inbox property, to retrieve the folder with the incoming or outgoing messages.

```
Set objSession = Server.CreateObject("CDONTS.Session")
objSession.LogonSMTP "Peter Evans", evans@proto.net
Set objInbox = objSession.Inbox
' Set objInbox = _
'    objSession.GetDefaultFolder(CdoDefaultFolderInbox)
```

(The commented lines are equivalent to the Inbox method.) The *objInbox* variable represents the user's Inbox, and you can use the properties and methods of the *objInbox* variable to access the messages in the Inbox folder. The Folder object exposes a single property (its name) and a single collection (the collection of messages in the folder).

In addition to the four properties listed in the section "Common Properties," the Folder object supports one more property, *Name*, which returns a string with the name of the selected Folder object.

The Messages Collection

The information in the Inbox and Outbox folders is exposed to the application through the Messages collection of the Folder object. As you will see, it is possible to create new messages by adding a new member to this collection with the Add method. We'll discuss first how you can access the items of the Messages collection and then how to create new messages by adding a new item to the Messages collection.

The Messages collection represents the messages in the Folder object, to which the Messages collection applies. This collection contains one member for each message, and each message is represented by a Message object. You can select a member of the Messages collection, assign it to a Message object variable, and then use this object's properties to access the selected message. The Message object's members are discussed later in this chapter.

To select a member in the Messages collection, use the Item property of the collection:

```
Set objMessage = objInbox.Item(i)
```

where *i* is the index of the desired message.

To find out the number of messages in the folder, use the collection's Count property:

```
MsgCount = objMessage.Count
```

To iterate through the members of the Messages collection, use a For ... Next loop like the following:

```
Set objSession = Server.CreateObject("CDONTS.Session")
objSession.LogonSMTP "Peter Evans", "evans@proto.net"
Set objInbox = objSession.Inbox
MsgCount = objMessage.Count
For iMsg = 1 To MsgCount
    Set objMsg = objInbox.Item(iMsg)
    ' STATEMENTS TO PROCESS CURRENT MESSAGE
Next
```

In the loop's body, you can access the items of the current message through the Message object's properties. objMsg.Text is the message's body, objMsg.Subject is the message's subject, and so on.

Alternatively, you can use a For Each ... Next loop, as shown next:

```
For Each objMessage In objSession.Inbox
    ' STATEMENTS TO PROCESS CURRENT MESSAGE
Next
```

The variable *objMessage* represents a different message at each iteration.

To access the messages in the Outbox folder, use the same statements, but replace the Inbox folder name with Outbox:

```
Set objOutbox = objSession.Outbox
```

After the execution of this statement, the *objOutbox* variable represents the messages in the Outbox folder and you can access individual messages through the Messages collection.

The Messages collection exposes two methods, which allow you to create new messages and delete existing ones. Notice that you can't edit, or add new messages in the Inbox folder; you can only delete selected messages with the Delete method.

Methods

Add

The Add method creates a new Message object and appends it to the Messages collection by means of the following syntax:

```
Set objMsg = objOutbox.Add(subject, text, importance)
```

The new message is represented by a Message object, and you can use this object's properties to set the items of the new message (its body, subject, and so on). To send the message, call the *objMsg* variable's Send method (see the description of the Message object, later in this chapter).

All arguments are optional, as you can set the message's items through the properties of the *objMsg* variable. *subject* is the message's subject, *text* is the message's body, and *importance* is a constant that represents the importance of the message. The importance argument can have one of the values listed in Table 16.2.

TABLE 16.2: The Values of the Importance Argument of the Messages.Add Method

Constant	Value	Description
CdoLow	0	Low priority (message will be delivered during hours of low system usage)
CdoNormal	1	Normal priority (message will be delivered during regular delivery schedule)
CdoHigh	2	High priority (message will be delivered immediately—if possible)

You must also set the message's recipient(s) through the Recipients collection of the Message object. After that, you can call the Message.Send method to actually send the message.

NOTE You can also create a new message with the NewMail object, which is discussed in the section "The NewMail Object," later in this chapter.

Delete

Just as you can add messages, you can delete messages from the Messages collection. The Delete method of the Messages collection deletes *all* the messages in the selected folder and cannot be undone.

```
' THIS STATEMENT WILL DELETE ALL
' MESSAGES IN THE FOLDER !!!
ObjInbox.Messages.Delete
```

To delete an individual message, you must extract the message you want to delete from the Messages collection, store it into a Message variable, and then call the Delete method of this variable. For more information about deleting individual messages, see the description of the Delete method in the section "The Message Object."

Chances are you'll never have to call this method, so now that you've learned what the Delete method does, you should probably forget about this method; use it only to implement a feature like "Empty Mailbox."

GetFirst, GetNext, GetPrevious, GetLast

You saw how to set up a For ... Next loop that scans all the members of the Messages collection. The Messages collection exposes a few more methods that allow you to navigate through its members. These methods are similar to the navigational methods of the Recordset object (see Chapter 9 for more information on the ADO Recordset object), and they're appropriately named GetFirst, GetNext, GetPrevious, and GetLast. In every case, the syntax is identical:

```
Set objMsg = objFolder.GetFirst
```

Notice that, unlike the ADO navigational methods, these methods return an object, which is the message they land on. If the navigational method doesn't land on a valid message, it will return the value Nothing. This will happen if you call the GetNext method while you're on the last message, for example.

The order of the messages in the Folder object is unknown, so there's no real advantage on using these methods in the place of the For ... Next loop.

The Message Object

This is the most important object of the CDONTS component; it represents a message. Message objects expose properties that correspond to the elements of a message. Two of the object's properties are actually collections, and they represent the message's recipients and the message's attachments. In addition, the Message object exposes two methods that allow you to either delete or send a message.

Properties

The properties of the Message object represent the items of a message, including its subject, body, and so on. Some of the properties are collections, which are described in their own sections after the properties. These properties are read-only for incoming messages; the mail server, wisely, doesn't allow you to change selected items of the incoming messages.

Attachments

A message may have one or more attachments, which are represented as members of a collection. This is the Attachments collection, made up of individual Attachment objects. Each Attachment object represents an individual attachment. See the description of the Attachment object, later in this chapter, for more information.

ContentBase

This property is the base of all URLs used in the message's body; ContentBase is used only with messages that contain HTML code (MIME HTML type).

ContentID

This is the Content-ID header of the message's body. Set this property to "text/html" for messages that are formatted as HTML documents.

ContentLocation

This property is the Content location header of a MIME attachment.

HTMLText

This is the message's HTML formatted body. See the description of the Text property (below) for more information on the message's body.

Importance

The Importance property is a constant that can have one of the same values as the importance arguments of the Message.Add method, shown previously in Table 16.2.

MessageFormat

This is a constant that specifies how the message was encoded. The settings of the MessageFormat property are:

Constant	Value	Description
CdoMIME	0	Message is in MIME format.
CdoText	1	Message is in plain text.

Recipients

This is a collection of Recipient objects that represent the message's recipients. (See the description of the Recipient object, later in this chapter, for more information.) The Recipients collection supports the Add method, which uses the following format to add a new recipient to the Recipients collection:

```
objMsg.Recipients.Add(name, address, type)
```

The *name, address,* and *type* arguments are the same as the properties with the same names.

The following statements create two new recipients for a new message using the Add method:

```
Set objMsg = Server.CreateObject("CDONTS.NewMail")
objMsg.Recipients.Add("Richard", "richard@earth.net", 1)
objMsg.Recipients.Add("M. Shuster", "mikeS@earth.net", 2)
```

The first recipient is the message's primary destination (the To field) and the second recipient is the message's carbon copy recipient.

To remove an entry from the list of recipients, use the Recipients collection's Delete method.

Sender

The Sender property is an AddressEntry object, representing the user that sent the message. The AddressEntry object is discussed in the section "The AddressEntry Object," later in this chapter. To find out the display name of the sender of the message represented by the *objMsg* variable, use the following expression:

```
Set objSender = objMessage.Sender
Response.Write objSender.Name
```

Size

This is the message's size, in bytes. The Size property includes the size of the attachments, in addition to the length of the message's body and subject.

Subject

This is a string with the message's subject. The following expression displays the message's size and subject:

```
Response.Write "Subject " & objMsg.Subject
Response.Write "Size " & objMsg.Size
```

Text

This is the message's body in text format. The CDONTS component maintains two copies of the message's body, one in plain text format and another one in HTML. When the Text property is edited, CDO adjusts the HTML-Text property to reflect the changes. For incoming messages, you can read either property.

TimeReceived

TimeReceived, naturally, is the date and time that the message arrived, for messages in the Inbox folder.

TimeSent

TimeSent represents the date and time that the message was sent, for messages in the Outbox folder. Notice that the TimeReceived and TimeSent properties are set by the mail server and you can't change the values of these properties.

Methods

The Message object exposes two methods that allow you to delete incoming messages and send outgoing messages (in effect, remove messages from the Inbox folder and add new messages to the Outbox folder).

Delete

The Delete method of the Message object deletes the message on which it's applied. Call it with the syntax:

```
objMessage.Delete
```

The message represented by the *objMessage* variable will be deleted as soon as you release the *objMessage* variable. You can still access the message's properties, even after you have called the Delete method. It's common to set the *objMessage* variable to Nothing immediately after calling the Delete method.

If you call the Delete method of a member of the Messages collection, as shown in the following example, the message will be deleted immediately.

```
objInbox.Messages(2).Delete
```

This time the message will be deleted upon execution of the Delete method.

The deletion of a message can't be undone, so you should prompt users before deleting a message. Notice that the deletion of a message can't be undone, not even by MTS, should the deletion be part of a transaction. You could store the message to another folder, like the Deleted folder, but the CDONTS component doesn't allow you to access folders other than the Inbox and Outbox folders. If you must save the deleted messages somewhere, send them to a special account. This account's Inbox folder will hold all deleted messages, for all users. To retrieve a specific user's deleted messages, you must scan the entire folder and isolate the messages of the user.

Example The following statements delete all the messages that were sent more than a month ago:

```
Set objSession = Server.CreateObject("CDONTS.Session")
objSession.LogonSMTP "Evans", "evans@proto.net"
Set objInbox = objSession.GetDefaultFolder(1)
For Each msg In objInbox
    If DateDiff("m", Now, Msg.TimeSent) > 1 Then
        msg.Delete
        DelMssgs = DelMssgs + 1
    End If
Next
Response.Write "Deleted " & DelMssgs &  " messages"
Set objInbox = Nothing
Set objSession = Nothing
```

Send

The Send method sends the selected message. To send a message, or add a new member to the Outbox folder (or create a NewMail object), set the items of the new message object accordingly, and finally send the message with the Send method. You can use the Add method of the Messages collection to create a new message, but the message won't be sent before you call its Send method. Once you call the Send method, the message will be sent according to the mail system's schedule. Also, the Send method applies only to messages in the Outbox folder, or messages created with the NewMail object. You can't apply the Send method to a message in the Inbox folder. The SMTP doesn't provide any methods for forwarding messages or replying to messages. These operations must be coded manually.

In the syntax objMessage.Send, *objMessage* is a Message variable representing a new message. Here are the steps to create and send a message:

```
Set objOutbox = objSession.GetDefaultFolder(2)
Set objMessage = objSession.Messages.Add
objMessage.Text = "the message's body"
objMessage.Subject = "the message's subject"
objMessage.Recipients.Add("Richard", "richard@earth.org")
objMessage.Send
```

The Recipients collection contains the list of recipients for the message to which it applies. For more information on the Recipient object, see the section "The Recipient Object."

After sending a message with the Send method, you can still access its items, as long as the *objMessage* variable remains in memory. This variable will be released when you set it to Nothing, or when the script terminates.

The Attachment Object

The Attachments collection contains one or more members that correspond to the current message's attachments. If the message has no attachments, this collection is empty. The members of the Attachments collection are Attachment objects, and you can use the members of the Attachment object to access the message's attachments, or create new attachments for an existing message.

Properties

Most of the properties of the Attachment object are very similar to the properties of the Message object.

ContentBase

This property is the base of all URLs used in the message's body and is used only with messages that contain HTML code (MIME HTML type).

ContentID

This is the Content-ID header of a MIME attachment.

ContentLocation

The ContentLocation property is the Content location header of a MIME attachment.

Name

This is the attachment's name (and it's usually the name of the attached file).

Source

If the attachment is a file, this property is not set. For embedded messages, the Source property returns (or sets) the Message object to be embedded.

Type

This is the attachment type; it can be 1 (the attachment is a file) or 4 (the attachment is an embedded message). The following statements iterate through the attachments of the message represented by the *objMessage* variable and display the names of the attachments:

```
Set objMessage = objInbox.Messages.Item(1)
For Each objAttch In objMessage.Attachments
    ' STATEMENTS TO PROCESS CURRENT ATTACHMENT
Next
```

The *objAttch* variable represents a different attachment at each iteration of the loop. To save the attachment to a disk file, for example, you can call the WriteToFile method, which is discussed in the following section.

Methods

The methods of the Attachment object allow you to process the attachments of incoming messages.

Delete

The Delete method removes the selected Attachment object from the Attachments collection. Notice that you can remove attachments only from unsent messages in the Outbox folder. You can't delete attachments from incoming messages.

Delete attachments with the statement:

```
objAttachments.Item(n).Delete
```

objAttachments is a properly declared Attachments collection. The attachment won't be deleted instantly. If you set a variable to represent the attachment you want to delete, as in the following statement, you will still be able to reference the attachment through the *objAttch* variable.

```
Set objAttch = objMessage.Attachments.Item(n)
```

ReadFromFile

This method reads an attachment's contents from a file and can be used only if the attachment is a file; use this format:

```
objAttch.ReadFromFile fileName
```

fileName is the file to be attached and *objAttch* is an Attachment object.

WriteToFile

This method saves an attachment to a file on the server's file system. The syntax of the WriteToFile method is:

```
objAttch.WriteToFile fileName
```

fileName is the path of a file, where the attachment will be saved. The WriteToFile method overwrites the specified file if it exists already, so make sure the file doesn't exist before you attempt to save an attachment to disk.

Example Let's say you want to store all the attachments of a message to the disk. You must set up a loop to iterate through the message's attachments and store each file attachment to a different file. Here's the loop that stores the attachments:

```
Set objSession = Server.CreateObject("CDONTS.Session")
objSession.LogonSMTP "Peter Evans", "evans@proto.net"
```

```
Set objInbox = objSession.GetDefaultFolder(1)
Set objMessage = objInbox.Messages.Item(1)
For Each objAttch In objMessage.Attachments
    If objAttch.Type = 1 Then
    objAttch.WriteToFile "C:\AttachDocs\" & objAttch.Name
    End If
Next
```

The Recipient Object

The Recipients collection is made up of Recipient objects, and each Recipient object represents a message's destination. The Recipient object does not represent a user, even though it has a Name and an Address property. Each Recipient object contains the information you need to set a message's destination, and it exposes three properties. In other words, SMTP doesn't allow you to create a collection of recipients and use them as destinations for your messages. Instead, you must create a new Recipient object for each recipient of the message. Some of the these objects may be used as primary destinations for the message, others as carbon copy recipients, and others as blind carbon copy recipients.

Properties

The Recipient object exposes a few properties that determine the attributes and the type of the message's recipient.

Name

This is the recipient's display name. For incoming messages, the display name is determined by the mail system on which the message originated. You set this property for outgoing messages; it may not match the real user's display name.

Address

This is the address of the recipient, and it must be a full address of the form user@domain.com, even if the destination is another user in the same domain.

Type

The Type property determines the type of the recipient (from the message's point of view), and its value must be one of these constants:

Constant	Value	Description
CdoTo	1	The Recipient object is the message's primary destination.
CdoCC	2	The Recipient object is the message's carbon copy destination.
CdoBCC	3	The Recipient object is the message's blind carbon copy destination.

Each message has a single primary destination, but it can have multiple CC or BCC destinations.

Method

The Recipient object exposes a single method, which removes a recipient from the Recipients collection.

Delete

The Delete method removes the selected recipient from the current list of recipients. Notice that the Recipients collection supports a Delete method as well, except that method deletes *all* the recipients in the collection. To delete only one recipient, use the syntax:

```
objRecipient.Delete
objMessage.Recipients.Item(index).Delete
```

When you delete a recipient represented by a Recipient object, the Delete method is called without an argument. If you want to apply the Delete method to an item of the Recipients collection, you must specify the index of the member to be deleted.

Example   Notice that the order of the recipients in the Recipients collection is unknown. We usually scan the entire collection and apply the Delete method to the items that meet our criteria. To remove the users that belong to a specific domain from the list of recipients, use the following statements:

```
For Each objRecip In objMsg.Recipients
    If Right(objRecip.Address, 11) = "@domain.com" Then
        objRecip.Delete
    End If
Next
```

The same operation can be implemented with the following loop:

```
For i = 0 To ObjRecipients.Count
    If Right(objRecip.Item(i), 11) = "@domain.com" Then
        objRecip.Item(i).Delete
    End If
Next
```

The result of the Delete method of the Recipient object is irreversible. The Recipient object you delete, however, is not removed instantly from memory. You can still access the properties of the deleted Recipient object, which will be permanently removed from memory when you release the object variable that represents the recipient.

The AddressEntry Object

Incoming messages have a sender too, and the sender's information is stored in an AddressEntry object. The AddressEntry object supports three properties, which are the Name (the sender's display name), Address (the sender's address), and Type properties. The Type property is always "SMTP."

To retrieve the sender of a message, use a statement like the following one:

```
Set objSender = objMsg.Sender
```

Use the *objSender* variable's properties to retrieve information about the sender, as shown in the following statements:

```
Response.Write "Message sent by " & objSender.Name
Response.Write "<BR>"
Response.Write "Reply to " & objSender.Address
```

Notice that the AddressEntry object can represent the message's Sender property, not the recipients of a message. Moreover, you can't use the Sender of an incoming message as the Recipient of an outgoing message. You must create a new Recipient object, copy the individual fields from an AddressEntry object, and then attach the Recipient object to a new message's Recipients collection.

The NewMail Object

The NewMail object allows you to send messages from within your Web application. To use this object, you must first instantiate it with the following statement:

```
Set objNewMessage = Server.CreateObject("CDONTS.NewMail")
```

The NewMail object exposes a single method, the Send method, whose syntax is shown here:

```
objNewMessage.Send(From, To, Subject, Body, Importance)
```

All arguments are optional and correspond to the fields of a new message. The simplest method to create and send a message is to call the New-Mail object's Send method:

```
ObjNewMessage.Send ("evans@proto.com", _
    "Richard@earth.net", _
    "Sample Message", _
    "This is the message's body")
```

Properties

The NewMail object supports several properties that correspond to the attributes of a message, like the From, To, and Text properties. In addition, the NewMail object exposes properties that are not mapped to arguments of the Send method.

Bcc

This property adds one or more recipients to the list of blind carbon copy recipients. Its syntax is identical to the syntax of the To property, which is described later in this section.

Body

The Body property sets the message's text and its syntax is:

```
objMessage.Body = message_text
```

message_text is the body of the message, and it's plain text. If the message includes HTML tags, set the BodyFormat property accordingly.

BodyFormat

This property determines the text format of a new message created with the NewMail object, using the syntax:

```
objMessage.BodyFormat = bFormat
```

bFormat is a constant that can have one of the values shown here.

Constant	Value	Description
CdoBodyFormatHTML	0	The Body property is to include Hypertext Markup Language (HTML).
CdoBodyFormatText	1	The Body property is to be exclusively in plain text (default value).

Cc

This property adds one or more recipients to the list of carbon copy recipients. Its syntax is identical to the syntax of the To property, which is described later in this section.

ContentBase

The ContentBase property specifies the base of all the URLs in the body of the message created with the NewMail object. It has the following structure:

```
objNewMail.ContentBase = cBase
```

cBase is the content base of the body of a MIME message. If the message is plain text, this property is ignored.

ContentLocation

This is the Content location header of a MIME attachment. If the Content-Location property is set, it's treated as an absolute or relative URL. If the

ContentBase property is also set, ContentLocation is treated as relative and is appended to the base provided by ContentBase to produce the absolute URL.

From

The From property sets the full address of the message's sender, as follows:

```
objMessage.From = sender
```

sender is a full address, like user@domain.com. A message can't have multiple senders, so each time you set this property its previous value is overwritten.

The From property is a string; you can't assign a Recipient or AddressEntry object to this property.

Importance

Use this property to set the message's priority. See the Importance property of the Message object for more information on the property's settings.

MailFormat

This property determines the encoding of a new message's attachments, in the following statement:

```
objMessage.MailFormat = msgFormat
```

msgFormat is a constant that's either 0 (the message is in MIME format) or 1 (the message is in plain text format). The names of the constants are CdoMailFormatMime (0) and CdoMailFormatText (1). This property applies to attachments and URLs you may include in the message's body.

Subject

The Subject property is a string that sets the message's subject.

To

Use the To property to add one or more recipients to a message created with the NewMail object, with this syntax:

```
objMessage.To = recipients
```

recipients is the full address of a recipient. To specify multiple primary recipients, supply multiple addresses separated by semicolons, as in the following statement:

```
objMessage.To = "user1@domain1.com;user2@domain2.com"
```

In addition to the To property, you can specify recipients with the To argument of the Send method as well. If you use both methods, then all the recipients will receive the message.

Value

Use the Value property to pass headers other than the ones that can be specified with the properties of the NewMail object. Most mail systems will recognize the "Reply-To" header. The Message object doesn't support a Reply-To property, but you can include your reply address as header with a statement like the following one:

```
objMsg.Value("Reply-To") = "Evangelos<EP@sybex.com>"
```

Version

This property returns the version number of the CDONTS component. The current version is 1.2.

Methods

The NewMail object exposes the methods you need to compose new messages and attach files to them, and then sends them to their destination.

AttachFile

The AttachFile method adds an attachment to the message. Use this method to attach files to the message. The attached files are separate from the message's body, and the recipient must open them on the local computer.

Syntax   The syntax of the AttachFile method is:

```
objNewMail.AttachFile(source, fileName, encodingMethod)
```

source is the path and filename of the file to be attached to the message; it's the only mandatory argument. *fileName* is the file's name, as it will appear in the list of attachments to the recipient. If this argument is omitted, the filename from the *source* parameter is used. The *encodingMethod* argument is also optional and determines the method of encoding for the attachment. It can have one of these values:

Setting	Value	Description
CdoEncodingUUencode	0	The attachment is to be in UUEncode format (default).
CdoEncodingBase64	1	The attachment is to be in base 64 format.

If MailFormat is set to CdoMailFormatMime, the default value is CdoEncodingBase64. However, if you add an attachment encoded in base 64 format, the value of the MailFormat property is automatically set to CdoMailFormatMime.

AttachURL

The AttachURL method adds a URL as an attachment to the message. Use this method to embed binary information in the message's body. If the message's body is in HTML format, for example, and references an image with the <IMG> tag, you must attach the image file to the message with the AttachURL method.

Syntax   Use this syntax to call the AttachURL method:

```
objNewMail.AttachURL(source, contentLocation, _
                    contentBase, encodingMethod)
```

source is the full path and filename of the resource to be attached to the message. *contentLocation* is the absolute or relative prefix for the attached URL. The following two arguments are optional: *contentBase* is the base for the URL used to reference this attachment; the *encodingMethod* argument is the same as for the AttachFile method and can have one of the values shown for AttachFile above.

The URL of the attachment isn't complete unless you specify at least the *contentLocation* argument. If you supply the *contentBase* argument as well, it is appended to the *contentLocation* argument to produce the full URL of the attachment.

Example   The following statements create a new message with the NewMail object, set the message's body to an HTML document and insert an image. The only reason we format this message's body as HTML is to include an image. The image is attached to the message with the AttachURL method.

```
Set objMail = CreateObject("CDONTS.NewMail")
HTMLstr = "<HTML>"
HTMLstr = HTMLstr & "<H1>It's a girl!</H1>"
HTMLstr = HTMLstr & "<CENTER>"
HTMLstr = HTMLstr & "<IMG SRC=Baby1.gif>"
HTMLstr = HTMLstr & "</HTML>"
objMail.Body = HTMLstr
objMail.AttachURL "C:\Images\Family\Baby1.gif", _
    "Cute baby"
myMail.From = "me@MyDomain.com"
myMail.To = "user1@Domain1.com;user2@Domain1.com"
myMail.Subject = "Baby Pics"
myMail.BodyFormat = 0
myMail.MailFormat = 0
myMail.Send
```

The first few lines set up the *HTMLstr* variable, which contains the message's body in HTML format. This string is assigned to the message's Body property. The message's BodyFormat is set to 0 to indicate that the body must be interpreted as an HTML document. The image referenced in the body is also attached to the message with the AttachURL method. The last statement calls the object's Send method to deliver the message.

You could have also specified the URL of the attachment using the ContentBase property, as follows:

```
ObjMail.ContentBase = "C:\Images\Family\"
objMail.AttachURL "Baby1.gif", "Cute baby"
```

This notation makes sense when the message contains multiple attachments, and they're all stored in the same folder.

Send

The Send method sends the NewMail object to the specified recipients, using the following syntax:

```
objNewMail.Send(from, to, subject, body, importance)
```

All the arguments of the Send method are optional; you can specify the same information by setting the corresponding properties of the NewMail object. For simple text messages, however, the Send method allows you to set up a message and send it with a single statement.

The *from* argument is the full address of the sender. The target mail server will use this address to reply to the message. The *to* argument is the full address of the message's recipient. You can specify multiple recipients by separating their addresses with a semicolon. The next two arguments, *subject* and *body,* are the message's subject and body. The last argument, *importance*, is the priority of the message and can have one of the values shown in Table 16.1.

Example   The following statements create and send the same message as in the example of the previous section, but without the attachment:

```
Set objMail = CreateObject("CDONTS.NewMail")
ObjMail.Send me@MyDomain.com, _
        user1@Domain1.com;user2@Domain1.com, _
        "Baby Pics" , _
        "Connect to my Web site to see the pictures", 1
```

SetLocaleIDs

The SetLocaleIDs method sets the user's locale. The locale determines the user's environment (language, date/time and currency formats, and so on). See the discussion of the SetLocaleIDs method of the Session object for more information.

chapter 17

The Counters and Page Counter Components

The two components discussed in this chapter maintain counter values for your Web applications. Web applications maintain a large number of counters to keep track of viewers, viewers that open certain pages, viewers that place items in their basket, and so on. *The Counters component* allows you to create any number of counter variables and access them from within any script of an application. *The Page Counter component* is quite similar, only it maintains a counter for each page of the site. It's still your responsibility to increase each page's counter, but you don't have to name the counters for each page. The Page Counter component maintains a counter variable for each page and all you need to access it is the page's path. If you don't need to access a page's counter from within another script, you don't even need that.

The Counters Component

There was a time when displaying the count of visitors to a Web site was considered a novelty. Nowadays, there are hardly any sites that display the number of visitors they have served. Internally, however, all sites keep track of the number of visitors. Not only that, but they deploy software to keep track of where the visitors came from (the site that referred them to your site), how much time they spend on your site, how many pages they view on the average, and so on.

As you recall from our discussion of the Session and Application objects, it's fairly easy to create and maintain counter variables. The implication with this approach is that you must save their values to a text file and reload them every time the application starts. The simplest method of maintaining counter variables is to use the Counters component. The Counters component is instantiated from within the GLOBAL.ASA file and it applies to the entire site. This means that you can't implement Session level counters with the Counter component, but then again, Session level counters are uncommon.

The values of the counters you set up with the Counters component are stored in the COUNTERS.TXT file and you can examine this file, if you want to. The counters are stored there every time they change value and their values are automatically reloaded every time the Web server starts, so you won't have to worry about losing your counters' values.

Using the Counters Component

To use the Counters component, you must create an object variable like the following one:

```
Set objCounters = Server.CreateObject("MSWC.Counters")
```

This statement is placed in the Application_OnStart event, so that the objCounters object variable will be accessible by all the scripts in the application. Here's a typical Application_OnStart event of an application that uses the Counters component:

```
Sub Application_OnStart
    Dim objCounters
    Set objCounters = Server.CreateObject("MSWC.Counters")
End Sub
```

Alternatively, you can insert the following tag in the GLOBAL.ASA file to create an instance of the Counters component:

```
<OBJECT RUNAT=Server SCOPE=Application
ID=objCounters PROGID="MSWC.Counters">
</OBJECT>
```

Although the scope of the object is Application, if you have multiple applications running on your Web server they will all see the *objCounter* variable.

Finally, if you're using the Personal Web Server, you don't have to explicitly create an instance of the Counters component. A Counters component is created by default in the GLOBAL.ASA file in the default virtual folder and you can access it as if it were a built-in ASP object.

As soon as you create an instance of the Counters component, the COUNTERS.TXT file will be created in the folder of the Web server as the COUNTERS.DLL file, which implements the Counters component. There's no reason to edit this file ever.

The names of the counters are Unicode strings, so you can practically name your counters anything you like. There is no limit on the number of counters you can use in an application either. Just remember that the counters are visible from within any script.

The Counters component exposes the members you need to read and increment (or reset) the counters. These members are methods of the

Counters component and their implementation contains all the logic to avoid concurrency issues. In other words, you don't have to call the Lock and Unlock methods of the Application object, as you should do when changing the values of regular variables.

The Counters component is commonly used to implement viewer-voting systems. Viewers can cast their vote on a subject on any page of the application. The script that intercepts the results need only increment the proper counter. Any other script can see the results by reading the values of the designated counters. For example, you may be polling viewers about the most popular software, or the next president. You can insert a short Form with the options and the Submit button on all the pages of your site. After a viewer has voted, you can stop including this Form to the following pages. You can also send a cookie to the client computer indicating that the specific viewer has voted, so that you won't prompt them again, either in the current session, or in a future session.

Or, you can give your viewers the chance to vote on various issues. Again, all you need is a set of counters, which will be incremented accordingly. For your polls to be meaningful, however, you must be able to leave a cookie to the client computer. If not, the same viewers will be asked again and again to vote on the same issue. This will not only bias the poll, it will make your site look less than professional.

As you will see in the following section, you can retrieve and display the results of the poll as they come in. All you have to do is retrieve the values of the appropriate counters and display them on a new page.

Methods

The Counters component exposes a number of methods to create, store, increment, and retrieve any number of individual counters. Each counter is identified by a name and you must specify this name along when you call any of the methods described in the following sections.

Get

The Get method returns the current value of a counter.

Syntax

```
ctrValue = objCounters.Get(counterName)
```

ctrValue is the current value of the counter *counterName*.

Example

Let's say you're polling your viewers about the software they're using. The items you're interested in are their operating system (Windows, Linux, and MacOS) and their browser (Netscape Communicator and Internet Explorer). You'll see how to set up the counters in the following sections. To read the value of all counters and display the results on a table, use the following statements:

```
<H1>The Results Are In!</H1>
<H2>Operating Systems</H2>
<TABLE>
<TR>
<TD>Windows</TD>
<TD> <% = objCounters.Get("OSWindows") %></TD></TR>
<TD>Linux</TD>
<TD> <% = objCounters.Get("OSLinux") %></TD></TR>
<TD>Mac OS</TD>
<TD> <% = objCounters.Get("OSMacOS") %></TD></TR>
</TABLE>
```

Increment

The Increment method increases the value of the specified counter by one. If the specified counter doesn't exist, a new one is created and its value is set to one.

Syntax

```
objCounter.Increment counterName
```

counterName is the name of the counter to be increased.

Example

Let's continue our polling example. In this section you'll see the statements that create the necessary counters.

First, you must create an instance of the Counters component in the GLOBAL.ASA file:

```
<OBJECT ID="objCounters"
    RUNAT="Server" SCOPE="Application"
    PROGID="MSWC.Counters">
</OBJECT>
```

You don't need to explicitly create the counters. The counters will be created automatically the first time you attempt to increase their value. When a viewer selects the Linux option, you must increase the OSLinux counter with the statement:

```
objCounters.Increment "OSLinux"
```

The first time this statement will be executed, the OSLinux counter will be created and set to 1. All subsequent times the OSLinux counter will be increased by one.

Remove

The Remove method deletes an existing counter.

Syntax

```
objCounters.Remove counterName
```

counterName is the name of the counter you want to delete.

> **NOTE** You shouldn't have to remove counters, but if you do, make sure you don't reference them any longer in your scripts. A reference to a counter that doesn't exist may cause a run-time error. If you attempt to increase the value of a counter that doesn't exist, a new one will be automatically created and set to one. If you attempt to read the value of a counter that doesn't exist, however, then a run-time error will occur.

Set

This method sets the value of a counter to a specified value. If the counter doesn't exist, a new one is created and set to the specified value.

Syntax

```
objCoutners.Set counterName, initialValue
```

counterName is the name of the counter you want to set and *initialValue* is the counter's initial value. Notice that the Set method should be called only once. If you call the method after using the counter for a while, you'll reset it back to specified initial value.

Example

Let's take the polling example a little further. If, for any reason, you want to start counting from a different value, use the Set method to set a counter's initial value. The following statements set the initial value of the OSWindows counter to 1000:

```
objCounters.Increment "OSWindows"
If objCounters.Get("OSWindows") = 1 Then
    ObjCounters.Set "OSWindows", 1001
End If
```

Notice that we increase the counter's value and then examine the value of the OSWindows counter. If its value is 1 (which means that the counter has just been initialized), we set it to 1001.

The Page Counter Component

Unlike the Counters component that maintains counters for the application, the Page Counter component counts visits to specific pages of your site. The values of the counters for each page are periodically stored to the Hit Count Data File, so you won't lose much information in the case of an unexpected server shutdown. The Hit Count Data File is a text file and you can retrieve the value of any page's count from within your scripts. You can also process the same file with an external application.

To use the Page Counter component, create an object variable with the following statement:

```
Set objPageCntr =
        Server.CreateObject("MSWC.PageCounter")
```

You use the *objPageCntr* variable to increase a page's hit counter, retrieve the number of hits for a page, or reset the number of hits. You can't assign a fake value to this variable and you can't increment it by more than one (unless you call the PageHit method repeatedly). You can only reset its value to zero, if you wish.

Methods

The Page Counter component exposes three methods, which are described next.

Hits

This method returns the hit count for a specific page.

Syntax

```
pageHits = objPageCntr.Hits(pagePath)
```

pageHits is the number of times the page specified by the *pagePath* argument was hit. If the *pagePath* argument is omitted, then the Hits method returns the count of hits for the current page.

Example

The hits for each page are usually reported by special software. However, you can use the Page Counter component to maintain the hits for each page and display these values on the pages of your site. The following few statements will display the number of hits at the upper left corner of each page, but only when the viewer WebManager is viewing them:

```
<%
If Session("UserName") = "WebManager" Then
    Response.Write "Page Hits " & objPageCntr.Hits
Else
    ObjPageCntr.PageHit
End If
%>
```

If you insert these statements at the beginning of each page (they must be ASP pages, not HTML pages), you'll be able to browse your site and view how many times each page was viewed (as long as you identify yourself as the WebManager). Notice that the page counter is not increased every time the WebManager views it.

You can create a separate file with the statements shown earlier and incorporate it in every page with the #include directive.

PageHit

This method increases the number of hits for a specific page.

Syntax

```
objPageCntr.PageHit
```

The PageHit method doesn't accept any arguments. This means that you can't increase the hot count for a page from within another page's script.

NOTE Unlike the Page Counter component of ASP 2.0, this version of the component doesn't automatically increase the page's hit counter every time the page is requested. The reason for this is that you may want to choose when to increase the hit counter. For example, you probably won't increase the page's counter every time a member of the development team opens it, or every time the page is requested from a workstation of your own LAN— use the first two or three group of digits in the IP address of the viewer (REMOTE_ADDR server variable) to find out if the page was requested from a member of the development team.

Reset

The Reset method sets the count of hits for a specific page to zero.

Syntax

```
objPageCntr.Reset pagePath
```

pagePath is the path of the page whose hit count you want to reset. If the *pagePath* argument is omitted, then the Reset method applies to the current page.

chapter 18

Other Components

T he last chapter of this guide describes several components with very specific functionality and a small number of members. These components are not used frequently in Web development, but you may find them useful in certain scripts. The components discussed in this chapter are simple and straightforward to use; and they are:

MyInfo   This component stores information about the site. It stores much of the information you provide as you build a home page with the Home Page Wizard of the Personal Web server.

Permission Checker   This component allows you to determine whether the current user has the right to access a specific page.

Tools   This component exposes a few useful methods, such as the generation of random integer values.

IISLog   This component allows developers to access the log files (which are maintained by the IIS). They contain information about the requests made to the server and its responses.

The MyInfo Component

The MyInfo component maintains a list of properties with personal information, such as the site administrator's name, address, and display choices. These properties are the settings you supply to the Home Page Wizard of the Personal Web Server, but you can use the MyInfo component to store additional pairs of keys and values.

The MyInfo object can have properties in addition to the ones documented here. IIS and the Personal Web Server implement the properties listed below, but you can add your own properties. The same information could be stored in Application variables, but the MyInfo component makes it simpler to maintain a list of personal properties that apply to the entire site.

Using the MyInfo Component

To use the MyInfo component in your script, you must first instantiate a reference of the component with a statement like the following one in the GLOBAL.ASA file:

```
Set Application("objInfo") = Server.CreateVariable("MSWC.MyInfo")
```

Since there's only one MyInfo object per site, the statement shown above must appear in the Application_OnStart event in the GLOBAL.ASA file and the *objInfo* variable must be treated as an Application variable. Alternatively, you can create an instance of the MyInfo component with the following <OBJECT> statement in the GLOBAL.ASA file:

```
<OBJECT
RUNAT=Server
SCOPE=Session
ID=objInfo
PROGID="MSWC.MyInfo">
</OBJECT>
```

NOTE For the Personal Web Server, the <OBJECT> declaration that creates MyInfo has already been included in the GLOBAL.ASA file in the default virtual directory. You can work with MyInfo as if it were a built-in object.

To set one of the MyInfo object's properties use a statement like the following ones:

```
Application("objInfo").PersonalName = "Your Name"
Application("objInfo").PersonalMail = "Your EMail"
```

You can also create new attributes by simply assigning a string value to a new key value. For example, you can create the *PersonalTitle* attribute, with the following statement:

```
<%
Application("objInfo").PersonalTitle = "Mr."
%>
```

This statement creates a new attribute, names it *PersonalTitle*, and assigns the value "Mr." to the new attribute. The new attribute will be stored along with the other MyInfo attributes. Despite the names of the MyInfo object's properties, you can use this object to store values that remain constant throughout a site.

The values of MyInfo properties are stored in XML format in the file MyInfo.xml. You can find this file in the INETSRV folder of your server. The last statement, for instance, will add the following entry to the MyInfo.xml file:

```
<PersonalTitle>Mr.</>
```

Properties

The MyInfo component exposes a number of properties only, which are listed in the following table. Notice that these aren't really properties of the MyInfo object; you can append as many keys, and their corresponding values, to the MyInfo object as you need. The Home Page Wizard of the Personal Web Server will add the keys in Table 18.1, if you have used it to create a home page.

TABLE 18.1: The Properties of the MyInfo Component

Property	Description
PageType	This property returns information about the page type, as you set it in the Home Page Wizard of the Personal Web Server and it can have one of the following values: 1 About My Company 2 About My Life 3 About My School 4 About My Organization 5 About My Community
PersonalName	Returns the site owner's name.
PersonalAddress	Returns the site owner's address.
PersonalPhone	Returns the site owner's phone number.
PersonalMail	Returns the site owner's e-mail address.
PersonalWords	Returns additional text associated with the site owner.
CompanyName	Returns the name of the site owner's company.
CompanyAddress	Returns the address of the site owner's company.
CompanyPhone	Returns the phone number of the site owner's company.
CompanyDepartment	Returns the site owner's department name.
CompanyWords	Returns additional text associated with the site owner's company.
HomeOccupation	Returns the site owner's occupation.

Continued on next page

TABLE 18.1 CONTINUED: The Properties of the MyInfo Component

Property	Description
Home People	Returns a string with the names of other people the owner lives with (for personal home pages).
HomeWords	Returns additional text associated with the site owner.
SchoolName	Returns the name of the site owner's school.
SchoolAddress	Returns the address of the site owner's school.
SchoolPhone	Returns the phone number of the site owner's school.
SchoolDepartment	Returns the site owner's department or class.
SchoolWords	Returns text associated with the site owner's school.
OrganizationName	Returns the name of the organization featured on the site.
OrganizationAddress	Returns the address of the organization.
OrganizationPhone	Returns the phone number of the organization.
OrganizationWords	Returns text describing the organization.
CommunityName	Returns the name of the community featured on the site.
CommunityLocation	Returns the location of the community.
CommunityPopulation	Returns the population of the community.
CommunityWords	Returns text describing the community.
URL(n)	Returns the "nth" user-defined URL—a collection that allows you to store multiple user-defined URLs for easy access. This property corresponds to the "nth" link description in the property URLWords.
URLWords(n)	Returns a string containing the "nth" user-defined description of a link. Corresponds to the nth URL in the property URL.
Style	Returns the relative URL (starting with '/') of a style sheet.
Background	Returns the background for the site.
Title	Returns the user-defined title for the home page.
Guestbook	Returns -1 if the guest book should be available on the site. Otherwise, returns 0.
Messages	Returns -1 if the private message form should be available on the site. Otherwise, returns 0.

The Permission Checker Component

Windows NT (and Windows 2000) has a well-defined security model, which allows system administrators to control what resources each user can access. The Permission Checker component extends this functionality to the Web. If users are forced to log on to the system with a user name/password combination, the Permission Checker component allows you to determine whether a user has been granted permissions to read a file.

You can use the Permission Checker component to customize an ASP-based page for different types of users. For example, if a Web page contains hyperlinks, you can use the Permission Checker component to test whether the user has permissions for the target Web pages and format as hyperlinks only the destinations the viewer has permission to view.

Using the Permission Checker Component

To use the Permission Checker component in a script, you must first instantiate the component with a statement like the following one:

```
Set objPermissions = Server.CreateObject("MSWC.PermissionChecker")
```

Then, you can use the *objPermissions* object variable's HasAccess method to determine whether the viewer has permission to view the page. The viewer is validated by the operating system and you don't have to maintain lists of user names and passwords.

NOTE This component is not installed with IIS in Windows NT. You can install it from the Microsoft Web site at: http://www.microsoft.com/iis/, or from the CD included with the IIS Resource Kit. The component is installed automatically with IIS under Windows 2000.

The HasAccess Method

The Permission Checker component exposes a single member, the *HasAccess* method. This method determines whether the user has permissions to access a specified file.

Syntax

```
objPermission.HasAccess( filePath )
```

filePath is the physical or virtual path of a file. If the Web user has access to view the file, the method returns True. If not, it returns False. The HasAccess method will also return False if the file doesn't exist.

Examples

The following example uses the HasAccess method to test whether the current user has access to the Enter.htm file, which can be viewed by members only. If the viewer hasn't logged in as a member, then the viewer is redirected to the NonMembers.htm page.

```
<%
Set objPermission =
            Server.CreateObject("MSWC.PermissionChecker")
FName = "c:\Site\Members\Members.htm"
If objPermission.HasAccess(FName) Then
    Response.Redirect "Members.htm"
Else
    Response.Redirect "NonMembers.htm"
End If
%>
```

IIS supports three types of password authentication in any combination. The types are the anonymous, basic, and Windows NT Challenge/Response method (NTLM). If you allow viewers to connect anonymously, then the Permissions Checker component will not be able to authenticate viewers (in anonymous authentication, all viewers use the same account). Use the PermissionChecker Properties window (under the Web site's Properties window) to disable the anonymous authentication.

Windows 2000 supports more password authentication methods, but it doesn't make any difference which one you use. The Permission Checker component requires that viewers do not connect to the server anonymously. Once a viewer has been authenticated by the operating system, you can use the HasAccess method to find out whether a viewer has access to specific documents.

If your site contains pages that can be viewed by the public, as well as pages that are restricted to members of an intranet, you should enable anonymous authentication and specify one of the other two password authentication methods (Basic or NTLM). For the secure pages, you can deny anonymous access. The server will attempt to authenticate the user by using either NTLM or Basic password authentication.

When a user attempts to read one of the restricted pages, you can examine the LOGON_USER server variable to find out whether the current viewer has logged in anonymously (the LOGON_USER variable will be empty). If so, set the Response.Status to the "401 Unauthorized" error message. This will cause IIS to attempt to identify the user by using NTLM or Basic authentication.

```
<%
If Request("LOGON_USER") = "" Then
    Response.Status = "401 Unauthorized"
End if
%>
```

The usual dialog box prompting the viewer to enter his ID and a password will appear on the client's screen. The login information will be transmitted to the server and Windows will authenticate the viewer.

The Tools Component

The Tools component provides a few methods that enable you to add specific functionality to your Web pages. The methods of the current implementation of the Tools component provide very specific functionality, but the component will most likely be enhanced with additional methods in the future.

Using the Tools Component

To use the Tools component, you must first instantiate the component in your script with the following statement:

```
Set objTools = Server.CreateObject("MSWC.Tools")
```

The *objTools* variable exposes a few useful methods, which are discussed in the following sections.

> **NOTE** In Personal Web Server for Windows 95, the Tools object is already included in the GLOBAL.ASA file in the default virtual directory. You can work with the Tools object as if it were a built-in object, without having to instantiate the component. If you're using IIS, the Tools component can be found in the IIS Resource Kit.

Methods

The Tools component exposes its functionality through the following methods.

FileExists

The *FileExists* method checks for the presence of a file and it returns True if the specified URL exists within a published directory. If not, it returns False.

Syntax

```
objTools.FileExists(URL)
```

URL is a string that specifies the relative URL of the file you are checking. The argument a relative URL, because FileExists only checks the existence of files published on the site to which the page belongs.

Example

The following code segment displays the image of the selected product. It assumes that the images are GIFs and named after the product's ID. If there is an image that matches the ID of the selected product, it's displayed. If not, a generic image (the NoImage.gif file) is displayed.

```
<%
ID = objRS.Fields("ProductID")
ImgFileName = ImgPath & "\" & ID & ".gif"
If Tools.FileExists(ImgFileName) then
    Response.Write "<img src=" & ImgFileName & ">"
Else
    Response.Write "<img src=NoImage.gif>"
End If
%>
```

Owner

The *Owner* method checks whether the current user is the site administrator. It returns True if the name and password submitted in the request header matches the Administrator name and password set in the Personal Web Server interface. Otherwise it returns False.

Syntax

```
objTools.Owner
```

Currently, the Owner method works with Personal Web Server for Macintosh only.

PluginExists

The *PluginExists* method checks whether the specified Macintosh server plug-in exists. It returns True if the specified Macintosh server plug-in name is currently registered, otherwise, it returns False.

Syntax

```
objTools.PluginExists(PluginName)
```

PluginName is a string that specifies the name of the server plug-in.

Currently, the PluginExists method works with Personal Web Server for Macintosh only.

ProcessForm

The *ProcessForm* method processes the contents of a form that has been submitted by a visitor to the Web site. The processing consists of writing the data to a local file on the server and is independent of any other processing that takes place in the script. The ProcessForm method reads a template file, inserts information that you specify in the template file and stores the result to the output file.

Syntax

```
objTools.ProcessForm outputFileURL, _
                templateURL, [insertionPoint]
```

outputFileURL is a string containing the relative URL of the file to which the processed data is written. If the specified output file does not exist, the server creates it. The *templateURL* argument is another string containing the relative URL of the file that contains the template, or instructions, for processing the data. The last argument, *insertionPoint*, is optional and it indicates where in the output file to insert the processed data. If omitted, the data is appended to the output file.

The template file is usually an HTML file, but it may contain ASP statements. The statement will not be executed by the ProcessForm method. Instead, any section statements between the <% and %> delimiters will be written to the output file as is. When the output file is accessed, the script sections will be executed as usual.

If you want to insert a script in the template file and have it executed while the ProcessForm method writes to the output file, you must use the delimiters <%% and %%> to mark these statements. These statements will not appear in the output file; instead, the output generated by the statements (if any) will be saved to the output file.

If the *insertionPoint* parameter is specified, but it does not exist in the output file, Tools.ProcessForm replaces the entire output file. If the *insertionPoint* parameter exists, and does not begin with an asterisk (*), Tools .ProcessForm finds the *insertionPoint* string in the output file and inserts the data immediately after it. If the *insertionPoint* string begins with an asterisk (*), Tools.ProcessForm finds the *insertionPoint* string in the output file and inserts the data immediately before it. If the *insertionPoint* string exists, but is not found in the output file, the data is appended to the end of the file.

Example

Let's say you have a site that requests viewers to register, in order to view certain pages. In addition to storing viewer registration information to a database, you may wish to store it to a text file. Instead of manipulating the text file yourself, you can create a template and then store the viewer's name, e-mail, and password to an output file. The template file could be something like:

```
Entry added on <%% Now() %%>
New Viewer ID <%% = Request.Form("ID") %%>
E-Mail <%% = Request.Form("Email") %%>
- - - - - - - - - - - - - - - -
```

The expression <%% = Request.Form("ID") %%> will be replaced by the value of the control named ID on the Form that was submitted to your page. Likewise, the expression <%% = Request.Form("Email") %%> will be replaced by the value of the control named Email. The dashes separate consecutive entries in the output file (you can use any character, except for the asterisk, because the asterisk can't be used as insertion point).

If the template file is named REGTEMPLATE.ASP, then you can insert the following lines in your script to add an entry to the output file (the REGVIEWERS.TXT file):

```
<%
    Set objTools = Server.CreateObject("MSWC.Tools")
        objTools.ProcessForm "REGVIEWERS.TXT", _
                        "REGTEMPLATE.ASP"
%>
```

Each time the script is executed, it will add a few lines like the following ones to the output file:

```
Entry added on 04/23/2000
New Viewer ID KeithA
E-Mail Keith@HiTex.com
- - - - - - - - - - - - - - - -
```

Random

The Random method returns a random integer in the range from –32768 to 32767.

Syntax

```
rndInteger = objTools.random
```

This method is similar to the *Rnd* function but returns an integer (where Rnd() returns a floating-point number from 0 to 1). To get a random integer below a specific value, use the Mod function. To get a random number between 1 and 50, use the following statement:

```
<% = 1 + (Abs( Tools.Random ) ) Mod 50 %>
```

The IISLog Component

The Internet Information Server (IIS) maintains a log of the requests made by the clients and the server's responses. Besides the standard entries, which are added automatically by IIS, you can add custom entries to the log file with the AppendToLog method of the Response object. However, none of the intrinsic ASP objects exposes any methods for reading the contents of the log files. To access the IIS log files you must use the IISLog component (also known as the Logging Utility component). The properties and methods of the IILog component allow you to read from the IIS log files. The IISLog component can be used from within scripts, or Visual Basic applications, to programmatically extract the desired information from the log files.

As you can understand, this component is not meant to be used on pages that can be viewed by anyone who connects to your site. The user accessing the ASP script that references the IISLog component must be authenticated as Administrator or Operator on the Web server.

Using the IISLog Component

To use the IISLog component in a script, you must first instantiate the component with a statement like the following one:

```
Set objLog = Server.CreateObject( MSWC.IISLog )
```

The *objLog* variable exposes the methods you need to access the log files and a number of properties that extract the desired information from the same files. The methods and properties of the IISLog component are described in the following paragraphs.

To read the entries of a log file, you must:

1. Use the OpenLogFile method to specify from which log file the IIS-Log component should read from.

2. Use the ReadLogRecord to read the appropriate log records. In most cases we're interested in the entries of specific dates, so you'll probably

apply a filter with the ReadFilter method, which filters records by date any time.

3. Use the IIS Log component's properties to retrieve specific information from the log records.

The log files for IIS are stored in the folder C:\WINNT\system32\Log-Files\W3SVC1 and they are named *exyymmdd*. You can specify how often IIS will create a new log file and how it will name it in the Web Site Properties window. Right-click the Web site for which you want to specify the log file properties and select Properties. On the Web Site Properties window that will appear, select the Web Site tab. At the bottom of the tab you will see the log file options: you can enable or disable logging, set the log file's format and set additional properties by clicking the Properties button. Click the Properties button to see the Extended Logging Properties window, where you can specify how often IIS will create a new log file and the location of the log files. If you select the Extended Properties tab, you can specify the type of information IIS will store in each log record. The extended logging options correspond to the properties of the IISLog object, which are discussed shortly.

FIGURE 18.1: The Web Site Properties window

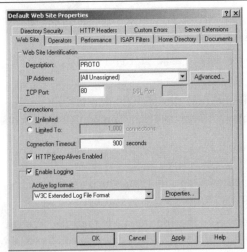

FIGURE 18.2: The tabs of the Extended Logging Properties window

Methods

The IISLog component exposes the following methods for opening, reading and closing the log files.

AtEndOfLog

This method indicates whether you have reached the end of the log file, or there are more records to be read in the log file. It returns TRUE after an attempt to read past the end of the file. See the description of the ReadLogFile for an example of using the AtEndOfLog property.

CloseLogFiles

This method closes all or selected log files that were opened in the same script. Call this method after you have read all the entries you're interested in, to release the resources to the system.

Syntax

The syntax for CloseLogFiles is:

```
ObjLog.CloseLogFiles IOMode
```

IOMode indicates which log file(s) and it can take one of the following values:

Constant	Value	Description
ForReading	1	Closes log files that have been opened for reading.
ForWriting	2	Closes log files that have been opened for writing.
AllOpenFiles	32	Closes all open log files.

OpenLogFile

This method opens a log file for reading or writing. The syntax for Open-LogFile is next:

```
ObjLog.OpenLogFile FileName, [IOMode],
                   [ServiceName], [ServiceInstance],
                   [OutputLogFileFormat]
```

All arguments of the OpenLogFile method are optional, except for the first one. *fileName* is the name of the log file to open. IOMode indicates whether the log file is opened for reading or writing and it can have one of the two values ForReading (1), or ForWriting (2). If the IOMode argument is omitted, the log file is opened for reading.

ServiceName is the name of the service, for which you want to view the log records. The default value is the string "W3SVC" and it corresponds to the log records of the Web server. *serviceInstance* is the name of the instance of the server for which you want to view the log records (the default value is "1"). The last argument, *outputLogFileFormat* indicates the format for log files opened for writing.

ReadFilter

Use the ReadFilter method select log records by date and time. The syntax for the ReadFilter is: ReadFilter [startDateTime], [endDateTime]. The two arguments are optional, but you should specify at least one of them. If not, all the records in the log file will qualify. *startDateTime* is the date and time after which log records are to be read. *endDateTime* is the date and time before which log records are to be read. Specify both arguments to select log records in an interval.

Example

The following statements open the file log EX000515 in the C:\WINNT\ system32\LogFiles\W3SVC1 folder and filter out all records except for the ones written by IIS in the last 24 hours:

```
Set objLog = Server.CreateVariable("MSWC.IISLog")
logFile = _
    "C:\WINNT\system32\LogFiles\W3SVC1\ex000515"
objLog.OpenLogFile logFile, ForReading, "W3SVC", 1
objLog.ReadFilter Now - 1, Now
' statements to read and process the selected records
```

ReadLogRecord

The ReadLogRecord method reads the next available log record. The syntax is: ReadLogRecord. Notice that you need not store the record in a variable; all the properties of the IISLog object apply to the current log record.

Example

The following loop scans all the log records specified by the ReadFilter method:

```
<%
Set objLog = Server.CreateVariable("MSWC.IISLog")
objLog.OpenLogFile logFile, ForReading, "W3SVC", 1
objLog.ReadFilter Now - 1, Now
While Not objLog.AtEnfOfLog
    objLog.ReadLogRecord
    ' statements to process current record
Wend
%>
```

WriteLogRecord

This method writes new log records that have been read from another IIS-Log object.

Syntax

```
WriteLogRecord IISLog
```

IISLog is an object variable that represents the instance of the IISLog object that provides the log records (the source records). To copy log records from one file to another, create two instances of the IISLog component, objLog1 and objLog2, open a file for Reading with the objLog1.OpenLogFile method and another one for writing with the objLog2.OpenLogFile, and then call the WriteLogRecord method as follows:

```
obj2.WriteLogRecord obj1.ReadLogRecord
```

This statement will copy the current log record. To copy multiple records, call the obj1.ReadFilter method to select the records and then iterate through them with a loop like the following one:

```
While Not objLog1.AtEnfOfLog
    ObjLog2.WriteLogRecord objLog1.ReadLogRecord
Wend
```

Properties

The methods of the IISLog component allow you to read the logs records. To extract the information you need from each record, use the IISLog component's properties, which are described in the following paragraphs.

All the properties listed below correspond to an attribute of the current record. The current record is the one read by the most recent call of the ReadLogRecord method.

BytesReceived

This property returns the number of bytes received from the browser during the request operation from the current log record.

BytesSent

This property returns the number of bytes sent to the client during the response operation referred to by the current log record.

ClientIP

This property returns the client's (or proxy server's) IP address for the operation referred to by the current log record.

Cookie

This property returns the value of the cookies that were sent to the server during the request operation referred to by the current log record.

CustomFields

This property allows you to retrieve any extra HTTP headers that were included in the operation referred to by the current log record. The extra headers are returned a two-dimensional array, consisting of key-value pairs, similar to cookies.

DateTime

This property returns the date and time the current log record was generated. The DateTime format is GMT.

Method

The Method property returns the HTTP operation type from the current log record and its value is one of the strings "GET" or "POST".

ProtocolStatus

The ProtocolStatus property returns the HTTP protocol's status code to which the operation of the current log record refers. For successful operations, the ProtocolStatus property is "200 OK".

ProtocolVersion

This property returns the protocol version string from the current log record. For HTTP requests and responses, this property is "HTTP/1.1".

Referer

This property returns the referrer URL for the page to which the current log record refers (the referrer is the page that initiated the request). This property is of interest if the referrer is not a page from the same Web site. The property's name is spelled as shown here.

ServerIP

This property returns the IP address of the server to which the current log record refers.

ServerName

This property returns the name of the server to which the current log record refers.

ServerPort

This property allows you to retrieve the port number that was used in the operation referred to by the current log record.

ServiceName

This property allows you to extract the name of the service from the current log record. It's "W3SVC" for Web operations and "MSFTPSVC" for FTP operations (these operations are logged by the FTP Service and not the Web service).

TimeTaken

This property allows you to determine the total processing time required for the operation referred to by the current log record.

URIQuery

This property enables you to extract any HTTP request parameters (also known as the query string) that were passed during the HTTP operation referred to by the current log record. They are the parameter values passed to the server by the client.

URIStem

This property allows you to extract the target URL from the current log record.

UserAgent

This property allows you to examine the browser user agent string.

UserName

This property enables you to discover the logon name for non-anonymous clients that participated in the operation referred to by the current log record.

Win32Status

This property allows you to determine the Win32 status code from the current log record.

appendix **A**

Windows Script
Components

The most commonly used words in this guide are probably "component" and "object." Objects are at the heart of modern programming, even with a simple language like VBScript, and you're more than familiar with the concept of object-oriented programming. Components are "pieces of code" that can be used by multiple applications and in different programming environments. To use a component in your script, you must first instantiate it with the Server.CreateObject method. This method returns an object variable that represents the component, and you can access the functionality of the component through the properties and methods of the object variable. The File Access component, for example, is the code you need to access a computer's file system. It's binary code that knows how to access the file system. Being able to manipulate the file system, however, isn't adequate. The component should also be able to communicate with other applications that need its services. This is made possible by a mechanism known as COM (Component Object Model). COM evolved into DCOM (Distributed COM) and recently to COM+. A COM component exposes its functionality to other applications through a programmatic interface, which consists of properties, methods, and events.

All the components you've read about in this book, including the ASP objects, are COM objects. In addition to the built-in and installable components, you can develop your own components for use in ASP scripts. You can develop custom components for use with your Visual Basic or VC++ applications, but this appendix discusses COM objects for ASP. Until recently, you could create custom components in high-level languages like Visual Basic or Visual C++. Now, you can develop custom components in VBScript and they are called Windows Script Components.

To simplify the development of script components, Microsoft has released the Windows Script Component package, which is on Microsoft's Web site at msdn.microsoft.com/scripting/. Download the package (the WZ10EN.EXE file) and run it to install the wizard on your system.

The Windows Script Component Wizard automates the process of creating script components by generating a skeleton WSC file. This file contains the XML elements for the script's members, the necessary information for registering the component in the Windows Registry, and the actual implementation of the component, either in VBScript or in JavaScript. You must edit this file to insert the code that implements the component's interface (its methods and properties) then register the component. If you have developed COM or COM+ components with Visual Basic, you're ready to develop your custom script components.

Along with the scripting wizard, you will get all the documentation you need to develop script components. I will not repeat the documentation in this appendix, which is a quick tutorial (but heavy on examples) to help you get started. Windows Script Components can be used in many different environments, but for the purposes of this guide I will focus on developing custom script components for use with ASP.

Once you've installed the Windows Script Component Wizard, the Microsoft Windows Script item will be added to the Start ➤ Programs menu. This command leads to a submenu with two options: Windows Script Components Documentation and Windows Script Component Wizard. Start the wizard, which will take you through six screens. This is where you'll specify the component's interface, and these screens will be discussed shortly. But first, let's see what a script component looks like and how to design a custom script component.

Designing a Script Component

The first step is the design of the component. You must decide the type of functionality you need from the custom component and then the properties and methods that will allow your applications to access this functionality. (Script components can also raise events, but since you can't take advantage of events in your ASP files we'll ignore this feature.)

Properties can be implemented either as public variables or as functions. To make a variable visible to scripts outside the component, declare it with the Public keyword:

```
Public Count, Length
```

When an application references a component that exposes these two public variables, the application will be able to read, or set, the variables. This method isn't very safe, because the component can't validate the values.

The second method uses the Get_Property and Let_Property procedures. When a property is set, the corresponding Let_Property procedure is invoked.

This procedure can validate the value and then assign it to the property (or ignore the setting and use a default value for the property). Likewise, the Get_Property procedure is invoked each time a property's value is requested.

The component's methods are implemented as public functions. Any public function in the component's code automatically becomes a method of the component. The parameters of the public function automatically become the parameters of the method.

You'll see how to implement properties and methods for script components. Before you start coding script components, it's very important to understand that the methods and properties exposed by the component constitute its interface. Script components don't have a visible interface and developers will use the component's members to manipulate it. Consider the functionality of the component and decide how this functionality will be best exposed to developers. Use properties to set attributes and methods to implement operations. Make sure all the information needed by a method to carry out its task is passed to the method in the form of parameters.

The MakeTable Component

In this section, we'll build a script component to automate the display of arbitrary Recordsets on Web pages, in tabular form. One of the most common operations in ASP scripts that access databases is the formatting of a Recordset as an HTML table. Here you'll develop a component that exposes this functionality in the form of properties and methods, and you'll be able to map Recordsets to HTML tables with a single line of code. You have a pretty good idea of the VBScript code involved (you've seen the actual code in Chapter 9, *ADO 2.5 for Web Developers*), but before you start coding the component, you must decide how the functionality of the custom component will be exposed.

Obviously, you need a method that accepts a Recordset as an argument, formats it as an HTML table, and writes the HTML code directly to the output. Let's call the method MakeTable. Its declaration should be MakeTable(RS).

The MakeTable method could also return a string with the HTML code, leaving it up to the calling application to write this string to the output stream with the Response.Write method. Since the calling application doesn't need this information (it's not going to process the HTML code any further), we can write it directly to the output stream.

In addition to the basic table-formatting method, we should be able to control the appearance of the table. Let's add two properties, TableWidth and ShowGrid, that control the width of the table on the page and the type of the grid that will be drawn around the information. The TableWidth property specifies the table's width as a percentage of the page; it's the same as the WIDTH attribute of the <TABLE> tag when expressed as a percentage. If the user sets the TableWidth property to 75, the component will generate the following tag for the table:

```
<TABLE WIDTH = 75%>
```

The ShowGrid property is a Boolean value that determines whether the table will have frames around the cells. If ShowGrid is True, the <TABLE> tag will be:

```
<TABLE WIDTH = 75% BORDER=FRAME>
```

Properties are implemented with the Get_PropertyName and Set_Property-Name procedures, which are equivalent to Visual Basic's Property Get and Property Set procedures. When an application attempts to set the value of the TableWidth property, for example, the Set_TableWidth procedure is invoked. The property's value is passed as an argument, and you can write the code to validate this value. When the application requests the value, Get_TableWidth is invoked. The value of the property is usually stored in a local variable. This variable changes value when the property is set, and its value is returned to the calling application when requested. Here are the two procedures that implement the TableWidth property:

```
Function get_TableWidth()
    get_TableWidth = TableWidth
End Function

Function put_TableWidth(newValue)
    If CInt(newValue) >=0 And CInt(newValue)<100 Then
        TableWidth = newValue
    Else
        TableWidth = 100
    End If
End Function
```

As you can see, if the application attempts to set the table width to an invalid value, the default value 100 percent is used.

The MakeTable method is implemented with the following statements:

```
Function MakeTable(RS)
    If ShowGrid Then
        Response.Write "<TABLE BGCOLOR = #" & _
                        Hex(TableColor) & _
                        " WIDTH=" & TableWidth & _
                        "% BORDER=FRAME>"
    Else
        Response.Write "<TABLE BGCOLOR = #" & _
                        Hex(TableColor) & _
                        " WIDTH=" & TableWidth &_
                        "%><TR>"
    End If
    For iCol = 0 To RS.Fields.Count - 1
        Response.Write "<TD><FONT=+1>"
        Response.Write "<B>" & RS.Fields(iCol).Name & _
                        "</B></FONT></TD>"
    Next
    Response.Write "</TR>"
    While Not RS.EOF
        Response.Write "<TR>"
        For iCol = 0 To RS.Fields.Count - 1
            Response.Write "<TD>" & _
                            RS.Fields(iCol).Value & "</TD>"
        Next
        Response.Write "</TR>"
        RS.MoveNext
    Wend
    Response.Write "</TABLE>"
End Function
```

These are the same statements we used over and over in Chapter 9, *ADO 2.5 for Web Developers*, to display Recordsets. As you understand, you can't just insert the definitions of the procedures and functions to make a custom script component. Windows Script Components have a rigid structure, so that they can be easily shared by multiple applications. This is what the wizard will do for you: it will create the structure of a working, yet useless, scripting component, which you must flesh out. You'll see shortly how you can edit the prototype generated by the wizard.

All COM components must be registered before they're used. This is exactly what the wizard will do for you. As you have seen, the implementation of the component's interface is quite simple: it's straight VBScript code that could appear in any script. The registration information requires a few additional steps, but the wizard will insert all the necessary information in the WSC file.

Using the Component Script Wizard

Let's build a custom component with the members discussed above. Open Start ➤ Programs ➤ Microsoft Windows Script ➤ Windows Script Component Wizard. The first screen of the wizard is shown in Figure A.1. Here you specify the name of the component; the wizard fills out the remaining fields as you type. You can overwrite the component's filename by supplying a different name.

FIGURE A.1: The first screen of the Windows Script Component Wizard

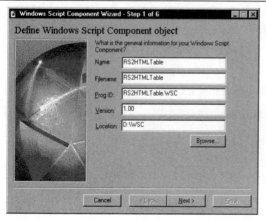

You can't open an existing component to edit its interface, so the Version field is of no use. A future version of the wizard will be able to open existing components and automatically update the version number.

The second screen of the wizard (Figure A.2) is where you specify the component's characteristics, such as the language in which the component will be implemented, whether the component will be used in ASP pages or DHTML behaviors, and the runtime options. Make sure the Support Active Server Pages option is checked and click the Next button to continue.

FIGURE A.2: The Specify Characteristics screen of the Windows Script Component Wizard

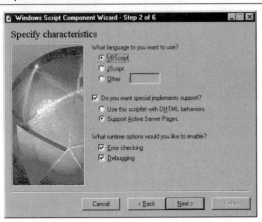

On the next three screens, you specify the component's interface. The Properties screen is shown in Figure A.3. Enter each property's name, select its access type (read-only, write-only, or read/write), and supply a default value (if any).

FIGURE A.3: The Properties screen of the Windows Script Component Wizard

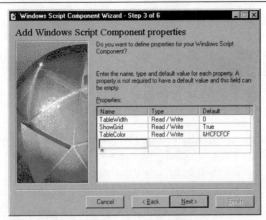

The default values of the properties are variants. The wizard, however, can't handle data types other than numbers and strings. If you set a property's default value to True, the code generated by the wizard will assign the value "True" to this property. This is a string, and not the Boolean value True. Likewise, the hexadecimal notation of a color value (&HCFCFCF) will also be treated as a string. Just keep in mind this behavior of the wizard and make the necessary adjustments in the code.

In the next screen (Figure A.4) you specify the methods of the new component. Each method has a name and may accept one or more parameters. VBScript is a typeless language, so you need not specify the parameter types, just their names.

FIGURE A.4: The Methods screen of the Windows Script Component Wizard

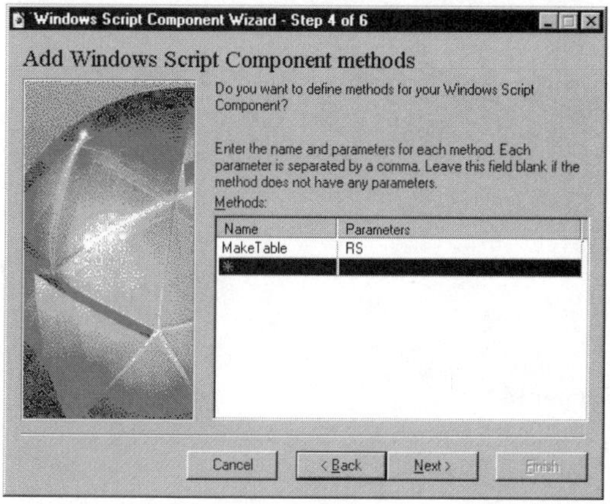

Click the Next button and you'll see the next screen, where you can enter the events of the components. Since we're not interested in events for our ASP components, skip this screen by clicking the Next button. The last screen summarizes the characteristics of the component and its interface members. Review the information and if everything looks OK click the Finish button to create the component.

The Structure of a WSC File

The wizard will produce the following code and store it in the RS2HTMLTable.WSC file in the specified folder. This script component is quite useless (it doesn't do anything at all). We'll add the code to implement the desired features of the component, but first we'll look at the structure of the WSC file produced by the wizard. Listing A.1 shows the code.

▶ *Listing A.1: The RS2HTMLTable.wsc File Generated by the Wizard*

```
<?xml version="1.0"?>
<component>
<?component error="true" debug="true"?>
<registration
    description="RS2Table"
    progid="RS2HTMLTable.WSC"
    version="1.00"
    classid="{abf278c0-142f-11d4-904d-004005e0f76e}"
>
</registration>
<public>
    <property name="TableWidth">
        <get/>
        <put/>
    </property>
    <property name="TableColor">
        <get/>
        <put/>
    </property>
    <property name="ShowGrid">
        <get/>
        <put/>
    </property>
    <method name="MakeTable">
        <PARAMETER name="RS"/>
    </method>
</public>
<implements type="ASP" id="ASP"/>
<script language="VBScript">
<![CDATA[
dim TableWidth
TableWidth = 0
dim TableColor
TableColor = "&HCFCFCF"
dim ShowGrid
```

```
ShowGrid = "True"
function get_TableWidth()
    get_TableWidth = TableWidth
end function

function put_TableWidth(newValue)
    TableWidth = newValue
end function

function get_TableColor()
    get_TableColor = TableColor
end function

function put_TableColor(newValue)
    TableColor = newValue
end function

function get_ShowGrid()
    get_ShowGrid = ShowGrid
end function

function put_ShowGrid(newValue)
    ShowGrid = newValue
end function

function MakeTable(RS)
    MakeTable = "Temporary Value"
end function

]]>
</script>
</component>
```

The WSC file breaks down as follows:

<registration> This section contains information needed for registering the component in the Windows Registry. Use the fields in the registration section to provide a short description of the component, its version, ProgID, and ClassID. The ProgID is a name you choose, but the ClassID must be a GUID string that identifies your component. This string is generated by the script wizard.

<public>   This section contains the definition of the control's interface. Here you insert the declarations of all members, so that other applications will know how to contact the component. The scripting engine consults this interface and it knows whether a member requested by an application exists or not. If not, the runtime error "Object doesn't support this method" is generated. The name property is the member's name, while the <get> and <put> tags indicate whether the property is read-only (if the <put> is missing) or write-only (if the <get> property is missing). A read-write property has both a <get> and a <put> tag. The <method> tags indicate the names of the methods. If a method accepts parameters, each parameter is specified with a <PARAMETER> tag followed by the parameter's name.

<implements>   By default, the scripting component implements a standard COM interface. To implement the ASP interface handler, insert the code `<implements type=ASP>`. This interface allows you to access the ASP objects and write components that send data directly to the Response stream. You need not specify an <implements> tag if you plan to use the custom component through a standard COM interface (if you use the component in a VB application, for example).

<script>   Following the <implements> tag comes the code that actually implements the component's interface (its properties and methods) in a <script> tag. This is straight VBScript code, and you can contact any COM component on the host computer. For example, you can include the ADO component to access databases, or the File Access component to access the host computer's file system.

A scripting component may include the following optional tags. None of them appears in the example WSC file shown in Listing A.1:

<object>   This tag contains information about objects you use in the script, such as another COM component (the ADO component, for instance).

<resource>   This tag contain values that need not be hard-coded into the code. Resources are usually strings that must be translated into a different language.

<reference>   This tag specifies type libraries you want to use in your code.

<comment>   This tag delimits comments, which are ignored when the script component is parsed and executed.

Editing the WSC File

Now that you understand the structure of the WSC file, you can step in and write the code that makes it do something useful. Start by changing the lines:

```
TableColor = "&HCFCFCF"
ShowGrid = "True"
```

to

```
TableColor = &HCFCFCF&
ShowGrid = True
```

The wizard treats all default values as strings, even if they're reserved keywords (like True) or hexadecimal numbers.

The implementation of the procedures of the TableWidth property is shown in Listing A.2. The put_TableWidth() procedure accepts as a parameter the value assigned to the TableWidth property by the application. The procedure validates the property's value and, if it's valid, stores the new value to the TableWidth local variable. The get_TableWidth procedure assigns the value of the TableWidth variable to the get_TableWidth function name. This value will be returned to the application when it requests the property's value.

▶ *Listing A.2: Implementing the TableWidth Property*

```
Function put_TableWidth(newValue)
    If CInt(newValue) >=0 And CInt(newValue)<100 Then
        TableWidth = newValue
    Else
        TableWidth = 100
    End If
End Function
```

```
Function get_TableWidth()
    get_TableWidth = TableWidth
End Function
```

The MakeTable method (Listing A.3) converts the fields of the RS Recordset variable to an HTML table and writes it directly to the output stream with the Response.Write method.

▶ *Listing A.3: The MakeTable Method*

```
Function MakeTable(RS)
    If ShowGrid Then
        Response.Write "<TABLE BGCOLOR = #" & _
                        Hex(TableColor) & _
                        " WIDTH=" & TableWidth & "% BORDER=FRAME>"
    Else
        Response.Write "<TABLE BGCOLOR = #" & _
                        Hex(TableColor) & _
                        " WIDTH=" & TableWidth & "%><TR>"
    End If
    For iCol = 0 To RS.Fields.Count - 1
        Response.Write "<TD><FONT=+1>"
        Response.Write "<B>" & RS.Fields(iCol).Name & _
        "</B></FONT></TD>"
    Next
    Response.Write "</TR>"
    While Not RS.EOF
        Response.Write "<TR>"
        For iCol = 0 To RS.Fields.Count - 1
            Response.Write "<TD>" & RS.Fields(iCol).Value & _
            "</TD>"
        Next
        Response.Write "</TR>"
        RS.MoveNext
    Wend
    Response.Write "</TABLE>"
End Function
```

Registering a Scripting Component

Before you can use the new component, you must register it. Although it's possible to register the component from within your code, the simplest method is to right-click the WSC file and select Register from the shortcut menu (as shown in Figure A.5). If the script doesn't contain syntax errors, it will be registered.

FIGURE A.5: Registering an ASP scripting component

After the component has been registered, you can use it in your scripts by instantiating it with the Server.CreateObject method. The following statement creates an object variable that represents the RS2HTMLTable component:

```
Set objHTMLTable = Server.CreateObject("RS2HTMLTable.WSC")
```

Then, you can use the *objHTMLTable* variable to access the members of the RS2HTML component. Assuming that RS is a properly initialized Recordset variable, you can display its rows on an HTML page in tabular format by calling the MakeTable method:

```
objHTMLTable.MakeTable RS
```

This line has replaced the loop that scans the rows of the Recordset and formats the fields as a tabular form for display on a Web page. Listing A.4 shows a short script that retrieves the first 25 titles from the BIBLIO database (ISBNs and titles) and formats the information as an HTML table. The last three lines set the properties of the table and call the MakeTable method of the RS2HTMLTable component.

▶ *Listing A.4: The HTMLTableTest.asp Script*

```
<!-- #include file="adovbs.inc" -->
<%
Set objHTMLTable = Server.CreateObject("RS2HTMLTable.WSC")
Set RS = Server.CreateObject("ADODB.Recordset")
RS.CursorLocation = adUseClient
RS.CursorType = adOpenStatic
RS.Open "SELECT Top 25 ISBN, Title FROM " & _
            "Titles ORDER BY Title", "DSN=BIBLIO"
objHTMLTable.ShowGrid = True
objHTMLTable.TableColor = &HE0E0E0&
objHTMLTable.MakeTable RS
%>
```

As you can see, developing a custom scripting component is fairly straightforward and simple. It's no more complicated than writing an ASP script; the Script Component Wizard takes care of the complicated part of the process. The next example is a little more complicated, but it demonstrates how script components are used to build real-world applications.

The NWModule Script Component

The last example demonstrated how to simplify the development of scripts that access databases. We'll build a component that isolates the script from the database by exposing methods that perform all the queries against the database. The developer need not know the exact structure of the database, or even how to manipulate the tables with SQL statements. The component exposes methods like GetCustomerByID, which retrieves a row from the Customers table, and GetCustomerOrders, which retrieves all orders placed by a specific customer from the Orders table. If you develop a component that exposes all the methods and properties needed to extract the desired information from the database, as well as the methods to update it, then all the developers in your team can use this component to access the database.

The NWModule script component exposes many methods to access the rows of the NorthWind database. Here are just a few of the methods:

Method	Description
GetCustomerByID(CustID)	Retrieves the row that corresponds to the specified customer ID
GetCustomerByName(CustName)	Retrieves all the rows that correspond to customer whose names match the supplied name
GetCustomerOrders(CustID)	Retrieves all the orders placed by the specified customer
GetOrderDetails(OrderID)	Retrieves the details of the specified order

There are too many methods to list in this appendix or to show the complete code. Any script that requires access to the NorthWind database can use these methods, instead of executing SQL statements against the database. You can call the GetCustomerOrders method to retrieve all the orders placed by a specific customer. One of the items returned by this query is the ID of the orders. You can isolate an order and use its ID to retrieve its detail lines with the GetOrderDetails method. The script doesn't "see" the database directly; instead, it sees the database through the methods of the custom component. These methods implement all the operations you need in an application that manipulates the database; they offer developers a high-level interface to the database.

Start the Script Component Wizard, create the NWModule script component, and define the methods shown in the previous table. Let the wizard produce the WSC file and then insert the following code for the various methods:

```
Function GetCustomerByID(CustID)
    Set RS = Server.CreateObject("ADODB.Recordset")
    RS.Open "SELECT * FROM Customers WHERE CustomerID='" & _
                custID & "'", "DSN=NWINDDB"
    Set GetCustomerByID = RS
    Set RS = Nothing
End Function
```

```
Function GetCustomerByName(CustName)
    Set RS = Server.CreateObject("ADODB.Recordset")
    RS.Open "SELECT * FROM Customers WHERE CompanyName LIKE '%" & _
                    custName & "%'", "DSN=NWINDDB"
    Set GetCustomerByName = RS
    Set RS = Nothing
End Function


Function GetCustomerOrders(CustID)
    Set RS = Server.CreateObject("ADODB.Recordset")
    RS.Open "SELECT * FROM Orders WHERE CustomerID='" & _
                    custID & "'", "DSN=NWINDDB"
    Set GetCustomerOrders = RS
    Set RS = Nothing
End Function


Function GetOrderDetails(OrderID)
    Set RS = Server.CreateObject("ADODB.Recordset")
    RS.Open "SELECT * FROM [Order Details] WHERE OrderID=" & _
                    OrderID , "DSN=NWINDDB"
    Set GetOrderDetails = RS
    Set RS = Nothing
End Function
```

Testing the NWModule Script Component

Let's test the NWModule component, using the code in Listing A.5. First, register the component as explained earlier. The script will call the methods of the NWModule component to retrieve a customer's orders and the details of these orders. As you will see, this script is much simpler than a script that would retrieve the same information from the database with SQL statements. We'll also use the RS2HTMLTable component to display the selected order's details (Figure A.6). The script is quite short for the tasks it performs, thanks to the functionality we have built into the script components.

▶ Listing A.5: The NWModuleTest.asp Script

```
<%
Set NW = Server.CreateObject("NWModule.WSC")
Set Orders=NW.GetCustomerOrders("BLAUS")
```

```
Set HTMLUtil=Server.CreateObject("RS2Table.WSC")
Response.Write "<TABLE>"
While Not Orders.EOF
    Response.Write "<TR>"
    For iCol=0 To Orders.Fields.Count - 1
        Response.Write "<TD>" & Orders.Fields(iCol) & "</TD>"
    Next
    Set Details = NW.GetOrderDetails(Orders.Fields(0))
    HTMLUtil.MakeTable Details
    Response.Write "</TR>"
    Orders.MoveNext
Wend
%>
```

FIGURE A.6: The output of the NWModuleTest.asp script

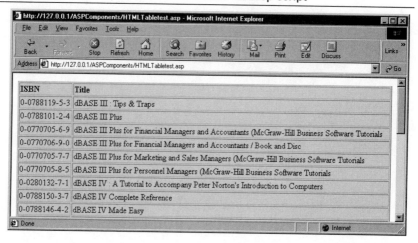

ASP Error Codes

The following table lists VBScript runtime errors. The error codes marked with an asterisk are new to VBScript 5.1, which is still in beta. All other codes apply to VBScript 5 and 5.1.

TABLE B.1: VBScript Runtime Errors

Code	Error
5	Invalid procedure call or argument
6	Overflow
7	Out of memory
9	Subscript out of range
10	Array fixed or temporarily locked
11	Division by zero
13	Type mismatch
14	Out of string space
17	Can't perform requested operation (*)
28	Out of stack space
35	Sub or Function not defined
48	Error in loading DLL
51	Internal error
52	Bad file name or number (*)
53	File not found
54	Bad file mode (*)
55	File already open (*)
57	Device I/O error
58	File already exists
61	Disk full
62	Input past end of file (*)
67	Too many files
68	Device unavailable (*)
70	Permission denied
71	Disk not ready (*)

Continued on next page

TABLE B.1 CONTINUED: VBScript Runtime Errors

Code	Error
74	Can't rename with different drive (*)
75	Path/File access error
76	Path not found
91	Object variable or With block variable not set
92	For loop not initialized
94	Invalid use of Null
322	Can't create necessary temporary file
424	Object required
429	ActiveX component can't create object
430	Class doesn't support Automation
432	File name or class name not found during Automation operation
438	Object doesn't support this property or method
440	Automation error
445	Object doesn't support this action
446	Object doesn't support named arguments
447	Object doesn't support current locale setting
448	Named argument not found
449	Argument not optional
450	Wrong number of arguments or invalid property assignment
451	Object not a collection
453	Specified DLL function not found
455	Code resource lock error
457	This key already associated with an element of this collection
458	Variable uses an Automation type not supported in VBScript
462	Remote server machine does not exist or is unavailable (*)
481	Invalid picture (*)
500	Variable is undefined

Continued on next page

TABLE B.1 CONTINUED: VBScript Runtime Errors

Code	Error
501	Illegal assignment
502	Object not safe for scripting
503	Object not safe for initializing
504	Object not safe for creating (*)
505	Invalid or unqualified reference (*)
5016	Regular Expression object expected (*)
5017	Syntax error in regular expression (*)
5018	Unexpected quantifier (*)
5019	Expected ']' in regular expression (*)
5020	Expected ')' in regular expression (*)
5021	Invalid range in character set (*)
32811	Element not found (*)

TABLE B.2: VBScript Syntax Errors

Code	Error
1001	Out of memory
1002	Syntax error
1003	Expected ':'
1005	Expected '('
1006	Expected ')'
1007	Expected ']'
1010	Expected identifier
1011	Expected '='
1012	Expected 'If'
1013	Expected 'To'
1014	Expected 'End'
1015	Expected 'Function'
1016	Expected 'Sub'

Continued on next page

TABLE B.2 CONTINUED: VBScript Syntax Errors

Code	Error
1017	Expected 'Then'
1018	Expected 'Wend'
1019	Expected 'Loop'
1020	Expected 'Next'
1021	Expected 'Case'
1022	Expected 'Select'
1023	Expected expression
1024	Expected statement
1025	Expected end of statement
1026	Expected integer constant
1027	Expected 'While' or 'Until'
1028	Expected 'While', 'Until', or end of statement
1029	Expected 'With'
1030	Identifier too long
1031	Invalid number
1032	Invalid character
1033	Unterminated string constant
1034	Unterminated comment
1037	Invalid use of 'Me' keyword
1038	'Loop' without 'Do'
1039	Invalid 'Exit' statement
1040	Invalid 'For' loop control variable
1041	Name redefined
1042	Must be first statement on the line
1043	Can't assign to non-ByVal argument
1044	Can't use parens when calling a Sub
1045	Expected literal constant

Continued on next page

TABLE B.2 CONTINUED: VBScript Syntax Errors

Code	Error
1046	Expected 'In'
1047	Expected 'Class'
1048	Must be defined inside a Class
1049	Expected Let or Set or Get in property declaration
1050	Expected 'Property'
1051	Number of arguments must be consistent across properties specification
1052	Cannot have multiple default property/method in a Class
1053	Class initialize or terminate do not have arguments
1054	Property set or let must have at least one argument
1055	Unexpected 'Next'
1056	'Default' can be specified only on 'Property' or 'Function' or 'Sub'
1057	'Default' specification must also specify 'Public'
1058	'Default' specification can only be on Property Get
32766	True
32767	False
32811	Element not found

TABLE B.3: ASP Error Codes

Code	Error
100	Out of memory
101	Unexpected error
102	Expecting string input
103	Expecting numeric input
104	Operation not allowed
105	Index out of range
106	Type mismatch
107	Stack overflow

Continued on next page

TABLE B.3 CONTINUED: ASP Error Codes

Code	Error
115	Unexpected error
190	Unexpected error
191	Unexpected error
192	Unexpected error
193	OnStartPage failed
194	OnEndPage failed
240	Script Engine Exception
241	CreateObject Exception
242	Query OnStartPage Interface Exception

TABLE B.4: ADO Error Codes

Code	Error
3000	The provider failed to complete the requested action.
3001	The application is using arguments that are of the wrong type, are out of acceptable range, or are in conflict with one another.
3002	An error occurred whilst opening the requested file.
3003	There was an error reading from the specified file.
3004	There was an error whilst writing to the file.
3717	The operation caused a security dialog to appear.
3718	The operation caused a security dialog header to appear.
3220	The provider cannot be changed.
3021	Either BOF or EOF is True, or the current record has been deleted; the operation requested by the application requires a current record.
3219	The operation requested by the application is not allowed in this context.
3246	The application cannot explicitly close a Connection object while in the middle of a transaction.
3251	The operation requested by the application is not supported by the provider.

Continued on next page

TABLE B.4 CONTINUED: ADO Error Codes

Code	Error
3265	ADO could not find the object in the collection corresponding to the name or ordinal reference requested by the application.
3367	Can't append. The object is already in the collection.
3420	The object referenced by the application no longer points to a valid object.
3421	The application is using a value of the wrong type for the current operation.
3704	The operation requested by the application is not allowed if the object is closed.
3705	The operation requested by the application is not allowed if the object is open.
3706	ADO could not find the specified provider.
3707	The application cannot change the ActiveConnection property of a Recordset object with a Command object as its source.
3708	The application has improperly defined a Parameter object.
3709	The application requested an operation on an object with a reference to a closed or invalid Connection object.
3710	The operation is not reentrant.
3711	The operation is still executing.
3712	The operation was cancelled .
3713	The operation is still connecting.
3714	The transaction is invalid.
3715	The operation is not executing.
3716	The operation is unsafe under these circumstances.
3719	The action failed due to violation of data integrity.
3720	The action failed because you do not have sufficient permission to complete the operation.
3721	The data was too large for the supplied data type.
3722	The action caused a violation of the schema.
3723	The expression contained mismatched signs.
3724	The value cannot be converted.
3725	The resource cannot be created.

Continued on next page

TABLE B.4 CONTINUED: ADO Error Codes

Code	Error
3726	The specified column doesn't exist on this row.
3727	The URL does not exist.
3728	You do not have permissions to view the directory tree.
3729	The supplied URL is invalid.
3730	The resource is locked.
3731	The resource already exists.
3732	The action could not be completed.
3733	The file volume was not found.
3734	The operation failed because the server could not obtain enough space to complete the operation.
3735	The resource is out of scope.
3736	The command is unavailable.
3737	The URL in the named row does not exist.
3738	The resource cannot be deleted because it is out of the allowed scope.
3739	This property is invalid for the selected column.
3740	You have supplied an invalid option for this property.
3741	You have supplied an invalid value for this property.
3742	Setting this property caused a conflict with other properties.
3743	Not all properties can be set.
3744	The property was not set.
3745	The property cannot be set.
3746	The property is not supported.
3747	The action could not be completed because the catalog is not set.
3748	The connection cannot be changed.
3749	The Update method of the Fields collection failed.
3750	You cannot set Deny permissions because the provider does not support them.
3751	The provider does not support the operation requested by the application.

Index

Note to Reader: In this index, **boldfaced** page numbers refer to primary discussions of the topic; *italics* page numbers refer to figures.

function to determine depth, 356
moving, 233, 335
parent, 346
  method to return name, 332
and Record objects, 230
recursive scan, **359–361**
for Web site documents, 9
Folders collection, **358–361**
For Each ... Next loop for iteration
  through collection elements, 43
  through Cookies collection, 77
  through Form collection, 101
  through Messages collection, 373–374
  through QueryString collection, 106–107
  through subfolders, 358–359
For ... Next loop, to populate Select control, 17–18
Form collection, 12, 33, **100–105**
Form property (Request object), 92–93, 102, 115–116
<FORM> tag (HTML), 12
  ACTION attribute, 91
  building URL as parameter for, 167–168
  METHOD attribute, 90
  for ParamsPost.asp script, 107
FormatDateTime() function, 7
Forms, 2, 8, **11–24**
  ACTION attribute, 12
  creation, 11–12
  HTTP Request header for page containing, 27
  METHOD attribute, 12
  methods to process contents, **414–416**
  NAME attribute, 12
  submitting parameters without, **93–94**
forward-only cursor, 202
frames
  banner destination page in, **275–276**
  browser support of, 282
  navigational, **304–306**
FreeSpace property (Drive object), 351, 352

frequency of banner display, 269
From property (NewMail object), 389
#fsize, 24
FSYS variable, 159, 342

G

GATEWAY_INTERFACE server variable, 111
GET method, 12, **90–93**
  of Counters component, **398–399**
  and Form collection, 100
  <FORM> tag using, 107
  QueryString property for parameters passed with, 117
GetAbsolutePathName method (FileSystemObject object), **328**
GetAdvertisement method
  of Ad Rotator component, **276–277**
  of AdObj variable, 271
GetAllContent method (Content Rotating), **316**, *316*
GetBaseName method (FileSystemObject object), **329**
GetChildren method (Record object), 233
GetChunk method (Field object), 243–244
GetDefaultFolder method of Session object (CDONTS), 366–367, **371**
GetDepth function, 356
GetDrive method (FileSystemObject object), **329–330**, 351
GetDriveName method (FileSystemObject object), **330**
GetExtensionName method (FileSystemObject object), **330**
GetFile method (FileSystemObject object), **331**
GetFileName method (FileSystemObject object), **331–332**
GetFirst method of Messages collection (CDONTS), **376**
GetFolder method (FileSystemObject object), **332**, 354
GetLast method of Messages collection (CDONTS), **376**

H

K

Key property
  of Application.StaticObjects collection, 47
  for Contents collection, 42–43
  of Request.Cookies collection, **99–100**
  of Response.Cookies collection, 130
  of Session.Content collection member, 60–61
  of Session.StaticObjects collection, 64
KeySet cursor, 202

L

language, and CODEPAGE, 23
LANGUAGE directive, 23
LCID directive, 23
LCID property (Session object), 37, **55–56**
Let_Property procedure, 427
Line property
  of ASPError object, 38, 170
  of TextStream object, 338
LineSeparator property (Stream object), 235
List control. *See* Select control
LoadFromFile method (Stream object), 237
local variables, 40
LOCAL_ADDR server variable, 113
locale ID, 23, 55
Locale.asp script, 56, *57*
Lock method (Application object), 31, **48**
LockType property (Recordset object), 206–207
Logging Utility component, **417–424**
LogOff method of Session object (CDONTS), **371**
LogonSMTP method of Session object (CDONTS), 366, **370**
LOGON_USER server variable, 113, 412

M

MailFormat property (NewMail object), 389
MakeTable component, **428–431**
  creation, **431–440**

MapPath method (Server object), 36, **165–166**
MarshalOptions property (Recordset object), 207
MAXLENGTH attribute (Text control), 14
MaxRecords property (Recordset object), 207
memory, eliminating object from, 187
Message object (CDONTS), 373, **376–381**
  methods, **379–381**
  properties, **376–379**
MessageFormat property
  of Message object (CDONTS), **377**
  of Session object (CDONTS), 369
Messages collection of Folder object (CDONTS), **373–374**
<META> tag, character set specified, 34
METHOD attribute of Form, 12, 90
Method property (IISLog component), 423
Microsoft Data Shape driver, 181
Microsoft Transaction Server, Object-Context object, 252–253
MIME attachment, Content location header of, 377
Mode property
  of Connection object, 180
  of Record object, 231
  of Stream object, 236
Move method
  of File object, 349
  of Recordset object, 221
MoveFile method (FileSystemObject object), **335**
MoveFirst method (Recordset object), 221
MoveFolder method (FileSystemObject object), **335**
MoveLast method (Recordset object), 221
MoveNext method (Recordset object), 221
MovePrevious method (Recordset object), 221
MoveRecord method (Record object), 233
MSDAOra provider, 181
MSDASQL provider, 181
MSDataShape provider, 181